ARMY OF THE
HEARTLAND

THOMAS LAWRENCE CONNELLY is a
native of Nashville. He is an associate professor of history at Mississippi State University. He is the author of *Will Success Spoil
Jeff Davis?*, a satire on the Civil War Cen-
tennial.

GREEN RIVER BRIDGE AT MUNFORDVILLE, KENTUCKY

ARMY OF THE HEARTLAND

The Army of Tennessee, 1861–1862

THOMAS LAWRENCE CONNELLY

LOUISIANA STATE UNIVERSITY PRESS ● BATON ROUGE

To HOWARD WHITE, *Scholar, Gentleman, and Teacher*

Acknowledgments

ONLY A FEW OF THE MANY PEOPLE WHO HAVE CONTRIBUTED TO THIS
project may be mentioned. Professor Frank Vandiver of Rice University
was responsible for the project's initiation, and has continually offered
advice and encouragement. Much help has been provided by Mrs. Harriet
Owsley, Tennessee State Archives; Dr. James Patton, Southern Historical
Collection, University of North Carolina; Mrs. Alene Lowe White, Western
Reserve Historical Society; Mrs. Dorothy Thomas Cullen, Filson Club
Historical Society; Mrs. Connie Griffith, Howard-Tilton Memorial Li-
brary, Tulane University; and Dr. William T. Alderson, director of the
American Association for State and Local History.

Other valuable assistance was provided by the staffs of the National
Archives, the Library of Congress, the United States Military Academy
Library, the Historical Society of Pennsylvania, the Chicago Historical
Society, the New York Public Library, Houghton Library of Harvard
University, the Alabama State Department of Archives and History, Fon-
dren Library of Rice University, the University of the South Library,
the Duke University Library, and the Missouri Historical Society.

Professor T. Harry Williams of Louisiana State University read the
manuscript and made valuable suggestions. Professor Grady McWhiney
of the University of British Columbia also offered good criticism, as
did the venerable Confederate historian Thomas Robson Hay. Professor
Harold Snellgrove, head of the History Department at Mississippi State
University, extended many courtesies, as did Professor Lyell C. Behr,
dean of the College of Arts and Sciences. Grants from Rice University,
the American Philosophical Society, and the Mississippi State University

Development Foundation aided greatly in the research. William Mc-Collister performed the arduous task of drawing the maps.

Dozens of people, such as Joe Henley of Paradise Ridge, Tennessee, extended great kindness and volunteered valuable information on local terrain as the writer covered the Army's trail through the western Confederacy. Above all, I extend sincere appreciation to my wife Sally Evelyn. Besides her constant encouragement, her abilities as a free-lance editor were very helpful. By now she must be weary of camp life in the Confederacy.

Preface

I REMEMBER THE BALMY SUMMER NIGHTS WHEN MY BROTHERS AND I SLIPPED onto the old battleground at Shiloh, half afraid of the young park rangers with their new Pershing hats and well-thumbed park guidebooks, and half fearful of the ghosts of the 23,000 casualties who everyone said roamed the field by night. I remember the many campfires we burned and the phantom Rebels we conjured up while camping and running foxes along the Cumberland and Tennessee rivers, on the ridges overlooking Stone's River, and on Shy's Hill, where the Army of Tennessee was destroyed at Nashville. Shy's Hill was a special haunt for Rebel ghosts before the county pushed through a road there and the local historical society blessed the hill with gaudy aluminum markers. Shy's Hill meant lying on your stomach in a stand of cedars and waiting for the Yankee XXIII Corps to swarm out of the glade below. It meant hunting for fragments of cartridge boxes that might have been some hobo's rusty sardine can—though you never gave that a thought. Most of all, Shy's Hill meant your three great-grandfathers staggering back with Bedford Forrest's cavalry into Alabama for one last campaign.

I could not prove they were with Forrest if I had to do so to get into the Sons of Confederate Veterans. My ancestors left no swords, tintypes, medals, pension records—not even a letter. Perhaps they could not even write. But they were with Forrest, because my grandfather said so. Sometimes the entire archives of a soldier's record in the Army of Tennessee consists of a grandfather's tales. I remember how he leaned on the whitewashed fence on his farm along Mingo Branch in the days before TVA came to Field's Hollow and when Western Electric was still king. He spoke quietly of my three great-grandfathers. All were buck privates in Forrest's cavalry. One was a blacksmith for Forrest, and another deserted. A third had come to America from Cork at the age of fifteen. He joined the cavalry, but quit to drive steel on the railroad till he literally dropped on the tracks, dead with pneumonia at the age of twenty-four. His wife was only four feet ten inches tall, but managed to lock two of Buell's foragers in the springhouse where they almost died, and also outran a company of Wilson's raiders who wanted the black horse she was riding.

Scores of personal experiences, a handful of tales related by an old man, and a shoe box of bullet fragments—such is one family's heritage in the Army of Tennessee.

Sadly enough, the historiography of that army is little more than a composite of such recollections. Except for a few regimental histories and printed reminiscences, and a recent outpour of poorly written battle accounts, there has been only one major book on the subject, Stanley Horn's *Army of Tennessee*. Horn's book is well written, but suffers from the author's heavy reliance upon memoirs and recollections, and from an almost total absence of manuscript sources.

The history of the Army of Tennessee, unlike that of its companion in arms, the Army of Northern Virginia, has been rather badly neglected. The influence of the "Lee tradition" in Confederate writing explains part of this neglect. Robert E. Lee and the Army of Northern Virginia have been deified by writers such as Douglas Southall Freeman and Clifford Dowdey as the epitome of what Southerners like to see in themselves— knightly manners, gentleness, planter society. The Virginia army has long been pictured as Stephen Vincent Benet's army of planters' sons. In contrast, the Army of Tennessee has always been associated with the roughness of the Old Southwest, where, as Henry Nash Smith points out in *Virgin Land,* the plantation myth did not carry over. For example, in the Virginia army, a man of the coarseness of a Jubal Early was considered something of an oddity. In the Tennessee army, a tobacco-chewing, cursing, hard-drinking general such as Benjamin F. Cheatham was an accepted fact.

Geography also explains the neglect. The Virginia battlefields are close to the largest concentrated population area in the United States. Visitors to these greatly outnumber those who travel to the widely scattered, generally unassuming western battle sites. Also, Southerners like a winner, and the Tennessee army rarely won. Had the western army possessed a number of colorful generals, the stigma of defeat might have been more bearable. But the high command of the Tennessee army leaves much to the imagination. Many of the western generals had a certain dullness and absence of color which fail to inspire writers.

Yet the basic cause of the Army's neglect is a paucity of good historical writing. The dominance of the Virginia army in Confederate scholarship began immediately after the war and became self-perpetuating. Beginning with John Esten Cooke and also the *Southern Historical Society Papers,* Civil War historiography became identified with the Virginia army. This monopoly was furthered by a shortage of available primary source materials on the Tennessee army. There has been no concentrated area in the West, as in Virginia, where manuscripts were available to historians. With a few exceptions, source materials were scattered widely and were often found in Northern libraries. Many of the states in the old Confederate Second Department, including Tennessee itself, failed to appropriate sufficient funds for the collection of papers. Many papers, especially those of some western generals, remain undiscovered except for isolated materials.

The Tennessee army does not deserve this neglect. Although it was not as successful as the Virginia army, it had to face obstacles which Lee did not have to face in Virginia. The western army had to defend a much larger territory, and with fewer men. It fought over an area of some 225,600 square miles, while the Virginia army only fought over an area less than a tenth as large. Lee's army never traveled more than sixty miles north of the Virginia border. In contrast, Braxton Bragg's campaign in 1862 alone took the Army of Tennessee eight hundred miles from Mississippi to the Kentucky-Ohio border, via Alabama and Georgia. The entire Confederate line in northern Virginia, from the western end of the Shenandoah Valley to Chesapeake Bay, stretched only about 125 miles. In Tennessee, the situation was reversed. The Army was forced to defend a line that extended some four hundred miles from the Mississippi to the Appalachians, with no east-west river to block a Federal army.

To maintain itself in this larger area, to concentrate rapidly, the Tennessee army needed mobility. The rail network in the West, however, discouraged concentration. There was no good east-west line. A body of troops that needed to move from Nashville to Knoxville, a distance of two hundred miles, had to move over a circuitous route of four hundred miles via Chattanooga. There was a line from Memphis to Nashville via Clarksville, Tennessee, but it was lost in early 1862, as was the Memphis and Charleston Railroad, which linked Memphis and Chattanooga. After these losses the Army was forced to rely on a third line 180 miles south of the Memphis and Charleston. This line, which ran from Atlanta to Vicksburg, Mississippi, via Montgomery, was incomplete between Atlanta and Selma. The route was also too circuitous. An army in northern Mississippi had to travel almost six hundred miles to reach East Tennessee, or ten times the distance Lee marched from the Virginia border to Gettysburg, Pennsylvania. In contrast, the Virginia army had three east-west railroads—the Manassas Gap, the Virginia Central, and the Southside—that afforded speedy concentration at Richmond, in the Shenandoah Valley or on the Washington front.

The Army of Tennessee was also burdened with the responsibility of defending the Heartland of the Confederacy. This region of Tennessee, north-central Alabama, northern Georgia, and northeast Mississippi contained the South's greatest concentration of food, livestock, iron, raw materials, and munitions production. To defend it, the Army was constantly undermanned. On the average, the western army had from twenty thousand to twenty-five thousand fewer troops during the war than the Army of Northern Virginia, and had to guard a much larger area. Not only was the Tennessee line much wider than the Virginia front, but the depth of the western theater, from Kentucky to southern Georgia and Alabama, meant there were more calls for dispersion of troops for local defense than in Virginia.

The Army of Tennessee was also hindered by a lack of governmental attention. Richmond developed a peculiar attitude toward the western force. Either it ignored the Army when aid was needed, as in the fall of 1861, or else it intervened and meddled in the Army's affairs, often without consulting the commander. Neglect was the more common policy. Jefferson Davis' strategy of departmental command was destined to isolate the West. According to Davis, each military department was to be self-subsisting and able to repel invasion within its borders. In Virginia, as compared with Tennessee, this was less difficult, for Lee had more men and less area to defend. But in the West, where one major army was responsible for the defense of several large states, the reinforcement problem was acute throughout the war.

When Richmond did intervene in western affairs, the results were usually disastrous. For example, in 1862 President Davis gave the young, ambitious Edmund Kirby Smith equal command with Braxton Bragg on the Kentucky expedition, and so made command discord inevitable. At the same time Davis, without Bragg's knowledge, gave Earl Van Dorn the command over Sterling Price in Mississippi. Bragg had intended for Price to assume command of Van Dorn's troops and lead a column to assist in the Kentucky invasion. Instead Van Dorn turned to attack Corinth and wrecked the Confederate force.

Despite all of these disadvantages, the Army of Tennessee fought well and left an admirable record. True, it was beaten two out of every three times it took the field. Yet it was this constant defeat which made it a great army. It required something special, an intangible *elan,* to come back from the humiliation of Missionary Ridge and fight heroically at Kennesaw Mountain.

This *elan* was at once both the triumph and tragedy of the western army. For the immense faith of the common soldiers in themselves sustained the Army through its worst disadvantage, weakness in the high command. Unlike the Virginia army, which depended for its morale upon a few individuals such as Lee or "Stonewall" Jackson, the men of the Army of Tennessee never attained a real *esprit* at a corps level. Instead, the peculiar western morale was usually most evident at the regimental or brigade level.

For four years the Army's high command was plagued with personality conflicts, a lack of communication and good relations between the Army and Richmond, and a lack of rapport between commanding generals and corps and division leaders. The list of arguments, hatreds, and near rebellions which occurred among the western commanders was indeed long. As a result, the command never attained cohesion. During its brief history the Army was under the command of at least nine generals. The turnover of generals and corps leaders was so great that the common soldier scarcely had time to anchor his devotion to any single leader.

This study traces the Army of Tennessee during its first two years, from its beginnings to its failures in the Kentucky invasion of 1862. These years have been the most neglected in the Army's history, yet they were probably the most vital and decisive. This was the period of the Army's high tide, for after the Kentucky campaign it never had logistical and manpower strength anywhere near equal to that of its opponents. This was also the period of the Army's molding—it was shaped by the influence of the Heartland, by the events of the summer of 1861, and by a succession of commanders who each left his influence upon the Army but failed to temper the newly-shaped force.

To tell the story of this first half of the Army's history has required a diligent examination of seldom-used manuscript materials. A major fault in much of the small amount of work in existence on the western Confederacy has been the heavy reliance upon old myths, reminiscences, and surface criticism furnished by the professional anti-Braxton Bragg school and other groups. Likewise, there has been a century of deification of some commanders which has clouded a fair estimate of their abilities. The influence of the University of the South in Southern literature and history, for example, has wrapped Leonidas Polk and Edmund Kirby Smith in protective mantles unmerited by their performance. In some studies, reminiscences written by embittered former generals such as John Bell

Hood and Joseph E. Johnston have been freely accepted without scrutiny of manuscript sources.

To avoid these dangers of hero worship and hindsight observation, this study not only attempts greater use of manuscripts, but also describes Confederate operations on the basis of information as it was available to the commanders. This method helps to eliminate past injustices against some generals who have been held responsible for information which they either did not have or could not have had at a certain time. It also allows a better understanding of certain more complex operations, such as at Fort Donelson and during the few days before the battle of Perryville, Kentucky. Occasionally, information unknown to the Confederate command, yet necessary to the reader's understanding of the book is included, but then only with proper notification that it was unknown to the Confederates. Other less essential information unknown to the Confederates is included in the footnotes.

Technically, the Army of Tennessee was not permanently so designated until November of 1862. Until then a number of names were used: the Western Army, Central Army of Kentucky, Army of the Mississippi, and others. To avoid confusion, the name Army of Tennessee is used interchangeably with these others.

THOMAS LAWRENCE CONNELLY
Mississippi State University

Contents

Illustrations and Maps

ARMY OF THE
HEARTLAND

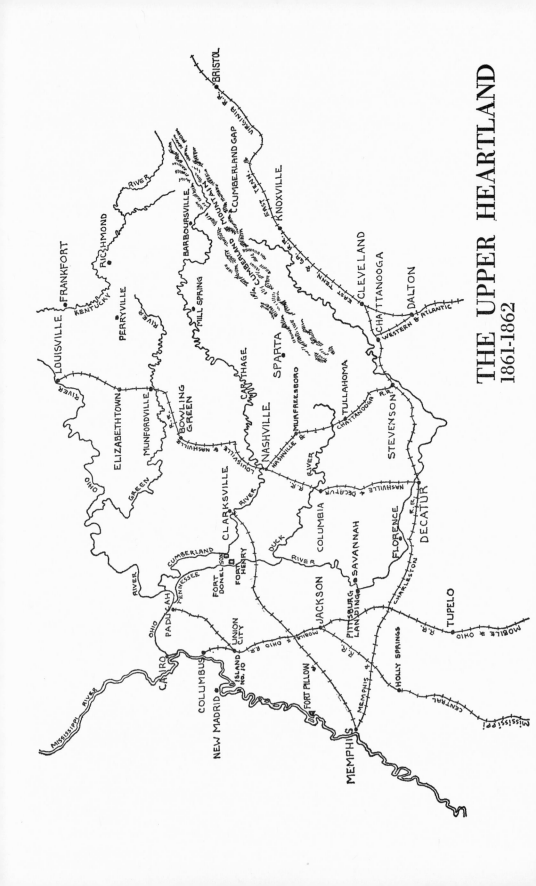

THE UPPER HEARTLAND
1861-1862

introduction

The Legacy of the Heartland

IT IS DOUBTFUL THAT ANY CONFEDERATE OFFICIAL BESTOWED THE NAME "Heartland" upon the region of Tennessee, north-central Alabama, north-central Georgia, and northeast Mississippi. Yet the name might well apply, for this large, irregularly shaped region of some 150,000 square miles was the physical heart of the Confederacy. If one traced the Heartland's boundaries on a map, a ragged square would be formed. The northwest corner of this square, Columbus, Kentucky, was also the northwest corner of the Army of Tennessee's defensive line in the fall of 1861. From Columbus the northern border extended eastward some four hundred miles to Bristol, Tennessee. From Bristol the border extended southward to Macon, Georgia, and from Macon the southern border ran west through Selma, Alabama, to the southwest corner at Jackson, Mississippi.

This region was not only the Confederacy's geographical heart but, more importantly, its logistical and communications heart as well. For the Heartland was a vital manufacturing center, an irreplaceable source of raw materials, livestock, food, and other items. Here was a heavy percentage of the South's iron works, munitions factories, gunpowder mills, and copper mines. Here were hundreds of Confederate, state, and private installations which manufactured artillery, firearms, tents, shoes, and other equipment. The Heartland also boasted a large number of the Confederacy's major supply depots and ordnance laboratories. Through it ran the South's main east-west rail lines, the western Confederacy's major north-south lines, and the key rail links between Virginia and the West. The area was also the heart of Confederate river traffic. On the western fringe lay the Mississippi. Through the Heartland

3

flowed the waters of the Tennessee, Cumberland, Alabama, Chattahoochee, Coosa, and other major rivers.

The history of the Army of Tennessee begins with the influence of the Heartland upon the Army and its commanders. Here the Army was organized, drilled, fed, armed, and equipped. Here the Army fought most of its major battles, for it was responsible for the Heartland's defense. Moreover, the crucial importance of this rich area and the geographical problems of its defense placed heavy burdens upon every commander of the Army of Tennessee. When Albert Sidney Johnston replaced temporary commander Leonidas Polk in September of 1861, Johnston soon discovered that the Heartland had bequeathed to him three important legacies—material, land, and attitude. These were to influence Johnston's defense of the West in the fall and winter of 1861–62, and would influence future commanders of the Army as well.

The Heartland was the largest concentrated area for the production of war materials in the Confederacy. When Johnston retreated to the edge of the Heartland in March, 1862, many believed that he should have turned east to Chattanooga to defend this important region instead of moving into the Mississippi Valley. Of that move Johnston's chief engineer, Major Jeremy Gilmer, commented, "I fear we will lose Middle and Eastern Tennessee—and most of the country producing a supply of grain and wheat." [1] Chief of Ordnance Josiah Gorgas wrote that the loss of the Tennessee sector of the Heartland was the great mistake of the war.[2]

Such laments indicate the overwhelming importance of the area to the South's war effort. There were several reasons for the region's logistical value. It was the principal area of munitions production in the Confederacy. At the beginning of the war, many of the South's makeshift ordnance installations were centered in this area until the government could provide permanent arsenals. Machine shops, foundries, and ordnance works quickly sprang up at Memphis, Nashville, Montgomery, Macon, and other cities. These were vital to the young Confederacy. Nashville installations manufactured powder, weapons, and equipment. Foundries at Rome, Georgia, undertook to cast rifled guns. Macon factories turned out

---

[1] Jeremy Gilmer to his wife, March 24, 1862, in Jeremy Gilmer Papers, Southern Historical Collection, University of North Carolina. The Southern Historical Collection is hereinafter cited as UNC.

[2] Frank E. Vandiver (ed.), *Civil War Diary of General Josiah Gorgas* (University, Ala., 1947), 3. See also Albert Sidney Johnston to Judah Benjamin, February 27, 1862, in Johnston Papers (Headquarters Book, 1861–62), Louisiana Historical Association Collection, Howard-Tilton Library, Tulane University, hereinafter cited as Headquarters Book, Tulane; and *The War of the Rebellion: A Compilation of the Official Records of the Union and Confederate Armies* (Washington, D.C., 1880–1901), Ser. I, Vol. VII, 900–901, hereinafter cited as *Official Records* (unless otherwise indicated all citations are to Series I).

large supplies of accouterments, while shops at Mount Vernon, Alabama, specialized in small arms.[3]

When Tennessee fell to the enemy in early 1862, many of these temporary installations were abandoned, and others were established deeper in the Heartland. Atlanta became a chief production center for caps and friction primers. Athens, Georgia, assumed the responsibility for manufacturing rifles and carbines of the Enfield model. Muzzleloading carbines and later breechloaders were assembled at Tallassee, Alabama. Small arms were repaired at Montgomery, and factories which manufactured leather articles were established. When Nashville fell, its ordnance shops were transferred to Atlanta.[4]

Not only makeshift installations but also permanent establishments of the War and Navy Departments were gradually located in the Heartland. Colonel G. W. Rains was commissioned to establish the Government Powder Mills at Augusta, Georgia, just outside the Heartland proper, and powder was being produced there by April, 1862. In September, 1862, the Ordnance Bureau decided to erect at Macon, Georgia, a Central Ordnance Laboratory for the production of artillery, small arms ammunition, and other equipment. Although the laboratory did operate during the war, the delay of some vital machinery in arriving from England limited the laboratory's service. The Ordnance Bureau also sought to establish a large central armory at Macon for the manufacture of small arms. Like the central laboratory, the armory never reached the planned production capacity; as the war ended before machinery from Virginia and North Carolina could be transferred there. The War and Navy departments also operated a foundry and rolling mills at Selma, Alabama. North of the town, high-grade iron ore deposits were accessible on the Selma, Rome, and Dalton Railroad. At Selma the naval foundry built ironclads for the defense of Mobile. Half of the cannon and two-thirds of the fixed ammunition used by the South in 1864 and 1865 were reportedly made at Selma. The fifty-acre government arsenal, which embraced over a hundred buildings, on short notice could turn out a 15-inch gun or a mountain howitzer, swords, rifles, muskets, pistols, and caps.[5]

This concentration of munitions plants was not planned merely to have

3 J. W. Mallet, "Work of the Ordnance Bureau of the War Department of the Confederate States, 1861–65," *Southern Historical Society Papers*, XXXVII (1909), 5–6; Josiah Gorgas, "Ordnance of the Confederacy: Notes of Brig. Gen. Josiah Gorgas, Chief of Ordnance, C.S.A.," *Army Ordnance*, XVI (January–February, 1936), 213–14; *Official Records*, Ser. IV, Vol. I, 622, 990–91.

4 Gorgas, "Ordnance of the Confederacy," 285–86; Mallet, "Work of the Ordnance Bureau," 6; *Official Records*, XVI, Pt. 2, pp. 740–41; Frank E. Vandiver, *Ploughshares into Swords: Josiah Gorgas and Confederate Ordnance* (Austin, 1952), 122.

5 Mallet, "Work of the Ordnance Bureau," 4–5; Gorgas, "Ordnance of the Confederacy," 286; Vandiver, *Ploughshares into Swords*, 148–76.

them safely behind the front lines. The Heartland was also the Confederacy's greatest source of raw materials. In 1861 the copper mines of East Tennessee contained the South's only supply of the precious reddish metal needed for field artillery and percussion caps. This copper region lay in the rugged Unaka Mountains on the southeastern border of Tennessee. In 1860 refining works had been built at Ducktown, Tennessee, and a copper rolling mill and wire works constructed west of Ducktown at Cleveland on the East Tennessee and Georgia Railroad. Until East Tennessee fell in 1863, the South relied upon these mountain plants for its copper supply. After that the Rebels scoured the mountains of North Carolina for the copper used in whiskey and turpentine stills.[6]

Three important saltpeter-producing regions, vital for the manufactured gunpowder, lay in the Heartland. Rich stores of saltpeter were in the cave regions of the Unaka Mountains of East Tennessee, the Cumberland Mountains of Tennessee, and the Sand Mountain area of northern Alabama. The most productive area for niter was northern Alabama. In 1862 the Nitre and Mining Bureau undertook the task of extracting the mineral from the area around Blue Mountain. Several hundred whites and slaves toiled in the Alabama limestone caves. By the autumn of 1864, the region had produced some 22,665 pounds of niter.[7]

The Confederacy's lead supply was derived from the Blue Ridge and Unaka Mountains, on the northeastern fringe of the Heartland. Lead mines at Wytheville, Virginia, yielded up to 150,000 pounds of lead each month. Ore from mines at Jonesboro, Tennessee, and the Silver Hill mines of western North Carolina was smelted at Petersburg, Virginia. A considerable amount of the precious metal was also mined in the knobs section, along the eastern fringe of the Great Appalachian Valley in East Tennessee. From Strawberry Plains to the Georgia border, small mines extracted lead ore.[8]

The Army of Tennessee was also responsible for the defense of the chief gunpowder production area of the South. The Confederacy's most important powder mills in 1861 lay along the Cumberland River near Nashville. These mills, established by the Military and Financial Board of Tennessee, were producing large quantities of powder as early as June,

[6] J. B. Killebrew and J. M. Safford, *Introduction to the Resources of Tennessee* (Nashville, 1874), 250–52; Mallet, "Work of the Ordnance Bureau," 10–11.

[7] Record Book, April 24, 1861–January 9, 1862 (MS in Military Board of Tennessee Papers, Tennessee State Archives, Nashville), hereinafter cited as Record Book, Tennessee Archives; *Official Records*, Ser. IV, Vol. I, 556; Walter L. Fleming, *Civil War and Reconstruction in Alabama* (2nd ed.; New York, 1949), 152–54, hereinafter cited as Fleming, *Alabama*; James Safford, *Geology of Tennessee* (Nashville, 1869), 502.

[8] Killebrew and Safford, *Resources of Tennessee*, 266; Safford, *Geology*, 484–85; Gorgas, "Ordnance of the Confederacy," 287; Vandiver, *Ploughshares into Swords*, 123; *Official Records*, Ser. IV, Vol. I, 555–56.

1861, and supplied the powder used by the Virginia army at the battle of First Manassas. In July, 1861, the energetic Colonel G. W. Rains of the Confederate Ordnance Bureau took charge of gunpowder production in Tennessee. More powder was sent to armies in Virginia, New Orleans, and Mobile, as well as the Army of Tennessee. In the fall of 1861 the Nashville mills were the only powder source for Albert Sidney Johnston's army.[9]

The Army of Tennessee also had to defend the vast network of Tennessee state ordnance, munitions, and accouterment manufacturing installations. Many of these factories were transferred to Confederate control in the summer of 1861, although some remained under state supervision. Defense of these factories was imperative. Throughout Tennessee a large number of factories were involved in the repair of older weapons; the manufacture of small arms, cartridges, percussion caps, and other equipment; and the casting of heavy ordnance. The Ordnance Department of Tennessee had established excellent foundries at Nashville and Memphis for the manufacture of field and siege artillery. By November, 1861, both foundries were turning out about six guns each week, including six-pounders, twelve-pound howitzers, and rifled artillery. Other foundries which made field artillery were private installations, contracted to the state government and scattered throughout Tennessee.

From Memphis to Nashville, other shops engaged in repair work and the production of small arms and equipment. Shops for converting hog rifles into military arms were established at Nashville, Memphis, Pulaski, Murfreesboro, and Columbia. By the fall of 1861 the Tennessee state munitions plants were among the most extensive in the South. Under the patient direction of Captain Moses Wright of the State Ordnance Department, Nashville plants turned out 100,000 percussion caps daily, and by October, 1861, some 1,300,000 caps were produced weekly in Tennessee. These, too, were used by the Virginia army at First Manassas. Powder, cartridges, sabers, caps, cannon, small arms, saddles, blankets—all were manufactured in state factories at Nashville and Memphis.[10]

The Army of Tennessee was also charged with guarding one of the

9 *Official Records*, LII, Pt. 2, p. 122; W. R. Hunt to W. W. Mackall, October 31, 1861, and M. H. Wright to Mackall, October 31, November 21, 1861, in Confederate Records, Record Group 109 (Western Department, Telegrams Received, September to December, 1861), National Archives, hereinafter cited as Telegrams Received, 1861, National Archives; Record Book, Tennessee Archives. All records cited as being in the National Archives are in Record Group 109.

10 Richard Steuart, "How Johnny Got His Gun," *Confederate Veteran*, XXXII (May, 1924), 166–67; *Official Records*, IV, 445–46, 512, 367; Record Book, Tennessee Archives; Weston Goodspeed and others (eds.), *History of Tennessee* (Nashville, 1887), 541; Gorgas, "Ordnance of the Confederacy," 213; Mackall to V. K. Stevenson, September 23, 1861, in Headquarters Book, Tulane; Richard Steuart, "Confederate Swords," *Confederate Veteran*, XXXIV (January, 1926), 12–13.

South's great stores of food. When the war deprived the South of its supply of beef cattle and grain from the northwestern states, only two areas of the Heartland remained to provide much of the Confederacy's wheat supply. These two areas, south-central Kentucky and Middle Tennessee, and East Tennessee, each produced more than two and a half million bushels of wheat annually. With the exception of Kentucky, largely held by Federals, the most important corn-raising district in the Confederacy east of the Mississippi River lay in Middle Tennessee. Each of the nine counties in this area had an average production of more than a million bushels of corn in 1860. [11]

The Heartland also boasted one of the two major Confederate sources of livestock. Middle Tennessee and the Shenandoah Valley of Virginia were the Confederacy's prime horse and mule centers. Tennessee supplied more mules than any other state in the Confederacy, and, except for Kentucky, produced more horses than any other Rebel state east of the Mississippi River. Northern Virginia and Tennessee were the most important wool-producing areas east of the Mississippi. More pork was raised in Tennessee than in any other Confederate state, save Missouri. When the war halted the South's supply of pork from the midwest, Richmond fell back upon the supply in Tennessee. In January, 1862, Lucius B. Northrop, commissary general of subsistence, reported to the War Department that Tennessee was the main source of pork for Confederate armies.[12]

The Army of Tennessee had to protect not only a center of agriculture but a region of coal smoke, sunrise whistles, open fires, and molten iron. With the iron resources of Pennsylvania and western Virginia lost to the Confederacy and with the western Kentucky furnaces in Union hands, the Cumberland River area from Fort Donelson to Nashville became the South's largest iron district. In 1861 this region was the Confederacy's largest producer of pig iron, iron blooms, and bar, sheet, and railroad iron. Before the war more than seventy-one furnaces and seventy-five forges and bloomeries were concentrated in this so-called Western Iron Belt. This fifty-mile-wide belt lay between the Tennessee and Cumberland rivers. It embraced thirteen counties, and encompassed 5,400 square miles from near the Kentucky border to the Alabama line. This was a land of abundant water power, of rough highland country dissected by

[11] A. L. Conger, "Fort Donelson," *Military Historian and Economist*, I (January, 1916), 56–58.

[12] Conger, "Fort Donelson," 58–59; United States Bureau of Census, *Agriculture of the United States in 1860: Compiled from the Original Returns of the Eighth Census* (Washington, 1864), 2, 6, 18, 62, 66, 84, 92, 108, 128, 136, 148, 162; *Official Records*, Ser. IV, Vol. I, 873.

the Cumberland, Duck, Buffalo, and Tennessee rivers and dozens of narrow, swift creeks which furnished power for the slave-manned forges. In 1861 thousands of slaves and whites labored at furnaces and forges in the iron belt, especially at the Cumberland Iron Works northwest of Nashville.

When the Federals swept across Middle Tennessee in the early months of 1862, a second line of iron works had already been established deeper in the Heartland. This more enduring iron belt was located in the hilly region of northern Alabama, south of the Tennessee River. A variety of items from cannon to cooking pots was manufactured here under the direction of the Nitre and Mining Bureau. The government employed several hundred white conscripts and several thousand Negroes in the mines and rolling mills of the nine-county iron belt. Blast furnaces, rolling mills, foundries, forges, and shops were established here even before the loss of the Cumberland district. During the war these mills and furnaces turned out thirty thousand tons of pig iron and ten thousand tons of bar iron annually.[13]

The concentration of water power, raw materials, and slave labor in the Heartland provided another burden for the western army. Hundreds of small private factories of great logistical or political importance were scattered throughout the area. All were anxious to have the Army's protection. Holly Springs, Mississippi, demanded protection because of the presence of a small arms arsenal and the vital railroad shops of the Mississippi Central line. At Huntsville, Alabama, were the precious shops of the Memphis and Charleston Railroad. Railroad wheels and axles were manufactured at Knoxville, Tennessee, while locomotives were made at Atlanta, Memphis, Nashville, and Holly Springs, Mississippi.

The entire Heartland seemed a maze of such small but crucial installations. Claiborne, Alabama, was the Confederacy's main supply wagon manufacturing source. Factories at Tallassee, Autaugaville, and Prattville, Alabama, manufactured five hundred yards of tent cloth per day in 1861. Shoes were manufactured at Tuscaloosa, Alabama, and salt was processed at the Upper Works near Old St. Stephens, Alabama, the Central Works near Salt Mountain, and the Lower Works near Sunflower Bend on the Tombigbee River. An entire county might contain a dozen vital factories. Lauderdale County, Alabama, alone contained rolling mills, cotton factories, tanneries, woolen factories, iron mills, and a navy yard. The dis-

---

13 J. P. Lesley, *Iron Manufacturer's Guide to the Furnaces, Forges and Rolling Mills of the United States* (New York, 1859), 130–36; Ethel Armes, *Story of Coal and Iron in Alabama* (Birmingham, 1910), 157–58; Fleming, *Alabama;* 154; Goodspeed (ed.), *Tennessee,* 262; Conger, "Fort Donelson," 60–62; J. B. Killebrew, *Middle Tennessee as an Iron Centre* (Nashville, 1879), 9–15.

persal of manufacturing plants and the ensuing cries for protection from every corner of the Heartland were to complicate the task of defending the region.[14]

The Army of Tennessee also had to defend Nashville, the great store-house and arsenal of the western Confederacy. The wisdom of placing such a vast depot and manufacturing center so near the front line was debatable. But when Albert Sidney Johnston came to Tennessee in September, 1861, as the first permanent western commander, the city's defense was a necessity. Already the city was the South's gunpowder center, a Confederate depot for small arms, ammunition, and artillery, and the chief ordnance laboratory of the Second Department. Tons of other equipment manufactured in state, Confederate, and private factories at Nashville were being stored in warehouses along the Cumberland River. Sabers, harness, muskets, pistols, saddles, gray jeans, clothing, tents, bacon, flour, artillery—all were manufactured and cached in Nashville.[15]

The Heartland was also vital as a source of manpower. This was one of Johnston's most serious problems in the autumn of 1861. To defend the Heartland, he had to rely for troops upon the frontline regions of the area. Tennessee not only contained much of the Army's main defensive line, but was also the key supplier of reinforcements. During the summer of 1861, when temporarily commanding the Army, Leonidas Polk was not allowed to call upon any states in the Western Department, except Tennessee and Arkansas, for reinforcements without consent from Richmond. By September, Tennessee had been repeatedly bled for manpower. Fifty regiments were in state or Confederate service, and thirty of these were on the Tennessee line. In September only three other states were represented on the western line by a total of seven regiments. Johnston asked Tennessee for even more men. On September 21 he asked Governor Harris for thirty thousand additional volunteers, and on November 21 he asked for every man in the state who could be armed. Harris was forced to call out thirty thousand state militiamen to meet his request.

Although the front line of Tennessee was almost drained of available

14 *Official Records*, Ser. IV, Vol. I, 881; Fleming, *Alabama*, 150, 154.

15 Wright to Mackall, September 24, November 9, 13, 1861, Stevenson to Mackall, September 27, 1861, Stevenson to Albert Sidney Johnston, October 2, 1861, all in Telegrams Received, 1861, National Archives; Wright to Josiah Gorgas, February 5, 1862, in Letters and Telegrams Sent, Ordnance Offices, Nashville, Tennessee, and Atlanta, Georgia, Ch. IV, Vol. 8, National Archives; Johnston to Harris, December 25, 1861, in Headquarters Book, Tulane; *Official Records*, IV, 441–42, Ser. IV, Vol. I, 618–22; Stanley Horn, "Nashville During the Civil War," *Tennessee Historical Quarterly*, IV (March, 1945), 3–8; James D. Porter, *Tennessee* (Atlanta, 1899), 8, Vol. VIII of Clement Evans (ed.), *Confederate Military History* (12 vols.; Atlanta, 1899).

troops, Johnston was forced to rely still upon Tennessee as his main reinforcement source. On November 19 the War Department rejected his requests for aid from Arkansas, Louisiana, and Georgia. He was restricted to calling out only *armed* men from Mississippi, Kentucky, North Alabama, and Tennessee. For all purposes, this restriction meant that Tennessee must continue to shoulder the burden. The state armies of Alabama and Mississippi were more poorly equipped than the State Army of Tennessee and generally could offer only unarmed regiments which Richmond would not allow Johnston to accept. Almost all of the Kentucky regiments which did come were organized in Tennessee camps. Even the Tennessee area was restricted. Most of the Tennessee troops were called from Middle and West Tennessee because of the uneasy situation in East Tennessee created by a heavy concentration of Unionists. Thus to abandon either Middle or West Tennessee would have been a severe blow to Johnston's efforts to obtain reinforcements.[16]

A similar logistical problem hampered the Army of Tennessee. Although it was responsible for defending the Rebel storehouse of food, munitions, and equipment which extended from the Kentucky border deep into Alabama, the western army was not allowed to use much of this food supply. Instead Johnston's force was expected to live off the country and send the collected stores to other areas. In October the War Department twice cautioned Johnston that food collected at Nashville was not for his army's use but for that of the Virginia army.

Such restrictions created an almost impossible situation. The Army had to obtain most of its subsistence from the northern border of Tennessee, in the very area where Johnston expected a Federal advance. This forced Johnston into a rigid policy of territorial defense, in order to protect his foodstuff supply. Even worse, in 1861 the rich Tennessee cupboard was almost bare, for the state was in the midst of a three-year drought. In Middle Tennessee what grain was raised and what meats were packed were sent to the Virginia lines. The Heartland's interior provided little aid. The fertile Tennessee Valley in Alabama was planted in cotton, and the food crops which grew there were hoarded by planters. The Chattanooga area was a region of pocketed mountain coves and mere subsistence

16 Johnston to Isham Harris, September 21, 1861, Harris to Jefferson Davis, July 2, 1861, W. C. Whitthorne to Judah Benjamin, January 8, 1862, General Order Twelve, Tennessee State Militia, November 19, 1861, all in Isham G. Harris Papers, Tennessee Archives; Johnston to Harris, September 21, 1861, in Headquarters Book, Tulane; Porter, *Tennessee*, 8–9; *Official Records*, IV, 452–53, 565, LII, Pt. 2, pp. 244–45, 253–54, Ser. IV, Vol. I, 626–31.

farming. The Cumberland Mountain region was too poor to support an army.[17]

Perhaps the richness of the Heartland eventually proved a hindrance to the Army of Tennessee. In the fall of 1861 the obligation to defend this vital area and the need to subsist his army on the front lines of the West forced Johnston into a policy of territorial defense with little possibility of maneuvering for a tactical advantage. If he surrendered territory, what territory could be spared? If Nashville were given up, the loss to Rebel logistics would be staggering. Abandon the area between the Cumberland and Tennessee waters, and the South's greatest iron center would be lost. Surrender East Tennessee, and precious copper and wheat stores would be swept away. A hundred towns and counties all seemed too vital to lose. There seemed to be no area to yield in the autumn of 1861; Johnston felt he must hold it all.[18]

If material resources produced heavy responsibility, the Heartland's geography beset the Army of Tennessee with defensive problems. The topography of the region seemed to work against Johnston's attempts at defense. When he took command, the western line extended from the Appalachian Mountains to the Mississippi River; the right flank rested in the Unaka Mountains.

In 1861 the Unakas were still a mysterious land of ice caves, bald summits, semi-arctic plants, April snow, and pure springs of icy water, with an average elevation of five thousand feet. They were not a single chain of high peaks. Had this been true, Johnston's problems in East Tennessee would have been less difficult. Instead, the Unakas were a series of parallel mountain belts, interspersed with deep valleys and hidden coves. An additional series of smaller ranges lay directly west of the main range. This was a prime Tory region of Tennessee, a land of irregular warfare, bridge burnings, and flights across the mountains to join Yankee armies. Topography had created the problem of the landlocked, non-slaveholding, small mountain farmers, and had also masked their activities. The result was a forced dispersal of Confederate

---

[17] *Official Records,* IV, 452, 444; *House Journal of the Second Extra Session of the Thirty-Ninth General Assembly of the State of Tennessee Which Convened at Nashville on Thursday, the 25th Day of April, A.D., 1861,* 19; Braxton Bragg to Edmund Kirby Smith, September 23, 1862, in William P. Palmer Collection of Bragg Papers, Western Reserve Historical Society, Cleveland, hereinafter cited as Bragg Papers, Western Reserve; Calvin Clack, "History of Company A, 3rd Tennessee Infantry" (MS in 3rd Tennessee Infantry Papers, Duke University Library) ; Transcript of Testimony of A. M. McCook (MS in Don Carlos Buell Papers, Fondren Library, Rice University) ; Don Carlos Buell, *Statement of Major General Buell in Review of the Evidence before the Military Commission Appointed by the War Department* (n.p., n.d.) , 13–14.
[18] Conger, "Fort Donelson," 55–62.

troops to guard railroad depots and bridges on the vital East Tennessee and Virginia Railroad link between the eastern and western armies. The mountains swallowed up the movements of the Union raiders who repeatedly lashed at the railroad. The Tories would debouch from the coves of Johnson and Carter counties to strike the East Tennessee and Virginia line north of Bristol. Others would come from the gorge of the French Broad River and the coves of Sevier and Greene counties to strike the Holston River bridge at Strawberry Plains. Farther north, others would steal from the coves of Roan and Iron Mountains to attack the Watauga River bridge. There was no chance of obtaining a single concentration of troops to fend off the mountain will-o'-the-wisps. Rebel troops badly needed on the Kentucky front had to be detached to guard numerous vulnerable points.[19]

West of the Unakas lay the Tennessee portion of the Great Appalachian Valley known as the East Tennessee Valley. This valley, some 220 miles in length and bounded by the Unakas and the Cumberland Plateau, extended from Bristol on the north to Chattanooga on the south. Drained by the Tennessee and its major tributaries, such as the Holston, Watauga, and Nolichucky, the valley contained rich soil with two growing seasons each year. This region was the principal food-producing area in East Tennessee for the western army.

In the fall of 1861 this valley produced more problems than wheat for Albert Sidney Johnston. The East Tennessee and Virginia and the East Tennessee and Georgia Railroads, a crucial link between Virginia and the West, ran the length of the valley from Chattanooga to Bristol. This exposed railroad line was extremely vulnerable to Tory harassment because of the valley's topography. The East Tennessee Valley was more than just a flat river bottom. Actually it was a series of smaller valleys divided by small mountain ranges which interlocked with the Unakas on the east and the Cumberland Plateau on the west. These buttressing ranges extended into the valley at right angles to the Unakas and the Cumberland Plateau and served to mask Union activities against the railroad.[20]

The valley presented Johnston with a still more serious problem. Should the Federals penetrate the northern part of the valley, they could move

[19] A. J. Lindsay to Mackall, W. B. Wood to Mackall, and Nashville operator to Johnston, November 11, 1861, Operator to Mackall, November 10, 1861, Operator to Johnston, November 9, 1861, all in Telegrams Received, 1861, National Archives; Henry Halleck to Buell, October 19, 1862, in Buell Papers, Rice; A. W. Hawkins, *Handbook of Tennessee* (Nashville, 1882), 5, 9; Arnold Guyot, "On the Appalachian Mountain System," *American Journal of Science and Arts*, Second Series, XXXI (March, 1861), 167, 169–71.

[20] H. C. Amick, "The Great Valley of East Tennessee," *Economic Geography*, X (January, 1934), 35–40; Conger, "Fort Donelson," 56–57.

by rail or road without difficulty down the valley to seize Chattanooga. This strategic town was the gateway to the lower Heartland and a great rail junction of the Western and Atlantic from Atlanta, the East Tennessee and Georgia from Knoxville, and the Nashville and Chattanooga from Stevenson, Alabama. If Chattanooga were lost, one of the two rail lines connecting Virginia and the West would be severed, and Atlanta would be vulnerable to capture. If Atlanta fell, the other rail link between Johnston and Virginia would be lost, and the munitions area of Georgia would be open to destruction. On the north and northwest, Chattanooga was protected from invasion by the Cumberland Mountains, or Plateau. On the west, both the Tennessee River gorge and the extension of the Cumberland range into Georgia and Alabama protected the town. The only vulnerable flank was on the east—the valley approach. Should the Yankees seize the upper valley, this flank was open to assault.

The Confederates hoped to block a Federal invasion of the East Tennessee valley by holding Cumberland Gap. The day before Johnston took command on September 15, 1861, General Felix Zollicoffer, the East Tennessee commander, seized and fortified this position. The gap was situated on the border of Tennessee, Kentucky, and Virginia, on the main road between the valley of East Tennessee and eastern Kentucky. The artillery which Zollicoffer placed there seemed to eliminate the threat of Yankee invasion.

Yet the strength of Cumberland Gap was a myth. There were five places at which a Federal army could cross the mountains between the gap and Nashville; three of these—Rogers' Gap, Big Creek Gap, and Wheeler's Gap—were all within forty miles of it. A Federal force could easily outflank Cumberland Gap by moving on these routes. There were two other potential invasion routes. One led by way of Albany, Kentucky, to Jamestown, Tennessee, and the other by way of Tompkinsville, Kentucky, to Gainesboro, Tennessee. A Federal advance on either road could easily sever communication between Confederates in Middle and East Tennessee.[21]

Indeed, the threat to Rebel communications was the great problem

21 John McCown to Bragg, September 14, 1862, in Letters and Telegrams Sent, Department of East Tennessee, March–November, 1862, Ch. II, Vol. 51, National Archives; McCown to Edmund Kirby Smith, September 15, 1862, in Endorsements on Letters Received, Department of East Tennessee, 1862–63, Ch. II, Vol. 51½, National Archives; Mackall to Felix Zollicoffer, September 23, 1861, in Headquarters Book, Tulane; James Rains to his wife, September 15, 1861, in Rains Letters, Tennessee Archives; Alexander Coffee to his wife, October 26, November 3, 1861, in Alexander Donelson Coffee Papers, UNC; Thomas L. Connelly, "Gateway to Kentucky: The Wilderness Road, 1748–1792," *Register of the Kentucky Historical Society*, LIX (April, 1961), 109–10; *Official Records*, IV, 195, 441.

in 1861 on that portion of Johnston's line between Cumberland Gap and the Tompkinsville area. Of this 128-mile stretch of the Army's line, guarded by General Felix Zollicoffer, 71 miles crossed the entire length of the Cumberland Plateau, or Cumberland Mountains. The mountain area was a country of thick forests, almost impassable roads, jagged rocks, and barren hillside farms. The land was so barren that a permanent Confederate force could not be stationed atop the plateau for lack of supplies. The mountain population from Cumberland Gap to Tompkinsville complicated the situation, for the strong Unionist sentiment produced much hostility. Guerrilla bands struck at Confederate communications; Unionists fed Confederates false information as to the Yankees' whereabouts; and citizens were uncooperative in furnishing the Rebels with subsistence.

Equally important, the topography of the area gave the advantage of maneuver to the Federals. An invading column could assemble at Somerset, Kentucky, and march toward either the Albany, Wheeler's Gap, or Big Creek Gap routes without the destination's being revealed until the Federals were in Tennessee. Zollicoffer had been able to blockade the five routes during the summer and fall of 1861. But when the autumn freshets of the Cumberland country changed to the icy rivulets of the mountain winter, the disadvantages of terrain would make Zollicoffer's defense even more difficult.[22]

West of Zollicoffer's position lay the great Cumberland River basin of Tennessee and Kentucky. The geography of this region strongly influenced Johnston's efforts at defense. When he first arrived in September, 1861, Johnston was troubled by the long curve of the Middle Tennessee line. The northeast salient was high on the Cumberland in the Mill Springs, Kentucky, area on a line fifty-five miles north of Nashville. The center of the line was at Nashville, and the northwest salient was at Fort Donelson on a line thirty miles north of Nashville. Both flanks were well in advance of the center, and Johnston found himself operating on an exterior line of communications.

22 Harriette Simpson Arnow, *Seedtime on the Cumberland* (New York, 1960), 13; Killebrew and Safford, *Resources of Tennessee*, 287; T. C. Hindman to Captain Pickett, January 17, 1862, in Western Department, Telegrams Received, January–May, 1862, National Archives, hereinafter cited as Telegrams Received, 1862, National Archives; Alexander Coffee to his wife, November 3, 9, 1861, in Coffee Papers, UNC; Diary of J. Stoddard Johnston, June 26–September 9, 1862 (MS in J. Stoddard Johnston Papers, Filson Club Historical Society, Louisville), hereinafter cited as Johnston Diary, Filson Club; Buell to Halleck, October 17, 1862, in Buell Papers, Rice; W. B. Wood to Mackall, October 26, November 5, 1861, Zollicoffer to Mackall, November 7, 1861, all in Telegrams Received, 1861, National Archives; *Official Records*, LII, Pt. 2, pp. 178–81, 190–91, IV, 442–43.

Confederate operations were also influenced by the peculiar attitude of the people in the Cumberland basin. The basin was a way of life, centered upon the Cumberland River and Nashville, the central town of the area. Northeast of Nashville 358 miles of navigable river water lay within Rebel hands from the city to the head of low-water steam navigation at Burnside, Kentucky. Northwest of Nashville only 117 miles of the river basin were within the Confederate lines. The fact that so much of the basin lay northeast of Nashville was significant. Most of the population of the Confederate-held sector of the basin lived in the northeastern part. Moreover, the eastern sector was navigable only six months of the year, while the river northwest of Nashville was navigable the entire year.[23]

The Confederate line in Middle Tennessee was to be colored by the aspirations of the river people to the east. To these people the most important item in their lives was running water. The Cumberland was news brought up from Nashville by packet steamer. The Cumberland was also sound: the wild roar of the river swollen by freshets high in the Cumberlands, the whistle of light steamboats, and the moan of the water as it raced over shoals. These were sounds of power and force, always surging away to the west. These people knew little of the meandering pace of the river northwest of Nashville. In the eastern basin the torrential, invincible river represented security. Security was also Nashville, the metropolis of the basin. A symbol of downriver strength, Nashville was their market, their legal and religious counsel, and their provider of salt, newspapers, and coffin nails.

The result was a curious state of mind among the people regarding the dangers of a Federal invasion up the Cumberland. The eastern basin folk were more concerned that the bluecoats might storm through the Cumberland Plateau area than that they might advance up the Cumberland River to Nashville. If such an advance did come up the river, it would probably come during the rainy months from December to June, when the heavy gunboats could pass over scattered obstructions below the city. Ironically, the people of the eastern basin eagerly awaited these months, for this was the only time of year when the river was navigable above Nashville. Even the people who lived along the river below the city seemed undisturbed by the danger of a Federal advance. These people also did their business at the town on the bluffs, and were caught up in the myth of the invincibility of Nashville. Much of the blame for the eventual failure to fortify the Cumberland River and Nashville ade-

[23] Arnow, *Seedtime*, 13; Killebrew and Safford, *Resources of Tennessee*, 287.

quately must go to the absence within the basin of a strong pressure bloc of people concerned with the river's defense.

The lethargic nature of the Cumberland basin residents was also felt at Fort Donelson, a hundred miles downriver from Nashville. It would be an easy matter, especially during the rainy season, for a Federal army to move up the Cumberland and take Nashville. When Johnston arrived in September, 1861, no guns were mounted at Donelson, no fortifications had been constructed, and the fort was abandoned.[24]

Even if Johnston had found a strong bastion at Donelson, still the terrain of the area would have frustrated the Cumberland's defense. Fifteen miles to the west, the Tennessee River followed a parallel course into Kentucky. The only force to protect the fort against a flank move from the Tennessee was a small garrison at Fort Henry, almost due west of Donelson. North of Fort Donelson a network of roads led south from Eddyville, Kentucky, and other potential embarkation centers into the region between the rivers. A Union force could descend upon either Fort Donelson or Fort Henry without even utilizing river transportation. South of Donelson a thin communications line, seventy-five miles long, connected the fort with Nashville. But the Nashville road crossed numerous creeks and stretches of Cumberland backwater which cut far inland; during the rainy season this road became impassable.[25]

The Tennessee was also difficult to defend. The river provided a good avenue for a Yankee advance, for it was navigable the year around from its mouth at the Ohio River to Florence, Alabama. If Florence were reached, the Confederate rail link between Chattanooga and Memphis, the Memphis and Charleston, would be severed. Yet the Tennessee River people were apathetic; few citizens demanded that the river be properly fortified. The reason for this lay with the river's geography. The Tennessee was actually not one river, but three. The upper river, some two hundred miles of water between Knoxville and Chattanooga, was an isolated region. For three months of each year, navigation was completely closed below Chattanooga, and was extremely hazardous during the remaining nine months. West of Chattanooga, the Tennessee thundered

24 Record Book, Tennessee Archives; Gideon Pillow to John B. Floyd, February 8, 1862, in Correspondence of Brigadier General J. B. Floyd, 1861–65, National Archives, hereinafter cited as Floyd Correspondence, National Archives; Mackall to Polk, October 8, 1861, in Headquarters Book, Tulane; Adolphus Heiman to Harris, October 14, 1861, in Harris Papers, Tennessee Archives.

25 *Official Records,* IV, 506–507; Johnston to Gustavus A. Henry, October 26, 1861, in Headquarters Book, Tulane; James L. Nichols, *Confederate Engineers* (Tuscaloosa, 1957) , 42–44.

through a gorge beneath the Cumberland Mountains in a morass of whirlpools, sucks, sandbars, and flint shoals which extended forty miles below the town. Such obstructions as Tumbling Shoals and the Suck were feared by even the boatmen of shallow draught vessels, and it was impossible for a gunboat to force its way through the gorge into Chattanooga. The people of the upper Tennessee seemed little concerned with a potential Federal naval invasion from below Chattanooga.[26]

The people of the central valley between Chattanooga and Florence also showed little concern for an upriver invasion. The cotton and corn planters of the central valley were almost completely isolated from the lower Tennessee River area. At Big Muscle Shoals, between Brown's Ferry and Florence, the river fell eighty-five feet within fifteen miles over a series of cascades and flint shoals. Here the river was navigable downstream for only three weeks during the year, and then only by light draught boats. In normal times a person could cross the Tennessee at the shoals without wetting his feet. Landlocked by these shoals and harassed by non-slave-holding Tory farmers in the sandy highlands overlooking the river, the central planters had no time to lobby for fortifications on the Tennessee.[27]

Yet even the people of the lower river, between Florence and Paducah, Kentucky, did not clamor for ample fortifications. The river's character was certainly different, for there were no serious obstructions below Florence and this portion was navigable all year. Still except for one ineffectual protest by a citizen's group from that city and Tuscumbia, Alabama, no pressure was exerted in this vulnerable section of the valley. The reason for this apathy was probably the lower valley's geography. The counties adjacent to the river contained poor land of thin topsoil. Few slaves were necessary and Union sentiment grew strong. These counties opposed secession in June, 1861, and responded only feebly to calls for Rebel troops. Henderson, Hardin, Wayne, and Decatur counties in Tennessee were hotbeds of Tory activity, and sporadic guerilla fighting flickered in the swamp bottoms along the lower river throughout the war.[28]

The defense of the Tennessee was further weakened by the site

26 S. H. Long, "Summary of the Tennessee River," *House Documents,* 29th Cong., 1st Sess., No. 167, pp. 3–95; William Gaw, "Report on the Examination and Survey of the Tennessee River," *House Executive Documents,* 40th Cong., 2nd Sess., No. 271, pp. 4–21, hereinafter cited as Gaw, "Survey of the Tennessee"; T. J. Campbell, *The Upper Tennessee* (Chattanooga, 1932), 41.

27 Gaw, "Survey of the Tennessee," 25–28; Fleming, *Alabama,* 109–16; William Martin, *Internal Improvements in Alabama,* Johns Hopkins University Studies in History and Political Science, XX, 4th series (Baltimore, 1902), 42–44, 48; Robert Somers, *Southern States Since the War: 1870–71* (New York, 1871), 113.

28 "Navigation of the Tennessee River," *Senate Documents,* 59th Cong., 1st Sess., No. 83, pp. 20–21; L. M. Jones to Harris, January 21, 1862, in Harris Papers, Tennessee

chosen for the river's protection. In May, 1861, when Tennessee authorities were searching for a place to locate a fort on the river, they passed up a strong position at the mouth of the Big Sandy River and instead began work downstream at Fort Henry. Yet Fort Henry had many geographical disadvantages. The Tennessee-Kentucky border was offset at the point where the Tennessee flowed into Kentucky. Fort Henry was on the eastern bank in Tennessee, but the west bank was in neutral Kentucky. Since politics forbade the construction of defenses on the Kentucky side, this made Fort Henry vulnerable to invasion both from the north and from the west bank.

The terrain surrounding the fort made for a poor defense. A range of hills on the west bank of the river commanded the few earthworks which had been constructed before Johnston arrived. These hills, within seven hundred yards of the fort, commanded the fort's parapet. On the east bank a line of hills north and west of the fort were within easy rifle range. Even worse, Captain Jesse Taylor, a seasoned artillerist, visited the fort in early September and uncovered some disturbing facts regarding rainfall. He noted that in an ordinary February rise of the Tennessee the highest point in the fort would be under two feet of water and the lower river batteries nine feet under water. Colonel Adolphus Heiman, commander of the Fort Henry garrison in October, 1861, was also aware of the fort's problem. Heiman particularly criticized the manner in which the fort's batteries had been mounted in the summer. All of the guns faced downstream and had a range of only a mile and a half. Once a Federal gunboat ran under the guns, the fort was helpless, and the boat would be free to steam upriver to Danville, Tennessee, where the vital Memphis, Clarksville, and Louisville Railroad crossed the river. Thus, when Johnston took command in September, the gateway to the Heartland was guarded by an incomplete Tennessee River fort constructed below the high water line and garrisoned by 870 men whose artillery would fire in only one direction.[29]

Between the Tennessee and Mississippi rivers, Johnston inherited the

Archives; Isham Harris to Albert Sidney Johnston, December 6, 1861, in Telegrams Received, 1861, National Archives; *Official Records*, VII, 888; Truman Strobridge (ed.), "Letters of D. C. Donnohue, Special Agent for the Procuring of Cotton Seed," *Tennessee Historical Quarterly*, XXI (December, 1962), 379–80; Mary Campbell, *Attitude of Tennesseans Toward the Union 1847–1861* (New York, 1961), 286–87, 292–93.

29 Wilbur Foster, "Building of Forts Henry and Donelson," in Bromfield Ridley (ed.) *Battles and Sketches of the Army of Tennessee* (Mexico, Mo., 1906), 65–66. Bushrod Johnson to Harris, June 11, 1861, and Harris to A. S. Johnston, June 14, 1861, in Harris Papers, Tennessee Archives; Captain Jesse Taylor, "Defense of Fort Henry," in Robert U. Johnston and Clarence C. Buel (eds.) *Battles and Leaders of the Civil War* (2nd. ed.; New York, 1956), I, 368–69, hereinafter cited as *Battles and Leaders;* Lloyd Tilghman to W. W. Mackall, January 23, 1862, in Telegrams Received, 1862, National Archives.

problem of defending an exterior line located in open terrain. In this area was the rail junction of the Mobile and Ohio, New Orleans and Ohio, and Nashville and Northwestern Railroads—Union City. A Federal seizure of the town would outflank Confederate forts on the Mississippi and would partially sever communications between West and Middle Tennessee. The level terrain of the Mississippi Plateau north of Union City provided no barrier to a Federal move. Also, north in Kentucky, on a line which extended east from the Mississippi River to Mayfield, there were a series of knobs which shielded Yankee operations.

When Johnston arrived, the Union City position remained vulnerable. Although Leonidas Polk had 22,000 men in West Tennessee in September, only 1,400 were on the Union City flank. The remainder were stationed at the Mississippi River forts at Memphis, Fort Harris, Fort Pillow, Island Number Ten, and Fort Wright. These defenses had been constructed by Tennessee authorities and by Polk in the summer.[30]

It was no accident that Johnston in September found that almost all of Polk's army was concentrated in the Mississippi River forts. Polk had succumbed to the pressure of the river bloc. While there were no such blocs of citizens who pressured for the defense of the Cumberland and Tennessee waters in the Heartland's center, there was a strong pressure group on the western fringe of the region. This group, centered mainly at Memphis, lobbied for strong fortifications on the Mississippi.

This Mississippi River bloc was partially a result of the martial atmosphere of Memphis. Despite Memphis' rapid growth between 1840 and 1860, during which the population increased from about two thousand to twenty-three thousand, the town had not attained the cosmopolitan atmosphere of Nashville, but remained a frontier community. Probably because of the town's location on the Mississippi, its citizens had shown unusually strong interest in the Texas War for Independence, William Walker's Latin American escapades, the Mexican War, and the territorial feud in Kansas. During the 1850's a large number of military outfits existed in the town. Even before Tennessee seceded, Memphis was an armed camp. Local merchants had resolved in a unanimous vote that West Tennessee, regardless of the opinion of the remainder of the state, should join the Confederacy. A powerful Committee of Public Safety was formed, more military companies were organized, and local manufacturers contracted for war materials.[31]

[30] *Official Records*, III, 651–52, 661, 681, 703–705, 712; Mackall to Joseph Dixon, September 30, 1861, in Headquarters Book, Tulane.

[31] Gerald Capers, *Biography of a River Town; Memphis: Its Heroic Age* (Chapel Hill, 1939), 143–44.

The pressure of the Mississippi River bloc was the product of something more than the warlike spirit of Memphis, however. The people of the town, as well as those in the Delta country further south, were fearful of a Federal invasion. This fear swelled into a chorus of demands for priority of Mississippi River defenses in state and Confederate appropriations. Sam Tate, president of the Memphis and Charleston Railroad, repeatedly warned Richmond that the Mississippi Valley would be overrun by Federals. The powerful Memphis Military Board badgered Polk, Johnston, Jefferson Davis, and others for more aid to Memphis. The board was so influential in its efforts that it drew funds from the legislature and was permitted to issue orders in Polk's name while he commanded the Second Department.[32]

No small element in the pressure groups were the people of the Yazoo–Mississippi Delta region. Throughout the war, Delta planters feared that a Union invasion would ignite a slave insurrection. Rumors of uprisings continually hindered Confederate recruiting in river counties in Mississippi. When Nashville fell in 1862, panic gripped the slaveholders on the Mississippi. General Gideon Pillow reported that both great excitement and depression were commonplace among the people.

When Johnston arrived in Tennessee, the evidences of the river bloc's pressure were seen in the dispersal of Polk's forces. By September, five river forts, manned by eighteen thousand men, guarded the river approach to Memphis: Forts Harris, Wright, Columbus, Pillow, and the Memphis fortifications. A sixth fort at Island Number Ten was under construction. Less than two thousand men guarded the vast lands between the Mississippi and the Tennessee, and Forts Henry and Donelson remained in a pitiful condition.[33]

In the second week of September, Johnston began his long trek through the Heartland to survey his new command. Though other people, events, and ideas created problems for the new Army of Tennessee during the spring and summer of 1861, the Heartland had bequeathed its own peculiar legacy of difficulties. Johnston felt the awesome sense of responsibility for protecting the food and munitions area

[32] Memphis Military Board to Harris, August 30, 1861, in Harris Papers, Tennessee Archives; Record Book, Tennessee Archives; Capers, *Memphis,* 132–35; *Official Records,* IV, 367.

[33] *Official Records,* Ser. IV, Vol. I, 276, Ser. I, Vol. VII, 908–909, LII, Pt. 2, pp. 214–16, 279; Memphis Military Board to Harris, June 11, 1861, and C. G. Dahlgren to Harris, June 18, 1861, in Harris Papers, Tennessee Archives. John Bettersworth, *Confederate Mississippi: The People and Policies of a Cotton State in Wartime* (Baton Rouge, 1943), 161–62; James Hall to his parents, May 28, 1861, in James Iredell Hall Papers, UNC.

of the Heartland. He sensed that he must defend a line of over four hundred miles in length, beset with geographical defense weaknesses. Communications between the eastern, middle, and western areas of his command were dissected by several rivers and a mountain range. Every inch of the uplands of the Heartland was vital country from which the Army must eat, procure its weapons, and fill its ranks. To the east he sensed the powerful Tory element in East Tennessee. Lethargy would harass his defensive works in Middle Tennessee, and harangues for local defense would color his efforts in West Tennessee. Such was the legacy given by the Heartland to Johnston and the Army of Tennessee.

PART I

the legacy of the summer

one

The Legacy of Isham Harris

IF ANY ONE MAN COULD CLAIM THE DISTINCTION OF BEING THE FATHER OF the Army of Tennessee, that man would probably be Governor Isham Harris of Tennessee. In the spring and summer of 1861 Harris not only led his state out of the Union, but organized the Provisional Army of Tennessee. That army, perhaps the best organized state force in the South, became the nucleus of the Army of Tennessee. When Harris transferred it to Confederate service, it boasted twenty-four regiments, ten artillery batteries, an Engineer Corps, Quartermaster and Ordnance departments, and an Ordnance Bureau.

Harris did even more for the war effort. Between May and December, 1861, he organized more than seventy-one regiments for Confederate service. Indeed, by the end of the summer he had already enlisted more than one hundred thousand men for state and Confederate duty. That autumn he dutifully responded to every request by Albert Sidney Johnston for reinforcements. Harris even joined Johnston's staff as a volunteer aide, and later served on the staff of every other commander of the western army and in every major battle except Perryville.[1]

Despite his energy and devotion, Harris in 1861 did considerable damage to the Army of Tennessee's future efforts. By the end of the summer he had created several difficult problems for Johnston to overcome. Harris tended to dabble in strategy without correlating his efforts with Richmond's. He possessed a naive trust in his own scant mili-

---

[1] S. R. Simpson's Reminiscences (MS in S. R. Simpson Papers, Confederate Collection, Tennessee Archives); Harris to Jefferson Davis, July 2, 1861, and Gideon Pillow to Harris, July 14, 1861, in Harris Papers, Tennessee Archives.

tary abilities and those of his state officers. His efforts were often colored by political design.

Had the governor possessed little military power before Johnston came to Tennessee, his mistakes might have been much easier to overcome. But Harris held three positions of influence and in each he caused future trouble for commanders of the Army. In the spring of 1861 he led the move for an independent state of Tennessee. Between April and July he organized the state army, and was actual commander in chief until Leonidas Polk arrived in July. Even after Polk's arrival, Harris commanded in Middle and East Tennessee for two months while these sections were not yet under Confederate authority. Only with Johnston's arrival in September did Harris' power diminish. By that time the governor had bequeathed a troublesome legacy to the Army.

Harris' influence began with the campaign to carry Tennessee out of the Union. In February, 1861, Tennessee voters had rejected a proposal to summon a convention which would consider secession. Anxious for secession, Harris and his colleagues devised the clever strategy of placing the state in an isolated position, neither in the Union nor in the Confederacy. Relations with Federal government would be severed, but Tennessee would not actually secede. Then, when the populace was convinced that an independent Tennessee was in danger from Federal invasion, Harris and his friends would remind the people that the state's security lay in the Confederacy.

Harris began this campaign in a message to the legislature on April 25 in which he urged that the people formally dissolve their ties with the Union. On May 6 the legislature complied and passed the "Declaration of Independence and Ordinance," a document subject to ratification by the people on June 8.

The secessionists were careful to keep an independent Tennessee and Tennessee as a Confederate state as separate ideas, at least superficially. Thus the legislature authorized a second vote on the same day to determine whether, if independence were ratified, Tennessee should accept the Confederate constitution. Confederate Commissioner Henry Hilliard explained to Secretary of War Robert Toombs that the object of the separate vote was to secure the hasty secession of Tennessee.[2]

Later military affairs would be influenced by the methods used by these

[2] *Senate Journal of the Extra Session of the Thirty-Third General Assembly of the State of Tennessee Which Convened at Nashville on the First Monday in January, A.D., 1861,* 9; *Senate Journal of the Second Extra Session of the Thirty-Third General Assembly of the State of Tennessee Which Convened at Nashville on Thursday, the 25th Day of April, A.D., 1861,* 15, 27, 32, 16, 23, 30, 60; *House Second Extra Session,* 43, 66, 57, 49, 54, 65; *Official Records,* LII, Pt. 2, pp. 57, 76–78.

promoters of the independent Tennessee project. In order to emphasize Tennessee's isolated condition as a border state, the secessionists played on the fear of a Federal invasion down the Mississippi. On April 29, the house resolved to authorize Harris to send such aid as he deemed advisable to protect the river town of Columbus, Kentucky, from any such invasion. On May 3, the senate kindled fears of a Yankee advance through West Tennessee. The lawmakers urged that troops be sent to Union City, Tennessee, because of the large number of Federal soldiers who were allegedly encamped at Cairo, Illinois. When a boat owned by a Tennessee firm was seized at Cairo, speeches from the house floor aroused the old fear that the free navigation of the Mississippi might be in jeopardy. The culmination of these warnings came on May 9 in a Harris-sponsored statement by a joint committee of the legislature. The statement was designed to explain why the legislature had entered into a military league with the Confederates. It stressed the exposed condition of West Tennessee, and warned again of a Federal advance from Cairo.

Yet there is some evidence that the propaganda boomeranged on Harris and his friends. In the attempt to stress the weakness of Mississippi River defenses as a reason for joining the Confederacy, these secessionists had become intrigued with river defense. Consequently, long after Tennessee had seceded, the main concern of Tennessee officials was the protection of the Mississippi. During the early summer, Harris and his army commander, General Gideon Pillow, placed the bulk of the state force on the Mississippi and hastened the construction of new forts on the river. On June 22, the legislature petitioned the Confederate Congress for defense appropriations to prevent a Union advance down the river. These fears, planted by the Harris bloc, were a major concern of the Mississippi River pressure group which was to hamper Albert Sidney Johnston's efforts by urging the defense of that waterway to the neglect of others.[3]

A second stage of the independent Tennessee move promised trouble for Johnston. On May 7, Tennessee and Confederate officials agreed upon a military league which was ratified that same day by the legislature. Evidently Harris' strategy was to place the state just far enough within the Confederacy to make it difficult for voters to refuse secession in the June referendum. Yet Tennessee would in the meantime remain officially out of the Confederacy, so that Harris could not be accused of doing what the voters had refused to do in the February election.

This hasty action of Tennessee officials in joining the league also boomeranged upon its designers. Harris soon discovered that Tennessee was more outside than inside the Confederacy. The league's terms were

3 *Senate Second Extra Session,* 44, 90, 117; *House Second Extra Session,* 85–105.

vague. While both state and Confederate authorities were to provide for common defense, Tennessee's military force would be controlled in wartime by the Confederacy.[4] Yet Confederate authority was not established in the state until July, and until then Harris had the responsibilities of defense. In May the state army was still in the process of being organized and was in no condition for such defense. The state militia had been abolished in 1857, and as late as January, 1861, Harris had reported that no military organization existed in the state. Thus the governor would have to build a state army to guard territory which had declared itself under Confederate military jurisdiction.[5]

The real dilemma, however, appeared with the arms situation in Tennessee. Commissioner Hilliard had promised that as soon as the Confederate government ratified the league, Tennessee would receive enough arms to place the state in a condition of war preparedness. These arms were vital, for the state had no Federal arsenal from which to seize guns, and the antique weapons in the state arsenal would not have beaten off an Indian assault. The public arms consisted of about 8,000 flintlock muskets of which more than half were damaged, 185 percussion muskets, 350 badly damaged Hall's carbines, and assorted other weapons. The artillery boasted one six-pound unserviceable iron gun, one damaged twelve-pounder bronze piece, and two other six-pounders. The arsenal even lacked tools needed to convert old country rifles from flintlock arms to military percussion weapons, and five days after the military league was agreed upon, only a thousand muskets in the Nashville arsenal were classified as fit for use.

The Confederacy was slow to send arms, and state General S. R. Anderson complained bitterly to Secretary of War Leroy Walker concerning the delay. Evidently the state authorities felt cheated; they had gone farther out on the limb than they had intended and were now faced with a genuine weapons shortage. There was no shortage of men, for volunteers could be obtained easily. By May 1, seventy companies had enlisted and the Military Board predicted that twenty-five thousand more would volunteer in May and June. Harris complained to Walker that the raising of troops was no problem, but that the state could not arm even the token regiments which had volunteered.[6] Finally the Confederate government sent four thousand muskets to Tennessee, yet

---

[4] *Senate Second Extra Session,* 35, 67–68; *House Second Extra Session,* 40–43, 79; *Official Records,* LII, Pt. 2, pp. 82–84, 88, Ser. IV, Vol. I, 296–98, 320, 330–31.

[5] *House Journal of the Extra Session of the Thirty-Third General Assembly of the State of Tennessee Which Convened at Nashville on the First Monday in January, A.D., 1861,* 15, 158.

[6] *House Extra Session,* 22, 155–56; *Official Records,* LII, Pt. 2, pp. 96, 281–82, XVII, 811–12; Harris to Leroy Walker, May 25, 1861, in Harris Papers, Tennessee Archives.

stipulated that these were to be used only by regiments which were to be mustered into Confederate service and not by state regiments. A bitter Isham Harris called this restriction unreasonable and urged that Walker relent and allow Tennessee troops to use the weapons, but Walker refused.

Again the secessionists found themselves in trouble. In the campaign for an independent Tennessee, they had warned the population that huge Federal armies threatened the state. The result was that many regiments which answered the governor's call refused to go into Confederate service, but desired instead to remain near their endangered homes. On May 28, Harris confessed to Walker that he could not induce a single regiment to go. The only alternative was to raise troops especially for Confederate service, while the Confederate weapons lay idle.[7]

The arms problem became even more involved. Not only were the arms sent to Tennessee designated for Confederate troops only, but those Confederate regiments first organized in Tennessee were sent to the Virginia front. Some companies not only refused to serve beyond the state's borders, but also would not serve at all unless they received the same equipment as those regiments going to Virginia. Meanwhile, the morale of the state troops suffered as they waited in instruction camps and fretted because they had no weapons. Hence, in May, 1861, Harris' force consisted of state regiments that refused to leave the borders of the state, regiments which were unwilling to join the Confederate army under any circumstances, Confederate regiments which were promptly shipped elsewhere, and state regiments which would have gladly entered Confederate service if arms had been made available.

The only suggestion received from the Confederate government was that Harris should arm his troops with the country rifle. Walker pointed out that it was the rifle which won victory for the infant Tennessee settlements at King's Mountain. The only problem was that most of these country rifles were old enough to have been at the battle of King's Mountain. Some of the state arsenal's weapons had been deposited there as early as 1808, and many state troops were armed with Tower of London muskets which had been used by Tennessee militiamen in the War of 1812. These weapons had no standard caliber, and many were in need of repair.[8]

The arms situation was indicative of an even more serious problem

[7] *Official Records*, LII, Pt. 2, pp. 103–105; Harris to Pillow, and Harris to Walker, May 28, 1861, in Harris Papers, Tennessee Archives.

[8] J. W. Robertson to Harris, June 17, 1861, Ed Pickett to Harris, August 1, 1861, S. R. Anderson to Harris, June 29, 1861, Walker to Harris, May 20, 1861, all in Harris Papers, Tennessee Archives.

created by the independent Tennessee project. A general lack of rapport
existed between Tennessee and Confederate officials. The hasty formation
of the military league created a communications lag between Richmond
and Nashville. The league contained no specific provisions as to the
methods and time of transferring the state army to Confederate service.
Probably Harris and his friends assumed that as soon as the people voted
for secession, the Confederates would assume command and responsibility
for the state regiments.

The Tennessee officials soon found they were mistaken. The Confederates were slow to assume such authority, and Tennessee was in a
more isolated condition than had been intended. As early as June 18
the legislature authorized Harris to place his Provisional Army at the
disposal of the Confederacy. When Richmond did nothing, the legislature became impatient and inquired on June 27 as to whether the
Provisional Army was now a part of the Confederate army. If it were
not, then the lawmakers desired to know the army's status. Two days
later an exasperated legislature asked Harris to make arrangements
to place the army under Confederate control and to insure that Richmond would now direct Tennessee's defense. Harris immediately dispatched a note to President Davis, but on June 30 he complained that
he had received no reply. On July 2, determined to obtain Confederate
support, Harris formally offered his Provisional Army to the Confederacy. Even then, the governor was unsure that the offer would be accepted.[9]

The lack of agreement on a transfer system produced a delay which
hampered the war effort in Tennessee. Leonidas Polk did not assume
command in Tennessee of the Confederate Second Department until July
13, and the transference of the Army did not begin until July 31. Then
followed a long and tedious process, as Confederate officers had to travel
to each camp and outpost of state troops to muster the men into Confederate service. The process was so awkward and slow that troops in eastern
Kentucky and East Tennessee commanded by General Felix Zollicoffer
were not mustered into Rebel service until the end of October.

Once more, Tennessee was in and out of the Confederacy. Although
technically all state troops had now been placed under Confederate
authority, the limits of Polk's command did not include Middle and
East Tennessee. During the summer this part of the line had to be

---

[9] *Senate Second Extra Session*, 100; *House Second Extra Session*, 157, 173; "Joint
Resolution to Transfer Volunteer Forces to the Confederate States," June 29, 1861
(MS in Miscellaneous File, Confederate Collection, Tennessee Archives); Harris to
Pillow, June 30, 1861, and Harris to Jefferson Davis, July 2, 1861, in Harris Papers,
Tennessee Archives.

personally superintended by Harris. Moreover, this sector was manned by state troops not yet in Confederate service but vaguely considered to be part of the Rebel force. Since they were state regiments, they must procure their arms and pay from the state. But Tennessee stopped paying its Provisional Army on July 31, the official date of transfer. The result was that these troops of the no-man's-land of Middle and East Tennessee were forced to go through the summer without pay. Not until October 16 could Johnston's headquarters report that the Confederate War Department had decided to pay Tennessee troops for their service since July 31.

By then the damage had been done. On September 28 Harris complained to the War Department that because no Confederate pay had reached these troops, the state had been forced to pay advances out of a treasury already depleted by the expenditure of five million dollars on the state army. The morale and effectiveness of the volunteers who waited idly at training camps from Camp Brown at Union City to Camp Cummings at Knoxville were crippled because of shortages in pay and weapons. Many soldiers drilled with sticks as they waited for guns, and a riot almost ensued at one Middle Tennessee camp when soldiers learned they could receive no arms.[10]

The failure to work out a transfer system created additional problems. Harris had neglected to make arrangements for the transference of the general officers and various departments of the state army into Confederate service. If the Provisional Army were to be the backbone of the Confederate Army of Tennessee, orderly transference of these men and supplies was essential. Instead, both delay and ill will resulted. Not until September 16 was a deed drawn up for the transfer of the vast store of commissary and ordnance supplies at Nashville, and Quartermaster Kensey Johns admitted to the War Department that it would still be weeks before the transaction would be completed.

No provisions were made for the acceptance into Confederate service of certain fine departments of the state army. The War Department indicated that such departments would be displaced by the transfer. Had this displacement been complete, Johnston would have had serious difficulties indeed. The surgeon-general's department of the state army was one of the best in the South. The quartermaster general, V. K. Steven-

10 *Official Records*, IV, 431, 436, 362–63, LII, Pt. 2, p. 176, Ser. IV, Vol. I, 427–28; Mackall to Leonidas Polk, October 16, 1861, in Headquarters Book, Tulane; Enoch Hancock to "Dear Doctor," June 16, 1861, in Enoch Hancock Letters, Confederate Collection, Tennessee Archives; S. McMahon to Harris, August 30, 1861, in Harris Papers, Tennessee Archives.

son, was chiefly responsible for the millions of dollars in stores accumulated throughout the state. Moses Wright, the captain of ordnance, had been the guiding force behind Tennessee's gunpowder and munition production. Fortunately these departments and personnel were retained by Johnston on an informal basis. Their retention was accomplished in spite of and not because of the manner of transfer.[11]

Harris also failed to arrange an orderly transfer policy for the state army's high command. This neglect created a personality conflict which would plague Johnston until the battle of Fort Donelson. As commander of the state army, Gideon J. Pillow held the rank of major general. In July the vain and overstuffed Pillow was informed that under the transfer terms he would hold the rank of a brigadier general in the Confederate army. This demotion came as a surprise to him, for nothing about comparative ranks had been mentioned in the military league agreement. Pillow lashed out at his reduction in rank. He bitterly argued with Harris that the governor should not place the state army in Confederate service, beyond Harris' control, without knowing who its commanders would be. Pillow maintained that in the agreement to transfer the state forces, the term "forces" should be interpreted to mean the aggregate body of the general staff and the army corps. While he would accept the rank of brigadier general, which he described to Harris as the lowest grade of Confederate general officers, he would rather be a common soldier in the ranks. Pillow's motives might have been selfish, but his argument only emphasized Harris' lack of forethought. This dispute over rank left an open wound in the high command of the Tennessee army. By the time of Johnston's arrival, this wound was a deep, permanent scar which promised trouble.[12]

Harris' efforts in building the state army were also to greatly influence the future Confederate Army of Tennessee. From April to July, 1861, Harris pieced together the Provisional State Army of Tennessee, the skeleton of Johnston's Confederate army. Indeed, many of the organizational problems experienced by Johnston in the autumn of 1861 can be traced to the manner in which the parent organization, the state army, was constructed.

On the surface, Harris' efforts in building an army were impressive.

[11] Harris to Walker, August 1, 1861, and L. G. DeRussy to Harris, August 20, 1861, in Harris Papers, Tennessee Archives; *Official Records,* IV, 375–76, 362–63, 371–73, 380–81, 388–89, 391–92, 398, 402, 410–11, LII, Pt. 2, p. 146, Ser. IV, Vol. I, 427–28; Leonidas Polk to Judah Benjamin, January 6, 1862, in Leonidas Polk Papers, 1861–64, National Archives.

[12] Pillow to Harris, July 14, 1861, in Harris Papers, Tennessee Archives; *Official Records,* Ser. IV, Vol. I, 427–28.

More than seventy companies volunteered for service after the governor's plea to the legislature on April 25 to put Tennessee on a war footing. By May 9 some five thousand men were in the state army. When Harris offered the army to Jefferson Davis on July 2, the governor boasted that the twenty-two infantry regiments and two cavalry regiments were fully armed and equipped. By October 7, Harris had raised for Confederate service some thirty-eight infantry regiments, seven cavalry battalions, and thirty-eight artillery companies. By December, 1861, seventy-one infantry regiments, twenty-one cavalry regiments, and twenty-two artillery batteries had been organized in Tennessee.[13]

However, this force was a "paper army," one that looked much stronger on the muster rolls than in the field. Harris had formed the state army from the militia, scattered companies that volunteered independently, troops which entered service under the Army Bill of May 6, and a reserve force of militia which did not enter active service. Technically, every white male in the state between the ages of eighteen and forty-five was in the militia, and there were supposedly 152 regiments of state militia. In April, 1862, however, when militia division commanders began calling for volunteer companies, the 152 regiments were far from being organized because the militia had just been reorganized in January. Various companies, some of which belonged in the militia, began drifting into recruiting centers. Instead of keeping these independent units in their rightful place in the militia, the state authorities welcomed these volunteers.

Simultaneously with these actions came the Army Bill of May 6, 1861. This bill supposedly provided the nucleus of the state army. Under the bill the state issued a call for fifty-five thousand volunteers, twenty-five thousand of whom were to be armed while the remaining thirty thousand were to be held in reserve. The entire force would be organized into regiments, brigades, and divisions.

Encouraged by the response to the Army Bill, Harris developed new areas of troop resources. In June a statewide plea urged county courts to organize local Home Guard units. On June 24, Harris announced that the state would receive into service every man who would volunteer. By this immense drive, almost a levy en masse, Harris actually crippled the later efforts of Johnston to raise forces, because the state army appeared to be much larger than it actually was. A person could be at once a member of the militia, of an independent company, of a

13 *Senate Second Extra Session,* 12; James McHenry to R. H. Chilton, July 2, 1861, in Harris Papers, Tennessee Archives; *Official Records,* LII, Pt. 2, pp. 81–82, 91–92, 119–20, VII, 811–12; Porter, *Tennessee,* 8–9; Robert White, *Messages of the Governors of Tennessee* (Nashville, 1952–63) , V, 341–42.

state regiment, and of the reserve corps. Except for the Army Bill, which was an excellent effort at organizing the logistical branches of the army, there was no uniform plan for raising troops. Men who went into service early in April as members of an independent company might be recounted when regiments were organized or transferred to Confederate service.[14]

In the course of transferring the army to Confederate service, still another opportunity was presented to misconstrue the size of Harris' force. Many of the state regiments were consolidated, once they were in Confederate service. These regiments had different names on the roster. For example, Colonel William Carroll's 1st East Tennessee Rifles was also the 37th Tennessee, as well as the 7th Regiment of the Provisional Army. Hill's 5th Infantry Regiment of the Provisional Army was also referred to as the 35th Infantry Regiment. The 43rd Infantry Regiment was also known as the 5th East Tennessee Volunteers, and, later, the Mounted Infantry.

Unless someone in the War Department at Richmond kept close watch on the numbering of the Provisional Army's regiments during its transfer to the Confederate Army of Tennessee, several regiments might be registered that did not exist or might disappear from the records entirely. In November, for example, the Adjutant General's office in Richmond lost count of the organized Tennessee regiments that were numbered between the 29th and the 40th regiments. Furthermore, the office requested that any Tennessee regiments which Harris chose to organize should begin their numbering after forty-one, regardless of whether the gap between twenty-nine and forty-one had been filled. In exasperation, V. D. Groner of the Adjutant General's office told Harris to give a full report on what regiments had been organized by the governor. Groner admitted that frequently months elapsed before Richmond received the muster rolls, and that regiments were in existence without Richmond's knowledge. Acting Assistant State Adjutant General W. C. Whitthorne could do no better. In November he confessed to Harris that he did not have a record of seven state regiments mustered into Confederate service, although he knew these outfits existed because he knew their commanders by name. These records had been misplaced among the morass of paper

14 "An Act to Raise, Organize and Equip a Provisional Force and for other Purposes," in Militia Laws of Tennessee, Ch. VIII, Vol. 278½, National Archives, hereinafter cited as Militia Laws, National Archives; Harris to Pillow, May 24, 1861, Walker to Harris, June 30, 1861, C. H. Dunn to Harris, July 4, 1861, all in Harris Papers, Tennessee Archives; Senate Second Extra Session, 48, 130, 156; Public Acts of the State of Tennessee Passed at the Extra Session of the Thirty-Third General Assembly for the Year 1861, 57–114; Official Records, LII, Pt. 2, pp. 85–86.

work involved in the transfer of the state army to Confederate duty.[15]

The lack of criteria for the organization of divisions and brigades in the Provisional Army also helped to produce an overestimate of size. Tennessee regiments were careless in their usage of the terms "division" and "brigade." In September, Leonidas Polk reported that his Tennessee troops consisted of four brigades, but later he reported they were comprised of three divisions. Polk's entire command structure was so disorganized that in December, 1861, he confessed to Johnston that he did not know just how many men he did have in his column. The lack of standardization which originated in the state army made Polk's corps appear stronger than it was. For example, Polk's third division was actually little more than a brigade of four regiments, plus an additional regiment.

Also, there was no consistent number of men in each of the twenty-two regiments which Harris proudly turned over to Richmond in July, 1861. Colonel Taz Newman's regiment at Camp Trousdale numbered 914 men, but Lucius Walker's regiment at Fort Wright numbered only 541 men. Colonel John Savage's regiment at Camp Trousdale listed 952 men, but Colonel Adolphus Heiman's regiment at Fort Henry, only 720. In July, none of the regiments of the state army was up to the generally accepted quota of a thousand men. Only two regiments had more than nine hundred troops. These inconsistencies were partially responsible for Richmond's later overestimation of Johnston's force.[16]

The most serious weakness of the state army, however, was a lack of armed men. In late May, 1861, several thousand troops in the state army had no arms whatsoever. Even Henry Hilliard, the smooth-talking Confederate commissioner who had promised the weapons that never arrived, admitted to the War Department in May that fifty thousand men could take the field in Tennessee if small arms were available.

Even those regiments which were reported as "equipped" actually had inferior weapons. The best armed state regiment had flintlock muskets. Sixteen of the twenty-two regiments which Harris boasted to Davis of being fully equipped were armed with flintlocks. In dry weather these weapons were fairly adequate, but they were useless in rainy weather. The meager supply of flintlock muskets in the Nashville arsenal was supplemented by a collection of eight hundred old rifles and double-barreled shotguns gathered at Memphis by ordnance officer W. R. Hunt. All of

15 Marcus Wright, *Tennessee in the War 1861–1865* (New York, 1908), 95, 97, 104–105; *Official Records*, LII, Pt. 2, pp. 205–206, 210–12, 220–21, VII, 808.

16 "Sketch of General Beauregard by J. F. H. Claiborne" (MS in J. F. H. Claiborne Papers, UNC), hereinafter cited as Claiborne Sketch, UNC; *Official Records*, III, 699, 723–24, VII, 905–906, LII, Pt. 2, pp. 122–23.

these firearms were broken. Field artillery was nonexistent in the state army. Harris was able to obtain a sizeable number of guns for river defense but no field pieces.[17]

Despite the serious underlying weaknesses of the state army, Harris did manage to hand over to Confederate authorities a compact force. The Quartermaster General's Department was organized under the command of Vernon Stevenson, president of the Nashville and Chattanooga Railroad. His efforts to accumulate stores at Nashville had been so successful by August that Harris urged that Nashville continue to be the general depot for Rebel stores in the West. The entire department was transferred to Johnston's command.[18]

The Army Bill of May 6 provided for an Ordnance Bureau, and Harris appointed Moses H. Wright as captain of ordnance. Wright was directly responsible for the manufacture of weapons for the state army, for the organization of a system to repair arms, for the establishment of ammunition factories at Nashville to supply the entire Confederacy, and for the development within the Nashville area of the powder mills which supplied all Southern armies in 1861. In August Polk recognized Wright's value and mustered the entire Ordnance Bureau into Confederate service. Wright continued his work under Johnston as head of the ordnance laboratory at Nashville.[19]

The Engineer Corps and the Miners and Sappers Corps were also transferred into Johnston's command. The commander of the Engineer Corps, Bushrod Johnson, was a former college professor and professional soldier who had fought from Florida to Vera Cruz. Johnson would eventually rise to the rank of major general in the Army. The Artillery Corps, commanded by John McCown, was also transferred. McCown had the misfortune in June, 1861, to command eight organized field batteries with no guns. Also a veteran of the Seminole and Mexican wars, McCown would later command a division in the Army. The major

[17] Pillow to John Pettus, May 12, 1861, Leroy Walker to Isham Harris, May 20, 1861, Harris to Pillow, May 25, 1861, Harris to Walker, May 25, 28, 1861, Milton Haynes to Pillow, June 11, 1861, Harris to Jefferson Davis, July 2, 1861, W. R. Hunt to Mackall, September 12, 1861, all in Telegrams Received, 1861, National Archives: Steuart, "How Johnny Got His Gun," 166; Stanley Horn, *Army of Tennessee* (2nd ed.; Norman, 1955), 60, 82; *Official Records*, LII, Pt. 2, pp. 88, 100–101, 122–23; W. J. Worsham, *Old Nineteenth Tennessee Regiment, C.S.A.; June, 1861–April, 1865* (Knoxville, 1902), 22; "Liddell's Record and Impressions of the Civil War in North America 1860 to 1866" (MS in St. John Liddell and Family Papers, Department of Archives, Louisiana State University), hereinafter cited as "Liddell's Record," LSU Archives.

[18] Militia Laws, National Archives; Record Book, Tennessee Archives; Robert C. Black III, *Railroads of the Confederacy* (Chapel Hill, 1952), 72, 138.

[19] M. H. Wright to Mackall, October 7, 1861, in Telegrams Received, 1861, National Archives; L. G. DeRussy to Harris, August 20, 1861, in Harris Papers, Tennessee Archives; *Official Records*, IV, 367, 445–46.

of the Artillery Corps, Alexander P. Stewart, commanded Polk's river batteries at Columbus. Stewart would later command a corps in the Army.[20]

An unheralded but vital contribution of the state army was Harris' establishment of the Medical Board of Tennessee and the office of surgeon-general. Under the vigorous leadership of Surgeon-General B. W. Avent a solid medical department was founded for Johnston's future needs. A tireless worker, Avent assigned surgeons to each state regiment and established central hospitals throughout Tennessee. When the rain-swollen waters of the Barren River country flooded Johnston's Kentucky camps in the winter of 1861–62, the intact, efficient medical department would be welcome.[21]

Few of the general officers of Harris' state army would distinguish themselves in the Army of Tennessee. Most of the appointments of general officers in the state force had been politically inspired. Although a Democrat, Harris had won the governorship in 1857 and again in 1859 with the aid of Whig elements in Nashville and Memphis. Thus he was careful to give the Whigs representation on the general staff. Although the two major generals, Gideon Pillow and S. R. Anderson, were Democrats, four of the five brigadier generals—Felix Zollicoffer, W. R. Caswell, John Sneed, and Robert Foster—were Whigs. Benjamin F. Cheatham was the sole Democrat among the brigadiers. All of these generals except Zollicoffer and Cheatham proved to be incompetents or troublemakers. Zollicoffer performed ably as Johnston's right wing commander in East Tennessee in the fall of 1861. Cheatham, a tenacious fighter, would eventually rise to the rank of major general and corps commander in the Army, and would fight in every major battle of the Army except Jonesboro, Georgia.[22]

This failure of many state generals to distinguish themselves in the Army of Tennessee only indicated another influence which the state army had upon the later Confederate force. For the roots of the *elan* at lower command levels, which would sustain the Army of Tennessee's morale amidst weakness and dispute in the high command, originated in the state army of Tennessee. Harris furnished the Army with many of the brigade and regimental commanders who were to keep up the morale. In the state

20 Militia Laws, National Archives; Porter, *Tennessee*, 318–19, 321; Tracy Kegley, "Bushrod Rust Johnson: Soldier and Teacher," *Tennessee Historical Quarterly*, VII (September, 1948), 249–58; Ridley, *Battles and Sketches*, 473–74; Milton Haynes to Pillow, June 11, 1861, in Harris Papers, Tennessee Archives.
21 "Report of Medical Board of Tennessee to Isham Harris, October, 1861," in Militia Laws, National Archives; Journal of the Tennessee Medical Board, in Medical Board of Tennessee Papers, Tennessee Archives.
22 Harris to Jefferson Davis, July 2, 1861, in Harris Papers, Tennessee Archives.

army these men were not generals, but were usually staff officers or on the regimental line. The adjutant-general, Daniel Donelson, would command a brigade and help smash the Federal line at Perryville and Murfreesboro. John C. Brown, colonel of the 3rd State Infantry and later a division commander in the Army of Tennessee, would be one of the most respected line officers in the West. George W. Gordon, drillmaster of the 11th Tennessee Infantry, would become a respected brigade commander in the Army. Adolphus Heiman, assistant adjutant-general, would command the Sons of Erin, the 10th Tennessee Infantry, which was one of the most colorful outfits in the entire Confederacy.[23]

The Army of Tennessee's peculiar spirit was also derived from the manner in which state regiments were organized. Regiments were organized on a county basis, in accordance with the 1840 militia law. Because individual companies were composed of soldiers from the same community, companies and the regiment as a whole became the object of community pride. Before the state regiments marched off to instruction camps, they were feted with rounds of speeches by local politicians, the invariable presentation of the regimental flag by the local belle of the community, band serenades, and fried chicken. Once in camp, the chickens and the belles were few, mud and sickness were abundant, but the local boys never lost touch with the people back home. Regimental commanders watched over their commands in a fatherly fashion.

The result was a cementing of regimental pride which began to take shape in the state army during the summer of 1861. The Dixie Rifles, Secession Guards, Maury Braves, and Forked Deer Rifles were only a few of the many units which had developed a company and regimental *elan* even before their transfer to Confederate service. As the war progressed, this *elan* would spread to the brigade and division level. Soldiers did not fight for army commanders such as Braxton Bragg or even for a corps commander. Instead they fought for outfits such as Pat Cleburne's division or Ben Hill's regiment.[24]

[23] "List of Officers of the Corps of Artillery of Tennessee" (MS in Benjamin Franklin Cheatham Papers, Tennessee Archives) ; John Frank, "Adolphus Heiman: Architect and Soldier," *Tennessee Historical Quarterly,* V (March, 1946) , 35; Porter, *Tennessee,* 287, 297–98, 300–303, 307, 309, 329–31.

[24] Captain H. Barber, "Company K, 3rd Tennessee" (MS in Papers of Third Tennessee Regiment, Duke) ; John Irion, "Fifth Tennessee Infantry" (MS in Fifth Tennessee Infantry Papers, Confederate Collection, Tennessee Archives) ; A. J. Vaughan to Elijah Danforth, n.d., in Thirteenth Tennessee Infantry Papers, Confederate Collection, Tennessee Archives; Thomas A. Head, *Campaigns and Battles of the Sixteenth Regiment, Tennessee Volunteers, in the War Between the States, with Incidental Sketches of the Part Performed by Other Tennessee Troops in the Same War, 1861–1865,* ed. Stanley Horn (2nd ed.; McMinnville, Tenn., 1961) , 226–28.

After the state force was organized, Harris continued to wield strong influence upon the military situation in the West. The governor's first move was to commit firmly the state army to the defense of the Mississippi River, while he neglected the defense of the Cumberland and Tennessee. Now that Harris was in command, he found he must back up the pledges that were made in the spring. This was not painful for him, for he was personally committed to the idea that the great danger of invasion lay in West Tennessee. As early as May 25 he warned his army commander, Gideon Pillow, that the Federals planned to descend the Mississippi. Pillow's influence was another reason for Harris' fixation on the Mississippi. The governor placed great trust in Pillow and on May 24 authorized him to take such steps as were necessary to protect Tennessee from invasion. Pillow was only too happy to have this free rein. Like Harris, he was an exponent of the theory that the Mississippi River was the danger spot. Already Pillow had warned Harris that Union forces at Cairo would advance on West Tennessee at any time.

The result of this agreement between the governor and Pillow was an unbalanced defensive line in Tennessee that was heavily slanted toward the western border. In May and June, 1861, Harris concentrated fifteen thousand men in those forts on the Mississippi which were under construction: Forts Harris, Wright, and Pillow, and the Memphis defenses. Fewer than four thousand troops guarded the valuable supply depot at Nashville and all of Middle Tennessee, and only a small post was maintained at Knoxville in East Tennessee. The Cumberland and Tennessee defenses suffered the most serious neglect. Although Harris had inaugurated surveys for defensive positions on both rivers, he did nothing to urge the completion of the forts. For a brief period in June, Fort Donelson was manned by forty unarmed men and then was abandoned until October. The Fort Henry defenses remained unfinished throughout the summer.[25]

The governor's lack of interest in providing defenses for the inland rivers and Nashville, probably his most serious blunder as commander of the state army, was also due to another policy which he devised without consulting Confederate authorities. Harris was convinced that there was no real need for strong defenses on the northern border of Tennessee. Under the neutrality policy adopted by Kentucky in the spring of 1861, neither Federal nor Confederate troops were allowed even to pass through Kentucky, much less to occupy the state. The gover-

[25] Harris to Pillow, May 24, 28, June 21, 1861, Harris to Walker, May 25, 1861, Pillow to Harris, May 22, 1861, Adolphus Heiman to Harris, October 14, 18, 1861, all in Harris Papers, Tennessee Archives; Ridley, *Battles and Sketches*, 64–66.

nor of Kentucky, Beriah Magoffin, assured Harris that an agreement had been reached between Simon B. Buckner, commander of the Kentucky militia, and Federal General George B. McClellan. Supposedly, McClellan had promised that no Federal troops would march across Kentucky soil. And Magoffin promised Harris that he would repel any such troop movements which might occur. On these slim assurances, Harris devised his policy of the "Legal Line." He believed that as long as Kentucky remained neutral, Tennessee's exposed northern border would need no defense. Harris wrote Pillow that he was satisfied the Federals would not attempt to quarter troops in Kentucky and warned Pillow to be extremely careful not to break Kentucky's neutrality by sending state troops into Kentucky.

Yet this policy was definitely shortsighted. There is no evidence that Harris ever considered what would happen to the defenseless Tennessee border if Kentucky's neutrality evaporated. And so it did in September, 1861, when Leonidas Polk broke the neutral barrier and entered Kentucky. Then Harris' neat theory of the inviolable line went up in smoke. Albert Sidney Johnston found that due to the governor's strategy almost no defenses existed on the Tennessee line.[26]

The overwhelming confidence which Harris placed in his theory of Kentucky as a buffer zone was demonstrated by a third policy devised in June, 1861. The combination of his fear of an invasion down the Mississippi and his trust in the safety of the Kentucky border induced him to turn completely the defensive line in Tennessee so that it faced west, and to become interested in campaigning in Missouri. It was not that he did not anticipate a Federal advance. He simply expected that if an advance from Cairo were made on Tennessee, neutral Kentucky would be bypassed and the Federals would move down the west bank of the Mississippi River before crossing into Tennessee and attacking Memphis.

Once Harris had concentrated the state army along the Mississippi, he even contemplated the idea of abandoning Tennessee, weak though its defenses were, and of conducting a campaign into Missouri and Illinois. On June 20 he suggested such an expedition to Pillow, and on the following day wrote Pillow that their line of offensive operations should be northward into Missouri along the west bank of the Mississippi. Harris' interest in Missouri again showed his lack of communication with Richmond. The governor was in essence holding the state army in trust until the Confederates took over. Weakened by a lack of arms and composed of green regiments, the state army was in no condition for an offen-

26 Harris to Pillow, June 12, 13, 1861, in Harris Papers, Tennessee Archives; E. Merton Coulter, *Civil War and Readjustment in Kentucky* (Chapel Hill, 1926), 98–99.

sive move. Not only did Harris' attentions toward Missouri further delay
the construction of a real defensive line in Tennessee, but also the seeds
of the idea of a Missouri offensive were planted in the minds of Pillow
and, later, General Polk. The continuation of such aspirations by Pillow
and Polk could only lead to further delays.[27]

Harris also devised a plan for the treatment of Unionist activity which
would plague Johnston. During the fall of 1861, East Tennessee Unionists
rose in rebellion against Confederate authority and forced Johnston to
divert troops from the Kentucky line to protect the railroad link to Virginia. The seeds of this flare-up can be found in the two completely
inconsistent policies which Harris maintained toward the Unionists in the
summer of 1861, one before, the other after, his re-election as governor in
August.

From April until August, Harris maintained a "soft" attitude toward
Unionist activity in the region. The reason was that he wanted East
Tennessee votes in the August election. In 1859 Harris had won re-election by a slim majority over John Netherland, an East Tennessean.
When the vote on secession was taken in June, 1861, thirty-four East
Tennessee counties rejected the separation plan by a vote of more
than two to one. Both of these facts looked ominous to Harris, for in
the summer of 1861, a powerful East Tennessee party led by Netherland, T. A. R. Nelson, and William G. Brownlow picked a candidate,
William H. Polk, and campaigned hard against Harris in East Tennessee. The party stressed the governor's leadership in the secession move.
Harris not only feared losing the governorship but also feared Polk's
election might bring about Tennessee's readmission to the Union.

Harris had already inaugurated one move to insure his re-election, but
evidently did not think it would be sufficient. The state legislature resolved that furloughs be granted to all soldiers who wished to come
home to vote, for many of the secessionists were in the army. Also,
William B. Bate urged Secretary of War Walker to let Harris recall
the Tennessee regiments in Virginia so they could vote.

Harris believed, however, that he must win the friendship of East
Tennessee if he were to be re-elected. A close friend of Harris', H. S.
Bradford, warned that candidate Polk would pander to the defection
in East Tennessee, and urged the governor to adopt a conciliatory policy
in the region. Harris had already decided upon this policy and had
determined to play down in East Tennessee the state's cooperation with
and admission to the Confederacy. In May, Harris stationed in East
Tennessee only fifteen companies of state troops and declined Leroy

[27] Harris to Pillow, June 13, 20, 21, 1861, in Harris Papers, Tennessee Archives.

Walker's suggestion that Confederate troops be stationed in that area of the state. Harris explained that such a step would not be advisable, and that it would be a more sound policy to garrison East Tennessee with state troops. Harris also pursued a lenient policy in the treatment of Tories in that region. A citizens' group at Cleveland, Tennessee, asked Harris to send a force there to quell Tory activities, but the governor refused, stating that he doubted the propriety of sending troops into East Tennessee unless absolutely necessary.[28] On June 30, he warned Pillow that there was an "overwhelming majority in most counties of that section" for a Unionist policy, and maintained that "forebearance and conciliation is the true policy to be pursued towards them. . . ." [29]

Up until the election, Harris gave the Unionists a free rein in their activities. "Parson" Brownlow's Unionist newspaper circulated freely. Thomas A. R. Nelson stumped the region, speaking against both Harris and secession. Andrew Johnson went from Cumberland Gap to Chattanooga in an attempt to whip up the East Tennesseans to rise in conjunction with an invasion from Kentucky. A perceptive onlooker, Colonel John C. Vaughan, on furlough in East Tennessee during July, saw the danger in Harris' soft policy. He warned that the East Tennessee commander W. R. Caswell was too lenient with the Unionists, and affirmed that a stern policy was the only true method of handling the Unionists.[30]

After the election on August 8, there was a remarkable change in Harris' attitude toward the treatment of the Unionists. Re-elected by a majority of twenty thousand votes, he nevertheless lost East Tennessee by almost twelve thousand votes. Eight days after the election, Harris announced a new and vigorous policy of repressing Loyalists. The new policy, which he described to Leroy Walker as "decided and energetic," [31] was a complete reversal of the old. In fact, Harris had repudiated the use of all forceful measures before the election. He now argued that more troops should be stationed in that portion of the state. He spoke of bringing in fourteen thousand troops to crush Tory activity, and of establishing recruiting camps in the region. He ordered the new East Tennessee commander, Felix Zollicoffer, to arrest Union leaders and banish them from the state if necessary. The new policy began on the night of the election, when the popular Thomas A. R. Nelson was arrested. Two days later a prominent Knoxville Whig, John Baxter, was seized. On August 26, Har-

28 Campbell, *Attitude of Tennesseans*, 210–11, 276–77: *Official Records*, LII, Pt. 2, pp. 79, 81; H. S. Bradford to Harris, July 12, 17, 1861, Harris to Walker, May 25, 1861, Harris to G. W. Rowles and others, July 4, 1861, all in Harris Papers, Tennessee Archives.

29 Harris to Pillow, June 30, 1861, in Harris Papers, Tennessee Archives.

30 John C. Vaughan to Harris, July 14, 22, 1861, in *ibid.*

31 Harris to Walker, August 16, 1861, in *ibid.*

ris began his first major purge of Loyalists when he ordered a regiment into Johnson County. The commander carried a list of names of prominent Loyalists whom he was to arrest or kill if necessary.[32]

The mountain Tories never forgot the shock of the sudden change of policy. Throughout August and September resentment smouldered, and then flared into open rebellion in October and November. The result was that Johnston was forced to divert troops badly needed on the eastern part of his line in order to stifle the rebellion. Much of the Unionist activity probably could have been avoided if Harris had been consistent. In July, Landon Haynes warned Leroy Walker that only a policy which mixed leniency and force would keep Loyalist sentiment from rising in East Tennessee. Instead, Harris' first policy was all leniency and his post-election policy all force. Political expediency and the absence of a joint Confederate-state policy on East Tennessee had sown the seeds of Unionist trouble for Johnston.[33]

During July and August, Harris managed to create additional problems for Johnston. In July, General Leonidas Polk arrived to assume command of the Second Department, but his jurisdiction extended only to the west bank of the Tennessee River. The responsibility for the defense of Middle Tennessee remained in the governor's hands until Johnston's arrival in September, when the Second Department was enlarged to include the middle and eastern portions of the state. There was much to be done in Harris' command district. The inland forts remained unfinished, and no defense line had been created to protect Nashville. In East Tennessee, no defenses had been established in the Cumberland Mountain passes to block an invasion from eastern Kentucky.

Still Harris failed to provide for Middle Tennessee's protection. Perhaps the reason was the awkward command arrangement whereby a governor was commanding state and Confederate troops in an area supposedly under general Confederate jurisdiction. Indeed, there were complaints to Walker that Harris was ineffective because he did not consider himself authorized either to act or to command Confederate troops. During the two-month period that Middle Tennessee was under Harris' jurisdiction, no defenses were constructed at Nashville and Fort Donelson stood abandoned. Fort Henry, its guns unmounted and its breastworks unfinished, continued to be manned by one poorly armed regiment.[34]

[32] Harris to Zollicoffer, August 16, 1861, in *ibid*.

[33] *Official Records*, IV, 364–65, 393; Oliver P. Temple, *East Tennessee and the Civil War* (Cincinnati, 1899), 367.

[34] Heiman to R. C. Foster, August 27, 1861, in Harris Papers, Tennessee Archives; *Official Records*, IV, 384–85, LII, Pt. 2, pp. 140–41, 146–47.

In the early summer, Harris' neglect of these positions might have been explained, though not justified, by his belief in the barrier of Kentucky neutrality. In August, however, Harris decided that this neutrality was a sham, and it is to his discredit that he still did nothing to bolster Middle Tennessee's defenses even after he abandoned his trust in the "Legal Line." As early as July a postal rider warned that Andrew Johnson was collecting an army at Cincinnati to invade East Tennessee. In early August, Harris learned that the Federals had established Camp Dick Robinson, south of Lexington, Kentucky, for the purpose of training and arming Kentucky Union recruits. Harris also knew that Union sympathizers had established Camp Andy Johnson only forty miles north of Cumberland Gap. This camp was a receiving station for hundreds of East Tennessee Tories who slipped through the mountain passes at night. Harris first expressed doubt as to the future of the Kentucky situation on August 4, when he ordered Zollicoffer to respect neutrality not a moment longer than the Federals did. By August 30, the governor was convinced that Federal soldiers were assembling at Camp Dick Robinson, Barboursville, and Williamsburg, and that day lashed out at fellow governor Beriah Magoffin for this "open violation of the neutrality of Kentucky." [35] Still Harris' change of mind produced no change in his actions toward Middle Tennessee defenses.

As district commander Harris was equally ineffective in his efforts to manage affairs in East Tennessee. Again the tangled command system hampered constructive efforts. Technically, General Zollicoffer was commander in the region. Yet, while Zollicoffer held a brigadier general's commission in the Confederate Army, his men were state troops which were not yet transferred into Confederate service. On August 4, Harris wrote Zollicoffer that a Confederate officer would soon be in East Tennessee for that purpose, "after which you will all pass from my command and be alone subject to the orders of the Confederate States." [36] However, the transfer was so slow that for all purposes Harris commanded in East Tennessee until Johnston's arrival. As late as September 26, W. R. Caswell at Knoxville confessed to Harris that he did not even know whether his brigade was in state or Confederate service. The

[35] Harris to Magoffin, August 30, 1861, in Harris Papers, Tennessee Archives. See also H. A. Monsis to Harris, July 1, 1861, Harris to Zollicoffer, August 4, 1861, Harris to Magoffin, August 4, 1861, in Harris Papers, Tennessee Archives; Arndt Stickles, *Simon Bolivar Buckner, Borderland Knight* (Chapel Hill, 1940), 85–87; Robert Kincaid, *Wilderness Road* (2nd ed.; Harrogate, Tenn., 1955), 228; *Official Records*, IV, 397.
[36] Harris to Zollicoffer, August 4, 1861, in Harris Papers, Tennessee Archives.

bulk of Zollicoffer's command was not transferred until mid-October.[37]

Because of this command confusion and lack of communication between Harris and Richmond officials, little work was done on East Tennessee defenses while Harris was territorial commander. The only notable achievement was the seizure of Cumberland Gap, which anchored the right flank of the line in Tennessee. Yet Cumberland Gap was seized by Zollicoffer, not by Harris. By this move, Zollicoffer prevented the weak right flank in East Tennessee from crumbling even before Johnston arrived in Tennessee.[38]

The legacy of Isham Harris to the Army of Tennessee was sizeable. Harris' lack of military experience, his eye for the political advantage, his haste in taking his state out of the Union, his absolute trust in his own strategy, and his failure to establish rapport with the Confederate government—all combined to make the governor's efforts far less successful than they could have been. True, several positive steps were taken while Harris directed affairs in Tennessee. A superb munitions and supply organization had been established, and a state army, well organized especially in logistical matters, was handed over to the Confederacy. Yet Harris also bequeathed an army with several basic weaknesses—a nonexistent defensive line at Nashville and on the inland rivers, an unbalanced interest in the Mississippi River defenses, and a defensive line in West Tennessee which faced west instead of north.

[37] W. R. Caswell to Harris, September 26, 1861, in *ibid.; Official Records,* LII, Pt. 2, p. 176.

[38] Harris to Zollicoffer, August 4, 1861, and Hume Fogg to Zollicoffer, September 1, 1861, in Harris Papers, Tennessee Archives.

two

A Season of Neglect

ON JULY 12, 1861, LEONIDAS POLK, EPISCOPAL BISHOP OF THE DIOCESE OF Louisiana, began a career of service with the Army of Tennessee which would last until he fell in the Atlanta campaign of 1864. Polk's first assignment was to command the Western Department until Albert Sidney Johnston arrived from California to assume permanent command.

Although the bishop only held the temporary command for two months, he managed to create enough problems to plague Johnston in the fall of 1861 and the Army of Tennessee for the entire war. During July and August, 1861, the seeds of bitter personality and command conflicts were planted in the Army. The feud which began in July between Polk and his subordinate, Gideon Pillow, was to rage throughout the autumn. During the summer Polk also began to exhibit a sullen aloofness which would hamper cooperation between Johnston and the bishop in the fall and winter of 1861–62. Also, Polk became so preoccupied with the defense of the Mississippi River and with potential operations in Missouri that he failed to build a defensive line in West Tennessee and did not use his influence with Governor Harris to see that defenses were constructed in Middle and East Tennessee. Finally, Polk, although well aware that Tennessee was devoid of a defensive line, broke the Kentucky neutrality barrier by seizing Columbus, Kentucky. This action, which occurred only a week before Johnston took command, deprived the unguarded Tennessee border of the slim but important protection neutrality had provided. The bishop's action also left Johnston an exterior line of defense in Tennessee.

During his temporary command, Polk exhibited personality traits which would later prove injurious to the Army. To the casual observer, Polk was a distinguished soldier who was idolized by his troops. True, Polk did present a striking appearance, and he was extremely popular with his men. Yet there was another side to his character that was dimly visible in the summer of 1861, only to emerge in full view when Johnston took command. On the one hand, Polk was the humble, sacrificing bishop who buckled the sword over his clerical robes out of a sense of duty to his fellow Southerners. But he was also a man of little military experience who could be stubborn, aloof, insubordinate, quarrelsome, and childish. As a bishop, Polk had been trained to lead; but, as a soldier, he never learned to follow. Beginning with Johnston, Polk would treat his superior officers in a manner that smacked of insubordination. Until his death in 1864, the bishop often chose to obey his commander only when it pleased him to do so. Yet throughout his career in the Army of Tennessee, Polk had a remarkable ability to evade the blame for situations that were the result of these flaws in his character. He knew how to manipulate Johnston, who was easily dominated by his old West Point roommate. He also knew how to play on the sympathies of another old schoolmate, Jefferson Davis, and to use his own popularity to combat Braxton Bragg's constant accusations that he was insubordinate—accusations that were probably true. With such a personality and with amazing abilities to escape responsibility, Polk in 1861 was the most dangerous man in the Army of Tennessee.[1]

A man like Polk was bound to clash with his sub-commander. Gideon Pillow, formerly head of the state forces, was retained by Polk as second-in-command because of his familiarity with the Army. In the summer of 1861, Pillow also exhibited traits of character which later would cause Johnston serious trouble. Pillow found it difficult to be second in power to anyone, for he was vain, ambitious, and easily offended. He had been raised in the snobbish, plantation clique of Columbia, Tennessee, which was the showplace of that state's antebellum society. Although he lacked military experience, Pillow received a brigadier general's commission from his old law partner, James K. Polk, when the Mexican War began. Pillow's war service was far from spectacular. He was extremely unpopular with his fellow officers, and his commander, Winfield Scott, accused him of insubordination. This war experience was significant, however, for it convinced Pillow that he

[1] Walter Lord (ed.), *Fremantle Diary: Being the Journal of Lieutenant Colonel Arthur James Fremantle, Coldstream Guards, On His Three Months in the Southern States* (Boston, 1954), 111; G. Moxley Sorrel, *Recollections of a Confederate Staff Officer,* ed. Bell Wiley (2nd ed.; Jackson, Tenn., 1958), 188; Sam Watkins, *"Co. Aytch" Maury Grays, First Tennessee Regiment or a Side Show of the Big Show,* ed. Bell Wiley (2nd ed.; Jackson, Tenn., 1952), 34.

was a military genius. His promotion to command the state army in the spring of 1861 only entrenched him further in this belief.

When, in his transfer to Confederate service, Pillow's rank was reduced from major general to brigadier general, he never let the incident be forgotten. During the fall and winter of 1861–62, he spent most of his time trying to prove that this reduction in rank was unjust, and thereby damaged Johnston's efforts in Tennessee. Part of the harm was done even before Johnston took command. Pillow, his vanity injured, became convinced that Polk and the other officers were always against him. Consequently, he quarreled with Polk, B. F. Cheatham, and almost everyone else in the Army. Also, Pillow's hurt pride generated an intense ambition to "redeem" his honor by conducting some glorious offensive campaign into Missouri, Illinois, and Kentucky. These traits in Pillow's character—vanity, a quarrelsome nature, and ambition—were to be partly responsible for the trouble that Polk's temporary command produced for Johnston.[2]

The trouble began with a personality conflict. The Polk-Pillow feud which broke out in July, 1861, not only diverted Polk from building defenses in Tennessee, but left a lasting bad taste among the Army's high command. During July and August, the stubborn Polk and the ambitious Pillow clashed repeatedly. One observer reported that "Polk and Pillow are at loggerheads . . . ,"[3] and another noted that Polk and Pillow "are pulling in opposite directions."[4] The quarrel centered on a proposed offensive into Missouri in July. Influenced by Isham Harris' desires for such a move, Pillow had longed to campaign in Missouri in June. Before he could get under way, he was relieved of command by Polk, who also soon became interested in the idea of a Missouri offensive. A few days after Polk assumed command at Memphis on July 13, the Confederate governor of Missouri, Claiborne Jackson, arrived at his headquarters determined to talk the bishop into a Trans-Mississippi campaign. In mid-June, the Union bloc had seized control of St. Louis, routed a disorganized Confederate force at Boonville, and chased Jackson out of the state. Anxious to return, Jackson gave Polk a misleading report of the Confederate strength on the Arkansas border that could join with Polk in a drive on Missouri. Jackson assured the bishop that Sterling Price and Ben McCulloch had twenty-five thousand troops on the Mis-

2 Pillow to Harris, June 23, July 14, 1861, Polk to Leroy Walker, July 20, 1861, all in Gideon Pillow Papers, Duke; John Henry to Gustavus Henry, August 31, 1861, in Gustavus A. Henry Papers, UNC; H. S. Bradford to Harris, July 12, 17, 1861, in Harris Papers, Tennessee Archives.

3 *Official Records*, III, 612–14.

4 John Henry to G. A. Henry, August 31, 1861, in Henry Papers, UNC.

souri border that were waiting to help, while William J. Hardee had seven thousand well-equipped troops in northeastern Arkansas that could also be used. Dazzled by the possibilities, Polk and Pillow formulated a bold invasion scheme to cross the Mississippi at New Madrid with six thousand troops, join the forces of Price and Hardee, and march on St. Louis. Jackson, who saw he was winning his point, promised ten thousand additional troops in Missouri for good measure.

The planned invasion never got started. The failure of the enterprise was indicative of Polk's lack of military experience. Because of sickness in the ranks, Pillow's force was in no condition for an offensive. Instead of having six thousand men, Pillow could muster only thirty-five hundred. Polk had also trusted Jackson's word too much. After Jackson left Memphis, Polk received news that Price and McCulloch had only half as many men as Jackson had reported them to have, and that Hardee had only twenty-three hundred poorly equipped troops instead of seven thousand well-armed men. Polk also had given little consideration to the command problems that such an expedition would have presented. He had no jurisdiction in Missouri and none in Arkansas except in the counties bordering on the Mississippi. And Hardee's force, although within Polk's territorial jurisdiction, received its orders directly from the Confederate secretary of war at Richmond. Moreover, Polk had made no provisions for reinforcements and supplies to sustain an offensive, and had not even formulated a plan for what he would do once the force reached St. Louis.[5]

Equally serious, the plan's failure gave the spark to Polk's and Pillow's mutual dislike which now flared into an open dispute. When Polk abandoned the idea and ordered Pillow to halt at New Madrid, Pillow protested bitterly. In late July, Pillow went ahead with preparations as if Polk had not suspended the offensive. Pillow styled himself "Commander of the Army of Liberation" and hinted that if Polk were a capable leader, he ought to be able to find enough troops to make the move. Polk retorted that he knew his business as department commander better than Pillow did. By the end of the summer, relations between the two generals had completely broken down. Pillow flatly informed Polk that he wished he had never been assigned to his command. Polk heartily agreed. Almost two months had been wasted in quarreling, and all that Polk had to show for his service was low morale among the high command. As yet, there was still no defensive line in Tennessee.[6]

[5] Pillow to Polk, July 23, 1861, Pillow Papers, Duke; *Official Records*, III, 617–19, 693–94, LII, Pt. 2, p. 115. Not until September 2 was Polk's command extended to cover Arkansas and military operations in Missouri.

[6] *Official Records*, LII, Pt. 2, p. 115, III, 693–94.

Polk never established a line in Tennessee, and thus bequeathed more trouble to Johnston. He simply was more interested in the defense of the Mississippi and, specifically, the strengthening of river forts. In fact, a concern for the river's defense was the prime factor in Polk's being appointed department commander. He had first come to Davis' attention as a possible choice for temporary commander when he wrote Davis to express concern over the defenseless condition of the Mississippi Valley. When Davis offered him the post, Polk at first refused until the president shaped the command so that it would include the territory in which he was interested. Under Polk, the department included West Tennessee and the counties in Mississippi and Arkansas which bordered on the Mississippi River. Again, no small influence on Polk's decision to accept the post were the entreaties of groups of prominent Mississippi Valley citizens who pressed the bishop to take the position.[7]

Polk's defensive policy was demonstrated by the provisions he made for Tennessee's defense. The vulnerable area of his department was the 100-mile-wide stretch of flat country between the Mississippi and Tennessee rivers. He made no effort whatsoever to concentrate troops or build defensive works there in order to protect against Union forces reportedly assembling at Cairo. Nor did he urge Harris to press forward the work on the Cumberland and Tennessee river forts that were not yet under Polk's jurisdiction. Instead, he continued Harris' policy of massing the Tennessee forces in the Mississippi River forts, and exhibited no interest in constructing fortifications on the west bank of the Tennessee, which was under Polk's jurisdiction. By mid-August, batteries commanded the Mississippi at Memphis and at Fort Harris, six miles above the city. Sixty-five miles north of Memphis, the powerful battery at Fort Wright swept the river. A few miles farther north, at the First Chickasaw Bluff, another battery was posted at Fort Pillow. The northernmost fort in Polk's chain of command was the strong work at Island Number Ten, located at the foot of a horseshoe bend in the river opposite New Madrid.[8]

There were two obvious faults in Polk's policy. There were too many forts on the Mississippi that were of moderate strength, and yet not one that could be termed a principal salient. Also, no matter how strong the river batteries were, unless Polk established a line in West Tennessee, the

7 William Polk, *Leonidas Polk, Bishop and General* (New York, 1915), I, 352–58, 369–79; Horn, *Army of Tennessee*, 49; Polk to Jefferson Davis, November 6, 1861, in Leonidas Polk Papers, UNC; Capers, *Memphis*, 144.

8 Harris to Pillow, June 21, 1861, Pillow to Harris, May 3, 1861, Milton Haynes to Pillow, June 11, 1861, all in Harris Papers, Tennessee Archives; *Official Records*, IV, 363–64; Capers, *Memphis*, 143–44.

river forts were vulnerable to being taken in flank by a land assault. Polk grasped the necessity for more concentration of firepower at a single fort, but did not see the need of establishing land defenses in West Tennessee. Two officers urged him to build such defenses. Asa Gray, his topographical engineer, argued that he should establish a line stretching from Union City to Island Number Ten, with a cordon of outposts in between. Gray argued that such a line would both provide a principal salient on the river and protect northwestern Tennessee, especially the vital rail junction at Union City. Colonel John McCown, commanding one of Polk's brigades, agreed and told Polk that such a line was the strongest possible in West Tennessee. Polk, however, rejected the possibility of an inland concentration and sought only a river salient to concentrate firepower. There was no doubt that Island Number Ten was the strongest position available in Tennessee. The island commanded the channel of the Mississippi in three directions. The eastern approach to the fort was guarded by the cypress-entangled, deep waters of Reelfoot Lake and by the Reelfoot and Obion rivers.[9]

Not only did Polk reject Gray's and McCown's arguments for a West Tennessee line, but he also ignored their argument to place the main river salient at Island Number Ten. Instead, he had his eye on Columbus, Kentucky, located on the Mississippi thirty miles north of the Tennessee border, at the railhead of the Mobile and Ohio line. The decision to seize Columbus and violate the neutrality of Kentucky was a combination of Pillow's ambition and Polk's stubbornness. While in command of the state army, before he had become interested in a Missouri offensive, Pillow had considered an expedition into Kentucky to seize Columbus. In fact, he had even written Governor Magoffin for permission to enter Kentucky. Rebuffed by Magoffin, Pillow had turned his eyes toward Missouri. Now that his Missouri aspirations had been dampened by Polk, he again saw a chance for glory by leading an offensive into Kentucky.

During the last week in August, Pillow began to pressure the bishop to allow him to seize Columbus. Pillow contended that Kentucky was a boiling caldron of Unionist sentiment and that Federal troops were ready to sweep downriver and take the city. Let him have three boats, and he would save Columbus. Pillow was actually more interested in saving his reputation. Just a few days earlier, he had argued that the river defenses in Tennessee were strong enough to allow him to abandon them and move into Missouri. When Polk stymied that aspiration, he suddenly became alarmed at the condition of the river forts. On

---

[9] *Official Records,* III, 651–52, 661, 703–705; John McCown to Bragg, September 14, 1862, in Ch. II, Vol. 51, National Archives.

August 28, he informed Polk that he had modified his view of the strength of the forts and had decided they could not withstand attack. The only salvation, according to Pillow, was to allow him to seize Columbus.[10]

While this argument helped win Polk over, a weakness in the bishop's character also influenced the decision. Polk had a habit of gathering a few facts on a situation, closing his mind to any alternative, and then dogmatically holding to his first idea. The decision to move on Columbus was an example of this weakness. Throughout August, Polk had caught brief snatches of information, though nothing conclusive, which indicated the Federals were planning to enter Kentucky. Information reached him of recruiting activities in Indiana and Ohio, and of a foray by a small Union party to disperse a pro-Confederate group at Ellicott's Mills, Kentucky. Finally, on September 2, he learned that a Union column had occupied Belmont, Missouri, opposite Columbus. Immediately Polk made a hasty decision and held to it. He ordered Pillow to take Columbus. There is no evidence that Polk ever considered whether the town was so valuable a position that it was worth damaging Confederate relations with Kentucky. He did not even inform the War Department that he was going to make the move. He did ask Governor Magoffin on September 1 to inform him of recent Federal activity, but did not wait for Magoffin's reply. A combination of ambition, lack of communication, and sheer dogmatism prompted the move that officially broke Kentucky's neutrality.[11]

Polk had made what was probably one of the greatest mistakes of the war, and in so doing, had created another problem for Johnston. There was a complete lack of communication between Polk, Harris, and the Richmond authorities on the matter of Kentucky neutrality. On August 30, Harris assured Magoffin that Tennessee troops would continue to respect Kentucky's neutrality. Three days later, these troops were moving into Kentucky. Richmond authorities knew no more than Harris. After the move had been made, Polk sent a letter of explantation and Harris sent a telegram of protest to Jefferson Davis.

[10] Pillow to Magoffin, May 13, 1861, and Harris to Pillow, June 12, 1861, in Harris Papers, Tennessee Archives; Coulter, *Civil War and Readjustment,* 106–107; *Official Records,* LII, Pt. 2, pp. 61–62, 99–101, III, 630, 685.

[11] On August 28, when John C. Frémont assigned U. S. Grant to command in the area, he wrote: "It is intended, in connection with all these movements, to occupy Columbus, Ky., as soon as possible." *Official Records,* III, 142. For accounts of activities of both belligerents in Kentucky, see Stickles, *Buckner,* 55–89; Coulter, *Civil War and Readjustment,* 100–110; Nathaniel S. Shaler, *Kentucky: A Pioneer Commonwealth* (Boston, 1885), 250–51. See also Edwin Porter Thompson, *History of the First Kentucky Brigade* (Cincinnati, 1868), 52, and "The Civil War Reminiscences of John Johnston, 1861–1865" (typed copy of MS in Confederate Collection, Tennessee Archives); S. R. Latta to "Mary," September 7, 1861, in Samuel Rankin Latta Papers, Tulane.

Affairs in Richmond were so confused that on September 4 the secretary of war, Leroy Walker, ordered Polk to withdraw to Tennessee, and Davis told Polk that he approved the move into Kentucky. Polk himself did not seem to be sure of what he was doing. On September 4, he stubbornly maintained he was going to hold Columbus at all costs. Four days later, he informed Magoffin that if the Federals withdrew from Paducah, which had been seized the day after the occupation of Columbus, he would withdraw. This confusion of orders and counter orders, indicative of an absence of policy on neutrality, gave political ammunition to the pro-Union element in Kentucky. On September 18, after using the incident for all the propaganda it was worth, the Union bloc managed to carry through in the legislature a formal abandonment of neutrality and a declaration of support for the Union.[12]

Polk's action also foiled the attempts of pro-Confederate Kentuckians to maintain the state as a neutral buffer zone to aid the Confederacy. Although the correspondence between these Kentuckians and the Confederates was vague on the subject, it appears that a group headed by men such as Simon Buckner, Blanton Duncan, and John Helm believed Kentucky as a neutral zone was worth fifty thousand troops to the Confederates. These men felt that two groups, the pro-Confederates and the strict neutralists, could be combined to keep the Federals out of the state. The group's philosophy was expressed by Buckner in his reaction to Polk's move. He urged Polk to withdraw, and argued that if he remained the neutral elements would be aroused against the Confederates as invaders. If Polk withdrew, the same neutral elements would force the Union troops to withdraw from Paducah.

Buckner realized something that the Confederates would grasp only after a year of unsuccessful cajoling and Bragg's Kentucky campaign. Kentucky people were Kentuckians first and Unionists or Confederates second. These people resented any meddling in their affairs from the outside, from friends as well as enemies. For example, in 1862 the same Kentucky legislature that condemned Bragg's invasion also condemned the issuance of Lincoln's Preliminary Emancipation Proclamation. Both acts were considered as interference from the outside. Pulled

---

[12] Harris to Magoffin, Harris to Polk, Harris to Davis, September 4, 1861, all in Harris Papers, Tennessee Archives. Harris told Polk that the move "is unfortunate as the President and myself are pledged to respect the neutrality of Kentucky." Harris to Polk, September 4, 1861, in Harris Papers, Tennessee Archives. Harris wrote Davis the move was "unfortunate, calculated to injure our cause in the State." Harris to Davis, September 4, 1861, in *ibid.* Polk told Davis that "I thought proper, under the plenary power delegated to me . . . ," to seize Columbus. Polk to Davis, September 4, 1861, in Jefferson Davis Papers, Louisiana Historical Association Collection, Tulane, hereinafter cited as Davis Papers, Tulane.

by economic and family ties toward both sides, many Kentuckians resisted both Union and Confederate invasion. Since Polk invaded first,
a combination of this neutral sentiment and Unionist propaganda depicted the Confederates as the aggressors. Any hopes for a neutral buffer zone, as envisioned by Buckner, were thus destroyed.[13]

The occupation of Columbus as a defensive position was also a
blunder. Some historians have praised the seizure of the town as a
brilliant piece of strategy that netted the Confederates a strong river
bastion. Actually, Columbus was a trap. Holding it provided no additional security against a Union advance. The stronger natural defenses
at Island Number Ten were better able to repel a move down the
river. Holding Columbus could not prevent an invasion of Tennessee
via the Tennessee and Cumberland rivers. If Polk had seized Paducah
instead, he would have sealed off these invasion routes and blocked
the Ohio River as well. Buckner later pointed out that any strategic
advantage Polk acquired in occupying Columbus was neutralized when
the Federals seized Paducah two days later. Also, the occupation of Columbus could not prevent a land advance down the New Orleans and Ohio
Railroad into West Tennessee. Indeed, the town could easily be flanked
and completely encircled by such a move. Polk could have stifled this
danger of a flanking operation if he had extended a line from Columbus
east to Mayfield, but he never attempted to do so. Not only was Columbus
a weak position, but its occupation placed the West Tennessee defenses on
an exterior line. Since the town was thirty miles in advance of the recruiting
center Polk had established at Union City, the Confederate line must face
east as well as north. Clearly, the whole operation was small compensation
for the defensive problems it posed.[14]

Leonidas Polk left few achievements as evidence of his summer's
work, but did bequeath many problems to his successor. The inland
rivers had still been ignored and no line had yet been established in
West Tennessee. The move into Kentucky had put Johnston on an exterior line and had violated the neutral line at a time when defenses
in Tennessee behind that buffer zone were almost nonexistent. Pillow

13 *Official Records*, IV, 179–93, 400. See also *ibid.*, LII, Pt. 2, pp. 94–95, 72; Stickles,
Buckner, 73; William Johnston to Rosa Johnston, August 8, 1861, in Mrs. Mason Barret
Collection of Albert Sidney and William Preston Johnston Papers, Tulane, hereinafter
cited as Barret Collection, Tulane. One soldier wrote ". . . since the neutrality of
Kentucky has been busted asunder, things have taken quite a change. . . . A great
many people throughout Kentucky believe we have come to wrong them. . . ." W. E.
Coleman to "Bert," October 6, 1861, in W. E. Coleman Letters, Confederate Collection,
Tennessee Archives.

14 W. W. Mackall to Joseph Dixon, September 30, 1861, in Headquarters Book,
Tulane; *Official Records*, IV, 189.

and Polk had initiated a personality conflict betwen themselves and with Johnston, a conflict that would severely hamper the army's effectiveness. In the future, when they were not fighting each other, Polk and Pillow would maintain a disinterested attitude toward Johnston's problems in Middle and East Tennessee. The ambitious Pillow and the stubborn Polk had only one interest and that was the Mississippi River defense. They would oppose and refuse cooperation with Johnston, and would remain aloof at Columbus as the Tennessee line threatened to crumble around them. Perhaps the bishop was also a prophet. In July he had made a statement that seemed to summarize this future attitude toward Johnston: "All we desire is to be left alone, to repose in quietness under our own vine and our own fig tree." [15]

15 Polk's Proclamation, July 13, 1861, in Barret Collection, Tulane.

PART II

the tempering of the johnston influence

three

An Uncertain Hand

IT WAS THE AUTUMN OF 1861. AT LAST ALBERT SIDNEY JOHNSTON HAD COME back to the South. Without fanfare he had arrived in Richmond and had hastened to the Confederate White House. There Johnston rang the bell and was admitted into the hallway. President Davis lay sick in bed, but, according to later accounts, when he heard Johnston's footsteps in the hallway below he exclaimed, "That is Sidney Johnston's step. Bring him up." [1]

There were many people in the Confederacy who had been waiting for Johnston to climb those stairs. The entire South, especially inhabitants of the Western Department, had anxiously followed Johnston's long, overland trek from Los Angeles to Richmond. Leonidas Polk had gone to the president again to insure that Johnston would be the bishop's successor. A delegation of prominent Memphis and North Mississippi citizens, including congressmen and railroad presidents, also journeyed to the capital to make certain Johnston would command the western force. They were not to be disappointed. After conferring with Davis, Johnston accepted the rank of major general and the command of the Second Department.[2]

If military success were conditioned upon appearance, Johnston was bound for glory. He was tall and muscular, very erect in posture, with

1 William Preston Johnston, *The Life of Gen. Albert Sidney Johnston Embracing His Services in the Armies of the United States, the Republic of Texas, and the Confederate States* (New York, 1879) , 291.

2 Leroy Walker to Johnston, August 31, 1861, and Johnston to Walker, September 11, 1861, in Headquarters Book, Tulane; Resolution of Memphis Committee of Safety to Jefferson Davis, September 3, 1861, in Barret Collection, Tulane.

strong shoulders, a powerful neck, and a square chin. A soft-spoken man, he sprinkled his conversations with humor. With his dark brown hair peppered with gray, with blue-gray eyes and a large moustache, Johnston was one of the South's most handsome generals.

Few generals could match his dramatic entrance into the conflict. In April, 1861, he had resigned as commander of United States forces in the Pacific Department in order to fight for the Confederacy. His last days in California had been a period of almost virtual captivity. His Southern sympathies were well known, and he was closely watched by Federal officers. In June, with a small band of comrades, Johnston had slipped into the desert to begin his new military career.

Gradually the news of his trek reached the Confederacy, and Southerners marveled at his daring. His party traveled by horseback, often by long night marches, through eight hundred miles of arid country between Los Angeles and the Rio Grande. The route led through hostile Apache country, and twice the group came upon the remains of stagecoach massacres. As they neared the Rio Grande, they also had to dodge Federal cavalry patrols. After weeks of waiting, the South learned that Johnston had safely run this gantlet of perils and was ready for new military service.[3]

Perhaps the South was a little too ready for Johnston. Polk assured Davis that he was the only available man capable of filling the position. Davis himself noted that at the time Johnston was his only sure hope of having a good general. Even Johnston's future enemy, U. S. Grant, would later state that in 1861 Johnston was considered by many Federal officers to be the Confederacy's most formidable general.[4]

Yet Johnston's past record did not merit such acclaim. He had never held a command which entailed responsibilities similar to those of the Second Department. In fact, he had come to the western army after years of disappointment in various interrupted careers of service. As a youth he had longed to go to sea. His family discouraged the idea, and sent young Johnston to Transylvania College at Lexington, Kentucky, not far from his birthplace at Washington. There he became friends with Jefferson Davis, a fellow student. Johnston later entered West Point, where he and Davis became closer friends. After graduation Johnston hungered for frontier service. In his first frontier duty, however, he spent most of his time in routine matters at Jefferson Barracks near St. Louis, where he married Henrietta Preston. Shortly after the birth of their sec-

---

[3] Johnston, *Life of Johnston*, 275–91; A. S. Johnston to his wife, July 5, 1861, in Barret Collection, Tulane.

[4] Charles P. Roland, *Albert Sidney Johnston: Soldier of Three Republics* (Austin, 1964), 259–61.

ond child, his wife became gravely ill, and asked her husband to quit the army to be near her; this he did. Henrietta died soon after.

For a time following her death, Johnston lived almost as a recluse on a farm near St. Louis. He then went to Texas to begin a new career in the Republic's army, and soon was commanding President David Burnet's army. But disillusionment with Texas affairs and a severe wound received in a duel cut short this new career. He returned to Kentucky, where he visited his family, and then returned to Texas to begin a new career as secretary of war in the government of Mirabeau B. Lamar. Financial difficulties, illness, and disillusionment with Texas politics cut his service short, and Johnston again went back to Kentucky. For several years he dabbled in real estate and Texas politics, and drifted across the United States. In 1843 he attempted a third career in Texas, as a planter on his newly-purchased China Grove plantation in Brazoria County. Later that year he took a new bride, Eliza Griffin, a cousin of his first wife. After struggling to overcome financial difficulties at China Grove, Johnston sought a new career with the outbreak of the Mexican War.

He continued to experience misfortune. Soon after the battle of Monterrey his period of enlistment expired. Unable to obtain a fixed rank, he returned to China Grove. Financial conditions remained gloomy, so gloomy that he was forced to board his two eldest children with Kentucky relatives. Poverty-stricken, he accepted a position as paymaster in the army for a portion of the Department of Texas. His new career provided only drudgery.

In 1855, after his friend Jefferson Davis had become secretary of war, Johnston eagerly accepted a new position as colonel of the 2nd Cavalry Regiment, and later as temporary commander of the Department of Texas. Again he felt disappointment. In 1857 he led the expedition into Utah against the Mormons. He saw no action, but struggled against mud, hard winters, and political animosity from Washington. In 1860, a bored and disappointed Johnston was relieved of the Utah command and given a long leave of absence. Later that year, when the chance for a new career as commander of the Department of the Pacific became available, he accepted the post. This service also proved to be short and unpleasant. A strong advocate of the Union, Johnston was troubled by the secession crisis. He determined not to resign his command unless Texas should join the Confederacy. In early April, when he learned that Texas had left the Union, he sent his resignation to Washington. Soon afterwards, he made plans to leave California and volunteer for Confederate service.[5]

5 Johnston, *Life of Johnston*, 1–291; Mrs. Susan Preston Hepburn to William Johnston, April 27, 1861, A. S. Johnston to his sister, June 1, 1861, Johnston to his wife, July 1, 1861, all in Barret Collection, Tulane.

Johnston's entire life had been frustrated by grief, disappointment, and the changing of jobs. Confederate service offered him an opportunity to prove to himself that he could succeed at a chosen career. He indicated this feeling in a letter to his wife, written while on the Arizona desert. "Never before have I had so many probabilities of success and better grounds for the belief that my star will continue to be in the ascendant." [6]

From the time Johnston assumed command of the Second Department on September 15, 1861, until the collapse of his Tennessee line the following February, his influence was to temper the newly molded Army of Tennessee. This influence, a complex of Johnston's personality, strategy, and the timeliness of his appearance in Tennessee, would in the following months act upon the strategic areas of the western line: Middle Tennessee and central Kentucky, the inland river forts, Columbus, and the Cumberland Mountain area. In January, 1862, when the Federal winter campaign began, the strength of the Tennessee line, tempered by Johnston's command, would be tested—and found wanting.

The most persistent of all factors which made Johnston's command structure weak was his personality. As far as human nature was concerned, Johnston seemed to live in a world to himself. He was never able to establish rapport with his sub-commanders, and never really grasped their personalities or command problems. Somehow he never felt the "pulse" of the Army's command system. He was insensible to command friction in the department, such as the quibblings of Polk and Pillow.

Even when Johnston recognized failure among his subordinates, he seldom corrected the situation. His overly gentle nature and his child-like faith in human goodness brought him much grief. He trusted lieutenants to accomplish difficult tasks when their backlog of conduct did not merit such trust. He was also an easy mark for an ambitious or insubordinate lieutenant. Johnston was too patient in dealing with such officers as Polk. Sometimes the degree of his patience indicated that his officers controlled the general, instead of the reverse.

Johnston's personality was also colored by a narrow outlook. He seemed able to grasp only one area of thought at a time, and unable to view the total command picture of his department. Often he became absorbed in menial details that were really the responsibility of a post commander or staff officer.

Johnston's ideas on strategy were also part of his tempering influence. When the Federals began their winter campaign in January, 1862, he was caught unprepared. He had no over-all departmental strategy, and there

6 Johnston to his wife, July 1, 1861, in Barret Collection, Tulane.

would be no coordinate defensive effort between his district commanders. Johnston's continual involvement in menial details and his difficulty in communicating with subordinates were partially responsible for the lack of defensive strategy.

Yet part of this failure was caused by the urgency of genuine problems on the Tennessee line. Before he devised a strategy, Johnston must first build an army. In September, 1861, he learned that there were only twenty-seven thousand troops in the Army. Some of these were totally unarmed and many were improperly armed. Of these, six thousand were scattered throughout East Tennessee, and almost twenty-one thousand were dispersed throughout West Tennessee from Columbus to Memphis. Johnston was convinced by mid-November that the Federals had fifty thousand men in central Kentucky to threaten Middle Tennessee. He also believed that from twenty thousand to twenty-five thousand Federals were concentrated around Cairo opposite Polk, and between ten thousand and twenty thousand more were facing Zollicoffer in eastern Kentucky and Tennessee. Johnston's only sure reserve was General William Hardee's paltry army of 3,600 effectives in the Upper District of Arkansas. Volunteers were plentiful in Tennessee, but there were no arms to equip them.[7]

Time needed for work on a strategic program would also be consumed by Johnston's attempts to mask the real weakness of the Army. Throughout the fall of 1861, Johnston would conduct a series of thrusts and parries designed to befuddle his central Kentucky opponent, William T. Sherman. The ruse utilized cavalry raids, infantry marches and counter marches, and infantry skirmishes, all designed to give the impression of a much larger force, especially in the Bowling Green area. Ironically, his success would prove to be part of his undoing. He would become so intrigued in his efforts to bluff Sherman and his successor, Don Carlos Buell, that Johnston would fail to see the danger of Federal movements in other areas.[8]

Out of these factors, some no fault of Johnston's, came no firm strategic plan but instead a medley of vague ideas as to what he hoped to accomplish. Johnston hoped to put into effect a form of the defensive-offensive strategy. He planned to remain on the defensive until he could both raise an army and stabilize his defenses. When he mustered sufficient logistical strength, he hoped to undertake an offensive in Kentucky and strike the Federals before they moved into Tennessee. He was also aware

[7] Johnston to Benjamin, November 15, 27, 1861, Mackall to Zollicoffer, October 21, 1861, all in Headquarters Book, Tulane; *Official Records*, III, 690, 712, IV, 425.

[8] Johnston, *Life of Johnston*, 363–66. See also B. H. Liddell Hart, *Sherman: Soldier, Realist, American* (New York, 1958), 100, 102, 107, 109.

that he had no second line of defense. When he visited Richmond in early September, it is probable that Davis cautioned him not to fight unless there were a reasonable assurance of victory (Davis did ask this of Joseph E. Johnston at the same time). The need to protect the new western commander's troop-recruiting and food-producing areas of Tennessee forced him into a strategy of dispersion. For example, to protect the fertile grain fields north of Nashville, Johnston posted his center corps at Bowling Green instead of behind the Cumberland River at Nashville. It is also possible that Confederate hopes for European recognition or intervention made Johnston careful only to commit his troops where victory was certain.[9]

The timing of Johnston's arrival in the West was also an element in his tempering influence. He assumed command at a peculiar time of hope, decision, and change. The hope was exhibited by the central government and the western people. With a degree of confidence unwarranted by Johnston's past record, everyone seemed sure that all would be well with Sidney Johnston at the helm. Consequently, public officials and citizens in the West, as well as authorities in Richmond, would be apathetic toward Johnston's pleas for support in the autumn of 1861.

Johnston also took command during a period of rapid and disturbing change. The limits of the Second Department had just been extended to include Middle and East Tennessee. The command of Forts Henry and Donelson was being transferred from Harris to Confederate authorities. Polk's command was now enlarged to include these forts. The seizure of Columbus had just laid bare Tennessee's defenseless border to Yankee invasion. This move, coupled with Zollicoffer's recent occupation of Cumberland Gap, had left Middle Tennessee on a recessed, interior line with both flanks far in the advance. Governor Harris' inconsistent treatment of East Tennessee Loyalists had already spawned murmurs of discontent in isolated mountain coves.

9 Johnston to Isham Harris, November 5, 1861, in Harris Papers, Tennessee Archives; Davis to Joseph E. Johnston, September 8, 1861, in Dunbar Rowland (ed.), *Jefferson Davis, Constitutionalist: His Letters, Papers and Speeches* (Jackson, Miss., 1923), V, 129–30; Simon B. Buckner to Johnston, September 19, 1861, and an added notation by W. W. Mackall, in Telegrams Received, 1861, National Archives. An explanation of the defensive-offensive is found in Frank Vandiver, "Jefferson Davis and Confederate Strategy," in Bernard Mayo (ed.), *The American Tragedy: The Civil War in Retrospect* (Hampden–Sydney, Va., 1959), 20–21. See also J. F. C. Fuller, *The Conduct of War, 1789–1961: A Study of the Impact of the French, Industrial, and Russian Revolutions on War and Its Conduct* (New Brunswick, N.J., 1961), 72, 103–104. For evidence that Tennessee military leaders followed closely diplomatic events, see Pillow to Harris, May 25, 1861, in Harris Papers, Tennessee Archives; W. P. Johnston to his wife, August 8, 1861, in Barret Collection, Tulane; Gilmer to his wife, December 20, 29, 1861, Gilmer Papers, UNC; Nashville operator to Johnston, December 18, 1861, in Telegrams Received, 1861, National Archives.

All of these problems demanded hasty decisions by Johnston. He must decide where to establish his central line and who would command the new central position which was so badly needed. He must also decide whether to keep the left and right flanks at Columbus and Cumberland Gap, or draw them back into Tennessee. More armed men and more officers must be found for the expanding army. All of these burdens rested upon the new commander's shoulders as he arrived at Nashville on September 14, hopeful of adding strength to the western army.

At Nashville, Johnston almost immediately made what would perhaps be his most important command decision: he established the center of his line at Bowling Green, Kentucky, seventy miles north of Nashville. After a conference with Governor Harris, hasty preparations were made for the advance. Simon Bolivar Buckner, former commander of the Kentucky State Guard, had resigned his post and had hastened to Nashville to offer his services to Johnston. Johnston urged Buckner to accept the command of the new Bowling Green sector. Buckner reluctantly agreed, and Johnston secured for him a commission as brigadier general in the Confederate army.

Almost overnight the line was pushed northward. Volunteer troops who had been patiently drilling for months at camps near the Kentucky border were alerted for duty, as were additional regiments assembling at Nashville. On the night of September 17, the regiments decamped and boarded Louisville and Nashville railroad cars. The trains rattled northward through the night into the Barren River country. On the morning of September 18 almost every available armed man in Middle Tennessee was arriving at Bowling Green.[10]

During the next four months, the defense of Bowling Green became an obsession with Johnston. He toiled over the routine matters of army management there as if he were merely a district commander. By late December this fascination worked two visible effects on him. He grew certain that a Federal army would advance upon Middle Tennessee via Bowling Green and Nashville. He also became convinced that Buell's army was the main threat to the Nashville basin, even though two other Federal armies threatened in Kentucky.

Johnston's preoccupation with Bowling Green affairs arose from several causes. One factor was that the move to Bowling Green was his first offensive thrust in his new command. Buckner's presence at Nashville had provided him with the opportunity for his first offensive move.

[10] Special Orders No. I, Department No. 2, September 15, 1861, in Headquarters Book, Tulane; William Johnston to Rosa Johnston, August 5, 8, 1861, in Barret Collection, Tulane; Barber, "Company K, 3rd Tennessee," Duke.

The capable Buckner was a native of the Green River country around Munfordville, northeast of Bowling Green, and knew the south-central Kentucky terrain. He was also an excellent organizer. As major general of the Kentucky State Guard, he had transformed the old "cornstalk militia" into a well-armed and well-equipped force of twelve thousand men. Such ability to organize would be needed at Bowling Green. The force to be assembled there was a disorganized combination of green regiments from Camps Trousdale and Brown, unarmed troops from Nashville, and scattered commands such as B. F. Terry's Texas Rangers, which drifted to Nashville. On September 18 more troops were obtained when William J. Hardee's tiny Arkansas army moved to reinforce Johnston.[11]

Buckner was a vigorous exponent of the offensive, and his move to seize Bowling Green almost assumed the nature of a massive drive into north-central Kentucky. Johnston's orders to Buckner were to seize the town and establish a defensive line. Buckner, however, wanted to press further into Kentucky. He saw the value of holding an advance post at Elizabethtown, forty miles southeast of Louisville. Elizabethtown lay south of the rugged Muldraugh's Hills, a range of bluffs which extended from the Ohio River into eastern Kentucky. If the Confederates held the Elizabethtown area, they could observe and counter Federal moves from Louisville more easily than could be done from seventy miles south. At Elizabethtown they could also draw supplies from the fertile Bluegrass region, and would be in a good position to strike the flank of a force which might try to move on Zollicoffer in east Kentucky. At Muldraugh's Hills, the Confederates could also command an excellent group of parallel turnpikes which extended south from the hills into the weak section of Johnston's line, between Zollicoffer and Buckner.[12]

Buckner saw the political advantage in such a move. He knew that a large force of Southern Rights Kentuckians allegedly had gathered in the Muldraugh's Hills region. He hoped to open communications with them, if for no other reason than to initiate guerrilla warfare in the area against the Federals. Major J. W. Hawes was ordered to establish communications while Colonel Roger Hanson's 2nd Kentucky Infantry was sent to hold the Green River crossing at Munfordville. Another column, led by Colonel Ben Hardin Helm, was sent northwest to strike at the Union Home Guards reportedly guarding the locks on Green River near Rochester. Helm led 1,500 men to Rochester, where the locks at the

11 Johnston, *Life of Johnston*, 298; *Official Records*, IV, 407–408; LII, Pt. 2, p. 149.
12 Buell to George McClellan, November 27, 1861, in Buell Papers, Rice; Basil Duke, *A History of Morgan's Cavalry*, ed. Cecil Fletcher Holland (3rd ed.; Bloomington, 1960), 66, 69–70.

mouth of Big Muddy were destroyed in order to prevent Federal boats from coming up Green River.[13]

Buckner's drive momentarily appeared to be on the verge of turning into a full-scale thrust on Elizabethtown. Then the offensive suddenly stalled. Johnston did not believe that Buckner's small force of four thousand men could be supported north of Bowling Green. Instead, Buckner was ordered to draw his troops back to the town. Hawes brought in as many Confederate sympathizers from north of Green River as he could, and the Munfordville bridge was destroyed. Hanson and Helm fell back to Bowling Green, and by September 25 the Federals occupied the country around Elizabethtown.[14]

Buckner's desire to press north of Green River produced significant results, even though his plan failed. The move completely panicked the Federals in Louisville. Hourly they expected to see the gray vanguard swing in toward Louisville from the pike below Salt River. The commander of the Department of the Cumberland, William T. Sherman, actually gathered the few Home Guards and volunteers available in Louisville and entrained for Muldraugh's Hills. Unknown to Buckner, Sherman not only expected a move on Louisville, but thought that Buckner was commanding a division instead of the thin brigade which the Kentuckian had at Bowling Green. The fear incited by the lightning move to Green River and by the destruction of the Green River locks proved to be of great help to Johnston in his efforts to mask the real weakness of his force.[15]

Another curious result of Buckner's operation was that it provided fuel for a pro-offensive bloc at Bowling Green. During the autumn of 1861 this group pressured Johnston to advance, and consequently held his attention on Bowling Green. Harris pressed for a winter campaign to drive the Federals into the Ohio River. Buckner urged that John C. Breckinridge, who had joined the Confederates at Bowling Green, be allowed to advance with a large column through eastern Kentucky. Chief Engineer Jeremy F. Gilmer, who had the ear of both Johnston and Hardee, repeatedly expressed his desire that Johnston should undertake a winter

13 Buckner to Johnston, September 18, 1861, in Telegrams Received, 1861, National Archives; *Official Records*, LII, Pt. 2, pp. 150–53, 155–56, 158, IV, 415–16, 424; Barber, "Company K, 3rd Tennessee," Duke.

14 Buckner to Johnston, September 19, 1861, in Telegrams Received, 1861, National Archives; Mackall to Buckner, September 19, October 11, 1861, Mackall to Hardee, October 21, 1861, all in Headquarters Book, Tulane; *Official Records*, LII, Pt. 2, p. 154.

15 Buckner's personal notes on Green River advance (MS in Telegrams Received, 1861, National Archives); Nashville operator to Leonidas Polk, October 1, 1861, in Polk Papers, National Archives; Thompson, *First Kentucky Brigade*, 65, 67–69; Liddell Hart, *Sherman*, 100; Johnston, *Life of Johnston*, 310.

campaign. General James L. Alcorn of Mississippi, who arrived with two regiments to reinforce Buckner, expected an offensive. Influential citizens in Memphis and Nashville also pressed Johnston for a move north from Bowling Green. For a time, Johnston himself hoped that he could build up his force to the extent that he could sustain an offensive drive from Bowling Green. By early December he had abandoned hope of building up his force to take the offensive because of his awe at the threat from Buell's army in north-central Kentucky.[16]

There was a less dramatic reason for Johnston's absorption in the problems of the salient. He had been forced into adopting the weak defensive position at Bowling Green, and now became involved in the struggle to improve its defenses. A better place to defend Nashville would have been the city itself. Federal engineers were to prove this later, when Nashville became one of the best fortified cities in the South. The city was situated on bluffs on the south bank of the Cumberland River. On the north bank the approaches to Nashville were cut by a series of steep hills and ridges. On the south bank the city was encircled by another range of hills. A third series of hills, which the Federals later fortified, were located within the business and residential sections of the city.[17]

Even though the position was strong, Johnston was unable to use Nashville, at least as a primary line. Polk's occupation of Columbus had placed the Confederate left wing in a dangerous angle which was vulnerable to an attack from the northeast. Either Polk must be withdrawn or the center must be advanced. Johnston did not believe it was possible to draw Polk back into Tennessee. He feared that the Federals would follow a retreat and discover that behind his facade of strength Johnston had no strong defensive line. Therefore, he decided to fortify Bowling Green, the first point north of Nashville which was defensible. Bowling Green, located on three hills, was an excellent site for fortifications. Johnston soon had artillery planted on these hills, and the guns commanded the surrounding area for a mile and a half in every direction.[18]

16 Harris to Jefferson Davis, October 15, 1861, Robertson Topp to Harris, September 16, 1861, Johnston to Harris, November 5, 1861, all in Harris Papers, Tennessee Archives; *Official Records*, IV, 445, VII, 922; Gilmer to his wife, October 17, 19, 23, 25, November 8, 14, 28, 1861, all in Gilmer Papers, UNC; James Alcorn to his wife, September 26, 1861, in James Lusk Alcorn Papers, UNC.

17 W. W. Clayton, *History of Davidson County, Tennessee* (Philadelphia, 1880), 193–94; Stanley Horn, *Decisive Battle of Nashville* (Baton Rouge, 1956), 24–29.

18 Johnston to Jefferson Davis, September 16, 1861, in Western Department, Letters Sent, 1861–62, National Archives, hereinafter cited as Letters Sent, 1861–62, National Archives; Mackall to Buckner, September 15, 1861, Headquarters Book, Tulane; Charles Mott (ed.), "Wartime Journal of a Confederate Officer," *Tennessee Historical Quarterly*, V (September, 1946), 236.

Yet the Bowling Green position was basically weak, and Johnston's efforts to remedy its weakness further claimed his attention. The main problem was the geography of the region. South of Bowling Green the rolling bluegrass country extended seventy miles to Nashville. North of Bowling Green the terrain was completely different. The town was located on the south bank of Barren River. North of the river lay the broken, sandy hill country of the Pennyroyal. Further north the terrain was intersected by the Green River, which flowed west into the Ohio. North of this river was the Dripping Springs Escarpment, a plateau formation several hundred feet above the country to the south. A poor, rocky plateau was broken by ravines and tributaries flowing down into the river. Even farther north was the Muldraugh's Hills region, which screened Federal activity in the Louisville and Bluegrass areas.[19]

Good reconnaissance was Johnston's primary need at Bowling Green. In order to defend Tennessee with his original skeleton force of twenty-seven thousand troops, he had to know the activities of the enemy beyond this series of topographical barriers, so that a concentration might be effected. Such reconnaissance was almost impossible in the seventy miles of rugged terrain north of Bowling Green. The people of the area, as well as the land itself, masked the enemy's operations. The country from Bowling Green north to Bardstown was Unionist territory. Confederate officers had difficulty in finding local citizens who would penetrate the enemy's lines north of Green River. A cordon of reconnaissance outposts was established from Hopkinsville on the west to Dripping Springs on the east, but Johnston's officers still complained of the difficulty in securing information. The problem became worse during the winter, when the rains and the mist rising off Green River produced fogs equaled only by the mental fog brought about by a lack of information.[20]

Bowling Green presented other defensive problems. To hold this position demanded a tremendous amount of the Army's manpower. South of Green River a network of turnpikes which an invading Union force could use spread into southern Kentucky. Only one, the Louisville–Cave City pike, passed through the Bowling Green area.

[19] J. Sullivan Gibson, "Land Economy of Warren County, Kentucky," *Economic Geography*, X (January, 1934), 74–98; Willard Rouse Jillson, *Topography of Kentucky* (Frankfort, 1927), 116; Carl Ortwin Sauer, *Geography of the Pennyroyal: A Study of the Influence of Geology and Physiography Upon the Industry, Commerce, and Life of the People* (Frankfort, 1927), 8–22.

[20] Johnston to Judah Benjamin, October 22, 1861, in Headquarters Book, Tulane. See also Gilmer to his wife, October 17, 1861, in Gilmer Papers, UNC; Thomas Speed, *Union Cause in Kentucky, 1860–1865* (New York, 1907), 173; Hindman to W. D. Pickett, January 20, 1862, in Telegrams Received, 1862, National Archives.

Should the Federals advance, there would be innumerable routes to be covered. On the northwest the Federals had their choice of the Owensboro, Brandenburg and Elizabethtown–Leitchfield pikes. On the north and northeast the enemy could move down the Cave City, Bardstown–Glasgow, Columbia–Liberty and Monticello–Bowling Green pikes. To cover all these routes and still maintain reconnaissance posts exerted a tremendous drain on Johnston's manpower.[21]

The manpower problem was intensified because the line around Bowling Green was a unhealthy place, especially for the troops from areas of warmer climate, such as Texas, Mississippi, and West Tennessee. North of the town lay the cave area of central Kentucky, a damp, unhealthful region of dripping springs, licks, sinkholes, and heavy rains. The problems of cold weather, dampness, and lack of camp sanitary facilities badgered the outposts. In October, 1861, epidemics broke out along this line. Johnston's efforts to obtain information were hampered and sickness reduced the number of effective troops.

The advance stations along Green River were the hardest hit by illness. In T. C. Hindman's command at Bell's Station, an epidemic of measles raged throughout the fall and early winter, and was accompanied by outbreaks of pneumonia and diarrhea. By January, 1862, half of Hindman's force was unable to walk. D. C. Govan's advance post at Drippings Springs was also disabled by a November epidemic of measles, as well as by outbreaks of scurvy. Terry's Texas Rangers, one of Johnston's best scout regiments, were decimated by an epidemic of measles in November at their Oakland post. By December, only one fourth of Terry's men were able to stand roll call. Johnston's northwest post at Hopkinsville, commanded by General James Alcorn, was hit severely by measles. By the end of November, eight hundred of Alcorn's men were in makeshift hospitals at Clarksville. Smallpox broke out along Barren River near Bowling Green, and B. W. Avent, Johnston's surgeon-general, was ordered to vaccinate every regiment. Typhoid fever and influenza were also contracted by the troops on the central line, especially by men not acclimated to the Kentucky weather. By the end of October, the military hospital at Nashville had provided accommodations for two thousand patients, most of whom were from the Bowling Green area.[22]

Geographical problems south of Bowling Green also kept Johnston's

21 Buell, *Statement of Major-General Buell,* 13; David B. Harris to Bragg, September 15, 1862, in David B. Harris Papers, Duke.

22 Hindman to Johnston, February 15, 1862, and Hardee to Johnston, February 15, 1862, in Telegrams Received, 1862, National Archives; W. E. Coleman to Parents, January 19, 1862, in W. E. Coleman Letters, Confederate Collection, Tennessee Archives; D. C. Govan to his wife, November 2, 1861, in Daniel C. Govan Papers, UNC;

attention on the district. Ninety miles to the southwest was the next salient in Johnston's line, Fort Donelson. The country between the fort and Bowling Green was flat, with no defensive works. Upstream from Donelson, the Cumberland River curved to the east until it reached Clarksville, where the river dipped south to Nashville. Clarksville was a vital position. If a Federal advance broke through the open country between Donelson and Bowling Green, Clarksville could easily be seized and the way to Nashville would be open. A further problem in this vulnerable area was the presence of Johnston's main line of rail communication with Polk in West Tennessee. The Memphis, Clarksville, and Louisville Railroad ran southeast from Bowling Green and crossed the Cumberland River at Clarksville. Should this line be seized, Johnston would have no other rail communication with Polk except the Memphis and Charleston line, far to the rear in northern Alabama and Mississippi. Also, northeast of Clarksville, a spur line, the Edgefield and Kentucky, extended from the Memphis, Clarksville, and Louisville tracks to Nashville. Hence the Federals did not even need to seize Clarksville both in order to cut Johnston's main rail line and procure a quick route to Nashville.[23]

The weaknesses of the position placed Johnston in a dilemma. Bowling Green, though inferior to Nashville as a defensive position, must be held. To withdraw to Nashville would expose Polk's flank and Johnston's ruse. If the line remained, however, an auxiliary line must be established, for the troops in Bowling Green alone were incapable of defending Nashville and Middle Tennessee. Caught between the line he must occupy and the more desirable Nashville position, Johnston became further enmeshed in the problems of a solitary district in his department. In October and early November, his attention was given to the planning of a second defensive line which he hoped could be established at Clarksville and Nashville.[24]

At a time when Forts Henry and Donelson badly needed supervision, Johnston sent his chief engineer, Jeremy Gilmer, to Nashville and Clarksville to survey the terrain for a second line. Gilmer, who despised

James Alcorn to his wife, October 8, 1861, in Alcorn Papers, UNC; Clarksville Military Board to Johnston, November 29, 1861, in Telegrams Received, 1861, National Archives; Enoch Hancock to his brother, November 22, 1861, in Hancock Papers, Tennessee Archives; Buckner to B. W. Avent, December 4, 1861, in Letters and Telegrams Sent and Circulars Issued, Central Division of Kentucky, September, 1861–February, 1862, Ch. III, Vol. 226, National Archives, hereinafter cited as Ch. III, Vol. 226, National Archives; Mackall to D. W. Yandell, October 21, 1861, in Headquarters Book, Tulane; Report of Tennessee Medical Board, October, 1861, Militia Laws, National Archives.
[23] Clarksville Military Board to Mackall, October 31, 1861, in Telegrams Received, 1861, National Archives; Official Records, VII, 742. See also Stephen Ambrose, Halleck: Lincoln's Chief of Staff (Baton Rouge, 1962), 20.
[24] Johnston to Benjamin, December 21, 1861, in Headquarters Book, Tulane.

the Kentucky climate, was happy to be in Nashville, and went about his duties at a leisurely pace. He spent almost the entire month of November surveying the Nashville defenses. By the end of the month he had decided on two positions. A river battery was to be constructed on the south bank of the Cumberland below the city. On the north bank of the river, a line of breastworks was to be dug on the range of hills that commanded the road approaches to the city. Actually, the land defenses would have demanded less work and would have required fewer troops to hold if Gilmer had laid them out on the steep bluffs on the south bank of the river. However, he wanted to make certain that the breastworks protected the village of Edgefield on the north bank of the river opposite Nashville. The cream of Nashville society lived at Edgefield, and the young, impressionable Gilmer was undoubtedly pressured to locate the defensive line north of the village.[25]

Satisfied with his work at Nashville, Gilmer went to Clarksville. He laid out the site for a river battery at the mouth of Red River. Plans for field works to be located north of the town were also formulated. After the initial surveys Gilmer left the details of construction to subordinates. He was assured by local officials that plentiful slave labor could be had to build the works. Confident that the line would soon be completed, he returned to Bowling Green.[26]

By early December, however, the construction of the secondary line began to create some problems. Gilmer had assumed that the Nashville citizens would be quite willing to lend their slaves for work on the land defenses and the river battery. On December 6, his assistant, G. O. Watts, complained that only seven slaves had been volunteered. At least three hundred laborers would be needed at each of the three road crossings north of the city. The next day, Gilmer told Johnston that most of the slaves had already been hired out for the season. He also reported no success in obtaining white laborers, for a large portion of the Nashville laboring class belonged to the militia which Harris had just called to the field to meet Pillow's "crisis" at Columbus.[27]

[25] Gilmer to his wife, November 3, 4, 6, 9, 13, 24, 1861, in Gilmer Papers, UNC; Johnston to Harris, October 26, 1861, in Headquarters Book, Tulane; Gilmer to V. K. Stevenson, November 26, 1861, Gilmer to Isham Harris, December 3, 1861, Gilmer to Mackall, December 4, 1861, all in Letters Sent, Chief of Engineers, Western Department, 1861–1862, Ch. III, Vol. 8, National Archives, hereinafter cited as Ch. III, Vol. 8, National Archives.

[26] Johnston to Major G. A. Henry, October 26, 1861, in Headquarters Book, Tulane; *Official Records*, IV, 554–55, LII, Pt. 2, p. 221.

[27] G. O. Watts to Hugh McKrea, December 6, 1861, Gilmer to Mackall, December 7, 9, 1861, Gilmer to Harris, December 11, 1861, Gilmer to R. C. Foster, December 13, 1861, Gilmer to V. K. Stevenson, December 23, 1861, all in Ch. III, Vol. 8, National Archives.

Gilmer was beginning to learn something about Nashville people which Johnston, preoccupied at Bowling Green, never realized. Leading citizens were not seriously interested in building a defensive line around the city. The reason for this unconcern lay in the self-assured, snobbish attitude of the influential Nashvillians. In 1861 Nashville, with the exception of New Orleans, was the largest and most cosmopolitan city south of the Ohio River. It was a city of five daily newspapers, gas lights, a steam fire department, and ten publishing houses. It was an educational center with one of the country's best medical schools at the University of Nashville, the university itself, a fashionable female academy, and the Western Military Institute. A group of Nashville families not only formed the social clique of Tennessee in 1861, but also controlled the city's affairs. These people, described by one writer as the "Nashville Gods," lived in elegance in such mansions as Belle Meade, Belmont, Two Rivers, Clover Bottom, and Burlington.[28]

The "Nashville Gods" were not interested in the need for laborers on Gilmer's fortifications, or in any other defensive problem of the city. They did not feel the same border complex that Louisville and even Memphis citizens felt. Few if any of the Nashville clique remembered the lean years of the 1780's when Dragging Canoe, the brilliant Chickamauga strategist, almost wiped out the Nashville settlement in the Battle of the Bluffs. The enormous prosperity which the city enjoyed in its golden years of the 1850's had erased these hard frontier memories, and had instilled a complacent, selfish attitude in the minds of the city's leaders.

There were other reasons for the apathy of the Nashville populace. There was no pressure bloc which demanded good defenses on the Cumberland. Also, Nashville was the Second Department's production center for war materials, and local businessmen were too busy getting rich on Military Board contracts to worry about the lack of fortifications. Those influential citizens who would have been concerned were away fighting. The newspaper editor Zollicoffer was in eastern Kentucky. Randall McGavock, the mayor in 1861, was with the Sons of Erin at Fort Donelson. Isham Harris was busy with his campaign to call out every available man in Tennessee to bolster Johnston's line.

There could also be seen in Nashville a lack of interest in the Confederacy's fortunes. Despite the bluster of the summer of 1861, when the Rock City Guards and Nashville Blues paraded the streets, many Nashvillians were for their city first and the Confederacy second.

[28] F. Garvin Davenport, *Cultural Life in Nashville on the Eve of the Civil War* (Chapel Hill, 1941), 32–55, 117–44, 145–59, 199–210; Henry McRaven, *Nashville: Athens of the South* (Chapel Hill, 1949), 93; Alfred L. Crabb, "Twilight of the Nashville Gods," *Tennessee Historical Quarterly*, XV (December, 1956), 291–99.

When the city eventually fell to Buell's army, there was much bowing and scraping on the part of Mayor R. B. Cheatham and other citizens. In March, 1862, Jeremy Gilmer would reflect bitterly on the amazing ease and rapidity with which the "Gods" adjusted to the horrors of Yankee occupation. Whatever its basis, the Nashville Myth, that absolute trust in the decisions of the "Gods," produced a lethargic attitude in the city that damaged Johnston's plans. By late December, planters still refused to lend their slaves, white volunteers were few, and Gilmer's plans remained on the sketch board.[29]

As dangerous as the myth itself was Johnston's belief that the defenses at Nashville were being constructed. There was an unjustifiable lack of communication between Johnston and Gilmer on conditions at Nashville. This communication lag, together with Johnston's preoccupation with menial details at Bowling Green and Isham Harris' repeated assurances that laborers could be had in abundance, completely misled Johnston as to the state of the Nashville defenses. There is no evidence that Johnston, before he retreated to Nashville in February, 1862, had any idea that the fortifications were not being built. In fact, on Christmas Day, 1861, he confidently wrote Judah Benjamin that the entrenchments "double the efficiency of my force for the defense of this line." [30] When he wrote this, there was not a single yard of fortifications constructed at Nashville.

Another reason for Johnston's fixation upon Bowling Green was that in early October, 1861, the first threat of a Federal advance against him was reportedly aimed at Bowling Green. When he first came to Tennessee, Johnston had ordered Buckner to Bowling Green and then had gone on to Columbus to confer with Polk. Johnston saw the weakness of Polk's Union City flank, and planned to order Polk to extend his Columbus line east to Mayfield to cover the weak condition. Had Johnston carried out this plan, Polk's line would have been much better prepared to give Johnston assistance in the early winter of 1862.

The extension of the line was soon forgotten. An urgent message from Buckner arrived at Columbus. A Union force of perhaps fourteen thousand men was reportedly preparing to cross Green River. Stunned, Johnston ordered every available reinforcement to Bowling Green. A regiment was called from reconnaissance duty on the Cumberland Plateau, every man in Nashville who had a weapon was put on the trains to Bowling

29 Crabb, "Twilight," 291–99; Stanley F. Horn, "Nashville During the Civil War," 3–8; Gilmer to his wife, March 6, 1862, in Gilmer Papers, UNC.

30 Johnston to Benjamin, December 25, 1861, in Headquarters Book, Tulane. See also Harris to Johnston, December 26, 1861, in Telegrams Received, 1861, National Archives.

Green, and Hardee's four thousand troops, already en route to Nashville, were diverted to the Kentucky town. By October 13, a worried Johnston had left Columbus to take command of the defense of Bowling Green. He would not leave the district until February, 1862.[31]

The threat of the advance proved a false alarm, but Johnston's attention was held in central Kentucky by the need to organize the assembled reinforcements. In fact, he was so completely engrossed in the work that he assumed personal command of the center corps, which he titled the "Army of Central Kentucky." The reason for his interest in the organization of the center corps was more than just a need to bring some order to the scattered commands. There was a heavy concentration of officer talent at Bowling Green. The state army had supplied the basis for the Army of Tennessee's *elan* and had given the Army many of its regimental and brigade commanders. By contrast much of the future high command of the Army was unknowingly assembled at Bowling Green. Buckner, retained by Johnston as commander of the first division, would later command a corps. Hardee, appointed commander of the second division, had more military experience than any other officer in the Army and was America's foremost authority on infantry tactics. T. C. Hindman, commanding a brigade, would command a division at Chickamauga. John C. Breckinridge, assigned to command the Kentucky Brigade, would command the Reserve Corps at Shiloh. The two exceptionally good officers at Bowling Green were Pat Cleburne, commander of Hardee's second brigade, and Nathan Bedford Forrest, who led an independent cavalry battalion. Cleburne became perhaps the finest infantry officer in the Army, and Forrest became probably the finest cavalryman in the Confederate service.[32]

Johnston's interest was also tied to Bowling Green by his attempts to conceal the Army's weakness from the Federals. In November, Cleburne was sent with 1,600 men on a wide sweep east to the mountains to create the impression that he was leading the advance column of a much larger force. Jacob Biffle's cavalry battalion was sent to make

[31] Mackall to Joseph Dixon, September 30, 1861, Mackall to Buckner, October 4, 1861, Johnston to Samuel Cooper, October 13, 1861, all in Headquarters Book, Tulane; *Official Records*, IV, 437; Johnston to V. K. Stevenson, October 4, 1861, and Mackall to Stevenson, October 6, 1861, in National Archives.

[32] T. B. Roy, "Sketch of the Life of Major-General William J. Hardee" (MS in Lieutenant General William Hardee Papers, Alabama State Archives), hereinafter cited as Roy, "Hardee Sketch," Alabama Archives; Gilmer to his wife, October 14, 1862, in Gilmer Papers, UNC; Lord (ed.), *Fremantle Diary*, 110; Colonel John Harrell, "Arkansas," in *Confederate Military History*, X, 396–98, 403–404; Watkins, *"Co. Aytch,"* 41; Johnston, *Life of Johnston*, 379–81; Robert Selph Henry, *"First with the Most" Forrest* (Indianapolis, 1944), 41.

a demonstration in the Glasgow area, and Forrest was sent as far north as Morganfield in a show of force. Infantry was marched back and forth between Bowling Green and Green River. In late December, Forrest smashed into a Union cavalry scouting party at Sacramento and sent the Union troopers reeling back with heavy losses and stories of a huge Rebel force. Terry's Rangers struck a Union column at Green River and fought a bloody engagement in which Colonel Terry was killed. From October to December, Johnston used every possible ruse to hold back the Federals while he tried to piece together an army to man the extensive Tennessee lines.[33]

Johnston soon found that his strategy might also work in reverse. In November he began receiving widespread reports of Federal advances along Green River. One force was rumored to be marching on Greenville, and another was said to be crossing Green River at Morgantown and Woodbury. Rumors had the Federals concentrating opposite Rochester to force a crossing of Green River, and another heavy column was allegedly gathering farther down the river at Calhoun. These reports were almost all false alarms, but the failure of Confederate intelligence to penetrate north of Green River and gain precise information worried Johnston. By December, the rumored concentration began to narrow to one point. The most consistent information came from T. C. Hindman's scout posts at Oakland and Bell's Station. His intelligence reports always located Buell's main force at the villages of Munfordville and Nolin, on the Louisville pike between Elizabethtown and Green River.[34]

Hindman's persistent reports disturbed Johnston. Already strained by three months' work at Bowling Green, Johnston was frustrated by the failure of reconnaissance north of Green River except in Hindman's area. The result of these pressures was dimly seen in December, only to emerge in full view in February, 1862. Johnston became absolutely certain that Buell was the only threat to Middle Tennessee, even though he knew that General Henry W. Halleck's army was in western Kentucky and that of General George H. Thomas in eastern Kentucky. By Christmas Day, Johnston was convinced that Buell was

33 Irving Buck, *Cleburne and His Command*, ed. Thomas Robson Hay (2nd ed.; Jackson, Tenn., 1959), 84–85; *Official Records*, VII, 732, 782, LII, Pt. 2, p. 229, IV, 545–48; Henry, *Forrest*, 43–44; Charles Clark to D. G. White, December 29, 1861, in Telegrams Received, 1861, National Archives; D. C. Govan to his wife, December 22, 1861, in Govan Papers, UNC.

34 Mackall to Tilghman, October 29, 1861, in Letters Sent, 1861–62, National Archives; T. H. Hunt to Mackall, November 13, 1861, and Clarksville Military Board to Johnston, December 5, 6, 1861, in Telegrams Received, 1861, National Archives; James Ollar to his wife, October 17, 1861, in James M. Ollar Letters, Confederate Collection, Tennessee Archives.

preparing to invade Tennessee with seventy-five thousand men. Hindman's intelligence had placed Buell's numbers at only twenty thousand, but Johnston was positive that Buell must have four times that number.

Not only did Johnston center his attention on Buell, but he also believed that when Buell moved, the advance on Nashville would come through central Kentucky. As early as mid-October, Johnston wrote Samuel Cooper that at Bowling Green the Federals "will make the greatest effort. . . ." [35] On Christmas Day, he wrote Isham Harris that the information "continues to convince me that a heavy concentration of force on this line has been made to invade Tennessee on the route to Nashville." [36] The same day, Johnston wrote Judah Benjamin that his information revealed that "every effort has been made by General Buell to concentrate all his strength for a movement upon Tennessee through Central Kentucky. . . ." [37]

As January, 1862, approached, Johnston held strongly to these convictions. If he had any doubts about his theory, they were erased by new intelligence which he received on December 28. Buckner sent him a curious document obtained from Buell's headquarters by a Louisville spy which supposedly listed Buell's complete regimental strength. Buckner gave the intelligence his whole support, terming it "beyond a doubt reliable. . . ." [38] Johnston also believed it, and described the document to Benjamin as "an accurate statement of the troops under General Buell's command." [39] This was the first concise bit of information Johnston had received from north of Green River, and it served to harden his belief that Buell was his main threat. The document listed Buell's strength as seventy-five thousand, precisely the number which Johnston had estimated. Johnston needed no further evidence. As the year ended, the commander of the Second Department more than ever focused his attention on the Bowling Green line, while other areas were neglected.

[35] Johnston to Cooper, October 17, 1861, in Headquarters Book, Tulane. This statement was deleted from the actual letter sent.

[36] Johnston to Harris, December 25, 1861, in *ibid.*

[37] Johnston to Benjamin, December 25, 1861, in *ibid.* See also Johnston to Benjamin, November 8, December 28, 1861, in *ibid.* Actually Buell was lobbying for a two-pronged advance. He wanted one force to advance on the inland river defenses while he marched on Bowling Green. The inland river area was under Halleck's jurisdiction, and he spent the months of November and December, 1861, and January, 1862, bickering with Buell as to what type advance would be made. By December 23 Buell's force, renamed the Department of the Ohio, boasted an aggregate of 70,000, with 57,000 men present for duty. On December 31, Johnston had 22,253 aggregate present for duty. *Official Records,* VII, 511–13, 520–21, 814, IV, 549, VII, 700, 761–62.

[38] Johnston to Benjamin, December 30, 1861, with notation by Buckner, in Headquarters Book, Tulane.

[39] *Ibid.*

four

The Land Between the Rivers

JOHNSTON HAD BEEN DEPARTMENT COMMANDER FOR OVER A MONTH WHEN Adolphus Heiman submitted to Polk and Harris a report on the Henry and Donelson defenses. The report indicated that little progress had been made since Johnston assumed command. Fort Donelson was manned by only three hundred untrained, almost completely unarmed, men. A small battery was finally mounted during the first week in October, but as late as October 17 not one artillerist was at Donelson. And, no defenses against a land approach had yet been constructed. Conditions at Fort Henry also showed little progress. Captain Jesse Taylor's warning to Polk in early September about the danger to the fort when the winter rains came had been ignored. Taylor had urged the relocation of Fort Henry and the building of another fort on the opposite bank of the Tennessee. Polk had given neither project any attention.[1]

During the fall of 1861, conditions at the forts failed to improve. The inexcusable weakness of this most vulnerable point in the Tennessee line did not go unnoticed. Heiman warned Polk that when the January and February rains came, the Cumberland would rise sufficiently to allow heavy draft gunboats to approach Donelson simultaneously with a move up the Tennessee. Others also warned Polk of the need to bolster the forts. But by January 1, 1862, these warnings had produced little change in the situation. No effort had been made to relocate Henry, and the guns of the river battery were still improperly mounted. An auxiliary

[1] Heiman to Polk and Harris, October 18, 1861, in Harris Papers, Tennessee Archives; F. A. Hannum to Johnston, October 17, 1861, and Randall McGavock to Johnston, November 9, 1861, in Telegrams Received, 1861, National Archives; *Official Records*, IV, 457–58; Taylor, "Defense of Fort Henry," 368–69.

position, Fort Heiman, had at last been planned for the river bank opposite Henry, but construction work had not begun. At Donelson, conditions were even worse than at Henry. The entire force of Lloyd Tilghman's command at the two forts numbered only 4,600 troops, of whom
almost 2,000 were unarmed. The total effective force at Donelson numbered six hundred. During the fall of 1861, some artillery instructors had
visited Donelson, but in January, 1862, there were still no trained men to
man the river batteries. Only a third of the planned earthworks were
under construction and none had been completed. In late December,
Tilghman warned that no other point in the entire Confederacy needed
more assistance than did the weak river forts.[2]

The neglect of Donelson and Henry was caused by Johnston's failure
to solidify and temper the command structure. A collapse of command
responsibility for the forts was evident in the fall of 1861. This breakdown occurred at three levels—the district command, the immediate command of the forts, and the department command.[3]

The neglect of the river defenses on the Cumberland and the Tennessee stemmed from the failure of the district commander, Polk, to meet
his responsibilities. Polk was retained as commander of the West Tennessee district when Johnston arrived, and his area was extended to include all defenses in Tennessee between the Mississippi River and the
west bank of the Cumberland. Polk knew the weak condition of the
forts, but he had become as fascinated with the defense of Columbus
as Johnston had with affairs at Bowling Green. Thus he ignored Captain
Taylor's warnings about the weakness of Fort Henry. When Heiman
commanded Henry and Donelson in September and October, 1861, Polk
sent him no aid except one regiment of infantry and a few cavalry companies, all badly armed. When Tilghman took command of the forts in
November, Polk sent him no troops despite his repeated pleas. In late
November, a group of North Alabama citizens appealed to Polk to
strengthen the Tennessee River defenses. They were told that they should
raise a home guard unit and defend the river themselves.[4]

Polk was not only personally disinterested in the problems of the
inland river forts, but also balked at cooperating with anyone else who
took any initiative in the matter. In October, 1861, there were only three

[2] Joseph Dixon to Mackall, November 14, 1861, and Gilmer to Mackall, November
15, 1861, in Telegrams Received, 1861, National Archives; J. W. Head to Mackall,
November 14, 1861, in Harris Papers, Tennessee Archives; *Official Records*, IV, 458,
519, VII, 817–18; Taylor, "Defense of Fort Henry," 369.

[3] *Official Records*, LII, Pt. 2, pp. 245–46.

[4] Special Orders No. 127, December 4, 1861, in Headquarters Book, Tulane; *Official
Records*, IV, 453–54, 481, 488–89, LII, Pt. 2, pp. 233–34.

engineers in the entire Second Department, and he had cornered all three for work on his Mississippi River forts. Johnston ordered one of them, Lieutenant Joseph K. Dixon, to go to Donelson and superintend the work there. Polk, in a manner that can only be described as insubordinate, first delayed the engineer's departure and then flatly told Johnston that neither Dixon nor the other two officers could be spared. Johnston had to issue two additional orders to Polk before Dixon was sent. In fact, except for some half-armed cavalry companies sent to Henry and four artillery officers sent to Donelson on a few days' loan, Polk did not volunteer to send any troops to the inland forts during the fall. The few other troops which were sent were ordered there by Johnston. Johnston was even forced to command Polk to send four companies of infantry to guard the Danville, Tennessee, bridge, where the Memphis, Clarksville, and Louisville Railroad crossed the Tennessee River.[5]

While there was a neglect of supervision of the forts at a district level, there was an excess of command in the Henry-Donelson area itself. In the fall of 1861, two officers were assigned commands in the area. Johnston ordered Gilmer to prepare defenses at Bowling Green, Nashville, Clarksville, Henry, and Donelson. Tilghman was assigned the command at Henry and Donelson. The two men held opposite views on the necessity of acting swiftly to provide good defensive works at Henry and Donelson. This conflict resulted in a maze of orders and counterorders that only hampered defensive efforts. Unfortunately, while Tilghman was more concerned than Gilmer with the weakness of the two forts, Gilmer was more influential with Johnston.

Gilmer exerted a great influence upon the condition of the Henry and Donelson defenses. In October, Johnston, with his usual manner of completely trusting an untried subordinate, assigned him to the task of supervising the works. Then Johnston, confident that a strong line would be built, turned back to affairs at Bowling Green. Though he was unaware of it, Gilmer almost completely ignored the Henry and Donelson defenses during the fall. There are several explanations for his lack of interest. For one thing, he was not happy in the Second Department. He had hoped to be assigned to superintend the Savannah defenses instead. Not only were his wife and many friends in Savannah, but he was partial to the warmer coastal climate.

When Gilmer came to Bowling Green, he was homesick, unhappy with his assignment, and bored. Nothing seemed to go right for him.

[5] Mackall to Dixon, September 27, 1861, Mackall to Polk, October 1, 1861, Johnston to Fisher Hannum, October 17, 1861, Polk to Johnston, April 1, 1862, all in Headquarters Book, Tulane; Polk to Mackall, October 7, 1861, in Polk Papers, National Archives.

He had had an unpleasant trip from Georgia to Kentucky, and complained of the "common cars" of the railroad and of the poor hotels en route. No sooner had he arrived at Bowling Green than the autumn rains began, and he developed a severe cold. Other occurrences continued to irritate him. His wife did not write often enough and he feared she was ill at Savannah. He was unhappy with his rank as major, and thought he should be promoted to brigadier. In his letters home, he showed no interest in his work on Johnston's line. The letters were filled only with detailed accounts of what he would do if he were fortifying Savannah and of wishes that he were there. Gilmer simply began his assignment with an indifferent, unpleasant attitude, characterized when he wrote: "This is a mean life for us to live my dear wife, *is it not?* And the worst is, this mean life may last a long time." 6

Gilmer did not think there was any need for hurrying along the work on the defenses. He considered himself an expert on the time and manner of the expected Federal advance into Tennessee. Privately, he formulated a dangerous opinion that would hamper work on Henry and Donelson. Gilmer expected Halleck's army to move down the Mississippi against Polk, but he did not think this move could be made until spring. Reports indicated that Halleck's predecessor, John C. Frémont, had all but wrecked the organization of the army, and Gilmer did not think that Halleck would "venture on an exploration so hazardous as the descent of the Mississippi—with such a rabble for an army." 7

Neither did he expect an advance on Middle Tennessee in the fall or in the winter. He was confident that snow, ice, and mud on Kentucky roads would make an advance by Buell impossible. As early as December 1, he remarked, "I consider the campaign in Kentucky essentially closed." 8 On December 4 he added that this cessation of operations would be to Johnston's advantage since the Confederates would be better prepared by spring to resist invasion. On January 10, Gilmer wrote his wife that he did not believe the Federal invasion would come until April or May of 1862. Confident that his time schedule was correct, he saw no urgency in bolstering the Henry and Donelson defenses.9 Gilmer also wasted much time

6 Gilmer to his wife, October 19, 1861, in Gilmer Papers, UNC. See also Gilmer to his wife, October 4, 13, 15, 25, November 24, December 1, 1861, in *ibid.*
7 Gilmer to his wife, November 24, 1861, in *ibid.*
8 Gilmer to his wife, December 1, 1861, in *ibid.*
9 Gilmer also wrote his wife: "The risk of attacking Bowling Green with its intrenchments is too great for them. . . . The result will be, most likely, that both armies will remain in *status quo* until next spring." January 5, 1862, in *ibid.* For additional evidence that Gilmer did not expect a Federal advance until the spring of 1862, see Gilmer to his wife, October 15, 17, 19, November 28, December 4, 6, 11, 29, 1861, January 2, 10, 29, 1862, in *ibid.*

sulking over Johnston's failure to take the offensive. When he came to Bowling Green, he saw only one bright spot in what appeared to him a dismal future: he hoped that Johnston would move north and take Louisville. On October 15, as he waited in Nashville for the train to Bowling Green, he wrote his wife that "it is by no means impossible—nor improbable, that we will winter in Louisville—the place you love so much." [10] Two days later at Bowling Green, he was shocked to learn that Johnston did not plan to move forward. Chagrined, he wrote, "I thought we would advance towards Louisville at once but I fear such is *not* to be the policy." [11] On October 19 Gilmer bemoaned that "I much fear our fall campaign will not be as active as I anticipated when I left you." [12] Only by the end of November had he reconciled himself to the fact that there would be no offensive that fall. Meanwhile, though chief of engineers, he behaved like a frustrated infantry commander.[13]

Even if Gilmer had been of a mind to work on the inland river defenses, it is doubtful that he would have accomplished much. His time had to be divided among too many other projects. The Bowling Green–Nashville line had first priority, and Gilmer spent weeks working on defenses there. He did not even go to Donelson and Henry until November.[14] Once at Donelson, he again delayed work on the fortifications.

Meanwhile, Joseph Dixon, supposedly assigned to work on the defenses at Donelson, had become intrigued with the idea of strengthening not only Donelson but several other points downriver as well. Fifteen miles below Donelson on the Cumberland was the river landing of Line Port. This site had two advantages which Donelson did not have. Fortifications there would guard the complex of iron works and rolling mills which lay between the Tennessee and the Cumberland rivers north of the landing. These iron works were owned by prominent Nashvillians who probably exerted pressure on the young officer to shift the defensive point from Donelson to Line Port. Also, three miles below Line Port the channel of the river was narrowed at Line Island. The narrow channel and shoals there rendered the river difficult for heavy gunboats to navi-

10 Gilmer to his wife, October 15, 1861, in *ibid.*
11 Gilmer to his wife, October 17, 1861, in *ibid.*
12 Gilmer to his wife, October 19, 1861, in *ibid.*
13 Gilmer to his wife, November 26, 28, December 4, 6, 8, 11, 14, 22, 1861, in *ibid.* See also Johnston to Cooper, January 22, 1862, and Johnston to Benjamin, November 8, 1861, in Headquarters Book, Tulane.
14 The relation between Gilmer's slowness to build defenses and his hopes for an offensive was shown when he wrote from Nashville, "My reconnaissance here is far from being complete—hence I expect to return here after a short time, unless we make a rapid advance towards Louisville. In that case Nashville will need no defenses I am sure." Gilmer to his wife, November 6, 1861, in Gilmer Papers, UNC. See also Gilmer to his wife, October 17, 19, 23, November 8, 24, December 20, 1861, in *ibid.;* Gilmer to E. B. Sayers, December 10, 1861, in Ch. III, Vol. 8, National Archives.

gate in ordinary stages of the river. Dixon thought Line Port was superior
to Donelson as a defensive position. Yet, instead of either relocating the
defenses or concentrating his energies to improve conditions at Donelson,
he committed a serious error: he divided his time and energy, as well as
the available manual labor, between Donelson, Line Island, and a third
position at Ingram's Shoals, farther downriver.

Gilmer fell into line with Dixon's ideas on spreading the river
defenses, even though Johnston had explicitly ordered him to Donelson
to work on the position there and at Fort Henry. In fact, Gilmer became involved in more projects than had Dixon. Not only were the two
projects downriver continued, but Gilmer began a third. He conceived
the idea of blockading the river channel below Donelson. Such a task
demanded not only his time but also a large force of laborers to handle
the blocks and ropes used to hoist the obstructions into the river. He
even experimented with the idea of converting a steamboat into a gunboat for defense on the Cumberland. Too many projects for him to
supervise were planned for the few slave laborers who were volunteered
to work at Donelson. The result was that by January, 1862, the most
vital projects had been neglected. Gilmer should have begun work on
land defenses at Donelson in November, but this work was not begun
until January. Gilmer should also have spent his energies in attempting
to rectify the poor location of Fort Henry. Fort Heiman had been
planned for this purpose, yet by January the auxiliary fort remained
only a plan. By repeating Dixon's error, Gilmer had neglected the areas
that were supposedly the reason for his being at Donelson.[15]

It was this neglect of vital areas which embroiled him in a controversy with Tilghman that also delayed work on the river defenses. Tilghman was one of the spokesmen in the Second Department for strong defenses at Henry and Donelson. While on duty at Hopkinsville, he became
concerned with the weakness of the inland river line, and began writing
letters to Johnston warning of its condition. On his own time, Tilghman
made a trip to the forts in early November to see what needed to be
done, and arranged a meeting with Gilmer to discuss the defense situation. Later that month, on Polk's recommendation, he was ordered by
Johnston to take command of Forts Henry and Donelson.[16]

When he arrived at the forts, Tilghman was shocked at the visible

15 *Official Records,* IV, 496–97, 501, 506, LII, Pt. 2, pp. 167–68, 229–30. Gilmer to
V. K. Stevenson, November 1, 1861, and Gilmer to Dixon, December 9, 1861, in Ch. III,
Vol. 8, National Archives; Gilmer to his wife, January 31, 1862, in Gilmer Papers, UNC;
Nichols, *Confederate Engineers,* 44.

16 Tilghman to Johnston, September 23, 1861, Mackall to Tilghman, October 23,
1861, Tilghman to Mackall, November 10, 21, 1861, Special Orders No. 89, November
14, 1861, all in Headquarters Book, Tulane; Tilghman to Polk, November 4, 1861, in
Polk Papers, National Archives; *Official Records,* IV, 491–92, 523, 527, 560, VII, 689.

neglect, and sent the first of a series of three warnings to Polk. He complained of the large number of unarmed men and the lack of land defenses. He begged for some field artillery, as well as additional heavy guns for the river works. Tilghman argued that the occupation of the ground across the river from Henry at the projected Fort Heiman was an absolute necessity. Field artillery would be required at Heiman, as would laborers to dig the fortifications. The only laborers available in the area were at Line Port and on the river below Donelson. Despite Tilghman's pleas, Polk sent him no troops, field artillery, river guns, or laborers.[17]

Tilghman's warnings went unheeded for two reasons. He was reporting to Polk, who cared little for the river forts. In April, 1862, Polk would all but admit that he had suggested that Tilghman command the forts in order to rid himself of the responsibility. Polk had hoped that since communications between Donelson and Bowling Green and Columbus were difficult, Tilghman would take his problems elsewhere. Tilghman, however, could not complain to Bowling Green. Not only was he supposed to report to Polk, but he had fared poorly in a dispute with Gilmer, because Johnston had such complete confidence in his chief engineer. When he first took command in November, Tilghman saw that manpower was being wasted on the various projects which Dixon and Gilmer had instigated. He realized that the slavepower which Gilmer was expending below Donelson was needed for the construction of breastworks at Donelson and Heiman. Consequently, he ordered S. P. Glenn, the civil engineer in charge of the project of obstructing the Cumberland, to cease work immediately. Glenn complained to Gilmer, who ordered him to continue the work and protested to Johnston that Tilghman was interfering with construction. Tilghman tried to explain that the obstruction project was badly planned and represented a waste of effort. He was curtly informed by Johnston's headquarters that in the future he was not to interfere with Gilmer's activities.[18]

For Gilmer, this was only one of many disputes that wasted valuable time and indicated the complete breakdown of command at the river forts. Even Gilmer was forced to admit that one commander should have the complete authority at the river defenses. Of course, he was quick to point out that he should have that authority.[19]

17 *Official Records,* VII, 719, 723–24, 731–32, LII, Pt. 2, p. 239.

18 Gilmer to Mackall, November 27, 1861, and Tilghman to Mackall, November 29, 1861, in Telegrams Received, 1861, National Archives; Gilmer to Mackall, November 28, 1861, and Gilmer to Dixon, December 4, 1861, in Ch. III, Vol. 8, National Archives.

19 Gilmer to Dixon, November 24, 1861, and Gilmer to Stevenson, November 29, 1861, in Ch. III, Vol. 8, National Archives; Dixon to Gilmer, November 24, 1861, in Telegrams Received, 1861, National Archives.

Polk's disinterest in the affairs of the eastern edge of his district and Gilmer's inexcusable neglect of his duties at Henry and Donelson both indicated a command failure at a departmental level. Throughout the fall and winter of 1861–62, Johnston was totally unaware of the debacle that existed at the inland forts. There is no evidence that he even knew that the forts were in a defenseless condition. Instead, his absolute trust in Gilmer and his preoccupation with menial tasks at Bowling Green led him to believe that the forts were strong. In November he assured Benjamin that Donelson "is in a state of defense," and that Fort Henry "is a strong work, and sufficiently garrisoned." [20] Of course, this ignorance of actual conditions at the forts was not all Johnston's fault. Polk volunteered no information to him as to the conditions at Henry and Donelson, and offered no aid to bolster the defense of that part of his own district. Gilmer failed to keep Johnston apprised of his work. Yet the final blame must rest with Johnston. He simply was unable to communicate with his subordinates. For example, he probably never knew that Gilmer did not believe the Federals would attack until April or May. Johnston himself did not hold this view, and on one occasion said that anyone who did not expect a winter advance by the Federals was deluded. Less absorption with central Kentucky affairs and a stronger hand with Polk might have forced Polk to meet his responsibilities at Henry and Donelson.[21]

By the end of December, the complex of command failures—district, area, and departmental—had combined to make the inland river defenses the most vulnerable spot on the Tennessee line.

[20] Johnston to Benjamin, November 8, 1861, in Headquarters Book, Tulane.
[21] Gilmer to Mackall, November 24, 1861, in Ch. III, Vol. 8, National Archives.

five

Tragedy in the Cumberlands

FELIX ZOLLICOFFER HAS BEEN ONE OF THE MOST CRITICIZED OF ALL CONFEDerate generals. He has been labeled an inept strategist, a political general, and a soldier incapable of leading troops. Zollicoffer has been accused of poor leadership at Mill Springs, and especially of stupidity in ordering an attack on the Union position there. All of these errors have been blamed on a general who was assigned to command the longest section of Johnston's line, with the smallest force and the largest percentage of unarmed men of any district commander in Tennessee. Zollicoffer's line lay in the most rugged terrain in Tennessee, the Cumberland and Unaka Mountain ranges. This area was also the poorest food-producing area in Tennessee, contained the largest amount of Unionist activity, and possessed the worst roads and other lines of communication. Moreover, "Zollicoffer's defeat" at Mill Springs occurred when the East Tennessee command had already passed to General George B. Crittenden. It was Crittenden, not Zollicoffer, who ordered the advance that ended with Zollicoffer lying dead in the pelting rains on Fishing Creek. Yet it would be Zollicoffer who would receive the blame of historians.[1]

It is true that Zollicoffer was a political general who had seen only limited military service in the Seminole War. Born in Maury County, Tennessee, in 1812, he achieved fame first as a printer and journalist; by 1842 he was editor of the powerful Nashville *Republican Banner.* A Whig, he later served in the United States Congress and in both houses of the state legislature. Despite his Whig affiliation, Zollicoffer in 1861 was given a brigadier general's commission in the state army by Isham Harris.

[1] Horn, *Army of Tennessee,* 50.

(He had been an outspoken member of the governor's secession bloc.) Later, he was commissioned a brigadier general in Confederate service and was sent to command in East Tennessee during the summer of 1861. When Johnston came to Tennessee, Zollicoffer was retained as district commander in the region. During the fall of 1861 he conducted an almost brilliant campaign in eastern Kentucky, only to have the army which he had built destroyed at Mill Springs in January, 1862. [2]

Although he was later severely criticized, Zollicoffer was actually a capable strategist. During the fall of 1861, his use of the defensive-offensive to stall a Federal drive on East Tennessee revealed exceptional ability. In September and October, after securing Cumberland Gap, he moved his force north of the gap along the old Wilderness Road. Zollicoffer hoped to relieve the pressure on Johnston's recently established line in central Kentucky, and also to keep the Federals on the defensive in his own area. He knew that a Union force of twenty thousand men led by General George H. Thomas was gathering at Camp Dick Robinson, the Rockcastle Hills, and other points with the intention of advancing on Cumberland Gap. He had information also that Thomas was to work in conjunction with East Tennessee Tories to capture the gap and cut the East Tennessee and Virginia Railroad.

To counter this threat, Zollicoffer could do either of two things. He could launch an offensive into the Kentucky Bluegrass to force Thomas back. He wished to do this, yet did not feel that he could logistically sustain an invasion that far into the state. His total force on the mountain line was only 3,549 troops, and his only reserves were 3,600 troops in East Tennessee. Almost 1,500 of the reserves were unarmed. Zollicoffer had only one battery of field artillery. In early October, his troops had less than five days' rations. The road from Cumberland Gap to the Bluegrass led through 150 miles of the most barren region in Kentucky, strong in Union sentiment but destitute of supplies.[3]

The only alternative was to begin a series of thrusts and jabs to keep Thomas occupied until the Confederates could assume the offensive. Cavalry was sent to Williamsburg and to Harlan County to break up pro-Union assemblies. In September, when news was received that Federal troops were at Barboursville, Zollicoffer sent a detachment of his force under Colonel Joel Battle to drive out the Federals. Battle

2 W. J. McMurray, *History of the Twentieth Tennessee Regiment Volunteer Infantry, C.S.A.* (Nashville, 1904), 380–88; Edd Winfield Parks, "Zollicoffer: Southern Whig," *Tennessee Historical Quarterly*, XI (December, 1952), 346–55.

3 James Rains to his wife, September 15, October 3, 4, 1861, in Rains Papers, Tennessee Archives; W. B. Wood to Mackall, October 26, 1861, in Telegrams Received, 1861, National Archives; *Official Records*, IV, 418–19, 424–26, 435, 439; Mackall to Zollicoffer, October 3, 1861, in Headquarters Book, Tulane.

ambushed the Union troops while they were foraging in one of the scarce corn fields south of the town, and pushed them out of Barbours-ville. On September 26 another column led by Colonel James Rains slipped into the mountain wilderness and struck sixty-five miles north of Cumberland Gap at Laurel Bridge. Union recruits were dispersed and their supplies were captured. Meanwhile, a second column under Colonel D. H. Cummings raided the valuable Goose Creek Salt Works.[4]

Zollicoffer found in October that he must revise his strategy. He learned that a column led by General Albin Schoepf was advancing on Cumberland Gap via London, Kentucky. To stall this drive, Zollicoffer launched his most vigorous threat. His entire division made a forced march eighty miles north on the Wilderness Road and fell on Schoepf's troops at Rockcastle Hills. The attack failed, for the Union position—protected by rocky gorges, steep bluffs, and fallen timber—was too strong to carry.

This setback convinced Zollicoffer that he must change his strategy. The loss demonstrated the difficulty of conducting defensive-offensive operations on the narrow, barren mountain roads in eastern Kentucky, where supporting columns were far to the rear in Tennessee and sub-sistence was scarce. Zollicoffer saw that he was in a dilemma. The farther north he moved to stall a Federal drive, the longer his supply line became, for he could not live off the desolate country. Yet if he chose to await a Federal column near his base at Cumberland Ford, he would lose the advantages of surprise and choice of field. Also, the Federal column would probably become stronger as it moved through eastern Kentucky, where Union recruiting was heavy.[5]

Another factor compelled Zollicoffer to revamp his strategy. By the end of October, his intelligence indicated a heavy buildup of Thomas' force and a change in Thomas' own strategy. Reconnaissance reported the Union drive would not come into East Tennessee via Cumberland Gap, but that Thomas would advance on one of the routes west of the gap which were on the unguarded portion of the line between the Bowling Green force and Zollicoffer. West of Cumberland Gap were

---

[4] R. R. Hancock, *Hancock's Diary: Or, A History of the Second Tennessee Cavalry* (Nashville, 1887), 28–51; Worsham, *Nineteenth Tennessee*, 14–15; James Rains to his wife, October 3, 1861, in Rains Papers, Tennessee Archives.

[5] See Francis F. McKinney, *Education in Violence: The Life of George H. Thomas and the History of the Army of the Cumberland* (Detroit, 1961), 108–23; *Official Records*, IV, 349; Zollicoffer to Mackall, October 21, 1861, in Telegrams Received, 1861, National Archives; Alexander Coffee to his wife, October 26, 29, 1861, in Coffee Papers, UNC; Hancock, *Second Tennessee Cavalry*, 55–67; Worsham, *Nineteenth Tennessee*, 16–17.

five routes into Tennessee, and Thomas might turn Zollicoffer's flank by taking any of them. Three of these routes—Rogers', Wheeler's, and Big Creek Gaps—were within fifty miles of Cumberland Gap, on the mountain ridges to the southwest. Two other routes were far to the west on the rugged Cumberland Plateau. One of these, the Albany (Kentucky)–Jamestown (Tennessee) road, was a good pike and also gave the Federals the advantage of maneuver. A force moving from Somerset, Kentucky, could advance either southwest via Albany or southeast toward the Cumberland Gap area. The terrain made it impossible to determine which route would be taken until the advance was long under way. A second route on the Cumberland Plateau, the Tompkinsville, Kentucky, road, intersected the main road leading between Knoxville and Nashville, and the Federals could easily cut communications between Middle and East Tennessee by moving this way.

By the first week of November, Zollicoffer was convinced the Federals would advance on the Albany route. To counter this expected move, he ordered a shift of his line—and his strategy. His troops were to be pulled back from eastern Kentucky into Tennessee, and then marched west to the Cumberland Plateau, where his army would again move north into central Kentucky. Zollicoffer's object was to strike Thomas before he could concentrate all of his forces in the central region. Zollicoffer knew that, once Thomas was entrenched in south-central Kentucky, the Federal railroad connections would allow a concentration either against Hardee's right at Bowling Green or against his own left. Also, he hoped that by moving closer to the Bowling Green sector, Buckner and Hardee would join him in the move to force Thomas out of the region.[6]

During November, the Confederates in eastern Kentucky began the move west. As he moved, Zollicoffer sealed off every entrance into Tennessee. Cumberland Gap was left in the hands of Colonel James Rains; with two regiments, breastworks, and a seven-gun battery, the gap was in a good defensive condition. Rogers', Wheeler's, and Big Creek Gaps were also blocked by small garrisons, breastworks, and felled timber. The Confederate force then crossed the Cumberland Plateau and turned north into the Cumberland River basin. Zollicoffer halted at Mill Springs, a village on the south bank of the river. There he hoped to receive sup-

[6] W. B. Wood to Mackall, October 26, November 5, 1861, and Zollicoffer to Mackall, November 4, 5, 1861, in Telegrams Received, 1861, National Archives; Mackall to Zollicoffer, September 23, October 20, 1861, Mackall to L. P. Walker, October 22, 1861, Johnston to Cooper, October 21, 1861, all in Headquarters Book, Tulane; *Official Records*, IV, 477–78, 486–88, 490, 493, 502, 516–17, 527, VII, 734.

plies from Nashville by steamboat rather than by road from Knoxville, as he had done at Cumberland Gap.[7]

At this point, he made a tactical error. He commandeered some rafts and crossed his troops to the north bank of the river. Circumstances seemed to justify the move. On the south bank, he could only observe the buildup of Thomas' army and had no chance to strike at scattered columns. Also, while he remained on the south side, it was possible for the Union army to veer to the southeast and attempt to force a passage in the area between Mill Springs and Cumberland Gap. To prevent such a move, Zollicoffer must either move north of the river and thwart it, or else remain on the Cumberland Plateau until he determined the enemy's route. The Plateau was a barren region and his army could not subsist there. Supplies could not be brought in, for the roads were impassable in winter. It was also a region of Unionist sentiment, and local residents offered little food or information to Confederates. Zollicoffer's only choice was to cross the Cumberland and strike Thomas' force before it became strong enough to drive his own troops back into the Cumberland River.[8]

Although the move to the north bank seemed necessary for logistical and reconnaissance purposes, it was extremely hazardous from a tactical viewpoint. Zollicoffer's troops were both badly armed and poorly disciplined. They had been in mountain service and were accustomed to operating in small, individual raiding parties. They had had little time for drilling, for most of them had been actively engaged in eastern Kentucky since their arrival in East Tennessee. They had little food, only a few artillery pieces, and almost no reserve ammunition. Entrenching tools, needed to dig fortifications on the north bank, must be sent from Nashville. Yet Zollicoffer confidently expected them to be capable of launching an offensive drive into central Kentucky.

His mistake was that his plan, though a good one, depended upon too many factors for success. His scheme was to cross the Cumberland, build entrenchments opposite Mill Springs at Beech Grove, await reinforcements from Knoxville, and then advance on that part of Thomas'

---

[7] Alexander Coffee to his wife, November 3, 9, 25, December 1, 17, 1861, in Coffee Papers, UNC; McCook's Testimony, in Buell Papers, Rice; Enoch Mitchell (ed.), "Letters of a Confederate Surgeon of the Army of Tennessee to his Wife, "*Tennessee Historical Quarterly,* V (March, 1946), 60–66; William T. Alderson (ed.), "Civil War Diary of Captain James Litton Cooper, September 30, 1861, to January, 1865," *Tennessee Historical Quarterly,* XV (June, 1956), 144.

[8] W. B. Wood to Mackall, November 5, 1861, in Telegrams Received, 1861, National Archives; Alexander Coffee to his wife, November 9, 20, 1861, in Coffee Papers, UNC; Buell to Halleck, October 17, 1861, in Buell Papers, Rice; Hindman to Ed Pickett, January 17, 1862, in Telegrams Received, 1862, National Archives; *Official Records,* XVI, Pt. 1, p. 110.

force concentrating at Columbia, Kentucky. Time became precious. Reinforcements and supplies must arrive before Thomas' army became too large to defeat. The longer Zollicoffer must wait, the less his chances for success became, and the greater the danger was that his undermanned division would be attacked while isolated on the north bank of the Cumberland.[9]

No sooner had Zollicoffer crossed the river than a series of problems began to delay his plan. These troubles were felt everywhere on Johnston's line, but especially at Mill Springs, where time was all-important. The first problem was a lack of arms. At Mill Springs, most of Zollicoffer's men carried old flintlock muskets and half of his Knoxville reserve force was totally unarmed. This shortage was a departmental one, for Johnston had inherited the arms dilemma of the state army. Men were available in abundance, but Johnston could not arm them. In September, he needed thirty thousand arms for men already in the Army who had no weapons. His force, like the state army, was a "paper army." Many of the regiments listed as serviceable were completely unarmed Polk had unarmed regiments at Forts Pillow, Donelson, and Henry; Trenton; Union City; and Henderson Station. Two regiments at Memphis were unarmed, as well as four at Columbus. Colonel W. A. Quarles' regiment at Clarksville could muster only 317 guns, two-thirds of which would not even fire. At Huntsville, Alabama, Leroy P. Walker's four regiments, intended to reinforce Zollicoffer, were completely without arms.[10]

During the fall of 1861, Johnston had used every available means to obtain both arms and men. Although he always had more troops than he could arm, he felt that more men were needed to effect the ruse of appearing to have a much stronger force. Johnston's idea was to place these unarmed men in training camps and arm them as guns became available. Requests for arms and men were sent to Harris, to Governors Thomas O. Moore of Louisiana, John Pettus of Mississippi, and A. B. Moore of Alabama, and to General Braxton Bragg at Pensacola.

9 *Official Records,* IV, 10-12, 108, 753; Worsham, *Nineteenth Tennessee,* 26.

10 Tilghman to Mackall, October 2, November 15, 1861, Harris to Johnston, October 22, November 12, 1861, L. M. Walker to Mackall, October 22, November 26, 1861, L. M. Walker to Johnston, October 24, 1861, A. J. Lindsay to Johnston, October 31, 1861, John Gregg to Mackall, November 1, 1861, Pillow to Mackall, November 23, 1861, W. A. Quarles to Johnston, November 29, 1861, W. C. Whitthorne to Mackall, December 13, 1861, all in Telegrams Received, 1861, National Archives; Johnston to Jefferson Davis, September 16, 1861, in Letters Sent, 1861–62, National Archives; Johnston to A. B. Moore, September 15, 1861, Johnston to Davis, September 17, 1861, Johnston to Pettus, October 12, 1861, Mackall to Neill Brown and W. B. Harding, October 23, 1861, all in Headquarters Book, Tulane; *Official Records,* IV, 524–25, VII, 825–26, 836–37, LII, Pt. 2, pp. 195–96.

None was able to give Johnston much assistance. Tennessee had been almost depleted of men and weapons. Governor Moore of Alabama explained that he needed the available men for seacoast defenses, and that no arms were on hand to send. Bragg said he had no extra guns to send. Moore of Louisiana replied that he could send no aid.[11]

East Tennessee felt the weapons shortage most keenly. Zollicoffer had been unable to equip a reserve force that was now needed at Mill Springs. Of the reserves in Knoxville, not a single regiment was fully armed. The 38th Tennessee had 998 men but only 250 guns, 200 of which were unserviceable. The 39th Tennessee had 771 troops but only 200 rifles, shotguns, and muskets, most of which had been classified as unfit for service. At Chattanooga, the 38th Tennessee, 850 strong, was armed with 500 flintlock muskets.[12]

These regiments were the best armed units in Colonel William H. Carroll's reserve brigade, which Zollicoffer was anxiously awaiting in December. Carroll, however, did not get to Mill Springs in December. He did not even leave Knoxville to join Zollicoffer until January 16, 1862, more than six weeks after Zollicoffer had planned the move for which he was needed. While Carroll delayed, Thomas continued to build his strength, and Zollicoffer's initial advantage of concentration slowly melted away. Carroll's delay was indicative of serious problems felt in Johnston's relations with Zollicoffer, and Richmond's attitude toward the West.[13]

Carroll was a typical victim of the arms dilemma. When he first organized his brigade in September, 1861, he obtained about two thousand old country rifles that needed repair. He put them in shops at Memphis, Nashville, and Murfreesboro, with assurances that the guns would be ready by mid-October. Yet when he was ordered to reinforce Zollicoffer in November, not a single gun had been fixed. Desperate for arms, Carroll found four hundred old weapons in the Memphis arsenal. These weapons were an almost totally useless collection of old double-barreled shotguns, muskets, and pikes. By December 13, Carroll was in Knoxville with four thousand men, but only three hundred were properly armed. Several

11 Johnston to Harris, September 21, November 19, 1861, Bragg to Johnston, September 27, 1861, Johnston to A. B. Moore, December 2, 1861, all in Headquarters Book, Tulane; General Order No. 12, Tennessee State Militia, November 19, 1861, and Harris to Pettus, November 20, 1861, in Harris Papers, Tennessee Archives; A. B. Moore to Johnston, September 23, 1861, in Barret Collection, Tulane; Johnston to Thomas Moore, November 20, 1861, Harris to Johnston, November 12, 1861, Buckner to Mackall, September 21, 1861, all in Telegrams Received, 1861, National Archives; Bettersworth, *Confederate Mississippi*, 23; Fleming, *Alabama*, 88–89; *Official Records*, IV, 449–50.

12 *Official Records*, VII, 749–52.

13 G. H. Monsarrat to Mackall, January 23, 1862, in Telegrams Received, 1861, National Archives.

hundred others carried old hunting rifles which Carroll labeled as worthless.[14]

Once in East Tennessee, Carroll was beset with more troubles. In the fall of 1861, the authorities in Richmond generally ignored Johnston's problems on the Tennessee line. There was little communication as to grand strategy, what was expected of Johnston, and what the Army's needs were. Occasionally, the central government would suddenly intervene in Johnston's affairs in a manner that crippled his efforts. In September, for example, after Johnston issued his call for troops and arms, he was rebuked by Judah Benjamin for calling on Arkansas, Louisiana, and Georgia for troops and arms. Benjamin informed Johnston that he was to restrict his calls to Mississippi, North Alabama, Kentucky, and Tennessee. Since Tennessee and Mississippi were already depleted of arms and Kentucky mainly in Federal hands, this left little territory for Johnston to scour.

Usually, Richmond authorities intervened in the West only when something was needed in another area. Benjamin ordered Johnston not to use the supplies at Nashville but to live off the country. Again, the commissary general ordered all meat stored at Nashville to be sent to Richmond, forcing a cancellation of Johnston's order for twenty-four thousand rations. This came late in September during Buckner's move into Kentucky, when rations were badly needed. The quartermaster general ordered all supplies at Nashville, such as tents and blankets, to be shipped to Richmond. Johnston protested that such a move would cause suffering among his troops, especially those from the Gulf states, during the Kentucky winter.[15]

Richmond's lack of understanding of Johnston's problems was due to poor communication. Johnston displayed a passive attitude toward pressing the government for things needed in his command. Also, Richmond did not realize how weak the Army of Tennessee was. In December, Judah P. Benjamin argued that Johnston must have twice the number of ten thousand effective men that were reported at Bowling Green. Benjamin did not realize that many of the regiments, even among the ten thousand, were poorly armed, if armed at all. Many were plagued with epidemics of measles and other diseases. Richmond's ignorance of the Tennessee situation was demonstrated in February, 1862, when Gen-

14 W. H. Carroll to Johnston, October 19, 1861, and Carroll to Mackall, October 26, 1861, in Telegrams Received, 1861, National Archives; Mackall to Carroll, October 20, 23, 1861, in Headquarters Book, Tulane; *Official Records*, VII, 764–66.

15 J. T. Shaaff to Mackall, October 15, 1861, Johnston to Judah Benjamin, October 18, 1861, Johnston to Cooper, October 19, 1861, all in Headquarters Book, Tulane; *Official Records*, IV, 452–53, 502–504.

eral P. G. T. Beauregard came to Tennessee. The general was shocked to find that Johnston's force was so weak, for he had been assured in Virginia that the Army of Tennessee had seventy thousand men, instead of forty-five thousand partially armed troops.[16]

Richmond seemed especially unable to comprehend the arms situation. Many of Johnston's regiments which had no arms were kept in instruction camps until local officials could find some private arms for them. Such procurement took time, for many of the weapons had to be repaired first. Yet Johnston wanted the unarmed troops in camp, both to effect his ruse and to keep them nearby so they would be available if some arms did come. The bulk of this unarmed force was composed of twelve-month volunteers raised in Tennessee and northern Alabama.[17]

In the fall of 1861, Richmond struck at the heart of Johnston's reserve force. Benjamin ordered Johnston to disband all unarmed, twelve-month regiments and not to muster any more such regiments in the future. In essence, this order meant that every soldier not already on the forward Kentucky line must be sent home. Johnston and Harris protested that such a policy would hurt the morale of the volunteers already in camp and would harm the prospects of future enlistment campaigns. Also, the order to disband the troops came at a critical time. In early November, Johnston believed that Buell and Thomas were combining for a strike at Bowling Green. Zollicoffer had already reported that the concentration on the eastern front was shifting westward as if to confront Buckner. Disturbed, Johnston even spoke of abandoning Bowling Green and retiring to Nashville. He wanted the unarmed troops in the camps at Red Sulphur Springs, Cheatham, and Trousdale to be available if conditions became grave. He hoped that if the Federals broke through at Bowling Green, these unarmed men could somehow temporarily stem the tide. Until the situation appeared calm again, Johnston suspended Benjamin's order.

Richmond unknowingly went further to hamper Johnston's efforts. Orders were issued that any Confederate arms sent to Tennessee must be given to those regiments which had volunteered for the duration of the war. Only after these men had been supplied could the twelve-month volunteers be armed. This restriction placed Johnston in a dilemma. Polk, for example, had at least eight unarmed twelve-month regiments, but no

16 Whitthorne to Benjamin, January 8, 1862, in Harris Papers, Tennessee Archives; Liddell to Hardee, January 19, 1862, in Telegrams Received, 1862, National Archives; *Official Records,* VII, 783–84; "Liddell's Record," LSU Archives; Horn, *Army of Tennessee,* 60.

17 Whitthorne to Benjamin, January 8, 1862, and Johnston to Harris, November 5, 1862, in Harris Papers, Tennessee Archives.

regiments which had enlisted for the war. In the autumn of 1861, almost all the troops raised in Tennessee were twelve-month volunteers. Since troops which enlisted for the war were almost nonexistent in Tennessee, the only alternative was to secure private arms for the twelve-month regiments. Under the terms of the earlier order, however, these regiments must be disbanded even before private arms could be found. Thus many of the reinforcements which Johnston had laboriously assembled had to be sent home.[18]

Zollicoffer became the victim of this lack of communication between Johnston and Richmond. While waiting at Knoxville for his guns to be repaired, Carroll was ordered by Richmond on December 12 to move for Mill Springs. He protested that if he went, he could only take three hundred armed men. Benjamin curtly replied that if Carroll's weapons did not arrive by January 10, unarmed companies and regiments would be disbanded. W. C. Whitthorne entered the dispute and said that if Benjamin really understood conditions in Tennessee, he would give Carroll time to procure private arms. Benjamin relented and cancelled the January 10 deadline order, but the interruption caused some delay in Carroll's efforts.[19]

Carroll again encountered misfortune, and Zollicoffer's hopes for reinforcement were dashed. By January 1, two regiments had been armed, and a third was expected to be armed in thirty days. On January 8 Johnston, unaware of Zollicoffer's predicament, ordered Carroll to send to Bowling Green all the armed men except one regiment. Therefore when Carroll reinforced Zollicoffer, he could only bring a solitary regiment and a battery. Johnston's action was indicative of the total lack of communication between Zollicoffer and his commander. Zollicoffer had urged some coordinated action with the central force, but with no success. Johnston made only one effort to support his lieutenant during the entire fall and winter of 1861–62. In October, Johnston sent two regiments to reconnoiter on the Cumberland Plateau, but gave them no instructions to combine action with Zollicoffer. Johnston knew almost nothing of what was going on along the eastern front. He did not even know that Zollicoffer planned

18 Johnston to Harris, September 23, November 2, 5, 16, 1861, Johnston to J. W. Head, November 6, 1861, Johnston to Benjamin, November 27, 1861, January 12, 1862, all in Headquarters Book, Tulane; Harris to Johnston, September 24, 1861, L. P. Walker to Mackall, October 31, 1861, W. R. Hunt to Polk and Johnston, December 20, 1861, all in Telegrams Received, 1861, National Archives; Johnston to Harris, September 24, November 2, 5, 16, 1861, Harris to Jefferson Davis, October 15, 1861, all in Harris Papers, Tennessee Archives; *Official Records*, VII, 770, 795, 798, 807, LII, Pt. 2, p. 144.

19 Carroll to Johnston, November 18, 1861, in Telegrams Received, 1861, National Archives; *Official Records*, VII, 771, 815, 834; Whitthorne to Benjamin, January 8, 1862, in Harris Papers, Tennessee Archives.

to cross the Cumberland at Mill Springs. When he learned of the move, he did not inform Zollicoffer whether he approved or disapproved.[20]

By the end of December, Zollicoffer's offensive plans, hampered by the arms situation, Richmond's interference, and Johnston's lack of communication, had completely collapsed. The expected reserves and supplies had not arrived. Had Zollicoffer been able to move out of his entrenchments in early December, he still might have been able to strike Thomas in detail, for information then indicated both generals had five regiments in the field. The *coup de grace* to this last hope of success was applied by Jefferson Davis. Unaware of Zollicoffer's plan, Davis ordered General Crittenden to take command of the East Tennessee district. Davis had grandiose visions of Crittenden's leading a column of ten regiments north from Cumberland Gap to redeem Kentucky. The only problem was that there were not ten armed regiments in the eastern district, and those that were armed were a hundred miles west of Cumberland Gap poised for another offensive. Crittenden was as ignorant of the situation as was Davis. In late November, when he arrived in East Tennessee, he did not know the extent of his district or what forces he was to command. He did know that there were no ten regiments in East Tennessee. Confused, he went to Richmond to discuss the matter with Davis once more.

Weeks of delay followed. On December 15, Zollicoffer informed Crittenden that Thomas' force had been increased to ten regiments. Then Zollicoffer's hopes faded. Instead of rushing every available man to Mill Springs, Crittenden ordered Zollicoffer back across the Cumberland, and dallied in Knoxville for two more weeks. Meanwhile, Zollicoffer could only remain in his breastworks at Beech Grove on the north bank, for to recross the river was impossible. The waters were almost at flood level, and the Confederates only had two small rafts which they could use.[21]

By January 1, Zollicoffer's chance of striking at Thomas with a hope of success had disappeared. Thomas moved out of Lebanon, Kentucky, on January 1 to unite with Schoepf's column at Somerset and drive the Confederates into the Cumberland River. As long as Zollicoffer remained in his fairly strong works on the north bank of the Cumberland, he would probably have the advantage should Thomas attack.

[20] *Official Records,* IV, 441, 493–94, VII, 825, LII, Pt. 2, pp. 182–83, 190–91, 196.
[21] R. Gerald McMurtry, "Zollicoffer and the Battle of Mill Springs," *Filson Club History Quarterly,* XXIX (October, 1955), 306–307; Peter Franklin Walker, "Holding the Tennessee Line: Winter, 1861–62," *Tennessee Historical Quarterly,* XVI (September, 1957), 242–43; Davis to Crittenden, October 25, 1861, in Rowland (ed.), *Davis,* V, 151–52; James Rains to his wife, November 25, 1861, in Rains Papers, Tennessee Archives; Alexander Coffee to his wife, December 17, 1861, in Coffee Papers, UNC; *Official Records,* VII, 740, LII, Pt. 2, p. 219; Hancock, *Second Tennessee Cavalry,* 29–126.

Reports indicated that Thomas did not have over 10,000 men, while Zollicoffer had some 6,500 troops behind fortifications.

Even this possibility of success was dashed when Crittenden arrived at Mill Springs on January 2. Crittenden was opposed to the idea of standing on the defensive, and sought to attack Thomas before he united with Schoepf. On January 18, Crittenden called a council of war and presented his views to his commanders. Thomas' column was encamped at Logan's Cross Roads, only ten miles north of the Confederate fortifications. Recent rains had swollen the waters of Fishing Creek, and the two Federal commands were separated by the unfordable waters. The rains were still falling hard in the upper Cumberland country, and Crittenden saw an excellent chance to crush Thomas in his isolated position.

But such an offensive would have been unwise, and there is evidence that both Zollicoffer and one of his regimental commanders, D. H. Cummings, opposed the plan. Crittenden did not understand the weaknesses of Zollicoffer's force. The men had confidence in Zollicoffer, while Crittenden was unknown to the troops. Confidence was sorely needed at Mill Springs, for the men were inadequately trained and badly armed. One brigade had never been drilled. Even the best armed regiments had flintlock muskets that always performed badly in rainy weather. Despite these weaknesses, Crittenden ordered the advance to begin at midnight on the eighteenth.[22]

At midnight the troops, already well soaked by the rain, were routed from their fortifications and were formed into a column on the road to Logan's Cross Roads. Zollicoffer commanded the lead brigade while Carroll's brigade followed. For six hours the shivering, poorly-clad infantry trudged along the muddy road in a driving rain. In that time the column covered only eight miles, for the artillery pieces frequently mired down in the road. By six o'clock on the morning of the nineteenth, Zollicoffer's skirmish line had struck Federal pickets about one mile south of the intersection of the Mill Springs and the Columbia–Somerset roads where Thomas' main column was encamped.

An eerie, three-hour fight commenced amidst the cold, driving rain, fog, and smoke which hung over Fishing Creek. The battle of Mill Springs was a battle in name only, for a combination of rough terrain, weather, and a lack of training produced total confusion in Crittenden's ranks. To reach Thomas' main line, the Confederates had to plunge through thick forests

22 See R. M. Kelly, "Holding Kentucky for the Union," *Battles and Leaders*, I, 387; McKinney, *Life of George Thomas*, 124–26; Johnston, *Life of Johnston*, 400. For evidence that Zollicoffer opposed advancing out of the entrenchments to attack Thomas, see Worsham, *Nineteenth Tennessee*, 20.

on both sides of the Mill Springs road. Brigade and regimental organization were soon lost, and the use of artillery was impossible because of
the thick forest cover. In the murky weather it was difficult to find the
enemy, for several of Crittenden's regiments wore blue uniforms similar in
color to those worn by Thomas' Kentucky regiments.[23]

The fighting had scarcely begun when the Rebel organization and morale
began to crumble. Colonel E. C. Walthall's 15th Mississippi Regiment
barely escaped disaster when, in the fog and smoke, Walthall mistook the
Union 4th Kentucky Regiment for a Confederate outfit. Shortly thereafter,
while it was still scarcely daylight, Zollicoffer committed the same error.
Clad in a white raincoat which concealed his own uniform, he rode into the
lines of the 4th Kentucky after he was convinced that one of his Tennessee
regiments was firing upon another Confederate regiment. As he conversed
with an enemy colonel, neither realizing the other's identity, a Confederate aide rode out of the fog and began firing at the Federals. In the return fire, Zollicoffer was killed instantly.[24]

When the news of Zollicoffer's death reached the troops, the men of
his brigade, holding the Confederate left flank, became demoralized and
began to retreat. Many of Crittenden's men were panic-stricken when their
weapons would not fire. The Confederates were armed with flintlock
muskets, together with a few double-barreled shotguns and percussion
squirrel rifles. Not one in five of the 20th Tennessee Regiment's flintlock
muskets would fire in the rain. Many of the weapons carried by men in the
19th and 17th Tennessee regiments also were useless, and many angry
soldiers in the 19th Tennessee broke their weapons on fenceposts in frustration. Carroll later charged that one half of Crittenden's weapons would not
fire at all.[25]

As the Confederate left wing began to fall back, Thomas hurled a
half dozen regiments against the weak flank, to strike a hammer blow. By
ten o'clock, the entire Rebel line had collapsed, and was streaming back
along the muddy Mill Springs road to the breastworks at Beech Grove.
There would be no defense. Thomas moved forward to Beech Grove during
the day and harassed the Confederates with sporadic artillery fire. Crittenden feared that the combined forces of Thomas and Schoepf would assault

23 Kelly, "Holding Kentucky for the Union," 387–88; Bennett H. Young, "Zollicoffer's Oak," *Southern Historical Society Papers*, XXXI (1903), 167; Johnston, *Life
of Johnston*, 400–401.

24 Young, "Zollicoffer's Oak," 167; Johnston, *Life of Johnston*, 401–402.

25 Murray, *Twentieth Tennessee*, 201; Worsham, *Nineteenth Tennessee*, 22; A. S.
Marks, "Seventeenth Tennessee Infantry," in *Military Annals of Tennessee*, ed. John
Berrien Lindsley (Nashville, 1886), 350; Young, "Zollicoffer's Oak," 166, 168; Alexander
Coffee to his wife, December 7, 1861, in Coffee Papers, UNC; *Official Records*, VII, 107–
108, 114.

the works on the following morning, and so decided to retreat to the south bank of the Cumberland.

The retreat was even more disastrous to the Confederates than the battle itself. At midnight on January 19, a tiny army began to cross the rain-swollen waters on a small steamboat and some barges which Crittenden had managed to commandeer. In his haste to save the small force, Critten-den left behind on the north bank all of his artillery, tents, blankets, mules, and a large amount of his food supply, as well as most of his wounded men. On the morning of January 20, the battered column began the dismal eighty-mile trek southwest along the Cumberland to Gainesboro, Tennes-see, where the remnants of Crittenden's force could receive supplies from Nashville. Crittenden had lost only five hundred men on the field, but his army was destroyed. His second in command was dead, and his ordnance and logistical strength were shattered. Even worse, once his troops reached the south bank of the river, they straggled in all directions. Weeks of re-building would be needed before the demoralized regiments could again take the field.[26]

More than an army had been lost. In the Tory counties of East Tennessee and Kentucky, where strength meant everything, Confederate prestige had been lost. Johnston's right flank had all but disappeared, and the only organized Confederate force remaining in East Tennessee was at Cumber-land Gap. A path was now open for a Federal advance into Tennessee through the undefended country between Bowling Green and the gap. New encouragement had been given to Yankee armies in the West, for this was their first real victory since the Bull Run disaster. In contrast, Johnston's army had suffered its first real defeat, even before the main Federal winter offensive had begun. The West had lost its first general, who was potentially an able commander.

When the firing died down in the murky drizzle around Fishing Creek, Johnston did not know of these events. The commander of the Second Department, busy with details at Bowling Green, first learned that his eastern district's defenses had collapsed when he read the news in a Louis-ville newspaper.[27]

26 McMurtry, "Zollicoffer," 313; Crittenden to Johnston, January 20, 1862, in Barret Collection, Tulane; Hindman to Hardee, January 22, 1862, Harris to Johnston, Jan-uary 23, 1862, A. J. Lindsay to Mackall, January 23, 1862, G. H. Monsarrat to Mackall, January 23, 1862, all in Telegrams Received, 1862, National Archives; Johnston to Crittenden, February 3, 1862, in Headquarters Book, Tulane; Worsham, *Nineteenth Tennessee*, 27–30; Hancock, *Second Tennessee Cavalry*, 80–113.
27 On January 22 Johnston informed Isham Harris that he had just read of the battle and of Zollicoffer's death in the Louisville *Democrat*. Johnston to Harris, Jan-uary 22, 1862, in Harris Papers, Tennessee Archives.

PART III

the decline of the johnston influence

six

A Season of Blunders

THE PERIOD OF TESTING FOR THE YOUNG ARMY OF TENNESSEE CAME IN February, 1862, when Union forces from western Kentucky struck at the land between the rivers, the weakest link forged in Johnston's defensive chain. For three weeks the command structure of Johnston's army broke down and showed the weakness of his tempering influence. Many of the conflicting reports and the confusion surrounding the fall of Forts Henry and Donelson are more intelligible if they are studied as an aspect of this total collapse.

The debacle began with the command failures of Polk in late autumn and early winter of 1861–62. Through a series of events which were initiated in November, Polk became totally immobilized in his Columbus fortress. He became so certain that the town was in daily peril of a Federal invasion that in February, 1862, he would not send aid to his sub-commander at Fort Henry, although he knew that the Federals were assaulting the fort in full strength. Polk's continued absence of concern for the inland forts, even when they had begun to fall, can only be understood, though hardly justified, by examining how he had become so immobilized at Columbus.

In November, 1861, Grant had been sent to the Missouri shore opposite Columbus in order to cover a Federal move being made on Jeff Thompson in southeast Missouri and prevent Polk from reinforcing him. Grant was unaware that Polk planned no such reinforcement. On November 7, Grant attacked a Confederate detachment on the west bank, but Pillow and Cheatham crossed the Mississippi with reinforcements and drove him

back to his transports. Although the battle was little more than a heavy
skirmish, it had important consequences. It badly frightened Polk, for he
interpreted it as the beginning of a campaign against Columbus. From
November until February, he constantly expected the Federals to advance
against him from Paducah and Mayfield, Kentucky. As early as the evening
after the battle at Belmont, he informed Johnston that he was expecting
an attack.[1]

The victory at Belmont also fortified Gideon Pillow's belief in himself
as a great strategist and tactician. Had Pillow been in a position where he
could do no harm, his super-inflated ego would have mattered little. On
November 11, however, he believed that his chance for glory had come.
At one of the Columbus river batteries, a large Dahlgren gun exploded
while Polk was standing nearby. The explosion blew away the bishop's
breeches, and unhinged his mind for a month. This ludicrous, if sad, episode left Pillow in command at Columbus while Polk recuperated. The
accident came at an unfortunate time for Johnston, since he had recently
ordered Pillow's division to central Kentucky, where reserves were needed
to strengthen Hardee's weak left flank at Hopkinsville. Pillow did not want
to go, for the encampment at Columbus was comfortable and pleasant. If
he went, he would lose his opportunity to command in Polk's stead. Pillow
now saw his chance to undertake the offensive campaign which he had
wanted to lead in the summer. He planned to concentrate the district's
forces at Columbus and move on Cairo.[2]

Pillow hoped that Polk's injury would induce Johnston to cancel the
transfer order. Johnston did consent to allow him to remain at Columbus, but informed him that his division must still proceed to Hopkinsville. Pillow was not happy with this arrangement, for he wanted his
own division for his invasion plan. To keep his men and also obtain
additional troops, Pillow devised a clever scheme. On November 13, he
began issuing almost daily reports of an overwhelming enemy force gathering in Kentucky to invade Columbus. According to his inflated estimates,
enemy strength gradually increased from a modest 25,000 to 100,000 men.
Pillow also issued a series of reports on the poor state of defenses at Columbus, and claimed his present force there would be unable to repel the
attack. The reports were issued throughout the Second Department, and

[1] Leonidas Polk to his wife, November 15, 1861, and General Orders 20, November
12, 1861, in Polk Papers, UNC; *Official Records*, III, 304–305; U. S. Grant, *Personal
Memoirs of U. S. Grant* (New York, 1885) , I, 269–71.

[2] Pillow to Johnston, November 6, 11, 1861, in Telegrams Received, 1861, National
Archives; Mackall to Pillow, November 11, 1861, in Polk Papers, National Archives;
F. A. Polk to Leonidas Polk, November 16, 1861, and Leonidas Polk to Sallie Polk,
in Polk Papers, UNC. *Official Records*, IV, 532; S. R. Latta to his wife, December 25,
1861, in Latta Papers, Tulane.

were so absurdly inflammatory that West Tennessee rang with his sensational alarms.[3]

Pillow's strategy was effective. Johnston believed his rumors, and not only cancelled his division's transfer but also asked Harris to call out the state militia to aid him. Harris, also impressed by the reports, responded by calling out thirty thousand men. No sooner had Johnston and Harris acted than Pillow changed the tone of his reports. The enemy threat miraculously ceased, and Pillow now reported that the Columbus defenses were impregnable. In fact, Pillow suggested that conditions in West Tennessee had improved enough to allow him to undertake an offensive campaign.[4]

On December 4, Pillow openly presented his plan for the Cairo expedition to Polk. When the latter refused to allow the move, the old summer feud flared up again. The dispute which ensued was an important influence on Polk's neglect of the inland river forts during late November and December. During late November, Polk spent most of his time arguing with Pillow over the proposed campaign. Polk maintained that his force was too weak for an offensive and that the Columbus works were not strong enough to be left behind. To back up his argument, he secured written statements from the division and brigade commanders. These men—among them B. F. Cheatham, John McCown, and S. F. Marks—agreed that Columbus was a weak position and that the army was not strong enough for an offensive.[5]

By the end of November the dispute had ended, but its repercussions further tied Polk to the Columbus position. The arguments his line officers had presented, especially their reports of Halleck's strength at Cairo and Paducah, did more than support his opinion. The force of their arguments convinced Polk that Columbus was in even greater danger than he thought. Thus, in December, he refused to send any reinforcements to the inland forts, and became completely absorbed in preparing the town against attack. He was positive that fifty thousand men would move any day on Columbus from Cairo and Mayfield.[6]

[3]Mackall to Polk and Pillow, November 14, 1861, in Polk Papers, National Archives; Pillow to Harris, November 17, 28, 1861, in Harris Papers, Tennessee Archives; Polk to Johnston, November 15, 1861, in Telegrams Received, 1861, National Archives; *Official Records*, III, 739, IV, 550–51, 557, 560–61, VII, 708, LII, Pt. 2, p. 222.

[4] Johnston to Harris, November 17, 1861, in Letters Sent, 1861–62, National Archives; Pillow to Polk, December 2, 1861, in Gideon J. Pillow Papers, National Archives; Harris to Thomas O. Moore, November 20, 1861, in Harris Papers, Archives; *Official Records*, IV, 553, VII, 703–704, 731, LII, Pt. 2, p. 221.

[5] John S. Bowen to Polk, December 4, 1861, and G. N. Hollins to Polk, December 7, 1861, in Polk Papers, UNC; *Official Records*, LII, Pt. 2, pp. 223–26, IV, 550, VII, 741–42; Samuel Weakley and others to Fellow Citizens of North Alabama and North Mississippi, November 23, 1861, in Headquarters Book, Tulane.

[6] Polk to Benjamin, October 10, 1861, and Polk to Johnston December 30, 1861, in Polk Papers, National Archives; J. F. Henry to his father, December 16, 1861, in Henry Papers, UNC; S. R. Latta to his wife, November 22, 1861, in Latta Papers, Tulane; *Official Records*, VII, 773–74, 797, 803, 828–29, LII, Pt. 2, p. 236.

By January, Polk's fear of attack had become almost pathological. On his front he had 21,000 men present for duty and had amassed 150 fixed and field guns. This force was by far the strongest on Johnston's line, and with it Polk might do several things. He could use it to glean valuable intelligence, or he could strike the flank of any Union force which threatened his weak right flank at Henry and Donelson. But instead, he announced his intentions of retiring into a state of siege at Columbus. He even declared to Johnston that any Federal force aimed at any point in his district other than Columbus would have to be the responsibility of the War Department and the people of the surrounding region. There was no excuse for Polk's neglect of his right flank, nor for Johnston's continuous weakness in handling the bishop. During January, Johnston made no effort to force Polk to be responsible for defending the eastern part of his district.[7]

An example of Polk's attitude toward the inland river forts came in late January, when a Federal reconnaissance force moved up the Tennessee in order to test the defenses of Fort Henry, which Polk knew were in poor condition. On the morning of January 17, three Federal vessels shelled Henry, while three transports landed a reconnaissance party on the west bank of the Tennessee. Tilghman estimated the force at about 5,500, and asked Polk and Johnston for assistance. Two days later, Polk sent a cavalry force to harass the rear of the Yankee column, which had already begun to withdraw. Tilghman had obtained cavalry from Harris and this force, eventually combined with the troops which Polk sent, followed the reconnaissance party almost as far as Paducah. Although Tilghman warned that the Yankee column was in a position to advance again on Fort Henry, a temporary calm descended on the inland rivers. With the exception of Tilghman, the Rebel high command considered the move a false alarm.[8]

The real attack came suddenly, and Tilghman pleaded with Polk for assistance. On February 3, Tilghman warned that the enemy was concentrating at Smithland, Kentucky, in preparation for another invasion. On the following day, four gunboats suddenly appeared in the river and opened fire on Fort Henry. Tilghman reported that the smoke of other

[7] Polk to Benjamin, January 6, 7, 1862, Polk to Johnston, January 12, 1862; Polk to Mackall, January 17, 1862, all in Polk, National Archives; Polk to Jefferson Davis, January 11, 30, 1862, in Leonidas Polk Papers, Duke; James Hall to his parents, January 16, 1862, in Hall Papers, UNC; J. F. Henry to his father, January 23, 1862, Henry Papers, UNC; *Official Record*, VII, 850-51, LII, Pt. 2, pp. 248, 257-59.

[8] This expedition, led by C. F. Smith, convinced U. S. Grant of the weakness of Fort Henry. See Bruce Catton, *Grant Moves South* (Boston, 1960), 122-24; Powhattan Ellis, Jr. to Harris, January 17, 1862, Harris to Tilghman, January 23, 1862, Tilghman to Harris, January 25, 26, 1862, all in Harris Papers, Tennessee Archives; James Sanders to Johnston, January 17, 1862, Tilghman to Mackall, January 22, 23, 25, 1862, all in Telegrams Received, 1862, National Archives; Taylor, "Defense of Fort Henry," 369-70; *Official Records*, VII, 847.

approaching boats was visible far down the Tennessee. Later that afternoon, five transports appeared downstream and landed troops on the east
side of the river within three miles of the fort. Tilghman drew in his troops
from the west bank of the Tennessee, where they had been desperately trying to dig entrenchments at the unfinished Fort Heiman. He warned Polk
that if he planned to aid the fort, he must do so at once. Polk informed
Tilghman that he had ordered some cavalry to the Tennessee. Tilghman
insisted that he must have infantry.[9]

Polk sent no help, and, after a courageous defense by Tilghman, Fort
Henry fell on February 6. The Kentuckian in charge of the fort's defenses did not have a chance to hold the position. The help in
building Fort Heiman which was promised by multiple sources never
came, and the fort remained unfinished. Tilghman's most outstanding
regiment, the 10th Tennessee, was put into battle line with Tower
of London muskets that were used by Andrew Jackson's militia in 1812.
Tilghman had warned Johnston and Polk that these were his only
weapons. Also, Captain Taylor's September warnings of the danger
resulting from the winter rains proved to be correct. On the day that
the Federals began to bombard the fort, the flagpole on the parade grounds
stood in two feet of river water. One third of the fortifications was inun-
dated, and the waters were lapping into the lower river batteries. Tilghman had also warned of the inadequate range of the fort's guns. In late
January, he reported to Johnston that he had only one gun at the fort
which was equal in range to that of the Federal guns which had fired on
the fort in the reconnaissance attack, a single ten-inch gun which had no
ammunition. Tilghman asked for ammunition and two additional ten-inch
guns.

The auxiliary firepower was never sent, and on February 6 the sixty-five
naval guns of the Union fleet easily disabled eight of Tilghman's twelve
guns. There was no possibility of sending his infantry to meet the Yankee
force which was moving down the east bank of the Tennessee to encircle
Fort Henry. Tilghman knew his 2,600 poorly armed troops were no match
for the 16,000 Federals reported to be moving on the fort. He sent all of his

[9] On January 29, Halleck ordered Grant to take Fort Henry. The latter attacked
Donelson independently, and Halleck eventually saw he must go along. Grant moved
on Henry with about fifteen thousand troops, finally leaving the fort on February 12
after a delay of several days. Meanwhile, Halleck had ordered Andrew Foote's fleet of
gunboats to steam up the Cumberland and attack Donelson. Foote brought with him
transports containing six regiments to reinforce Grant, whose total force at the surrender of Donelson numbered about twenty-seven thousand. See Lew Wallace, "The
Capture of Fort Donelson," *Battles and Leaders*, I, 401–29; Ambrose, *Halleck*, 23–40;
Grant, *Memoirs*, I, 298; Tilghman to Polk, February 4 (10:30 A.M., 1:30 P.M., 4:30 P.M.,
5:30 P.M.) , 5, 1862, all in Polk Papers, National Archives.

command to Fort Donelson while he remained with eighty men. Later in the day, the white flag was raised over Fort Henry, and Federal officers rowed straight through the sallyport into the fort. The Tennessee River was now open to the interior of Alabama.[10]

While Fort Henry was being attacked, Polk continued to hold back the badly needed reinforcements. On February 5 he finally ordered a meager force of two infantry regiments and four cavalry battalions to move towards the Tennessee River. That same day Polk announced to Johnston that he could furnish none besides these. He dallied in ordering the aid to Tilghman, and before the reinforcements left Columbus he learned that Fort Henry had been surrendered.[11]

Polk's failure to defend his own district was only an indication of a command breakdown at a higher level. Johnston was well aware of the weak condition of Fort Henry and of the situation at Fort Donelson. He had been sent a copy of almost every warning which Tilghman had delivered to Polk after the February advance began. Johnston realized that Tilghman's small force had inadequate weapons, that water was rising in the fort, and that mounted guns provided ineffective firepower. Johnston was also aware that there was insufficient ammunition for the one ten-inch gun at the fort, and that additional ten-inch guns were needed. When the nine transports began unloading to invest Fort Henry, he knew exactly when the move commenced and the comparative strength of Tilghman and the enemy. He also realized that Polk planned to send Tilghman little aid from Columbus.

Yet Johnston failed to aid Fort Henry. His habit of preoccupation with a single object had blinded him to his departmental responsibilities. His weakness in handling subordinates resulted in his not ordering Polk to reinforce Tilghman. His habit of completely trusting a subordinate caused him to expect confidently that Polk would defend his district, the inland forts, during the crisis on the Tennessee.[12]

[10] Tilghman to Mackall, January 17, 25, February 6, 1862, in Telegrams Received, 1862, National Archives; John Holcombe and Walter Buttgenbach, "Coast Defense in the Civil War, Fort Henry, Tenn.," *Journal United States Artillery*, XXXIX (1913), 83–90.

[11] Polk to Mackall, February 5, 1862, and Polk to Johnston, February 6, 7, 1862, in Telegrams Received, 1862, National Archives.

[12] Tilghman to Mackall, January 6, 17, 18, 19, 20, 21, 22, February 3, 4 (1 P.M., 1:15 P.M., 1:30 P.M., 4 P.M., 5 P.M.) , 5, (8 A.M.) , 1862, Polk to Johnston, February 6, 7, 1862, Whitthorne to Johnston, January 15, 1862, William Quarles to Hardee, January 16, 1862, Harris to Johnston, January 17, 1862, Powhattan Ellis, Jr. to Mackall, January 19, 1862, Clarksville operator to Johnston, January 22, 1862, Danville operator to Mackall, January 23, 1862, Heiman to Mackall, February 4, 1862, Polk to Mackall, February 5, 1862, James Chalmers to Mackall, February 5, 1862, all in Telegrams Received, 1862, National Archives.

Johnston's apparent disinterest in the Fort Henry situation marked the beginning of the collapse of his leadership. In January and February of 1862, he became further entrenched in conclusions which he had formulated in the autumn of 1861. He completely divided the expected Federal advance into rigid compartments. He considered Buell to be the enemy of Middle Tennessee, and Halleck's force to be the threat to Polk at Columbus. By February, Johnston believed that Buell would advance on Nashville in two columns via Bowling Green and South Carrollton, Kentucky. Johnston was convinced that Halleck would advance directly on Columbus. Another force would move up the Tennessee River against Fort Henry and would then turn west toward Columbus. When Grant moved on Fort Henry in early February, Johnston then expected him to turn west and strike Polk on the flank. There is no evidence that before Grant moved into the lines around Donelson, Johnston considered that he might go east instead of west to Columbus. Instead, Johnston waited at Bowling Green and watched for Buell to advance on Middle Tennessee.[13]

Johnston expected Buell to move against him from two bases—the main base in the Nolin–Munfordville area and the South Carrollton base on Green River. The Nolin force was encamped on the Louisville–Bowling Green pike, and threatened Bowling Green. The South Carrollton force had camped on the pike which led south through Greenville and Hopkinsville to the north bank of the Cumberland opposite Fort Donelson. Johnston had been observing the Nolin force since October. In January, the other force moved up the Green River to South Carrollton, and Johnston considered this a threat to the weak flank west of Bowling Green. He shifted three brigades commanded by Brigadier General John Floyd, who had recently arrived from western Virginia, to bolster the left flank at Russellville, Kentucky. Johnston did not order this move, as some historians would later argue, because he expected a combined move up the Tennessee and the Cumberland and wanted to put troops in position to reinforce Donelson. On the contrary, he expected the Donelson threat to come from the force at South Carrollton and prepared to oppose this

---

[13] See Gilmer to his wife, January 19, 23, 1862, in Gilmer Papers, UNC; Johnston to Benjamin, December 8, 21, 1861, January 22, 1862, in Headquarters Book, Tulane; *Official Records*, VII, 831, 834, 839, 859, LII, Pt. 2, p. 261; W. A. Quarles to Hardee, January 15, 1862, in Telegrams Received, 1862, National Archives. For other evidence of the believed split of the Federal advance, see Harris to Johnston, January 22, 1862, and Bushrod Johnson to Johnston, January 22, 1862, in Harris Papers, Tennessee Archives; Tilghman to Mackall, January 9, 18, 21, 1862, Polk to Mackall, January 22, 1862, James Starnes to Hardee, January 20, 1862, Charles Clark to Hardee, January 20, 1862, Donelson operator to Mackall, January 18, 1862, all in Telegrams Received, 1862, National Archives.

move with troops commanded by General Charles Clark at Hopkinsville, thirty-five miles northeast of the fort, and with Floyd's brigades at Russell-ville.[14]

But in early February, for two precious weeks, Johnston lost trace of Buell's army. Since November, he had had trouble in receiving news of Buell's movements. Geography, Union sentiment, illness, weather, over-eager reconnaissance commanders—all had masked his position. Buell was reported to be at multiple sites—Greensburg, Columbia, Campbellsville, Rochester—but always at Nolin. In late January, even the intelligence from the Nolin area was sparse. Hindman, commanding the main recon-naissance outpost at Bell's Station, said that it was becoming harder to observe Buell's movements. Numerous reports of a Federal advance came from widely divergent areas, from South Carrollton in western Kentucky to Burkesville in eastern Kentucky. A Federal column was said to be at Burkesville, and to be perhaps advancing into Tennessee in order to flank Johnston on the right. But Johnston could not determine if the reports were reliable. Other Federal troops were reported to be at Camp-bellsville and at Greensburg preparing to drive into Tennessee on the heels of Crittenden's force that had just fallen back from Mill Springs.[15]

The lack of dependable information on the Nolin and South Carroll-ton fronts became critical by early February. Reports in January had indicated that Buell was rebuilding the railroad bridge across the Green River at Munfordville, a few miles south of Nolin, and had already sent advance units across. In the last week of January, scouts said that the troops were pulling back to Louisville and that trains could be heard arriving and leaving Munfordville at short intervals. By February 1, however, intelligence reported that the Munfordville–Nolin force was not leaving, but rather that it was increasing. New encampments were ob-served, and the old camps were reported to have floored tents and chim-neys, as if they were to remain there for the winter.

The Federal activity at South Carrollton also puzzled Johnston. In late January, Bedford Forrest reported the enemy was repairing the Rochester locks in preparation for moving out of South Carrollton. Then, a rumor came which indicated that the force had already left the area in order to

14 Mackall to Hardee, January 20, 1862, John B. Floyd Papers, Duke; Hardee to Charles Clark, January 18, 1862, Clark to Hardee, January 19, 1862, Hindman to Ed Pickett, January 22, 1862, all in Telegrams Received, 1862, National Archives; *Official Records*, VII, 840–41.

15 "Memorandum of Reports of Spies and Scouts as to Federal Strength in Ken-tucky" (MS in Barret Collection, Tulane) ; Johnston to Cooper, January 13, 1862, in Headquarters Book, Tulane; Hindman to Pickett, January 20, 21, 1862, Harris to Johnston, January 20, 1862, James Bennett to Hardee, February 10, 1862, in Telegrams Received, 1862, National Archives.

move on Hopkinsville and Russellville. Scarcely had this been determined false when another report said that the troops were not moving south but were retreating toward the Ohio River. At the same time, another forward movement from Munfordville was reported to be under way. Confused, Johnston called for more reconnaissance in order to determine Buell's exact location. It was clear that he had lost his opponent.[16]

Not only had Johnston lost sight of Buell, he had also lost track of the Union force which moved on Fort Henry. Between February 5 and February 7, a communications "blackout" occurred. On the fifth, telegrams informed Johnston that heavy firing was being heard from Fort Henry and that transports were on the Tennessee River. On the same day, the Clarksville operator excitedly reported that heavy firing was also being heard from Fort Donelson and that the Clarksville-Donelson telegraph was out of order. Other reports said the Federals were pouring from transports into the land between Henry and Donelson. The Cumberland City operator repeatedly cut into the wire to report more heavy firing at Donelson. The Danville operator, after a hasty conversation with boatmen from downriver, said that a white flag was flying over Fort Henry. Finally, on the night of the sixth and the morning of the seventh, messages were received from Fort Donelson which severely jolted Johnston. The force which had overwhelmed Fort Henry was not turning toward Polk. Instead, it had turned to Donelson, where an attack was expected as early as the eighth.[17]

Johnston had not expected this move. Reports still indicated that Buell was on the Green River line, and Johnston could not comprehend that another force was attacking on the Cumberland River. Already confused as to Buell's location, he was staggered by the realization that he had miscalculated the Federal advance. There was still more confusion, for Johnston could not even find his own army. After the first shock of the report that Donelson was expecting an attack, he had blindly thrown troops into the area around Clarksville, thinking that the real advance would be there. Pillow, who had resigned at Columbus and then had rejoined the army at Bowling Green, was sent to Clarks-

16 Charles Clark to Hardee, January 22, 1862, and Hardee to Floyd, February 5, 1862, in Floyd Papers, Duke; Hindman to Pickett, January 5, 19, 21, 28, 30, 31, and February 7, 1862, Clark to Hardee, January 23, and February 2, 1862, Floyd to Hardee, February 2, 1862, Buckner to Johnston, February 3, 1862, "Army Spies" to Hardee, January 20, 1862, all in Telegrams Received, 1862, National Archives; *Official Records,* LII, Pt. 2, pp. 246–47.

17 Ellis to Mackall, February 5, 1862, W. A. Quarles to Mackall, February 5, 1862, Quarles to Hardee, February 5, 1862, Cumberland City operator to Mackall, February 5, 6, 1862, Danville operator to Mackall, February 6, 1862 (5:40 P.M.), J. S. Bailey to Johnston, February 6, 1862, all in Telegrams Received, 1862, National Archives.

ville to gather all available forces. Floyd, with his own and Buckner's troops, was ordered south to join Pillow. In his state of anxiety,
Johnston could not locate these forces which he had hastily sent to the
Cumberland area. He did not know where Floyd and Buckner were or
what their strength was. Johnston also did not know how many troops
were already at Clarksville and at Donelson, or Pillow's plans, strength,
and needs.[18]

Totally confused, he reached two curious decisions that were to have a
far-reaching influence on the fate of Fort Donelson. He was still unwilling
to believe the infantry force at Henry was moving to attack. He became
convinced that the main threat to the fort was the Federal fleet reported
to be steaming up the Cumberland, and for him defense became a question of whether the fort could hold out against the gunboats. At first, he
did not think that the fleet could be stopped and issued orders for Hardee
to fall back to Nashville. Johnston's strange belief that Donelson would
be safe if the gunboats could be stopped perhaps explains why he ordered
troops there even after he stated on February 7 that the fort was not
long tenable. To him, "untenable" meant not being able to withstand
gunboats. There is no evidence that during this critical period he ever
realized that the real danger to Donelson might be from the land side.
Hence, on February 7 he ordered Pillow to take his troops to the fort,
hold it as long as possible, and then retreat to Nashville, as if the Yankee
land force did not exist. Blinded to a fact that he did not want to accept,
Johnston saw only one side of the danger at Donelson—the river.[19]

Johnston also abdicated command responsibility for Donelson. Confused by Buell's movements, startled by the sudden advance on the fort,
and unable to locate his own troops, he tried to relieve himself of defending the Cumberland. On February 8, he gave up the command in
the area to John Floyd. Johnston told Floyd to make his own plans for
defense, and added, "I cannot give you specific instructions and place
under your command the entire force." [20] He then turned to busy himself
with preparations for evacuating Bowling Green. When he shunned the
Donelson responsibility, he gave indication that he was losing command
of himself and of the Army.

The Federal troops advancing on Donelson did not get into position

[18] Hardee to Floyd, February 5, 12, 1862, and Johnston to Floyd, February 12, 1862,
in Floyd Papers, Duke.
[19] Johnston to Floyd, February 11, 14, 1862, Mackall to Floyd, February 8, 1862,
Mackall to Gilmer, February 8, 1862, all in Floyd Papers, Duke; Pillow to Mackall,
February 7, 1862, and Tilghman to Mackall, February 7, 1862, in Telegrams Received,
1862, National Archives; Johnston to Benjamin, February 8, 1862, in Headquarters
Book, Tulane.
[20] Johnston to Floyd, February 8, 1862, in Floyd Papers, Duke.

before the fort until the morning of February 13, seven days after Fort Henry was surrendered. During this crucial time, a failure of command also occurred at the Clarksville post. When Johnston gave up the command, the problem of determining where to defend against the Federals fell to Pillow and Floyd. Johnston could not have made a worse choice in commanders. These two men, one of whom had retired from the army to sulk and then had returned with the hope of retrieving glory, and the other a new, untried general in the Second Department, were given responsibility for the fate of Middle Tennessee. The command confusion and delay in their preparations spoiled an excellent chance of striking the Federals while they were toiling on the muddy, narrow road between Henry and Donelson. This country was well suited for an ambush, because it was dotted with flooded creeks, ravines, and underbrush. Pillow, who was at Clarksville before Floyd arrived there, twice advocated concentrating Floyd's and Buckner's troops and striking the Yankees on the flank as they marched between the forts. Forrest, who came back to Tennessee with Floyd and Buckner, had operated in the area before being sent to Kentucky and knew the terrain well. The time seemed ripe for an ambush.[21]

Such a move never was attempted. It was prevented by a morass of confusion and personal ambition that entered the vacuum created by Johnston's passing of the command to Floyd. When Pillow wanted to make the move, he did not have enough troops, nor the cooperation needed. Charles Clark's brigade, ordered to Clarksville from Hopkinsville, was delayed by poor road conditions and Clark's own slowness. When Clark did reach the town, a quarrel began over whether Pillow outranked him. Clark declined to turn over the brigade to Pillow. Valuable time was lost before Johnston finally intervened to order Pillow to take command.[22]

When Pillow did have the necessary troops available, another confusion in command provided a further delay. Floyd was slow to realize the meaning of Johnston's assigning him on February 8 to command the Cumberland area. Not until February 11, when Johnston repeated and clarified the order, did Floyd take command at Clarksville. In that crucial three-day interval, an event occurred which changed Pillow's opinion about the proposed offensive. Although he knew nothing of the situation at Donelson, on the ninth Johnston ordered Pillow to

[21] Pillow to Mackall, February 6, 1862, and Pillow to W. D. Pickett, in Telegrams Received, 1862, National Archives; *Official Records,* VII, 758.

[22] Pillow to Mackall, February 6, 7, (5:30 P.M., 6 P.M.), 1862, Pillow to Johnston, February 7, 1862, Clark to Hardee, February 5, 1862, all in Telegrams Received, 1862, National Archives.

take Buckner's and Clark's troops, both at Clarksville, and proceed
to the fort. Pillow knew that the troops at Clarksville were deficient in
weapons, and that only one seventh of the friction primers in his troops'
possession were considered effective. He also was aware that Donelson
was low on ammunition, and that, since the fort had no storehouse, there
was not one day's rations there. All supplies were kept at the little town
of Dover near the fort. Also, with Floyd's troops coming up, Pillow
realized that the combined force would be strong enough to make the
flank attack that he had suggested.[23]

Though he knew Donelson was a weak position and despite the
fact that he had earlier pressed for a flank offensive, Pillow did not
protest Johnston's order. The move would provide another opportunity
for him to hold an independent command. To remain at Clarksville
would only mean serving under Floyd. His excellent plan for a flank
attack was forgotten. Instead, Pillow left immediately for Donelson,
after issuing his battle cry: "Liberty or Death."

But when Pillow surveyed the works, he realized the full extent of
the fort's weakness. Donelson had not been designed for land defense.
The fort was on a rise of high ground about 1,400 yards northwest of
Dover. North of the fort, Hickman's Creek, filled with backwater, formed
an impassable barrier. South of the fort, swollen Indian Creek intersected
the Confederate line and isolated the left flank. South of Indian Creek
and just above Dover, a third stream filled with backwater, Lick Creek,
flowed into the Cumberland. To supplement the weak defenses on the
land side, Gilmer in January had begun work on a line of rifle pits extending from Hickman's Creek along a series of ridges west of the fort,
and curving back to the river above Dover, a total distance of three miles.
Less than a third of these rifle pits had been constructed when Pillow
arrived. Even if they had been finished, they would not have strengthened
the fort. A garrison might hold the bastioned parapet which comprised
the primary work, but an army would be required to man the entire line
of rifle pits. Pillow saw these weaknesses, and confided to Floyd that the
works were not only incomplete but were badly planned.[24]

In contrast to his private views, most of the reports which Pillow

23 J. W. Head to Pillow, February 7, 1862, Pillow to Mackall, February 7, 1862, Pil-
low to Hardee, February 6, 1862, Pillow to Johnston, February 8, 1862, all in Telegrams
Received, 1862, National Archives; Mackall to Floyd, January 27, 1862, in Headquarters
Book, Tulane. See also H. L. Bedford, "Fight Between the Batteries and Gunboats at
Fort Donelson," *Southern Historical Society Papers*, XIII (1885), 165–73.

24 Pillow to Floyd, February 8, 1862, in Floyd Correspondence, National Archives;
"Missouri *Democrat* Narrative," in *Rebellion Record*, ed. Frank Moore (New York,
1861–68), IV, 176–77; *Official Records*, VII, 867–68.

sent were full of exaggerated assurances that Donelson could be held. He told Floyd that he felt confident of protecting the fort from an infantry assault, and that he could resist the gunboats. Johnston was informed that, if a little time were available, the batteries would be made bombproof. On February 12, Pillow sent a grossly misleading dispatch to Johnston, boasting that the fort could be held with the men Pillow already had. Pillow also informed Johnston that there was not any danger of the enemy's outflanking Donelson, since such a move would make the Union flank vulnerable to attack.[25]

These misleading statements about Donelson's strength were the product of command squabble and Pillow's ambition. When Floyd arrived at Clarksville, Pillow found that his independent command status at Donelson was threatened. Floyd had agreed with Pillow that the entire Confederate force in the area should be concentrated at Donelson, but then changed his mind. He decided that the weak condition of the fort and the nature of the terrain south of it made Donelson a trap. The line of communications from Donelson to Nashville was via the Wynn's Ferry Road. This road was intersected by the high backwaters of Indian and Lick creeks, already swollen by the February rains. Instead, Floyd revived Pillow's old idea—keep a token force to hold the fort, concentrate the main army at Cumberland City, and strike the Federal column on the flank as it moved to Donelson.

For an instant, the prospects of success on the Cumberland seemed bright. Then the command structure broke down, and the opportunity for the flank offensive slipped from Floyd's grasp. Pillow no longer had any enthusiasm for his own idea. He had only suggested the move when, as commander at Clarksville, he would have headed the expedition. He had no interest in a Floyd-led attack. Floyd intended for Pillow to hold Donelson while Buckner's troops joined his at Cumberland City. Not only would this rob Pillow of a chance for glory, but it would take from him a part of his Donelson command. Unable to sacrifice his personal ambition for the army's good, Pillow refused to send Buckner's men to Floyd. The result was a bitter quarrel that raged during the crucial days when the Federals were approaching Donelson. Floyd, a weak individual given to indecision and lack of force in dealing with a subordinate, made no attempt to coerce Pillow to obey the order. Pillow took advantage of Floyd's weakness. While Floyd pondered what to do, he bombarded Johnston with another batch of optimistic dispatches. To convince Johnston

25 Pillow to Floyd, February 12, 1862, in Floyd Papers, Duke; Pillow to Johnston, February 12, 1862, in Telegrams Received, 1862, National Archives.

that Buckner's troops should be retained, Pillow assured him that Fort Donelson would be safe against a land attack *provided* Buckner's men remained with Pillow.

While Floyd hesitated, Pillow won the argument. Johnston knew nothing of conditions in the Donelson area, but was impressed by Pillow's boasts of his ability to hold the fort. He ruled in favor of Pillow, and not only revoked Buckner's transfer but also sent Floyd's troops into Donelson. Again, Floyd demonstrated his indecision. Several hours before Johnston's order arrived, he had already put his troops in motion toward Donelson. Pillow had persuaded him to concentrate there against Floyd's better judgment. As his troops marched into Donelson in the early morning hours of February 13, Floyd's heart was not in the move, for he had no confidence in the works at the fort. Only a few days earlier at Russellville, both Floyd and Buckner had agreed that Donelson was a trap.[26]

Three days after Floyd arrived, the fort was surrendered to Grant. A command breakdown at Donelson between February 13 and February 16 proved to be the final blow. The leadership structure collapsed because in physical resources, morale, and leadership, the fort was completely unprepared to withstand an attack. The river batteries were not finished. The series of ridges a few thousand yards west of the fort presented Floyd with a dilemma. If the enemy seized them and planted artillery there, the Confederates in the river batteries and at the principal salient of the fort would be cut to pieces. The alternative was to complete the rifle pits already begun along the ridges to prevent the Federals from seizing the position. Only a third of the pits had been dug when Floyd arrived, and to hold even that mile of entrenchments would spread the Donelson garrison too thin.

Conditions inside the fort were no better. Ammunition and food were short. Blankets and tents were almost nonexistent. This shortage of cover was not noticed by the men until the morning Floyd arrived. Prior to February 13, Donelson had enjoyed unseasonably warm weather, but on that day, conditions changed drastically. By mid-afternoon, a warm drizzle had become a cold, sleeting rain. That night an icy gale brought two inches of snow and the temperature plunged to ten degrees. The rifle pits, already filled with rain, became pools of ice.

26 Stickles, *Buckner*, 131–32; Pillow to Floyd, February 9, 10, 12, 1862, and Mackall to Floyd, February 6, 1862, in Floyd Papers, Duke; Floyd to Johnston, February 8, 1862, Pillow to Johnston, February 9, 1862, Gilmer to Mackall, February 10, 1862, Pillow to Mackall, February 10, 1862, S. T. Peters to Moses Wright, February 13, 1862, all in Telegrams Received, 1862, National Archives; Pillow to Harris, February 12, 1862, in Harris Papers, Tennessee Archives; Johnston to Floyd, February 12, 1862, in Floyd Papers, Duke; Floyd to Johnston, February 13, 1862, and Floyd to Buckner, August 15, 1862, in Floyd Correspondence, National Archives.

Further digging of entrenchments in the frozen ground was impossible. There were few shelters on the three-mile line, and the wet half-frozen men huddled together during the miserable night.[27]

The suffering provided the finishing touch to an atmosphere of defeatism which permeated the entire fort on the eve of the struggle for Donelson. Morale had been low for several days, and troops and commanders were mentally unprepared to resist an assault. Floyd had no confidence in the position. Despite his telegrams to Johnston, Pillow admitted to Floyd privately that the fort was in a weak condition. The infantry which straggled in from Fort Henry was in deplorable shape, having lost camp equipment, provisions, and many weapons. The Donelson camp was filled with lurid tales of the invincibility of the Yankee force which battered Fort Henry into submission. Ugly rumors swept through the trenches that Fort Henry had been surrendered needlessly, and some wondered if Donelson might not suffer a similar fate. Tilghman was reported to have hauled down the flag when the enemy vessels were a quarter of a mile away. Tempers flared as supporters of the Kentuckian branded the rumors as lies. The argument spread into a bitter dispute between Kentucky troops who backed Tilghman and the Tennessee regiments. The quarrel had been brewing for some time, for feeling between the regiments from the two states ran high.[28]

Yet a peculiar air of serenity was present among the high command on February 13 that indicated a serious weakness of leadership. The problem was that Floyd simply did not know what Johnston expected him to do at Donelson. Floyd, a newcomer, sensed his own lack of familiarity with conditions in the Army, and his weakness of decision made him even more cautious. Also, Johnston's orders contained no instructions whatsoever. As a result, Floyd did nothing and, consequently, lost one of the greatest opportunities of the campaign. On February 13, the Confederate force at Donelson numbered about fifteen thousand. Pillow told Floyd that morning that the Federals approaching Donelson had between ten thousand and twelve thousand. Except for a brief and unsuccessful

[27] Pillow to Floyd, February 8, 1862, in Floyd Papers, Duke; Pillow to Harris, February 11, 1862, in Harris Papers, Tennessee Archives; Clark, "History of Company A," Duke; *Official Records*, VII, 278, LII, Pt. 2, p. 268. One participant observed, "It was raining, snowing, and freezing, accompanied by a sharp wind. We had no tents. . . . I understood that a number of soldiers froze to death in the breastworks." John Guy, "Movements of the Goochland Light Artillery," in *Donelson Campaign Sources* (Fort Leavenworth, Kan., 1912) , 142.

[28] Powhattan Ellis, Jr. to his mother, February 11, 1862, in Munford–Ellis Papers, G. W. Munford Division, Duke; Head to Pillow, February 7, 1862, and Pillow to Mackall, February 7, 1862, in Telegrams Received, 1862, National Archives; *Official Records*, LII, Pt. 2, p. 268.

foray against two Confederate batteries, the Federal land force remained inactive. If Floyd thought the fort was a trap, the situation gave him the opportunity to get his troops out. If he planned to stand and fight, the Federal inactivity and the numerical superiority of the Confederates provided a chance of success. Unable to make a decision, Floyd did nothing, and the Confederate infantry remained idle on this crucial day.[29]

Floyd's inactivity indicated something even more serious than the loss of opportunity. Like Johnston, Floyd and Pillow had become blind to the danger posed by the Federal land force. On the thirteenth, despite information that the Federals were moving into a semicircular position around Donelson that threatened to break contact with Nashville, Floyd made no effort to keep the communication lines open south of the fort. In fact, both Floyd and Pillow almost completely ignored land operations. Like Johnston, they were convinced that the threat to Donelson lay in the gunboats on the Cumberland. This fascination with the gunboat threat filled the vacuum created by the lack of instructions from Johnston.

This peculiar blindness to land operations was intensified by the success of Donelson's water batteries on February 13. Rumors of the invincibility of the gunboats proved a sham. During the afternoon, a duel ensued between the Confederate batteries and the gunboat Carondelet. For two hours the batteries and the vessel's guns hammered away at each other. After a 128-pound solid shot tore into the gunboat's port casement and burst the steam lines, the battle was all but over. Sporadic firing continued until dusk, but it was evident that the land batteries had gotten the better of the fight. Pillow and Floyd were jubilant, and both repeatedly telegraphed Johnston their assurances that Donelson could be held.[30] Floyd boasted, "We have maintained ourselves fully by land and water." [31]

29 Peter F. Walker, "Command Failure: The Fall of Forts Henry and Donelson," Tennessee Historical Quarterly, XVI (December, 1957), 347–48; Pillow to Harris, February 12, 1862, in Harris Papers, Tennessee Archives.

30 Henry Walke, "The Western Flotilla at Fort Donelson, Island Number Ten, Fort Pillow and Memphis," Battles and Leaders, I, 434; Floyd to Johnston, February 13 (9 A.M.), 1862, in Floyd Correspondence, National Archives; Pillow to Johnston, February 13 (9:50 A.M., 11:38 A.M.), 1862, Telegrams Received, 1862, National Archives; Pillow to Harris, February 13 (11:30 A.M., 2:45 P.M.), 1862, in Harris Papers, Tennessee Archives. Grant's army formed in battle line on February 13. C. F. Smith's division held the left, or north flank; Lew Wallace's division was in the center; and John A. McClernand's division was on the right. Grant did not attack on the thirteenth or fourteenth for he planned to use the same strategy with which he took Henry. Foote, commanding the gunboats, would batter the fort into submission while Grant blocked the escape routes on the land. The latter ordered his division commanders not to initiate action that would bring on a general engagement. Grant, Memoirs, I, 300–304.

31 Floyd to Johnston, February 13, 1862, in Floyd Correspondence, National Archives.

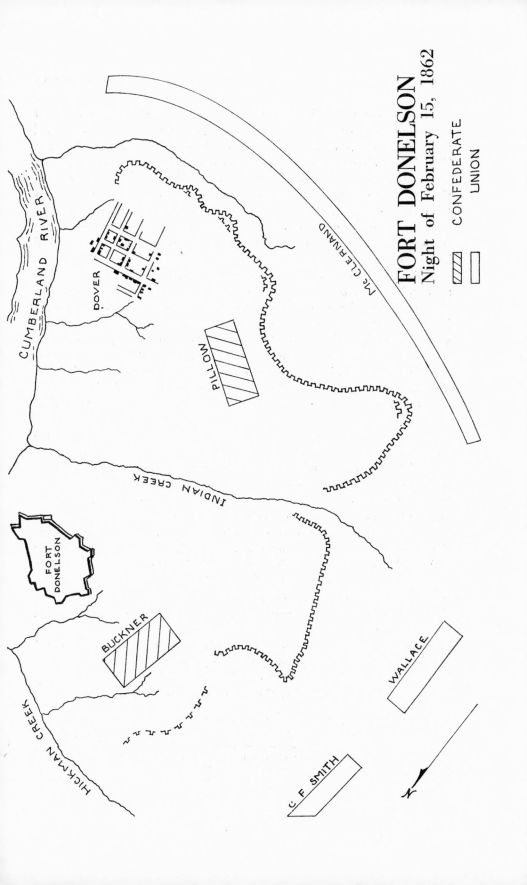

FORT DONELSON
Night of February 15, 1862

CONFEDERATE
UNION

CUMBERLAND RIVER

DOVER

PILLOW

Mc CLERNAND

INDIAN CREEK

FORT DONELSON

BUCKNER

HICKMAN CREEK

WALLACE

C. F. SMITH

N

On the morning of the fourteenth, command weakness again wasted opportunity. Floyd had the chance to fight while the odds were still fairly even, to open his communication line, or to abandon the fort. The Federals had gotten across the Wynn's Ferry Road, Floyd's line of communications to the south. If he were going to attack or retreat, the fourteenth appeared to be his last chance to do so with any certainty of success. Intelligence reported that fifteen Yankee transports carrying twenty thousand reinforcements were in the Cumberland. If the transports were unloaded, Floyd estimated the total Union force would be forty thousand.

Again Floyd did nothing. In the absence of instructions from Johnston and because of his interest in a new gunboat attack, the infantry remained idle. The least he could have done was to reopen the Wynn's Ferry Road. On the morning of the fourteenth, a halfhearted attempt was made to open that route, but when Pillow curiously protested that it was too late in the day for the move to succeed, Floyd gave in and cancelled the operation. The morning wore into afternoon, and Floyd himself observed Union reinforcements arriving on the field. Then he turned his attention back to the river, after he had wasted another opportunity.[32]

During the afternoon, a tremendous assault of five of the Federal gunboats on the river batteries kept Floyd's attention away from the Federal buildup on land. This assault was so fierce and its outcome so surprisingly favorable that Floyd remained convinced the fort would be safe if it could withstand a river attack. A determined Yankee fleet bombarded the river batteries with a deafening barrage. The firepower was so awesome that even Forrest, who never wavered in the face of the enemy, became excited and told an aide the fort could not possibly withstand the onslaught. Floyd telegraphed Johnston that the fort could not hold twenty minutes. But the fort did hold, and the plucky river batteries put four of the gunboats out of commission. Floyd was elated. With renewed confidence, he again sent Johnston assurance that the fort would stand.[33]

During the late afternoon and evening of the fourteenth, Floyd drastically altered his opinion of the situation. For the first time since he arrived there, he seemed to realize that the threat to Donelson was on the land side. During the afternoon, reports indicated that the

---

[32] Floyd to Johnston, February 13, 14, 1862, in *ibid.*

[33] John A. Wyeth, *That Devil Forrest: Life of General Nathan Bedford Forrest* (2nd ed.; New York, 1959), 40; Bedford, "Fight Between the Batteries and Gunboats at Fort Donelson," 171. See also Floyd to Johnston, February 14 (5:15 P.M., 8:15 P.M.), 1862, in Telegrams Received, 1862, National Archives.

Union buildup was increasing. Some reports even said the Federals were assembling fifty thousand men. Scouts on the Confederate left flank near Lick Creek told Floyd that the hold on Wynn's Ferry Road had been tightened by the arrival of reinforcements. After two days of doing nothing, Floyd suddenly decided that the fort was a trap which must be evacuated. A telegram from Johnston provided some impetus for this decision. Johnston's dispatch, which indicated how little he knew of the situation at Donelson, ordered Floyd to march to Nashville if he could not hold the fort. Thus, on the evening of February 14, Floyd called a council of war and made his first positive decision since arriving at Donelson. The Confederates would strike the Union right flank early on the morning of the fifteenth and open the Wynn's Ferry Road. When the road was open, Floyd's army would escape to Nashville.[34]

On the morning of the fifteenth, for the third consecutive day, Floyd exhibited his weakness as a commander. Briefly, the jaws of the Federal trap around Donelson were forced open. As the mists of dawn sifted over the icy backwaters of Indian Creek, the men of Bushrod Johnson's brigade rose up out of the gullies and creek bottoms and fell upon the Union right wing at the Wynn's Ferry Road crossing. With Forrest screening the far left of Pillow's line and the capable Johnson striking the crucial point, the Federal right began to buckle. After three hours of stiff fighting, a general attack along the Confederate left was launched by Pillow. Forrest's troopers crashed into the wavering Yankee line on the flank and rear and the Union flank crumbled. One hour later, the Federal right wing rested at right angles to the left and center, and the Confederates scrambled into the abandoned positions. A lone Yankee battery remained to command the Wynn's Ferry Road. About noon, Forrest again smashed into the Yankee position and the artillerists were sabered at their guns. The Yankee right wing was streaming back to the rear, and the road to Nashville was open.[35]

At this critical moment, the Confederate command wavered. Commanding on the left, Pillow ordered Buckner, who was attacking the Federal

[34] Floyd to Johnston, February 13, 1862, in Telegrams Received, 1862, National Archives; Stickles, *Buckner*, 140–41; *Official Records*, VII, 268, 387.

[35] Bushrod Johnson's attack mauled McClernand's division on Grant's right. Early that morning, Grant had gone to visit Captain Foote on his flagship, leaving specific instructions to each division commander not to move from his position without Grant's explicit consent. Lew Wallace sent to Grant's headquarters for permission to help McClernand but there was no one to give it. Only after Johnson had driven McClernand back two miles to Wallace's division could the Federals send reinforcements. Wallace later said that Floyd could have "put his men fairly en route for Charlotte before the Federal commander could have interposed an obstruction to the movement." Wallace, "The Capture of Fort Donelson," 419. See also Harris to Polk February 15, 1862, in Polk Papers, National Archives.

center, to break off the fight and return to his trenches on the right.
Surprised, Buckner refused—and argued that Floyd was in command of
the operations. He then rode off to urge Floyd to continue the retreat.
Floyd told Buckner to wait until he consulted Pillow. When Floyd found
Pillow, the latter persuaded him that Federal reinforcements were arriving on the field and that neither Pillow's nor Buckner's men were able
to continue the operation. Again Floyd's inability to decide lost the Confederates an excellent opportunity. Without checking with Buckner on
the conditions in his division, Floyd ordered him back into the trenches
on the right flank. Reluctantly, Buckner ordered a return to the entrenchments, but before he could get back to his old position the Federal left
wing counterattacked and seized the vacant rifle pits on the ridge. Soon,
Yankee batteries were in full command of the right flank of the Donelson
line.[36]

Floyd had made two errors in command. One was listening to Pillow.
After the retreat had started, it was almost a necessity that it be carried
to completion. This was demonstrated by the fate of the right flank
which crumbled in Buckner's absence. Pillow later explained that, after
a temporary repulse by the Yankee battery commanding Wynn's Ferry
Road, Buckner's troops were too demoralized to continue the fight. Actually, because of the icy ground and the slowness of the lead regimental
commander, Buckner's line had scarcely advanced when the ferry road
was opened and only two of his regiments had seen action. Even in Pillow's division, Bushrod Johnson, who commanded the main striking
force, did not report heavy casualties in the morning operation. Although
bold in words, Pillow lacked the determination needed to command the
lead escape column. When the road was first opened, he seemed to believe
the action was over. Elated at the victory his troops had won, he sent a
flowery telegram to Johnston boasting, "On the honor of a soldier, the day
is ours." [37] After sending this report, Pillow did nothing.

The failure of Floyd to make clear the details of the escape also
explains Pillow's stopping the move. Floyd and Buckner later claimed
that the purpose of the move was to open the line of communications
to Nashville as well as to retreat when that line was open. Pillow in-

36 Stickles, Buckner, 143–44; Henry, Forrest, 55–56. Despite the failure of the plan,
encouraging news, which was misleading, was sent to Johnston of the day's action. Floyd
telegraphed "we maintained a successful struggle which continued for nine hours and
resulted in driving him from the field. . . ." Floyd to Johnston, February 15, 1862, in
Floyd Correspondence, National Archives. Pillow boasted that they "carried the whole
field inch by inch and driving the enemy from every position." Pillow to Johnston,
February 15, 1862, in Telegrams Received, 1862, National Archives.

37 Walker, "Command Failure," 352. See also Pillow to George Randolph, November
8, 1862, in Pillow Papers, National Archives; Official Records, VII, 290, 362.

sisted that the only purpose agreed upon was to open the line, and that retreat was not discussed. Heiman, who was also present at the meeting, stated that the objective was only to open the line. Major Jeremy Gilmer later said the plan was to secure a line of retreat and then either to retreat or continue the fight. Forrest reported that nothing was said about a retreat, no order was given to that effect, and no preparations were made among the troops. Some regimental commanders, including Colonels John C. Brown and William Palmer, took an opposite viewpoint. They reported that their troops had been ordered to carry three days' rations as well as blankets with them.

It appears that Floyd planned to retreat, for on the fifteenth he sent to Clarksville and Nashville every available boat filled with the sick and wounded. Yet he failed to provide any system for evacuating the fort, such as the withdrawal of artillery, and did not make it clear to his subordinates that he intended to retreat. Once the Wynn's Ferry Road was open, a lack of understanding as to what Floyd intended doomed the expedition to failure.[38]

The command breakdown became complete during the night of the fifteenth and the early morning hours of the next day. Floyd, Buckner, and Pillow gathered at Floyd's headquarters at Dover Inn to discuss future plans. The lack of orders from Johnston, the exaggerated reports of the enemy's reinforcements, the two days' concentration on the gunboats without keeping open a communication route, the lack of a positive plan devised by Floyd—all began to take effect. Thirteen transports were reported to have arrived, and the high command was now convinced that the Yankee force at Donelson numbered more than fifty thousand. Tension mounted as Pillow and Buckner lashed out at each other for the morning's failure. All three agreed that the move which had failed should be attempted immediately. Floyd's scouts, however, reported that the Wynn's Ferry Road had been recaptured that evening by the Federals, and that campfires of the enemy could be seen flickering along the roadside. The only escape route was a river road to Cumberland City, but the scouts reported that at the Lick Creek crossing it was under three feet of water and was impassable to infantry.[39]

[38] *Official Records*, VII, 266, 302, 338–39, 347, 352. Pillow maintained later that "Gen. Buckner is in error in stating that any purpose was ever determined upon in council, or indeed elsewhere previously to the battle, to retreat from the battlefield. . . ." Pillow to Randolph, November 8, 1862, in Pillow Papers, National Archives.

[39] The rumor at Donelson on the fifteenth was that Grant had fifty thousand troops. W. H. Allen to Harris, February 15, 1862, in Telegrams Received, 1862, National Archives. Floyd had received information as early as the night of the thirteenth that fifty thousand troops were concentrating. Floyd to Johnston, February 13, 1862, in Floyd Correspondence, National Archives.

For the fourth consecutive day, Floyd failed to stand by his decision. When it was learned that the Wynn's Ferry Road was apparently re- taken, Buckner mentally went to pieces and advocated immediate sur- render. He argued that his troops were worn by four days without sleep and a day of hard fighting. Actually, Buckner was the one who must have been exhausted, for when the surrender did come his line officers and troops were shocked. Buckner's defeatism was shared by his two col- leagues. All three were worn by the pressures of the past three days, and were puzzled as to what Johnston expected of them.

Soon Forrest was summoned for his views. The cavalryman was startled to learn that surrender was being discussed, and protested that it was still possible to escape by the Wynn's Ferry Road. To prove it, Forrest sent two of his own scouts to reconnoiter. They reported that they saw no enemy, only fires burning by the side of the road. Forrest argued that these were the old fires that had been whipped into flames by the strong night winds.[40]

Forrest's protests were to no avail, for the three commanders seemed completely demoralized. Buckner continued to hammer away at the need to surrender. He argued that even if Forrest were correct, his troops had little ammunition and were physically exhausted. Floyd agreed, and Pillow, who put up a feeble argument for the retreat, agreed to surrender.[41]

In the early morning hours of February 16, the Cumberland defenses fell and the way was open for the Federals to move on Nashville. The surrender had more repercussions than merely the collapse of John- ston's center line. The manner in which the fort capitulated left a bit- ter memory among the troops that four years of valor would not erase. Although he was in command and he agreed to the surrender, Floyd did not remain with the troops. He feared that he would be tried for treason because of the alleged removal of Federal arms to Southern arsenals while he was James Buchanan's secretary of war. Instead, he commandeered the only available steamboat and ordered a Mississippi regiment to guard it while his own two Virginia regiments boarded. Dutifully the Mississippians obeyed, expecting then to be put on board

[40] Major Nat Cheairs of the 3rd Tennessee wrote bitterly from Fort Warren prison in Boston Harbor that the surrender was ordered "to the utter astonishment of many of the soldiers and officers." Statement of Major Nat Cheairs (MS in John C. Brown Autograph Book, Confederate Collection, Tennessee Archives). Forrest later reported that two thirds of the army could have marched out without loss. He also stated that the road was open as late as 8 A.M. on the sixteenth; see *Official Records*, VII, 386. Gilmer wrote his wife that it was possible to save a remnant of the army, February 22, 1862, in Gilmer Papers, UNC.

[41] Stickles, *Buckner*, 156–57; *Official Records*, VII, 386.

themselves. To their chagrin, the Mississippi troops found themselves standing on the dock when the steamboat puffed upriver.

Pillow's conduct was no better. Although second in command, he refused to surrender on the dubious grounds that there was no general in the Confederacy other than Floyd whom the Federals would rather have as a prisoner than himself. Actually, Pillow was worth more to the Federals when he was commanding Confederate troops than he would be as a prisoner of war. The bluster that he had demonstrated in the council of war by calling for the troops to cut their way out soon disappeared. Pillow handed the command of the fort to Buckner and, together with Gilmer, unceremoniously escaped in a rowboat. Buckner sent a note to Grant, and the fall of Fort Donelson was complete. The only consolation was the conduct of the gaunt, bearded Forrest, who stormed out of Floyd's headquarters and refused to surrender. Forrest gathered his troopers and, with many infantry riding double, led them through the freezing backwaters to safety in Nashville.[42]

---

42 Floyd to Johnston, February 16, 1862, and Buckner to Johnston, February 16 (4:10 A.M.), 1862, in Telegrams Received, 1862, National Archives; Floyd to Johnston, February 16, 1862, in Floyd Correspondence, National Archives; Buckner to Major Cosby, February 16, 1862, Buckner to Grant, February 16, 1862, Grant to Buckner, February 16, 1862, all in Simon B. Buckner Letters, Pennsylvania Historical Society, Philadelphia. The background of Floyd's fear of Federal reprisal is found in Floyd to James Buchanan, July 31 and October 26, 1857, and August 5, 1858; Floyd to S. A. Peugh, June 15, 1858, all in John B. Floyd Letters, Pennsylvania Historical Society. See also James Chalmers, "Forrest and His Campaigns," *Southern Historical Society Papers*, VII (1879), 457. General Bushrod Johnson, as late as February 18, escaped through the Federal lines by merely strolling out. See *Official Records*, VII, 364–65.

seven

The Death of an Image

WHEN JOHNSTON'S BOWLING GREEN GARRISON TRUDGED SOUTH WITH SNOW swirling around the Nashville pike, the move indicated more than just a retreat across the Cumberland River. Three months before his death in the Shiloh ravine, Johnston was steadily losing control of the Army of Tennessee, as evidenced by the factors which motivated the retreat: confusion concerning the situation at Fort Donelson and the rising influence of General P. G. T. Beauregard.

Johnston's attitude concerning Donelson operations ran from complete despair to dangerous optimism. When he ordered the retreat from Bowling Green, he did so partly because he did not think the fort could hold against the Union gunboats. In fact, prior to the early morning hours of February 16, he ignored the Federal infantry force, not comprehending that Floyd's garrison might be trapped at the fort by this land column. Several days earlier Johnston had described Donelson as not being tenable for long. That he was referring only to gunboats was evident when he informed Judah Benjamin that he thought only the gunboats, and not the Federal infantry, would be engaged at Donelson. All of Johnston's dispatches to Floyd before the battle were concerned with the gunboat danger—not with the hazards Grant's land force might create. Johnston asked Floyd if he could repulse a naval assault, but never asked if he could repel a land attack. Floyd could give him no assurances of the fort's security, and so a disheartened Johnston ordered the retreat before the battle had started.[1]

[1] Johnston to Benjamin, February 8, 1862, in Headquarters Book, Tulane; Hardee to Floyd, February 13, 1862, in Floyd Papers, Duke; Tilghman to Johnston, February 7, 1862, in Telegrams Received, 1862, National Archives; *Official Records*, VII, 869.

En route to Nashville, Johnston's despair turned to jubilation, and an unhealthy optimism replaced his defeatist attitude. Numerous telegrams sent by Floyd and Pillow on the night of February 13 and on February 14 changed his mind about Donelson's fate. The fort had not only held out against the dreaded gunboats, but had smashed the Yankee fleet and sent it limping back to Paducah.

Thus, when the infantry clashed on February 15 Johnston was so confident of Floyd's success that he did not send a single reserve, nor did he offer to go to the fort. Part of this lack of concern was Johnston's belief in his gunboat theory; part was caused by misleading information which Floyd and Pillow telegraphed. On the evening of the fifteenth both generals sent Johnston glowing accounts of a brilliant victory over the Federals. Of the half dozen telegrams sent, not one reported that the fight had occurred while the garrison was attempting to cut their way out of the fort—and that the evacuation attempt had failed. In fact, Johnston did not know until after the fort had surrendered on the sixteenth that any attempt was being made to leave Donelson.

Indeed, late on the night of the fifteenth, while the Donelson commanders huddled in conference at Dover Inn, Johnston telegraphed Benjamin that Floyd had won a brilliant victory that day. Before he received the surrender news early on February 16, Johnston was completely deluded as to what was happening at the fort. His ideas on the naval threat, his shock at the land move on Donelson which he still was unwilling to believe, and a lack of communication with Floyd had created a dangerous situation. Johnston was setting himself up for the same type of shock which Grant's move from Henry had produced. Clearly, he was losing control.[2]

There was a new arrival in the West who wanted command of the Army. On February 4, Beauregard came to Bowling Green to report as new commander of the left wing at Columbus. Although his most powerful influence upon Johnston would not be felt until later, the seeds of a major power shift were sown at this meeting.

The curious episode of Beauregard's transfer began in late January, at his headquarters in Centreville, Virginia. Colonel Roger Pryor, a former Beauregard aide, had come from Richmond with a semi-official offer for Joseph E. Johnston's second-in-command. The Military Committee of the Confederate Congress wanted to know if Beauregard

2 Johnston to Floyd, February 13, 1862, in Floyd Papers, Duke; Harris to Polk, February 1, 1862, in Polk Papers, National Archives; Johnston to Benjamin, February 15 (5:15 P.M., "Midnight"), 1862, and Floyd to Johnston, February 16 (3:45 A.M.), 1862, in Telegrams Received, 1862, National Archives; *Official Records*, VII, 878–79, 883; Johnston, *Life of Johnston*, 495.

would consent to a transfer to the West. His new command would be Johnston's left wing, then under Polk. Pryor assured Beauregard that Richmond authorities favored the idea. According to Beauregard, Pryor also assured him that Johnston's total force numbered seventy thousand, of which Polk's wing boasted thirty thousand.

Almost immediately the general's friends urged him to reject the offer, which they believed to be an administration trick to rid Virginia of Beauregard. Robert Toombs warned that the government would not force Beauregard to leave Virginia, but that if he chose to go elsewhere, he would not be allowed to return. The warnings were to no avail. On January 23, the same day on which the Georgian penned his warning, Beauregard wrote his acceptance to Pryor. Even after receiving Toombs' warning, Beauregard telegraphed him that he had decided to accept the transfer.[3]

This transfer, destined to have a great impact on the western army, has raised many unanswered questions. The entire matter smacks of intrigue. Just who was most anxious for Beauregard to leave Virginia? Beauregard claimed that he was at first unwilling to accept the assignment. He said he told Pryor that he would go provided certain conditions were met: the western army must be reinforced strongly enough to allow an offensive campaign; when his western duties were finished, he could return to Virginia; and he could take his personal staff, together with a dozen minor officers from the Virginia army. Pryor realized his lack of authority to grant such conditions, but promised he would ask the War Department. On January 23 he sent a vague telegram to Beauregard which stated that a Richmond friend of Pryor's was certain Jefferson Davis would accept the stipulations. One biographer of the general has noted that Beauregard may have been interested in the idea from the start, and was merely trying to appear unwilling to leave Virginia.[4]

Just why and how much Richmond authorities wanted Beauregard to go to the West is also a mystery. His friends sensed an anti-Beauregard plot, and suspected that his enemies were flattering and misleading him in order to be rid of him. One supporter, W. F. Alexander, felt that Beauregard should decline "all proposals and solicitations." [5] Pryor's role

---

[3] Benjamin to Beauregard, January 26, 1862, in Barret Collection, Tulane; Special Orders 24, February 5, 1862, in P. G. T. Beauregard Papers, Duke; Special Orders No. 21, February 5, 1862, in Order Book, Tulane; T. Harry Williams, *P. G. T. Beauregard: Napoleon in Gray* (Baton Rouge, 1955), 113–14; Alfred Roman, *Military Operations of General Beauregard in the War Between the States 1861 to 1865 including a Brief Personal Sketch and a Narrative of His Services in the War With Mexico, 1846–1848* (New York, 1883), I, 210–12, 489–91.

[4] Roman, *Beauregard Military Operations*, I, 212; Williams, *Beauregard*, 113; "Claiborne Sketch," UNC.

[5] Roman, *Beauregard Military Operations*, I, 489.

elicits suspicion. For one so interested in Beauregard's welfare, Pryor did little to ascertain that the general's transfer conditions would be understood and accepted by Richmond. In fact, Pryor seemed a little too eager for Beauregard to make the transfer. In his note of January 23 he seemed in great haste to brush off Toombs's warning and to commit Beauregard to the project, possibly before Toombs changed the general's mind.[6]

Probably, as Pryor stated, western influence had much to do with the proposal. Pressure was rising for Richmond to give more attention to defense problems in the Mississippi Valley. The old Mississippi River bloc, so vocal during Polk's command in the previous summer, was again exerting force. In fact, Pryor told Beauregard that he had been sent to Centreville not only by his own Military Committee but by congressmen from the West. President Davis undoubtedly felt this pressure, and may have thought Beauregard's assignment would ease the criticism.

It would have been advantageous for the administration also if Beauregard were to leave Virginia. True, his rank would suffer no loss. He was second-in-command in Virginia, and would be second ranking officer in the West. Yet in Virginia he was steadily becoming an important member of a combined civilian-military anti-administration bloc. Along with such leaders as Toombs, Alexander Stephens, and Joseph E. Johnston, Beauregard openly criticized Davis' policies.

In fact, Beauregard already had a long record of clashes with Davis, Benjamin, Lucius Northrop, and other administration officials. In personal letters, open letters in Richmond newspapers, and battle reports, Beauregard and the administration had exchanged blows since the battle of First Manassas. The bickering had covered many topics, from the general's criticism of the Commissary Department to whether administration blunders prevented a more complete victory at Manassas. Davis may have thought it wise to isolate Beauregard from both his anti-administration friends and from the attention he received from the anti-administration press in Virginia by sending him to the West. Perhaps Beauregard's Richmond enemies did think they were duping him into accepting "exile" in the West.[7]

If the transfer scheme were a plot to strip Beauregard of power, then the plan boomeranged. For, beginning with the Johnston-Beauregard conference at Bowling Green on February 4, the command of the Army began to slip gradually from Johnston's hands to Beauregard's, until eventually the latter obtained virtual control. If Johnston was a man easily swayed by subordinates, Beauregard was a man who

[6] *Ibid.*, 489–91.
[7] Williams, *Beauregard*, 96–115.

could wield such influence. When he came to Bowling Green he had already planned an offensive which he believed would win the plaudits of the government. Evidently he partially considered the West as a place of exile, a field where he would show Richmond that he had been misjudged. He hoped to prove the government wrong by uniting Polk's left wing at Columbus with Earl Van Dorn's force, and then move on Cairo. With his usual modesty, Beauregard described the scheme as a "brilliant programme." [8]

Yet the Creole wanted more than the command of the left wing. For while he might have felt he was partly in exile, Beauregard also envisioned himself as the savior of the entire Second Department. He evidently believed he would be the real leader behind the scenes. In a confidential note to Pryor, written after his first conferences with Johnston, he described himself as "taking the helm when the ship is already on the breakers. . . ." [9] He did not specify which helm, but his treatment of Johnston showed his desire to take over the Army of Tennessee.

Indeed, Beauregard had strong motivation for wanting to take command. Even before Fort Donelson fell, the people of the West seemed to be losing faith in Johnston. Some were angry because he had not launched an offensive drive through central Kentucky. Beauregard received a hero's welcome in the West; from Centreville to Nashville, people gathered at railroad stations to see him. At Nashville he was presented to the state legislature, and he spoke at a public gathering. Leroy Walker wrote enthusiastically, "The whole country looks up to you as a forlorn hope." [10]

At Bowling Green, Beauregard learned he must revise his plans. Immediately after he arrived on February 4 he went into conference with Johnston, and the two generals toured the town's fortifications the following day. Beauregard's hopes for an offensive from Columbus were dashed. Instead of the expected seventy thousand, Beauregard learned that Johnston's total force numbered only some forty-eight thousand. Polk did not have the assured thirty thousand, but instead only about seventeen thousand. Equally serious, Beauregard found that Johnston's flanks at Columbus and Cumberland Gap were far in advance of Forts Henry and Donelson, thereby forcing the Confederates to operate on an exterior line. Thus any offensive from Columbus would be endangered by a flanking move by Federals along the Tennessee rivers.[11]

[8] Official Records, VII, 900.

[9] Beauregard to R. A. Pryor, February 14, 1862, in Beauregard Papers, Duke.

[10] Walker to Beauregard, February 19, 1862, Official Records, LII, Pt. 2, p. 275.

[11] Beauregard to Johnston, February 12, 1862, in Barret Collection, Tulane; "Claiborne Sketch," UNC.

After surveying the situation, Beauregard hastily revised his plans. To Johnston he proposed a concentration of the approximately thirty-thousand men gathered at Bowling Green, several towns southwest of that salient, and at Henry and Donelson. Still hoping for an offensive campaign, he desired to concentrate these around the inland river forts and strike any enemy coming up the Tennessee. Johnston opposed the plan. Evidently he was still unwilling to accept the fact that another force besides that of Buell was threatening Middle Tennessee, and he argued that such a move would tempt Buell to advance on Nashville.

The fall of Fort Henry forced another revision in the Beauregard strategy. This capture dimmed his hopes for a Middle Tennessee offensive, and now he groped for a new plan. Again he began to advise Johnston. Some of his advice was very sound. He warned Johnston that Fort Henry's capture gave the Yankee gunboats access to the Tennessee as far upriver as Florence, Alabama. He also made Johnston aware that, should the Federals penetrate up the Cumberland, Johnston's center corps in the Bowling Green area would be isolated on the north bank. Yet some of Beauregard's advice seemed colored by his ambition. He suggested that, since Fort Henry's surrender had for all purposes severed communications between Middle Tennessee and Columbus, he should operate as an independent commander at Columbus until the corps was reunited.[12]

Johnston was in a receptive mood for Beauregard's ideas. On the night of February 6 and during February 7 he received messages not only confirming Fort Henry's surrender but indicating that the Federal army was sweeping east against Donelson. Stunned by the news which had proved his theory of the Federal advance to be wrong, Johnston seemed in a daze as he gradually handed more power to Beauregard. On February 7 he and Hardee met at Beauregard's headquarters, and the three generals drew up a memorandum. Johnston's unwillingness to admit the danger to Donelson on the land side, coupled with his fear that the fort could not withstand gunboat fire, led him to believe that it could not hold long. Therefore the Bowling Green position would be abandoned, and Hardee's troops would fall back to the south bank of the Cumberland at Nashville. There Johnston hoped to make a stand. Meanwhile, Beauregard won his freedom of command. It was agreed he would act independently until the wings reunited.[13]

Even before Beauregard left Bowling Green for Columbus more power began to slip from Johnston's grasp. On February 12 Beauregard re-

[12] Roman, *Beauregard Military Operations*, I, 213–21; "Memorandum of Agreement," February 7, 1862, in Headquarters Book, Tulane.

[13] Johnston to Benjamin, February 8, 1862, and "Memorandum of Agreement," February 7, 1862, in Headquarters Book, Tulane.

minded him that Fort Henry's surrender greatly endangered the Columbus position, which was now extremely vulnerable to a flank assault.
Beauregard recommended that the garrison be evacuated to some point
deep into western Tennessee, preferably Jackson. On February 14, as he
was passing through Nashville en route to Columbus, Beauregard received
Johnston's approval, provided Richmond consented.[14]

While the danger of a flank attack was real, Beauregard had two less
unselfish reasons for this suggestion. Secretly, he was planning another
offensive movement. Immediately after he left Johnston, Beauregard sent
urgent calls for reinforcements to the governors of the Second Department and to Van Dorn in Arkansas. He spoke of moving north on an
offensive against Cairo or St. Louis. Thus his primary concern was not the
danger of being outflanked at Columbus, for such a move would only
heighten the danger of a flank attack. Instead, Beauregard wanted to draw
the left flank back so that he could build it up for an offensive campaign.[15]

Beauregard's other reason for desiring the evacuation of Columbus was
seen only dimly at Bowling Green, only to be seen more clearly when
Johnston later abandoned Nashville. Beauregard evidently wanted the
left wing drawn back so that he could eventually join forces with Johnston—and possibly take control of the Army's operations. A hint of this
was seen in the February 7 memorandum, which stated that if Johnston
had to abandon Nashville, he would retreat to Stevenson, Alabama, "and
thence according to circumstances." [16] On February 12 Beauregard's request for temporary independent command said that this condition would
exist until either the Tennessee River was recaptured or the Confederates
"combined the movements of the two armies in rear of it." [17] This was as
far as Beauregard would commit himself at the time. However, his later
pleas for Johnston to join him, which came immediately after Johnston
announced he was retreating to Alabama, seem to indicate that Beauregard never wanted Johnston to move to Stevenson. Such a move would
place Johnston far from Beauregard, and Beauregard's later telegrams
indicated he hoped to draw his commander farther west.

Armed with independent command and filled with prospects for the
future, Beauregard left for Columbus. His chance for greater things
came even sooner than he had probably thought. Shortly after 5 A.M.

[14] Johnston to Floyd, February 14, 1862, in Floyd Papers, Duke; Beauregard to
Johnston, February 12, 1862, in Barret Collection, Tulane; Roman, *Beauregard Military
Operations*, I, 223–24.
[15] *Official Records*, VII, 900–901, 905–906; Roman, *Beauregard Military Operations*,
I, 240–42.
[16] "Memorandum of Agreement," February 7, 1862, in Headquarters Book, Tulane.
[17] Beauregard to Johnston, February 12, 1862, in Barret Collection, Tulane.

on February 16, a messenger awakened Johnston at his headquarters in Edgefield, on the north bank of the river opposite Nashville. A candle was lighted, the dispatch was read, and the Nashville–Fort Donelson line began crumbling around the commander. Only three hours after he had telegraphed Johnston additional news of the great victory over Grant on the fifteenth, Floyd now reported that the officers had agreed to surrender the fort and the garrison. Stunned, Johnston ordered Hardee to fall back immediately to Murfreesboro, where a decision would be made as to what to do.[18]

There was no chance of making a stand at Nashville, as Johnston had planned to do if Fort Donelson fell. On Christmas Day, 1861, Johnston had assured Isham Harris that the Nashville defenses guaranteed the city's safety. Yet, when the commander arrived at Nashville, he learned for the first time that the city's line of defense had never been built.[19]

Gilmer had failed to build the Nashville–Clarksville defenses, just as he had failed to bolster those at Fort Donelson. Nashvillians still had not responded to the requests for slave laborers to build the fortifications north of the Cumberland. Now that the river was open to Nashville, such fortifications were no longer of any benefit. Gilmer never seemed to have anticipated this problem, and thus had not planned a defensive line on the south bank. The oversight was a great error, and to compensate for it, independent efforts were made during late January and early February to build some fortifications there. These projects, like the earlier ones, did not receive public support, were uncoordinated in effort, and remained only a dream when Donelson fell. A twenty-gun battery was placed on the bluff below the city, and a submarine battery was planned for the river. Some advisers suggested stretching a large chain across the river. A local inventor came forward with a quack machine that supposedly fired submarine batteries located more than a mile away. Harris began organizing independent companies to be put into line below the city. There was just not enough time to build the line that Johnston had assumed was already there.[20]

18 Floyd to Johnston, February 16 (3:45 A.M.), 1862, in Floyd Correspondence, National Archives; Johnston to Benjamin, February 18, 1862, Cumberland City Operator to Johnston, February 7, 1862, Mackall to Crittenden, February 16, 1862, W. H. Allen to Johnston, February 17, 1862, Hardee to Mackall, February 18, 1862, all in Headquarters Book, Tulane.

19 Johnston to Isham Harris, December 25, 1861, in Headquarters Book, Tulane.

20 V. K. Stevenson to S. Bransford, January 17, 1862, and Gilmer to Mackall, January 28, 1862, in Ch. III, Vol. 8, Engineer, National Archives; Mackall to Captain Lindsay, February 9, 1862, and W. H. Armstrong to Shaaf, February 12, 1862, in Barret Collection, Tulane; Harris to Johnston, February 7, 1862, Johnston to Harris, February 10, 1862, Moses Wright to Mackall, February 10, 1862, all in Telegrams Received, 1862, National Archives; Johnston to Benjamin, February 14, 1862, in Letters Sent, 1861–62, National Archives.

Gilmer had also failed at Clarksville. As late as February 6, Pillow reported to Johnston that none of the Clarksville fortifications, supposedly begun in November, was complete. Only four guns were even available, and not one was mounted. The only battery site which effectively commanded the river was placed below the high water level, and the river was already rising. Desperate last-minute efforts were made to build defenses. Plans for blocking the river channel were discussed. The soldiers at the Clarksville post were set to digging fortifications, but the tools they needed were not available. Negroes could not be obtained during December and January to work on the fortifications, and when Donelson fell there was absolutely nothing at Clarksville that would even slow the progress of the gunboats, much less prevent their passage upriver. Yet Johnston had definitely relied on fortifications there to provide delaying tactics for gaining time needed at Nashville in the event of any emergency. Such time was not to be had. On February 19, the telegraph operator at Clarksville reported that from his key he could see the Union gunboats steaming up the river.[21]

At Nashville, Johnston also first realized the truth of Beauregard's warnings about being outflanked in Middle Tennessee. As early as February 7, the telegrapher at Florence excitedly reported that a steamboat had been chased there from Fort Henry by gunboats. The next day, five gunboats were in the Tennessee at Florence, and reports began coming from points all along the river. The Memphis, Clarksville, and Louisville railroad bridge at Danville was burned. Gunboats were reported at Clifton. Tennessee. A rumor sprang up that troops had disembarked from the gunboats at Florence and were marching on Tuscumbia to sever the Memphis and Charleston Railroad. Although this proved false, the threat was real. The Memphis and Charleston line ran west from Tuscumbia near the river for a distance of about thirty miles, and the Federals could easily land and cut the railroad line.[22]

Other intelligence indicated that Buell was preparing to move on Nashville, and that another force was moving to outflank Johnston on the east. Johnston believed that Buell had eighty thousand men on the

21 Pillow to W. D. Pickett, February 6, 1862, in Pillow Papers, National Archives; W. H. Armstrong to Floyd, February 12, 14, 1862, G. N. Quarles to Floyd, February 15, 1862, W. H. Allen to Mackall, February 19, 1862, all in Floyd Papers, Duke; *Official Records*, VII, 841–42.

22 Florence operator to Johnston, February 7, 1862, S. D. Weakley to Johnston, February 8, 1862, R. M. Patton and S. D. Weakley to Johnston, February 10, 1862, M. J. Ross to Johnston, February 8 (1:20 A.M.), 1862, Nashville operator to Johnston, February 8 (5 P.M.), 1862, Cumberland City operator to Johnston, February 9, 1862, L. P. Walker to Johnston, February 2, 1862, all in Telegrams Received, 1862, National Archives.

Green River line, and scouts reported the Henry-Donelson activity was only a diversion to hold Johnston's attention while Buell moved south on Nashville. Meanwhile, another column was to move into East Tennessee. At Lexington, Kentucky, nine hundred wagons were supposedly being loaded for this flank move. Johnston's fourteen thousand men at Nashville, even when supplemented by the estimated four thousand men who escaped Donelson, were no match for the army Buell allegedly had. Intelligence further said that the Federal army at Donelson alone was between sixty thousand and seventy-five thousand strong. After Johnston evacuated Nashville, Captain John Hunt Morgan's troops penetrated the Yankee lines there and reported that sixty-five thousand Federals were in the city. Johnston concluded that he was being encircled by two pincers while Buell moved against him with the main force. Already, pickets on the rear guard south of Bowling Green reported that they were being driven in by Buell's troopers.[23]

Johnston also found at Nashville that his logistical support was swept away. Since the city's fall was not expected, no measures had been taken to collect the valuable stores scattered at numerous depots between Bowling Green and Nashville. Some advisers had warned that the supplies should be moved. On February 8, Isham Harris suggested moving the Nashville meat stores farther south, and two days later Moses Wright suggested the same for munitions. Their advice was not heeded by Johnston, and thus when Donelson fell the logistical situation became hopelessly entangled. The few railroad cars available were being used to evacuate sick troops still in Kentucky. The winter rains had washed away many bridges and miles of track. The Nashville and Chattanooga Railroad alone had at least 1,200 broken rails. The railroad's president, V. K. Stevenson, also in charge of the Nashville supplies, abandoned his post and took a train for Chattanooga. During the week after Donelson's fall, a washout on the line between Nashville and Chattanooga blocked all traffic over the road south of Nashville.[24]

Johnston's supplies were lost through confusion, inadequate preparation, and a lack of patriotism. At Clarksville, the commandant abandoned his post and order broke down. A wagon train of between seventy-five and a hundred wagons was stranded, as were several boatloads of pork.

23 Johnston to Benjamin, January 8, 1862, in Headquarters Book, Tulane; John Morgan to John C. Breckinridge, February 25, 1862, in John Hunt Morgan Papers, UNC; Report of Captain John H. Morgan, March 10, 1862 (MS in Barret Collection, Tulane) ; J. W. Fisher to Johnston, February 16, 1862, and W. H. Allen to Johnston, February 18, 1862, in Telegrams Received, 1862; Official Records, VII, 864–65, 867.

24 Harris to Johnston, February 8, 1862, and Moses Wright to Mackall, February 10, 1862, in Telegrams Received, 1862, National Archives; V. K. Stevenson to Hardee, February 19, 1862, in Floyd Papers, Duke; Black, Railroads of the Confederacy, 138.

No boats or railroad cars were available to move the supplies. Eight days' provisions were stranded at Bowling Green. At Franklin, Kentucky, ten thousand bushels of wheat were abandoned. Stores in large quantities remained at Bell's Station, Kentucky, and at Mitchellville, Tennessee. Twenty carloads of government stores were isolated at Columbia.

At Nashville, the supply service totally collapsed. About seventy thousand pounds of bacon were piled on the Cumberland River wharf, and vast quantities of this supply floated off on the rising waters. John B. Floyd had been as poor at handling a post as he was at commanding a fort. On February 18, Bedford Forrest was called in to restore order. Looting of government stores was widespread, as depots and warehouses were sacked and wagons laden with supplies were spirited away into the countryside.[25]

Forrest exerted superhuman effort to remove all valuable supplies before the Federals arrived. He hauled to the depot 250,000 pounds of bacon, 600 boxes of army clothing, and thousands of pounds of flour. Rifling machinery was dismantled and taken to Atlanta. Forty wagons loaded with ammunition were taken to a secure place south of Nashville. Despite his superb efforts, however, Forrest could not save a fraction of the supplies at Nashville. The pork on the wharves was turned over to local citizens because it could not be moved. The railroad depot was filled with pork and other stores which could not be sent south for lack of transportation. These tremendous losses were never estimated officially, but Colonel St. John Liddell, an aide to General Hardee, speculated that, because of negligence, poor transportation and weather, and panic, half of the supplies of the Army of Tennessee were lost when Johnston abandoned Nashville. Whatever the figure, it is certain that when Hardee's corps left the city, the Army's logistical strength no longer existed.[26]

It was panic that had hampered Forrest's efforts most severely. The effects of the collapse of the Nashville myth of invincibility, of the first

25 E. M. Bruce to Floyd, February 13, 1862, S. Peters to Floyd, February 15, 1862, Alexander Winn to Floyd, February 19, 1862, Pillow to Hardee, February 19, 1862, all in Floyd Papers, Duke; Hindman to W. D. Pickett, February 6, 1862, A. J. Lindsay to Mackall, February 10, 1862, John Claybrooke to Johnston, February 11, 1862, Harris to Johnston, February 12, 1862, Hardee to Johnston, February 14, 15, 1862, W. S. McLemore to Johnston, February 15, 1862, L. M. Thomas to Johnston, February 16, 1862, Clarksville quartermaster to Johnston, February 16, 1862, Hindman to Johnston, February 16, 1862, D. P. Buckner to S. B. Buckner, February 16, 1862, all in Telegrams Received, 1862, National Archives.

26 Forrest complained that a large amount of stores was stolen before he took command, and that all the public stores might have been saved had the Confederates been more diligent. See "Colonel Nathan B. Forrest's Responses to Interrigatories [sic] of Committee of Confederate House of Representatives," in Ridley, Battles and Sketches,

battle lost in Tennessee, and of the first surrender by a Confederate army all combined to produce in the people of the Heartland both fear and a loss of confidence in Johnston. The panic was felt chiefly by the Nashvillians and by the people of the Yazoo–Mississippi Delta country. In the Nashville area, morale broke down completely. At Clarksville, Confederates attempted to burn the railroad bridge to prevent the Federals from having a clear line from Bowling Green to the Tennessee River. A local citizens' group headed by the mayor overpowered the hapless six Confederates who remained at their Clarksville post and would not allow them to burn the bridge. One bold lieutenant wriggled free and managed to set the bridge afire.

When it was learned that the Confederates planned to abandon Nashville, a mob stormed Johnston's headquarters. By the time Forrest arrived, a lawless element had taken control of the town, and his efforts to remove supplies were impeded by the need to restore order. He felled the ringleader of one mob with his pistol butt, and turned firehoses on another unruly crowd. When these more gentle resources had been exhausted and the mobs continued to surge through the streets, Forrest's troopers charged into their midst, and the colonel himself used the flat side of his saber to discourage further pillaging. Self-interest was evident everywhere in Nashville. Citizens who had earlier been loud in their support of Johnston's army now vigorously protested the destruction of the suspension bridge over the Cumberland, despite the fact that such a move would help delay Buell's occupation of the city and bring Johnston a little extra time in his retreat. When the Federals did appear on the north bank of the Cumberland, the mayor and his "committee" broke all records in rowing across the river to receive Buell's army officially.[27]

The panic eventually subsided, but the bitterness toward Johnston remained. Hailed as the man who could save Tennessee, Johnston had been expected to accomplish too much. Now the people were ready to look elsewhere for a savior. At Murfreesboro, St. John Liddell observed, "Here the conclusion is almost universal that he [Johnston] is totally unfit for the position he holds in the Confederate army, and if he does nothing to retrieve his character very soon, he will be regarded as hopelessly embicile [sic]." [28]

72; Wyeth, *Forrest,* 58–59; Duke, *Morgan's Cavalry,* 116; Horn, "Nashville During the Civil War," 10; R. B. Cheatham to Floyd, February 19, 1862, in Floyd Papers, Duke; Nashville operator to Johnston, February 16, 1862, B. R. Johnson to Mackall, February 21, 1862, A. K. Richards to Breckinridge, February 22, 1862, all in Telegrams Received, 1862, National Archives.

27 Crabb, "Twilight of the Nashville Gods," 291–99; Horn, "Nashville During the Civil War," 9–11; Lt. Brady to Floyd, February 18, 19, 1862, and J. W. Fisher to Hardee, February 19 (6:40 A.M., 1:45 P.M.), 1862, in Floyd Papers, Duke.

28 Liddell to his wife, February 28, 1862, in "Liddell's Record," LSU Archives.

In the Confederate Congress, the Tennessee delegation asked for Johnston's removal, and charged that "confidence is no longer felt in the
military skill of General A. S. Johnston. . . ." [29] The delegation argued
that the commanders and citizens of the West had lost all confidence
in him. The influential Charles Ready, member of a prominent Murfreesboro family, complained to Jefferson Davis that only the latter's
presence could save the Army from demoralization. Other citizens wired
the president that Johnston and Hardee should be removed.[30] When he
reported Donelson's fall to Richmond, Johnston's adjutant had uttered
almost prophetic words: "We lost all." [31]

When Johnston left Nashville, his control of the troops was visibly
slipping from his grasp. He had planned to move to Stevenson, Alabama, as previously agreed, while Beauregard acted independently. Johnston never reached Stevenson, however. Instead, by progressive steps, he
and the Army moved west to come under Beauregard's control. The
initial step occurred when Beauregard drew him out of the central
Tennessee Valley into the Mississippi Valley area. He first persuaded
Johnston to change his destination from Stevenson to Decatur, Alabama,
by warning him that the Federals were moving up the Tennessee and
that a great battle in West Tennessee was imminent. On February 24,
Johnston informed Davis that he was moving to Decatur. This change
was significant, for if Johnston had gone to Stevenson, he would have
operated from the base at Chattanooga, only forty miles east. Decatur,
however, was 110 miles west of Chattanooga and was just as close to
Beauregard's position in West Tennessee.[32]

Once Johnston had made this initial change in destination, he was
steadily drawn into Beauregard's territory. On February 26, even before
Johnston had left Murfreesboro, Beauregard sent two telegrams asking him
to move to West Tennessee, where a Federal advance was expected. The
pressure of the Louisiana general was too strong. The next day, Johnston
informed Judah P. Benjamin that he was moving to unite with Beauregard in the defense of Memphis and the Mississippi River area. Johnston

[29] Tennessee delegation to Davis, March 8, 1862, in Gustavus A. Henry Papers, Confederate Collection, Tennessee Archives.

[30] Charles Ready to Davis, February 21, 1862, and W. H. McCardle to Albert Gallatin
Brown, March 1, 1862, in Headquarters Book, Tulane.

[31] Mackall to Beauregard, February 16, 1862, in Telegrams Received, 1862, National
Archives. See also Johnston to Davis, March 18, 1862, in Barret Collection, Tulane.

[32] "Claiborne Sketch," UNC; Johnston to Davis, February 24, 1862, in Telegrams
Received, 1862, National Archives; Beauregard to Mackall, February 22, 22, 1862, in
Correspondence between General A. S. Johnston and General P. G. T. Beauregard,
Manuscripts Division, Tulane, hereinafter cited as Johnston–Beauregard Correspon-
dence, Tulane; Johnston to Beauregard, March 7, 1862, in Albert Sidney Johnston
Papers, Pennsylvania Historical Society; Johnston to Benjamin, February 27, 1862,
in Headquarters Book, Tulane.

had chosen to defend the Mississippi Valley instead of Middle Tennessee. On February 28, Hardee's corps took up the march for Decatur.[33]

If Johnston had any qualms about giving up Tennessee, Beauregard's persuasion soon eased them. No sooner had he left Murfreesboro than Beauregard exerted pressure for him to bring Hardee's corps to a desired rendezvous point at Corinth, Mississippi. While Beauregard drew back the troops from Columbus to Jackson, Tennessee, reinforcements commanded by Generals Braxton Bragg and Daniel Ruggles began assembling at Corinth. Beauregard then urged Johnston to come there also, and the latter complied with his request. Benjamin was informed that Hardee's troops would move for Corinth. Not only was Johnston allowing Beauregard both to draw him out of Tennessee and to select the rendezvous area, but also he began to allow Beauregard to manage departmental affairs. When Johnston stated he was moving to unite with Beauregard, the language used indicated that he referred to the Creole general as a commander equal in rank, and not as a district commander serving under him.[34]

This tendency became more pronounced in the following weeks. On March 6 Beauregard told Johnston to spread rumors that Hardee's men were going to Chattanooga instead of Corinth. Two days later Beauregard told, rather than asked, Johnston to send him General Bushrod Johnson immediately, and Johnston complied. When told that he should not use any more cars and locomotives on the Memphis and Charleston Railroad than were absolutely necessary to move his troops to Corinth, Johnston meekly replied that he would endeavor to form a junction with Beauregard. Beauregard answered by ordering him to send to Corinth any available surplus ammunition. On March 15, he asked Johnston to send him a brigade and two additional regiments. Johnston sent Hindman's brigade and the requested regiments. Beauregard even asked for Johnston's own adjutant, W. W. Mackall, and for his chief engineer, Jeremy Gilmer.

Even after Beauregard and Johnston met at Corinth, the former continued to manage the Army's affairs. Although only in command of Polk's troops, he took it upon himself to telegraph the War Depart-

---

33 Beauregard to Johnston, February 26, 1862, in Barret Collection, Tulane; Beauregard to Johnston, February 26, 1862, in Johnston–Beauregard Correspondence, Tulane; Pillow to Johnston, February 26, 1862, and Memphis Committee of Safety to Johnston, February 27, 1862, in Telegrams Received, 1862, National Archives; Johnston to Benjamin, February 27, 1862, in Headquarters Book, Tulane; Confidential Orders, Western Department, Order Book, Tulane; *Official Records*, VII, 911–12; Gilmer to his wife, February 27, 1862, in Gilmer Papers, UNC.

34 Beauregard to Johnston, March 2, 1862, and Beauregard to Mackall, March 4, 1862, in Johnston–Beauregard Correspondence, Tulane; Johnston to Benjamin, March 5, 1862, and Johnston to Davis, March 7, 1862, in Headquarters Book, Tulane.

ment to send a major general and four brigadiers to be used by Bragg's troops, as well as by Polk's.[35]

The method by which Beauregard managed to obtain such control was also the method he used to complete the final stage of his assumption of leadership. Repeatedly he bombarded Johnston with threats of a Federal invasion up the Tennessee River. He warned that such an invasion would either isolate Johnston in northern Alabama or strike Beauregard in West Tennessee. Whether he intended to or not, Beauregard, by using this same method of sending alarming notes, gathered under his wing not only Johnston's immediate command but also almost all the reinforcements which were sent to Tennessee. In a series of dramatic statements, he excited the attention of the Mississippi Valley people as well as the authorities in Richmond. For the first time, Richmond hastened to answer pleas from the West. The reinforcements were sent to Beauregard's district, where they were assimilated into his command. The result was that Beauregard became the commander of an army instead of a corps.[36]

Beauregard was simply more adept at stirring public opinion than Johnston had been. In his call to the governors of the Second Department for troops, he promised an invasion to the Ohio River. Shortly thereafter, he made his famous call for plantation bells to be gathered in the Mississippi Valley to be melted down and cast into cannon. Such a project was impractical but was excellent propaganda. Fiery telegrams were sent to Richmond warning of a Federal sweep down the Mississippi Valley. Richmond, already shocked by the Middle Tennessee disaster, sent large numbers of reinforcements to Beauregard. Four regiments commanded by Ruggles were sent from General Mansfield Lovell's command at New Orleans. Recruits began to assemble in both Alabama and Mississippi. In early March, Braxton Bragg, with ten thousand troops from Mobile and Pensacola, moved north to Corinth.[37]

Beauregard not only had the ability to obtain reinforcements but also managed to take complete charge of them. Although it was not in his agreement with Johnston, he styled himself as the commander

[35] Beauregard to Johnston, March 6, 8, 10, 12, 15, 17, 24, April 2, 1862, and Johnston to Beauregard, March 11, 1862, all in Johnston–Beauregard Correspondence, Tulane; Johnston to Beauregard, March 11, 1862, Johnston to Bragg, March 19, 1862, Johnston to Jefferson Davis, March 15 and 25, 1862, all in Headquarters Book, Tulane; Special Orders 10, Western Department, March 10, 1862, Order Book, Tulane.

[36] Beauregard to Mackall, March 8, 1862, and Beauregard to Johnston, March 16, 1862, in Johnston–Beauregard Correspondence, Tulane; Beauregard to Johnston, March 13, 1862, in Barret Collection, Tulane; Gilmer to his wife, March 9, 15, 1962, in Gilmer Papers, UNC.

[37] Benjamin to Bragg, February 8, 1862, and Johnston to Lovell, February 10, 1862, in Barret Collection, Tulane; Benjamin to Johnston, February 23, 1862, in Telegrams Received, 1862, National Archives; *Official Records,* VII, 862–63, 872, 890, 892–94, 899–900.

of the Army of the Mississippi Valley. He referred to the command to which he had originally been assigned, Polk's corps, as the First Grand Division, and to Bragg's and Ruggles' reinforcements as the Second Grand Division. Also unauthorized by Johnston, Beauregard even created districts within the district to which he had been assigned, and appointed Polk and Bragg to command them.[38]

Despite his penchant for the extravagant, exemplified in his invasion plan which was formulated at a time when the Army was already facing short rations, Beauregard provided a stabilizing influence which was badly needed. He brought to the Army ideas of departmental coordination. Under Johnston, the subcommanders had operated loosely, with no combined effort. Beauregard established forage and ordnance depots, and made provisions for better distribution of supplies to the troops. His organization of Polk's troops into the Army of the Mississippi Valley, though it went further than Johnston had intended, did bring a tightly knit organization to the left wing. In the matter of regimental and division organization, both Polk and Johnston had been poor housekeepers. Beauregard provided for a complete revamping of Polk's command into an organized system of regiments, brigades, and divisions.

For the first time, the Army of Tennessee began to give evidence of cohesion. Johnston's organization had been determined according to geographical lines more than according to a system of army corps. The commands of Polk, Hardee, and Zollicoffer bore only the slightest resemblance to an army consisting of three corps. In every command, regiments were of minimum strength, and brigades contained no uniform number of regiments. Beauregard's "Confidential Notes of Reference," issued on March 5, were designed to cement the existing Army's organization, to rebuild its shattered logistical structure, and to assimilate into the main command the reinforcements that he had garnered. A unity which Johnston had been unable to achieve began to form in early April, 1862. [39]

This unity was not all beneficial, for the control of the Army was passing into the hands of a general to whom the defense of the Heartland was perhaps secondary to that of the Mississippi Valley. In the opinion of some, this move was a mistake, for it lost the rich storehouse of Middle Tennessee, practically conceded northern Alabama and the Memphis and Charleston Railroad, and placed in jeopardy the bastion at Chattanooga and all of East Tennessee.[40]

38 General Orders No. I, Army of the Mississippi Valley, March 6, 1862, in Barret Collection, Tulane; *Official Records,* VII, 920–21.
39 "Confidential Notes of Reference of P. G. T. Beauregard," March 4, 1862 (MS in Barret Collection, Tulane) ; Williams, *Beauregard,* 120–23.
40 Gilmer to his wife, March 3, 21, 1862, in Gilmer Papers, UNC.

Johnston's impact on the Army of Tennessee during his period of command had thus far left much to be desired. His preoccupation with Buell, his concentration of attention upon the Bowling Green district, his failure to insure that Polk meet his command responsibilities, and his failure to develop more effective cooperation between Hardee and Zollicoffer all resulted from weaknesses in his personality. His difficulty in communicating with people, his absorption in one task at a time, his lack of sternness in handling unruly subordinates—all were factors which helped to weaken the Tennessee line.

Ironically, the most constructive influence Johnston had on the Army was a result of his failure and not of any success he might have had. His failure to solidify the high command helped to produce the individual *elan* that welded the Army together for four dark years. The debacles of Mill Springs and Donelson wounded the pride of the individual soldiers, probably more than historians have recognized. Some thought their comrades had been sold out too cheaply at Fort Donelson; others believed they had not been given a real chance to show their fighting qualities. Perhaps these attitudes help explain the exceptional valor and tenacity with which the private soldiers usually fought.

Even Johnston's abandonment of much of Tennessee wrought a constructive influence. The Army had always been a Tennessee-oriented force. Its nucleus was the state army of Tennessee, and the first defensive line stretched the length of Tennessee. Throughout the war, Tennessee remained, at least in spirit, the Army's home. When Johnston left Middle Tennessee, many soldiers were bitterly disappointed and a new element was added to their spirit—a determination to retake Tennessee. From Shiloh to Franklin, Rebel commanders would whip their regiments into a fighting spirit by reminding them that the battle was to regain Tennessee. "Home to Tennessee" would be the Army's battle cry and morale booster throughout the war.

But Johnston's influence now faded, at least on the surface, as the force marched toward Corinth and a junction with Beauregard. Back on the Arizona desert, Johnston had seen a comet quickly flash across the sky and had pondered whether it was an omen of future success. Perhaps the rapid disappearance of the comet was a more accurate sign, for while Johnston had come to Tennessee with the acclaim of a hundred thousand lips, he was now an object of scorn. Weeks before the guns opened at Shiloh, a new rising star and a new influence were being felt in the Army. The command was still Johnston's—but the control was Beauregard's.

PART IV

the beauregard interlude

eight

In Need of a Napoleon

ALL DAY LONG ON MARCH 24, HARDEE'S TROOPS SLOGGED OVER THE RAIN-swollen Mississippi roads into Corinth. Johnston also arrived that day and met with Beauregard, Polk, and the newcomer Bragg. They talked of Grant's gathering force at Pittsburg Landing on the Tennessee and of the need to strike before he was reinforced by Buell from Nashville. They agreed that the Army would move against Grant as soon as the forces were reorganized—a process expected to require weeks of work. The conference ended, and Johnston wrote President Davis the following day. It was a hopeful note that assured Davis "my force is now united." [1]

Either Johnston was simply expressing optimism or he was operating in the same peculiar fog which engulfed him during the Fort Donelson period. For the one notable mark of the Corinth concentration was discord. The Army's morale had waned from the enthusiasm of the previous autumn. After the Mill Springs disaster, accusations of incompetence and even disloyalty were directed at Crittenden. Crittenden was still with Johnston, commanding a division in Hardee's corps. The inland river forts were gone, thirteen thousand Rebels were bound for Yankee prisons, and Floyd and Pillow were under attack for their conduct. Johnston's own popularity had declined, and the public's fickle admiration had turned to Beauregard. The praised bastion at Columbus—the last position on Johnston's old line—had been abandoned in mid-February. The key fortress at New Madrid had been left without a fight in early March. Beauregard's planned offensive to Cairo or St.

---

[1] Johnston to Jefferson Davis, March 25, 1862, in Headquarters Book, Tulane.

Louis had fizzled. Position after position had fallen, and Johnston had little to show after seven months of work.

These constant setbacks had not gone unnoticed by the citizenry. The Confederates observed a new attitude among many Tennesseans as the Federals swept into the state. St. John Liddell complained that in Nashville many people received the Federals with open arms. Even the rabid Confederate Isham Harris told President Davis that the confidence of Tennessee people in their security from invasion was a prerequisite to full cooperation with the Confederacy.[2]

The loss of morale was visible in the ranks, where the rate of stragglers and deserters was high. A large chunk of Crittenden's force melted away into the Cumberland Mountains after Mill Springs. After Nashville fell, some of Hardee's troops broke ranks to plunder the abandoned military stores, or straggled south into the shelter of the Duck River Ridge wilderness.

The high command's morale was no better. When Bragg arrived in early March to command the area around Corinth, he minced no words in voicing his disgust with the condition of Beauregard's troops. He complained of poor discipline and habitual plundering, intimated that Beauregard was partly responsible, and accused Polk himself of plundering. A first-rate scandal broke out in the hapless Crittenden's division posted at Iuka. Crittenden was arrested for drunkenness and relieved of his command, while one of his brigadiers, Charles Carroll, was arrested for drunkenness and neglect of his troops. A smaller scandal occurred in the medical corps over the removal of the wounded from Donelson, and there were reports that many wounded were hastily abandoned when Nashville fell.

Johnston's confidence in his own abilities had also declined. The general never seemed to recover from the shock of Grant's move on Donelson. Johnston's movements from Nashville to Corinth had shown the same indecision he had exhibited in the Donelson situation. Despite apparent misgivings, he had allowed Beauregard to draw him westward out of the Heartland, and on the march had let Beauregard all but direct his movements. At Corinth he even offered the general the command of the Army. The offer was refused, and defenders of both generals would long argue Johnston's motive. The importance of the proposal was its indication that Johnston's confidence seemed to have waned, and rumors were widespread that he would resign his command.[3]

2 Liddell to his wife, February 28, 1862, in "Liddell's Record," LSU Archives; Harris to Davis, October 15, 1861, in Harris Papers, Tennessee Archives.

3 Pillow to Johnston, February 18, 1862, and Harris to Johnston, January 31, 1862, in Telegrams Received, 1862, National Archives; George Johnson to Albert Sidney

The Army's logistical strength was also disorganized. The thin Corinth ranks showed the results of the Mill Springs and Middle Tennessee disasters. After Nashville fell, Richmond finally responded to the West's pleas for aid. Reinforcements from New Orleans, Mobile, Pensacola, and elsewhere totaled almost 20,000. Still these were not enough. Battlefield casualties at Donelson and Mill Springs, the 13,000 captured at Donelson, the sick and wounded left at Nashville, the stragglers and deserters on the retreat—all had severely reduced Johnston's force. In January, Johnston's effective force on the Kentucky line numbered some 55,000 but on April 1, the Army had only about 39,500 effectives. Hardee's old Central Army had boasted 24,500 present for duty in January; now Hardee could muster only 13,000 troops. At Columbus, Polk's force had 14,000 effectives, but at Corinth had scarcely over 9,000. [4]

Supplies were also low. Huge amounts of ordnance and small arms had been lost in the past few months. All of Crittenden's artillery and some one thousand stands of arms were lost at Mill Springs. Some twenty thousand small arms and sixty artillery pieces were lost at Donelson. At least twenty-three artillery pieces were captured at Fort Henry, and probably twenty-one heavy guns seized at New Madrid. Nashville, the chief ordnance plant and storehouse for the West, was lost, along with the powder mills and iron works on the inland rivers. Army supplies had been abandoned at Columbus, New Madrid, Nashville, Clarksville, Bowling Green, Columbia, and other points. Such heavy losses could only be countered by weeks of rebuilding. [5]

There was also discord in the high command's strategy. The wisdom of sacrificing the Heartland for the Mississippi Valley was debatable. Middle Tennessee's great corn, wheat, iron, ordnance, and livestock centers were lost. East Tennessee was in greater danger. Northern Alabama was threatened by Grant's move up the Tennessee. If Grant seized the Memphis and Charleston Railroad, the Federals would at last have a continuous communication link from Paducah to near Chattanooga, and the East Tennessee city would be endangered. Yet most of the high command, colored by ties with the Mississippi Valley, agreed with Johnston's

Johnston, March 22, 1862, in Barret Collection, Tulane; H. C. Burnett to John B. Floyd, March 1, 1862, and J. A. Forbes to Floyd, March 8, 1862, in Floyd Papers, Duke; *Official Records*, X, Pt. 2, pp. 339–40, 379, 341–42; Davis to Johnston, March 12, 1862, and Johnston to Davis, March 18, 1862, in Barret Collection, Tulane.

4 *Official Records*, VII, 762, 824, 852–53, 855, X, Pt. 2, pp. 377–78, 382.

5 *Ibid.*, VII, 81, 130, 180, 436–38; Liddell to his wife, February 28, 1862, in "Liddell's Record," LSU Archives; Alexander Winn to Floyd, February 19, 1862, in Floyd Papers, Duke; A. K. Richards to Breckinridge, February 22, 1862, Hindman to Johnston, February 16, 1862, L. M. Thomas to Johnston, February 16, 1862, all in Telegrams Received, 1862, National Archives.

choice. Johnston was a Texan by residence and sentiment. Beauregard, Bragg, and Polk were Louisianians. At least half the division and brigade commanders had business or residence ties in the Mississippi Valley.

The wisdom of the choice remains a moot question. Even if the decision were wise, Johnston erred in not making provisions for northern Alabama's defense. As early as February 8, he knew that Yankee gunboats were near Florence; on March 9, he was warned the Federals might land below Tuscumbia; and on March 16 he was warned that Grant might cut the Memphis and Charleston Railroad near the Great Bend of the Tennessee. Still Johnston made no defensive efforts. Also, he dawdled on the march to Corinth. His route took him to Huntsville and then west to Corinth, with his flank constantly exposed to attack from the river. It was a month from the time Johnston announced his decision to move until he joined Beauregard. Bad weather and the need to collect supplies were partly responsible—but Johnston also moved too slowly.[6]

His slowness, as well as his confused state of mind, may well have been results of his bewilderment at Beauregard's constant reversals in strategy. When Beauregard abandoned Columbus, he established a new line at Jackson, Tennessee, and explained to Johnston that he would remain on the defensive there. Yet a few days later he reversed his plans and spoke of attacking Paducah, Cairo, or even St. Louis. In early March, Beauregard again changed his mind. He lost his taste for an offensive when New Madrid and Fort Henry fell, and so went back to Corinth. There he told Johnston he would take a defensive position and wait for Grant to attack him; then Beauregard would counterattack and cut Grant off from his river base. But when Johnston met with Beauregard, the latter had again changed plans. Instead of awaiting attack, Beauregard proposed to strike before Buell joined Grant. In slightly more than a month, the Creole general had changed from a defensive to an offensive, then to a defensive-offensive, and finally to an offensive against Grant.[7]

These changes in strategy may well have been partly caused by a lack

[6] Johnston to Davis, March 7, 1862, and Johnston to Benjamin, February 27. 1862, in Headquarters Book, Tulane; Beauregard to Johnston, February 22, March 12, 16, 1862, and Beauregard to Mackall, March 8, 1862, in Johnston–Beauregard Correspondence, Tulane; Gilmer to his wife, March 3, 9, 1862, in Gilmer Papers, UNC; W. C. Whitthorne to Johnston, February 8, 1862, in Telegrams Received, 1862, National Archives.

[7] Beauregard to Johnston, February 12, 1862, in Barret Collection, Tulane; Beauregard to Johnston, February 7, 1862, and Johnston to Judah Benjamin, February 8, 1862, in Headquarters Book, Tulane; Beauregard to Bragg, March 17, 1862, in Johnston–Beauregard Correspondence, Tulane; Johnston, *Life of Johnston*, 538–39, 549–50; P. G. T. Beauregard, "The Campaign of Shiloh," *Battles and Leaders*, I, 578–79.

of knowledge of Federal activity. Johnston's move to Corinth produced dire effects on his intelligence network. In Kentucky he had used chiefly citizen scouts and Rebel infantry to probe the Green River area, as the cavalry was still ineffective at reconnaissance. Bedford Forrest and Joseph Wheeler were yet relatively unknown as cavalrymen, while John Morgan was erratic amid flashes of competence. Even this makeshift system was impossible at Corinth. The field of operations now embraced a wider and deeper area, for the Federal line extended from the Ohio River to near the Tennessee–Mississippi line. Scouts could not cover such an area and good cavalry remained scant. Other sources proved unreliable. Private citizens drifted into Johnston's lines with estimates of Federal strength colored by inexperience or even disloyalty. Nervous telegraphers at stations along the Tennessee River flashed every rumor of Federal activity to Johnston's headquarters.

Up until the night before their departure for Pittsburg Landing, the Confederates were not absolutely sure that Buell was moving to reinforce Grant. John Morgan had been unsuccessful in his efforts to penetrate the Federal cavalry screen around Nashville and gain information. The first definite report Johnston received indicated that Buell would not move to aid Grant. In early March a Texas doctor passed into the gray lines from Nashville with news that Buell would move on Florence to cut the Memphis and Charleston Railroad. Bragg forwarded the note to Johnston, and added that the essential points of the doctor's report were given consistently to him and his inspector-general in separate interviews. This report was bolstered on March 15, when General James R. Chalmers reported from Iuka that his scouts had learned that Buell was moving on Florence. Three days later the situation became critical. Buell moved some forty miles south from Nashville to Columbia. Morgan's cavalry held him on the north bank of Duck River by burning the turnpike bridge.

At Columbia the road forked: south to Decatur, southwest to Florence, and west to Savannah and Grant. For twelve agonizing days Morgan held Columbia and watched Buell's engineers build pontoon bridges. On March 20 Johnston learned that Morgan's right wing had been driven in at Shelbyville, southeast of Columbia on the road to Huntsville. All reports indicated a strong Yankee push to the south and southeast of Columbia.

Johnston was in a dilemma. If Buell broke through into northern Alabama, Corinth would be outflanked. If he moved west and joined Grant, the Confederates would face a combined force which reports placed somewhere between sixty-five thousand and a hundred thousand men. If Buell did plan to unite his troops with Grant's, it was imperative to strike before the junction could be made.[8]

Grant's plans also baffled the Confederates. As early as late February, they expected him to move up the Tennessee and strike rail communications in northern Mississippi or Alabama. Since Corinth was the junction of the Mobile and Ohio and the Memphis and Charleston, it was also expected that Grant would move there. Yet Corinth could become a trap for Johnston. There were multiple landing points on the Tennessee between Crump's Landing near Savannah and Muscle Shoals that Grant could use to outflank Corinth. The Federals could land at Tuscumbia; they could land at Eastport and march on a good road to Iuka; or they could land at the mouth of Yellow Creek and move between Corinth and Iuka to the Mobile and Ohio Railroad south of Corinth.

Even if Grant aimed for Corinth, his route would be a puzzle. Between Yellow Creek and Crump's Landing there were a half dozen good landing spots. The Federals could disembark at Chambers Creek and march via Farmington; land at Hamburg and march on a good ridge road; move from Pittsburg Landing over several good roads; or even land at Crump's Landing, some thirty miles northeast of Corinth.

Grant's actions added to the mystery. As early as mid-March, Beauregard knew that 120 Federal boats had passed up the Tennessee from Fort Henry, but could not determine their destination. On March 12, gunboats shelled Eastport, but that same day scouts reported that Grant was preparing to land at Hamburg. On March 14 transports were reported unloading at Yellow Creek, but the next day thirty thousand Federals were reported at Crump's Landing. On March 16, Bragg reported Grant was unloading troops at Pittsburg Landing, and three days later, he was certain that between twenty-five thousand and fifty thousand of the main force were there. Still Beauregard was uncertain. On March 18 a gunboat attack was expected near Florence, and three days later reports placed the Federals at both Yellow Creek and Eastport. By March 24, Beauregard was sure the main force was at Pittsburg Landing. Yet as late as April 2, Johnston had information that Yankee transports were at Eastport, some fifty miles southeast of Pittsburg Landing.[9]

8 Morgan to Breckinridge, February 25, 1862, and Johnston to Hardee, March 18, 1862, in Morgan Papers, UNC; Bragg to Johnston, March 7, 1862, and Morgan to Hardee, March 10, 1862, in Barret Collection, Tulane; John Scott to Johnston, March 19, 1862, and Johnston to Scott, March 20, 25, 1862, all in Headquarters Book, Tulane; *Official Records*, X, Pt. 2, p. 362, 373, 387.

9 Gilmer to his wife, March 9, 15, 21, 24, in Gilmer Papers, UNC; Johnston to Davis, March 15, 25, in Headquarters Book, Tulane; S. A. M. Wood to Bragg, April 1, 2, 1862, in Bragg Papers, Western Reserve; "Movements of Enemy's Boats on Tennessee

All of this confusion only indicated continuing disunity in the Army's high command. At Corinth, Johnston continued to allow Beauregard to control matters. Had Johnston been more sensitive, the Corinth meeting could have turned into a gray Donnybrook. A less patient general would have resented Beauregard's unauthorized action in creating his own miniature department in West Tennessee, and in forming his own "Army of the Mississippi" with Beauregard as a self-styled "general commanding." Instead, Johnston passively allowed the troops he brought to Corinth to be assimilated into Beauregard's force, instead of the reverse. The Army retained Beauregard's chosen name, and the organization pattern of four corps commanded by Hardee, Polk, Bragg, and Breckinridge was a Beauregard idea. Johnston also agreed that the Louisiana general would draw up the marching and battle orders for the planned offensive. Modestly, Beauregard accepted the title of "Second in Command" of the Army, but Johnston's failure to stand up to his lieutenant still left him commander in name only.

There were other command problems among the ranks. At best, the Army was inexperienced. Bragg's troops were well trained but raw, and the New Orleans reinforcements were green. Many of Polk's men had seen no combat, and Hardee's troops had spent their time on picket duty around Bowling Green. For the first time, Johnston and Beauregard would work together in a campaign. Bragg was new in the Army, as were many brigade and regimental commanders. All of this newness must be ironed out in the midst of a surprise offensive campaign, with scarcely two weeks of preparation. In matters of morale, logistics, strategy, intelligence, and command, the Army was in poor shape for an offensive.[10]

Though weeks of preparation were needed at Corinth, on April 2,

---

River" (MS in Beauregard Papers, Duke) ; Taz. Newman to Breckinridge, April 3, 1862, in John C. Breckinridge Papers, Chicago Historical Society; *Official Records*, X, Pt. 2, pp. 316–17, 319, 327, 329–32, 338, 341, 351–53, 357. Shortly after the fall of Fort Donelson, Grant had been temporarily relieved of his command by General Henry W. Halleck. By March 13, when Grant rejoined his command, the army was concentrated at Savannah and Pittsburg Landing. Grant gathered his force at Pittsburg Landing, except for Lew Wallace's division, which remained five miles downriver at Crump's Landing. At Pittsburg Landing, Grant had 41,543 present for duty while Wallace had 7,771 troops. Grant planned to await Buell's 25,000 men to join him, and then move on Corinth and the Memphis and Charleston Railroad. See U. S. Grant, "The Battle of Shiloh," *Battles and Leaders*, I, 465–66; Don Carlos Buell, "Shiloh Reviewed," *Battles and Leaders*, I, 489–90; Johnston, *Life of Johnston*, 684–85.

10 Edmund Kirby Smith to Johnston, March 2, 1862, in Letters and Telegrams Sent, Department of East Tennessee, Ch. II, Vol. 52, National Archives, hereinafter cited as Ch. II, Vol. 52, National Archives; Beauregard to Polk, March 6, 1862, in Barret Collection, Tulane; *Official Records*, X, Pt. 2, pp. 325, 354.

Johnston found that he had no more time to prepare. The Army must now meet Grant at Pittsburg Landing. The ensuing campaign has long been a battle of metahistorical "ifs" and "might have beens." Writers would argue about how close the Rebels came to victory. Much of this speculation has been based on the assumption that the Confederates launched a powerful attack which, for reasons debatable, failed in its execution. Yet the campaign seemed doomed from the start. Confusion and indecision marked the three-day approach to Pittsburg Landing and the battle itself. Failure to solve the problems faced at Corinth, added to unexpected problems encountered en route, spelled out defeat from the outset.

The confusion began in the early morning hours of April 3. Word came from Cheatham's advance division at Bethel Station, twenty miles north of Corinth. Grant was evidently dividing his force to strike the Mobile and Ohio Railroad. Other information reported that Buell had finally left Columbia and was moving thirty thousand men to join Grant. Beauregard sent Cheatham's note to Johnston by Colonel Thomas Jordan, his chief of staff, and added an endorsement which suggested that the time had come to advance and strike Grant at Pittsburg Landing. Johnston mused over the note and conferred with Bragg. Bragg agreed with Beauregard, but Johnston protested that the Army was unready for an offensive. Colonel Jordan, well versed in Beauregard's offensive hopes, argued that such a move was vital before Grant and Buell combined to move on Johnston.[11]

Perhaps unwisely, Johnston assented, and Jordan began to prepare the elaborate plans for the march. Using a table in Bragg's chambers, Jordan wrote a circular order for the corps, directing that each corps should be under arms and with three days' rations by 6 A.M. on April 3. After Johnston approved of the rough draft, copies were sent to the corps commanders about 1:30 A.M. on the third.

Soon the preparations became confusing. Jordan roused another aide and told him to wake Beauregard at daylight and tell the general that the order to advance at midday had been issued. Here Jordan may have erred. The order to the corps said nothing about moving out at noon, but only to be ready to move by 6 A.M. By sunrise, Beauregard was busy framing the orders for the advance and attack. Dazzled by prospects for a grand offensive, the Creole rose to the occasion with an impossible set of maneuvers ill-suited to raw troops and unfamiliar terrain.

11 "Claiborne Sketch," UNC; Thomas Jordan, "Notes of a Confederate Staff Officer at Shiloh," *Battles and Leaders*, I, 594–96; Roman, *Beauregard Military Operations*, I, 270; Beauregard to Johnston, March 22, 1862, in Johnston–Beauregard Correspondence, Tulane.

Then Jordan took Beauregard's notes and framed the complicated Special
Order Number Eight, the march and battle plan. True to his superior's
taste, Jordan drafted the order with a copy of Napoleon's orders for
Waterloo before him.

Before Jordan could finish, he went to Beauregard's quarters for
another meeting with Johnston. Beauregard explained to Johnston the
road system. The paucity of information was evident, for Beauregard
had only one map of the roads, which Jordan had left in his own
quarters. Instead, Beauregard sketched the roads on a table top, as
Bragg, Polk, and Hardee joined the council. Since it would take Jordan
some time to complete the marching orders, Beauregard explained orally
the first day's march. He told the corps leaders not to wait for written
orders, but to move at noon.[12]

Beauregard's plan failed to consider the rough country north of Corinth. The land between Corinth and Pittsburg Landing was thickly
wooded, cut through with creeks, ravines, swamps, and dirt roads which
resembled a confusing patchwork. The presence of Grant's army had
worsened matters, for the land around Pittsburg Landing was now cut
up into numerous wagon trails leading in every direction through the
wooded country. Frequent spring rains had turned the clay roads into
quagmires.

The Federals were camped on a high, timbered bluff above the river
landing. On the north, Grant's right flank was protected by Snake Creek,
which ran east into the Tennessee River. Two miles to the west of the landing, Owl Creek flowed northeast and emptied into the Snake. South of
the landing, the Federal left flank was anchored on Lick Creek which
emptied into the Tennessee. All of these creeks were swollen by the
spring rains, aiding to protect the Union army's flanks. The entire area
between Snake and Lick creeks was a maze of underbrush, swamps,
gullies, ravines, old fields, and fences.

The road system which the Confederates must use to reach Grant's
strong position was confusing enough to tax well-trained soldiers, much
less Johnston's inexperienced column. Several roads led to Pittsburg
Landing from Corinth—the Ridge or Bark Road, the Monterey–Purdy
road, and the Monterey–Savannah road. Around these Beauregard devised complicated maneuvers. Hardee would move on the Ridge Road
and bivouac on April 3 at Mickey's. At 3 A.M. on the fourth, Hardee
would advance and deploy in battle line between Owl and Lick creeks.
Bragg was to march to Monterey. His right wing would advance on
the Monterey–Savannah road to Mickey's. Bragg's left wing would move

12 Jordan, "Shiloh Notes," 594–96; Beauregard, "Campaign of Shiloh," 579–81.

on the Monterey–Purdy road to the Ridge Road junction. On the morning of April 4, after Hardee had passed, Bragg would turn onto the
Ridge Road behind Hardee, and deploy in battle line some one thousand
yards to his rear. That part of Polk's corps which was at Corinth was to
move on the Ridge Road and bivouac behind Hardee on the night of April
3. Then Polk would wait at Mickey's for Cheatham's division to rejoin
the corps, and then would form a third battle line. When someone
pointed out that Bragg and Polk might collide on the Ridge Road, Polk
was ordered to halt at the junction of the Monterey–Purdy road to allow
Bragg's left wing to move ahead of him. Breckinridge was to assemble
his corps at Monterey, and then move in the general direction of the
Army.

Such complicated moves demanded excellent road information and
weather. Neither Johnston nor Beauregard knew the road system well.
Yet Beauregard was depending on a rapid, secret move of heavy artillery and supply wagons over country roads which crossed acres of
swampland. If the heavy wagons bogged on the miry roads, the campaign could fail. The weather was not promising. The country north
of Corinth was already soaked by rain, and several rivers in the area
were at flood level.[13]

The battle plan was also confusing, and ill-suited to the brief planning
of the April 3 council. Instead of assigning each corps a section of the
line, Beauregard devised a curious arrangement. Hardee's corps occupied the entire first line, followed consecutively by Bragg, Polk, and
Breckinridge. Such a plan would make it difficult for a corps commander to maintain discipline and communications along the length of
the battle line. Also, this formation seemed to frustrate the Confederate
tactical plan. The plan called for the most severe attack to be made
against the Union left flank, to drive the Federals away from the Tennessee River into the pocket of Snake and Owl creeks. Yet the linear
formation gave no extra strength to the Confederate right flank, where
the strongest blow was to be delivered.

Johnston's son, William Preston Johnston, together with Jefferson
Davis and Braxton Bragg, would later maintain that Johnston originally
planned to attack in a formation in which the corps would attack
abreast, but that Beauregard deliberately changed those plans and issued the order for a linear attack. Johnston's son based his claim on a

13 Ephraim A. Otis, "The Second Day at Shiloh," in *Campaigns in Kentucky and
Tennessee, including the Battle of Chickamauga, 1862–1864* (Boston, 1908), 184, 186,
Vol. VII of *Papers Read before the Military Historical Society of Massachusetts* (Bos-
ton, 1881–1912); Henry Stone, "The Battle of Shiloh," in *ibid.*, 47; Roman, *Beauregard
Military Operations*, I, 270–74.

telegram sent by Johnston to President Davis on April 3 which stated the positions as "Polk the left, Bragg the centre, Hardee the right wing, Breckinridge the reserve." [14] William Preston Johnston claimed that after the April 3 council Beauregard changed the tactical formation, and that Johnston discovered it when it was too late to revert to the original plan. Beauregard's supporters later maintained that the plan as drawn up and the one explained to Johnston in the morning council of April 3 were the same. It is probable that Johnston simply did not understand all the details of Beauregard's plan, for he did not even see a written copy of Beauregard's orders until April 4. [15]

If the planning was confusing, the execution of the scheme was chaotic. The Army did not reach its destined bivouacs for the night of April 3. In fact, it almost failed to get out of Corinth. Although verbal orders were given at the morning council to move at noon, the Army was still idle by early afternoon. Beauregard later blamed Polk, and charged that the bishop's trains blocked Hardee's march. Polk claimed he was clear of the road and was waiting for Hardee to move. For some reason Hardee waited for a written order to move, which he did not receive until after 3 P.M.

Whatever the cause, the delay cost a precious day's time. Beauregard had probably intended to attack Grant on April 4, and had the Army made good time on the third this could have been done. But the delay forced Beauregard to postpone the attack to the fifth. The exodus from Corinth was so slow that Polk's rear column was still in town on the night of the third. All of Bragg's corps did not reach Monterey until late on the fourth, and Hardee did not reach Mickey's until the morning of the fourth.

The confusion increased on April 4. Bragg found only bad roads, poor guides, and raw troops in his move on Monterey. Due to these conditions, he was forced to route both his divisions onto the Ridge Road via the Monterey–Savannah road. This move threw the Rebel column into more turmoil. Hardee was slowed, for Bragg asked him to wait until his corps moved up in support before Hardee deployed. Even worse, Polk and Bragg became entangled in a jam which took hours to clear. Polk accidentally marched ahead of Bragg, and before Bragg

14 Johnston to Davis, April 3, 1862, in Headquarters Book, Tulane.

15 William Preston Johnston, "Albert Sidney Johnston at Shiloh," *Battles and Leaders,* I, 552–54; Alexander Robert Chisholm, "The Shiloh Battle-Order and the Withdrawal Sunday Evening," *ibid.,* 606; Memorandum for the Commanders of the Corps and Reserves, April 3, 1862, Special Orders No. 8, Army of the Mississippi, April 3, 1862, in Headquarters Book, Tulane; Roland, *Johnston,* 321; Bragg to William Preston Johnston, December 16, 1874, in Barret Collection, Tulane.

could deploy behind Hardee, he had to march through Polk's corps. By night of April 4, Hardee was concentrated at Mickey's, ready to move out in battle line at 3 A.M., but Bragg and Polk trailed in the rear.[16]

In the early hours of April 5, Confederate hopes again flickered dimly. About three hours before Hardee planned to deploy in battle line, a fierce rainstorm swept the Rebel lines. The swamp country became almost impassable. Rivulets became roaring streams, and the dirt roads became deep quagmires. Hardee could not move, and postponed his advance until dawn.

At daylight Hardee advanced, and by 10 A.M. his vanguard neared the Federal pickets. Again the Rebel attack stalled. Hardee lacked the men needed to fill the long battle line. To fill the gap between Hardee's right and Lick Creek, Johnston advanced Gladden's brigade of Bragg's corps. But another problem arose. Bragg's left division, commanded by Ruggles, was nowhere in sight. By 11:30 A.M. Ruggles still had not appeared. Now irritated, Johnston sought out Ruggles' division. It was far in the rear, blocked by Polk's column. Hurriedly Johnston untangled the mess, but the road still was not clear until 2 P.M. By four the Army was at last in battle line.

The strain of the march now began to take its toll. More confusion erupted as Bragg and Polk moved into formation. Columns accidentally marched across the path of other columns, causing frequent delays. Many troops were tired before the battle began, worn by rain, mud, and forest roads. Worse, a food shortage developed on April 5. Two days' rations remained in the supply wagons, and more time was spent in bringing up the scant supplies.[17]

For the third straight day, Beauregard's plans faced revision. About 4 P.M., a casual conversation between Bragg and Beauregard swelled into a full-scale war council which included Breckinridge, Polk, Johnston, and Gilmer. Tempers and nerves were frayed—especially Beauregard's. He implied that Polk was to blame for the day's delays, and Polk vigorously denied the charge. Discouraged, Beauregard argued that the Army should abandon the campaign and return to Corinth. Rations were low. Some units already had no food, and by April 7 the whole Army would have no rations. The green troops were exhausted. It was too late to begin an

---

[16] Braxton Bragg's Official Report of Shiloh (MS in Bragg Papers, Western Reserve) , hereinafter cited as Bragg's Report, Western Reserve; Roman, *Beauregard Military Operation*, I, 275–76; Bragg to Johnston, April 4, 1862, Johnston to Breckinridge, April 14, 1862, in Headquarters Book, Tulane.

[17] Bragg's Report, Western Reserve; *Official Records*, X, Pt. 1, pp. 400, 464; Johnston, *Life of Johnston*, 562–64; John Taylor, "Twenty-Seventh Tennessee Infantry," in Lindsley, *Annals*, 418–19.

attack on the fifth. Surely the Federals had discovered the Army by now. Cleburne's brigade had repulsed a Yankee reconnaissance force on the fourth with artillery and infantry fire. On April 5 many troops, nervous at the rain and the delay, fired their weapons to test them. Johnston himself was forced to ride along the lines to quiet the firing.

Beauregard's arguments were of no avail. In a rare moment of decision, Johnston, supported by Polk and Bragg, calmly announced that the Army would attack at dawn the next day. His new-found stability may have been misguided. Weary and hungry, poorly trained and disorganized, the Army was in no shape to launch an attack.[18]

Through the night of April 5, the Army lay in the river bottom dampness, waiting for daylight. At dawn, the commanders huddled around Johnston's fire for another council. Even with a battle only minutes away, the high command showed the discord and indecision which haunted the Army for four years. Beauregard again pressed for a retreat, repeating his fears of the Army's condition. Again Johnston stood firm. Even while they spoke, skirmish fire opened on Hardee's front.

Johnston's sudden decisiveness was surprising. On the night of April 5 and early the next day he spoke with unusual optimism and daring. Johnston muttered to his aide, Colonel William Preston, *"I would fight them if they were a million."* [19] To others he boasted, "To-night we will water our horses in the Tennessee River." [20] Yet Johnston also spoke with the desperation of one whose reputation was at stake. His old command structure had lost face badly in the winter campaign in Tennessee, and already there were misgivings about the new organization. From Corinth, Gilmer had written of Johnston and his new organization, "Among them all, I fear, there is not a Napoleon." [21] Possibly Johnston saw the impending battle as a chance to mend the frayed edges of his public image. He was not too sure of the undertaking, however, for in the hours before the battle he sought assurances from staff members that his decision to fight was right. He exclaimed to Colonel Randall L. Gibson, *"We must win a victory,"* [22] and confided to his old friend Colonel John C. Marmaduke that "We must this day conquer or perish." [23]

18 Johnston, *Life of Johnston,* 567–69; William J. Hardee's Official Report of Shiloh (MS in William Hardee Papers, Chicago Historical Society), hereinafter cited as Hardee's Report, Chicago; Hardee to Bragg, April 4, 1862, in Headquarters Book, Tulane.
19 Johnston, *Life of Johnston,* 569.
20 Johnston, "Albert Sidney Johnston at Shiloh," 557.
21 Gilmer to his wife, March 29, 1862, in Gilmer Papers, UNC.
22 Johnston, "Albert Sidney Johnston at Shiloh," 557.
23 *Ibid.*

nine

Another Storm, Another Helmsman

LONG AFTER THE LAST GUN COOLED ON THE SHILOH FIELD, WRITERS WOULD
bitterly argue the nearness of a Confederate victory on April 6. Supporters
of Johnston would depict the battle as a near Rebel success, stymied only
by assorted factors on which few could agree. Yet, even if Johnston's
hopes for a victory were conceded a chance after the confusion of the
three days prior to the battle, probably the Army was beaten at Shiloh
almost from the outset. During the morning and early afternoon of April
6, Johnston's force encountered insurmountable problems. By night, the
Army was anything but close to victory, and instead resembled an armed
mob. Again, the shibboleth of the Army of Tennessee—a faulty command
structure—was to blame.

The Army was harassed by command problems from the outset of the
day's fighting. Although Johnston commanded the Army, during the
early hours of the battle he behaved more like a brigade or regimental
commander than an army chieftain. In a manner reminiscent of his old
days at Bowling Green, he expended hours of valuable time in matters
better left to subordinates. He personally led brigades and regiments
into position, made front-line reconnaissances, and performed other such
tasks.

Nor did Johnston establish a smooth working relationship with Beauregard. The two men evidently failed to reach a solid agreement on what
the latter was to do. Johnston's supporters later claimed that Beauregard
had little control over the battle's operations, and that, by an agreement
made at a dawn meeting, he was to remain in the rear to forward men
and supplies, while Johnston was to ride to the front. After the war,
Beauregard gave a different account of the meeting: Johnston said that

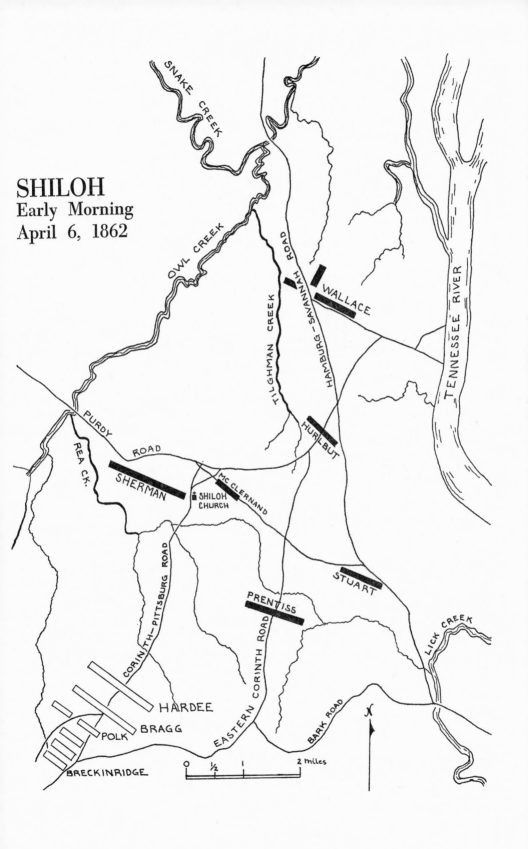

SHILOH
Early Morning
April 6, 1862

SNAKE CREEK

OWL CREEK

TILGHMAN CREEK

HAMBURG – SAVANNAH ROAD

TENNESSEE RIVER

WALLACE

HURLBUT

PURDY
ROAD

REA CK.

SHERMAN

MC CLERNAND

SHILOH CHURCH

CORINTH – PITTSBURG ROAD

STUART

PRENTISS

EASTERN CORINTH ROAD

LICK CREEK

HARDEE

BRAGG

POLK

BARK ROAD

BRECKINRIDGE

0   ½   1   2 miles

N

he planned to ride to the front and leave Beauregard with the general direction of the battle. While Beauregard probably exaggerated the authority given him, it appears that during the morning and early afternoon he behaved more like the Army's leader than did Johnston. He repeatedly sent staff officers to all parts of the battle line to procure information by which he could determine where reinforcements were needed, and probably had a better overall view of the situation than did his commander. Colonels Thomas Jordan, George Brent, and Jacob Thompson and a host of other aides combed the field for information.[1]

The informality of the Shiloh command was also indicated by the activities of Beauregard's chief of staff, Colonel Jordan. Shortly after 7:30 A.M., Jordan was ordered by Beauregard to go to the front. He was given free rein to reconnoiter the field and urge on the assault. Jordan proceeded to gather his own miniature staff around him at Shiloh Church and, independent of Johnston and Beauregard, to send men into action. Jordan employed such staff members as Bragg's chief aide, Colonel David Urquhart, and Johnston's chief aide, Colonel Preston, to press Confederate reinforcements toward the sound of the heaviest fighting.[2]

The lackadaisical manner in which troops were directed toward the field only further indicated the fragmentation of the Army's command. Although the avowed battle plan was to strike the enemy's left flank, a haphazard "make yourself useful" policy was utilized throughout the day. When Beauregard first ordered Polk's and Breckinridge's corps into action, he ordered them to march toward the sound of the most severe fighting. Evidently Beauregard gave Jordan the same advice. Other commanders adopted this same loose policy. During the early afternoon when General Patton Anderson's brigade needed direction, Anderson's orders from Bragg were to go wherever the fight was the thickest. Some whole brigades wandered the field without orders. Colonel R. M. Russell's brigade, having no orders, moved to where the firing was concentrated. Some units were almost forgotten in the command confusion. Colonel George Maney's crack 1st Tennessee Infantry and Bedford Forrest's cavalry had been posted on the south bank of Lick Creek, on the crucial right flank, to guard against any possible enemy move from Hamburg, and were then forgotten. By 11 A.M., still having received no orders, Maney and Forrest, on their own initiative, sought out the enemy.[3]

1 Roland, *Johnston*, 326–27; Beauregard, "Campaign of Shiloh," 586; Roman, *Beauregard Military Operations*, I, 524–34.

2 Jordan, "Notes," 599–601.

3 Roman, *Beauregard Military Operations*, I, 285; *Official Records*, X, Pt. 1, pp. 497, 417, 421, 533; Henry, *Forrest*, 77; Thomas P. Jordan and J. P. Pryor, *Campaigns of Lieut. Gen. N. B. Forrest, and of Forrest's Cavalry* (New Orleans, 1868), 121–26; Bragg's Report, Western Reserve.

Even the battle's objective was perhaps not properly explained to the high command before the fighting began. Johnston's memorandum issued to the corps leaders on April 3 stated that the battle plan was to turn the Union left flank, cut the Yankee line of retreat to the Tennessee River, and throw Grant's army back on Owl Creek.[4] Yet in his official report of the battle, written on April 11, Beauregard did not mention Johnston's memorandum, and stated that it was expected that the enemy "would be beaten back into his transports and the river, or captured." [5] There is other evidence which indicates a possible lack of rapport between the two generals as to the battle's objective. When he sent Polk and Breckinridge into action shortly after 7:30 A.M., Beauregard ordered them to march toward the sound of the heaviest fighting. At that hour, the fighting was thickest on the Rebel left and center, and not upon the far right. In his official report of the battle, Beauregard wrote that by late afternoon the Confederates were "successfully pushing the enemy back upon the Tennessee River," [6] hardly the direction intended according to Johnston's battle order.

Even if the battle plan were fully understood by the high command, the alignment of the Army for the April 6 attack made the success of Johnston's plan almost impossible. It was bad enough that the linear attack formation of the corps placed no extra strength on the Lick Creek flank which Johnston planned to turn. Equally serious, the successive lines of the corps were improperly aligned to carry out this maneuver. Hardee, commanding the first wave, had massed his power on the left and center. His right wing was so weak that General Adley H. Gladden's brigade of Bragg's corps had been moved up onto the right of his line on the evening of April 5. On the second line, Bragg had massed three brigades on the left and center, and only two on the right. Polk's entire corps was placed in reserve on the west side of the Corinth–Pittsburg road, behind the Confederate left, while Breckinridge's reserve corps was massed behind the center. When the attack began, ten brigades were massed on the left and center, and only four on the right flank.

There was another serious alignment error which Johnston failed to remedy. During the daylight hours, when the battle's initiative and the advantage of surprise still belonged to him, the hammer blow against the Union left near Lick Creek did not come. The faulty alignment of Johnston's right wing was partially to blame. Johnston, prior to the battle, had only scant knowledge of the Shiloh terrain and the Yankee position. On the march from Corinth, a lack of knowledge of the tangled

4 Memorandum for the Commanders of the Corps and the Reserves, April 3, 1862, in Headquarters Book, Tulane.

5 *Official Records*, X, Pt. 1, p. 385.

6 *Ibid.*, p. 387.

road system had cost the Army at least one day's march. Again, a lack of topographical information was evident, for Johnston knew little of the location of the Union line. Not until after the informal council of war on the night of April 5 did he move to obtain such intelligence. He ordered Bragg's chief engineer, Colonel S. H. Lockett, to steal forward early on April 6 and reconnoiter the enemy's left flank near the river. But Johnston's order called for Lockett not even to begin his search for the enemy until 4 A.M., and the attack was planned for daybreak. The daring engineer could not possibly have had time to return before the battle opened. In fact, Lockett's report, which warned that the Federal left flank overlapped Johnston's right, did not reach the general until almost 9:30 A.M.[7]

Without adequate reconnaissance, Johnston did not know that his battle line was so arranged that the right wing would be delayed in its assault. The main Federal line extended from near Lick Creek westward across the Corinth–Pittsburg road to Owl Creek. Except for a slight recess by William T. Sherman's division on the Owl Creek flank, the Federals' front line faced southward. Sherman's division, posted between the Corinth–Pittsburg road and Owl Creek, bent slightly to the northwest. General Benjamin Prentiss' division occupied the center, slightly in advance of Sherman, on the east side of the Corinth–Pittsburg road. The meager Federal left, manned by Colonel David Stuart's lone brigade which had been detached from Sherman, was posted along the Hamburg road on heavily timbered bluffs near Lick Creek.

Yet Johnston's line was attacking in a northeastward direction, along the general alignment of the Corinth–Pittsburg road. Thus Prentiss and Sherman would be reached much sooner than Stuart. Prentiss was under heavy fire by 6:30 A.M., but Stuart was not assaulted until five hours after the battle started.[8]

The meanderings of Lick Creek also promised trouble for the Confederates. The extension of Hardee's line by the addition of Gladden's brigade was not sufficient. As Hardee's line moved forward, Johnston soon discovered he had been sorely in need of reconnaissance. Lick Creek diverged towards the northeast, creating a wide space between the creek and the Confederate right. Johnston had tried to remedy the matter by borrowing another brigade from Bragg. General James Chalmers' troops were hurriedly marched into the vacant space. But the creek continued to veer even more sharply eastward, and a gap of perhaps a mile was

7 S. H. Lockett, "Surprise and Withdrawal at Shiloh," *Battles and Leaders*, I, 604; Johnston, *Life of Johnston*, 572–73, 581; Hardee's Report, Chicago.
8 Roman, *Beauregard*, I, 292.

left between the Tennessee River and Johnston's line. In this gap lay the true Federal left. Only after receiving Lockett's report did Johnston grasp the problem and extend more brigades into the gap.[9]

Had Johnston given strong direction to the battle, many of these command faults might have been rectified. Yet throughout the morning, Johnston became absorbed in matters on the left and center. Affairs in the center first held his attention. By 6 A.M. the bulk of Hardee's command had driven back the Federal pickets and had smashed into the surprised Federals of Prentiss' division and Sherman's left flank. General S. A. M. Wood's brigade of Hindman's division hastened along the Corinth–Pittsburg road and fell on Sherman's left. On Wood's right, Colonel R. G. Shaver's brigade and Gladden's brigade stormed through the thickets east of the road and surged onto Prentiss' drowsy command.

Johnston rushed to the center. After a brief meeting with Beauregard, he soon caught up with Wood's brigade and rode to the center, personally urging on the attack. While Sherman's left was crumpling, Shaver and Gladden repeatedly forced back Prentiss. Casualties were horrible in the thick underbrush; Gladden himself was mortally wounded. Now Johnston became absorbed in the fight against Prentiss. He personally rallied stragglers and ordered up the brigades of Generals James Chalmers and John K. Jackson from Bragg's corps. Chalmers and Jackson smashed into Prentiss, the blue line buckled, and by 8 A.M. the Rebel center had swept through Prentiss' camps. Untouched breakfasts still on mess tables, and unpacked baggage indicated Prentiss' men had indeed been surprised.[10]

Still, the far right must wait for proper direction. The Confederate command now became involved in matters on the far left. General Patrick Cleburne's brigade had been assigned the task of driving in Sherman's right flank near Owl Creek. Cleburne had moved more slowly than the attacking units to his right because of the difficult terrain. As he moved across the marshy ground near Owl Creek, he discovered that Sherman outflanked him. The more Cleburne advanced, the more Owl Creek veered away from his line. Sherman's flank was anchored in this gap, and Cleburne found that he was outflanked by the length of half a brigade. After calling for aid, he moved forward about 8 A.M.

By 10 A.M. the far right of Sherman's line had been driven back toward the Purdy road, but at an awful cost to Johnston's plans. Cleburne's brigade was a shambles. Sherman's artillery had caught the Irishman's brigade as it advanced across a marshy field and into a ravine which fronted the Union position. Cleburne's brigade was so badly

9 Johnston, *Life of Johnston*, 592, 597.
10 *Ibid.*, 587–90; *Official Records*, X, Pt. 1, p. 568.

pulverized that it was of little use for the remainder of the day. He lost almost 50 per cent of his command, and the 6th Mississippi regiment alone lost 300 of its 425 troops.[11]

But the more severe loss was to Johnston's plans for the right flank. After observing the fight in the center, Johnston rode to the left to observe Cleburne's advance, a trip which only wasted valuable time. He then returned to the center and sent Colonel Jacob Thompson to Beauregard with a suggestion that strong reinforcements be sent to Cleburne's aid because the enemy was in great force there. Beauregard responded to Johnston's wishes by ordering Breckinridge's corps to march to the left flank. Later, Johnston changed his mind and sent a second message to Beauregard which stated that he had overestimated Sherman's strength. Meanwhile Beauregard, concerned for the right, had sent Colonels Numa Augustin and George Brent to reconnoiter the right flank. Augustin reported that the right wing was weak, that it did not reach Lick Creek, and that it was overlapped. Immediately Beauregard countermanded his previous order to Breckinridge, and ordered two of that corps' three brigades to hasten to the right. He later ordered a brigade of Polk's corps to march in the same direction.[12]

Still other precious reinforcements were wasted in the attempt to storm the wrong flank. Colonel Preston Pond's and General Patton Anderson's brigades were thrown into the fight to aid Cleburne. Colonel Robert Trabue's brigade from Breckinridge's corps and Colonel Russell's brigade of Polk's corps were also directed into this struggle.[13]

Meanwhile, Johnston was again occupied with matters in the center. After Prentiss' command abandoned their camps, the Yankee center fell back stubbornly, as did the supporting Federal division on Prentiss' right, that of General John A. McClernand. Johnston soon became involved in menial details on this sector of the line. For a time he directed a charge by Gladden's brigade. Later he led Jackson's brigade into line. Then Johnston directed a charge by Joe Wheeler's 19th Alabama regiment, and then personally led the 2nd Texas regiment into position. At other times he visited deserted camps, encouraged the wounded, and tried to reorganize stragglers. While these activities were admirable, they were more rightfully the responsibility of lesser officers.

Finally, by mid-morning, Johnston remembered the right flank. About

11 Johnston, *Life of Johnston*, 593; *Official Records*, X, Pt. 1, pp. 581–83; Roman, *Beauregard Military Operations*, I, 287.

12 Johnston, *Life of Johnston*, 593; Roman, *Beauregard Military Operations*, I, 286–89, 529.

13 Hardee's Report, Chicago; *Official Records*, X, Pt. 1, pp. 516–17, 494–95, 613, 416.

9:30 A.M., he received Lockett's delayed report which warned that the Confederate right was badly overlapped. Only then did Johnston personally move to the far right. Ordering Breckinridge's brigades to that sector, he took two of General Jones Withers' brigades, Chalmers' and Jackson's, and moved toward Lick Creek. Shortly after 10 A.M., the Confederate right was at last ready for battle.[14]

Still, command disorder stalked the field. Johnston remained on the far right only long enough to view the first attack upon Stuart. By 11 A.M. he had moved back toward the right-center to oversee Breckinridge's activities. In Johnston's absence, the Confederates lost not only an opportunity to turn the Yankee flank, but also to seize Pittsburg Landing as well. The first assault drove Stuart back several hundred yards to a heavily timbered ridge which was protected by thick underbrush on both flanks and an open field in front. For almost three hours, Withers' division was stymied by this lone brigade. Finally, the remnants of Stuart's brigade skillfully withdrew across a maze of wooded ravines to Pittsburg Landing.[15]

The Union left was now open, but a lack of command robbed the Confederates of another opportunity. When Johnston left Withers, he evidently failed to explain exactly what Withers was supposed to do. There is no evidence that he suggested that Jackson and Chalmers should attempt to seize the river landing, a move which would have prevented any possible reinforcement by Buell's army in that quarter. Evidently he also did not suggest that Withers should attempt to gain the rear of the Union center. In fact, Withers seemed to know little except that Johnston's April 3 memorandum had spoken of a turning move, and that Beauregard had suggested on April 6 that, when in doubt, troops should move to where the firing was most severe. Thus, after pursuing Stuart until within range of Federal gunboat fire from the Tennessee River, Withers seemed hesitant as to his proper course. Uncertain, he halted his advance, and his division soon became absorbed into the fight against the Federal center.[16]

This new absence of command on the right flank was due to new matters on the center of the line. By late morning, Prentiss had withdrawn the remnants of his brigade to an old wagon trail opposite the Confederate right center. There, in the "Hornet's Nest," he stalled the

---

14 Johnston, *Life of Johnston*, 595, 597; *Official Records*, X, Pt. 1, 532.

15 *Official Records*, X, Pt. 1, pp. 258–59, 532; Johnston, "Albert Sidney Johnston at Shiloh," 562.

16 Beauregard, "Campaign of Shiloh," 588; *Official Records*, X, Pt. 1, pp. 533, 550, 553.

general Rebel advance for several hours while the Confederates attempted in eleven separate attacks to storm the position. By early afternoon, the bulk of Johnston's army was occupied in the attack upon a position which could probably have been flanked with much less loss of men and time. Though Bragg had agreed to supervise matters on the right, he became involved with this same attack and did not reach Withers' position until late afternoon. Beauregard, on the advice of Augustin, had moved the bulk of Breckinridge's corps to the right. The last reserve available to Johnston, Breckinridge would have been valuable to Withers' efforts. Instead, after Breckinridge had slowly moved into position on Withers' left, Johnston moved to the former's line and assumed the direction of that corps' attack on the Hornet's Nest. More precious hours were wasted by the Confederates as Prentiss bought time for the remnants of Grant's other units to regroup at Pittsburg Landing. Only when he was almost completely encircled did the dogged Prentiss surrender.[17]

Johnston did not live to enjoy this surrender. Shortly after 2 P.M., while he was urging Breckinridge's attack on, a musket ball had ripped the sole from one of Johnston's boots. Isham Harris, serving as a volunteer aide, anxiously inquired if Johnston were wounded. Johnston joked about the affair, and ordered Harris to convey a message to a nearby commander. As Harris rejoined the general, he noticed that Johnston was reeling in his saddle. When Johnston murmured that he feared he was seriously wounded, Harris immediately dispatched an aide to bring Dr. D. W. Yandell, Johnston's staff surgeon. Harris meanwhile guided Johnston's horse into a nearby glade, and eased the semi-conscious general to the ground. Frantically, Harris tore at Johnston's shirt in an attempt to find a wound. Soon Johnston's old friend Preston appeared and attempted to arouse the now unconscious Johnston. It was of no use. The Kentuckian had bled to death from a severed artery below the knee of his right leg. Some have speculated that he may not have noticed the wound because he suffered from recurrent numbness in the leg due to an old duel wound incurred while in the service of the Republic of Texas. Johnston's Confederate career, like his Texas career and many others, had ended in heartbreak.[18]

Beauregard received the news of Johnston's death shortly after 3 P.M. at his headquarters near Shiloh Church. Though hampered by a recurring throat ailment, he quickly moved to press the attack. Critics

[17] Johnston, *Life of Johnston*, 609–611; Williams, *Beauregard*, 138; Bragg's Report, Bragg Papers, Western Reserve.
[18] Roland, *Johnston*, 335–36, 338–39.

would later assert that Beauregard knew little of the battle's progress because he remained in the rear. Probably, however, he was one of the best informed men on the field. A stream of aides had continually supplied him with reports of the situation. When he took command, Beauregard knew that the remnants of the Union right and left were falling back toward the river landing, and that Prentiss' division was the last pocket of resistance. Hastily, Beauregard reorganized the command for a final assault on the Hornet's Nest. Ruggles was to push the attack on the center, and Bragg on the right.[19]

Later, Beauregard's critics would make much of a lull in the fighting which ensued on the far right flank after Johnston's death, and would blame him for the alleged one-hour respite. A recent writer has implied that when Bragg rode to the far right about 4 P.M., he did so because he believed Beauregard knew little of the situation, and that when Bragg arrived he discovered that Withers' and Cheatham's divisions were idle.[20] If there were such a delay, it could hardly be blamed on Beauregard. Had Bragg been in his assigned position sooner, the far right might have had better direction after Johnson's death. Exhaustion was another factor. Withers' division was so weary that Withers was forced to give them a rest. Also, some time was probably lost in reorganizing for the final push against Prentiss' line.[21]

After a hasty reorganization, the Rebel line again surged forward through the timber which surrounded Prentiss' bastion. About 5:30 P.M., Prentiss was finished. Amidst loud cheers from the Rebels, his men, some 2,200 strong, were marched to the rear. Then the weary Confederates wheeled towards Pittsburg Landing, where the remnants of Grant's force had formed a strong new line. A large number of guns had been collected on a steep ridge above the river landing. To reach the position, the Confederates had to plunge into a deep ravine and scale the ridge. Meanwhile, murderous artillery fire from the ridge and a flanking barrage from gunboats in the Tennessee raked the attackers. Until 6 P.M., isolated assaults were made by the weary Rebels, but all failed. Jackson's and Chalmers' men repeatedly stormed across the ravine, but were thrown back. Finally, as it was getting dark, Beauregard

19 Beauregard, "Campaign of Shiloh," 589–90; Johnston, "Albert Sidney Johnston at Shiloh," 567–68; Roman, *Beauregard Military Operations*, I, 297–98; *Official Records*, X, Pt. 1, p. 472; Williams, *Beauregard*, 140.

20 Grady McWhiney, "Braxton Bragg at Shiloh," *Tennessee Historical Quarterly*, XXI (March, 1962), 26.

21 Bragg's Report, Western Reserve; Roman, *Beauregard Military Operations*, I, 297–99.

sensed the disorganized condition of his army and ordered the attack halted for the night.[22]

Beauregard would later be severely criticized for halting the battle. Yet his real mistake, judging from the Army's condition, was not in merely halting the action but in not retreating to Corinth. The corps were completely disorganized. A combination of the rough terrain and the peculiar attack plan had taken a heavy toll. As early as 10 A.M., there were probably only two places on the line where two brigades of the same corps were contiguous. By late afternoon, the organization of a large number of brigades had melted away, and regiments had become separated from their commands. The brigades of A. P. Stewart, Bushrod Johnson, Patton Anderson, Pat Cleburne, and others had disintegrated.[23]

The Army was also disorganized by desertions and plundering. Just how many troops sulked in the rear, or halted to plunder the rich Yankee camps was not ascertained. Ironically, Confederate success in capturing enemy camps may have been the Army's undoing. As early as 8 A.M., soldiers had dropped out to feast on prepared breakfasts in Sherman's advance camps. By nightfall, whole brigades were in the rear, plundering the Yankee camps of clothing, jewelry, money, apples, butter, coffee, sugar, preserves, hams, and flour.[24]

Other factors contributed to the chaos. Because of the dense underbrush on the field and the lack of a standard color for Rebel uniforms, accidental firings upon fellow soldiers became common by late afternoon. The brigades of Pond and Russell were repulsed on separate occasions by

[22] Grant, "Battle of Shiloh," 474–75; *Official Records*, X, Pt. 1, pp. 534, 551, 555, 387. The Confederate attack had been almost a complete surprise. When the assault began at dawn, Grant left his headquarters at Savannah, Tennessee, and moved by boat upriver to Pittsburg Landing, pausing en route to order General Lew Wallace's division at Crump's Landing to hurry forward. After the first attack, Sherman was reinforced by General John A. McClernand's division, which also failed to stem the attack by the Confederate left wing. By 10 A.M. Prentiss had been reinforced by the divisions of Generals W. H. L. Wallace and S. A. Hurlbut; the bulk of Prentiss' division, together with the right wing of Hurlbut's division and the left wing of Wallace's division, comprised the defenders of the Hornet's Nest. By late afternoon, the remnants of Sherman's and McClernand's divisions, together with parts of Wallace's and Hurlbut's command, had fallen back to Pittsburg Landing. There, Colonel J. D. Webster had arranged a strong battery of reserve artillery. Hurlbut took position on the right of the battery, his line being extended westward by McClernand and Sherman. Wallace's division was so badly shattered that it did not take a place in the last line. See Grant, "Battle of Shiloh," 467–75.

[23] *Official Records*, X, Pt. 1, pp. 427–28, 444–45, 499; 581–82, 448, 454, 416–17; Bragg's Report, Western Reserve; Roman, *Beauregard Military Operations*, I, 305, 551, 305.

[24] Bragg's Report, Western Reserve; Hardee's Report, Chicago; Roman, *Beauregard Military Operations*, I, 551; James M. Merrill (ed.), " 'Nothing to Eat But Raw Bacon': Letters From a War Correspondent, 1862," *Tennessee Historical Quarterly*, XVII (June, 1958), 144.

other Rebel units. One hapless regiment in Wood's brigade moved to the charge only to be shot at from the rear by other Confederates. Several officers were wounded. A regiment in Hindman's brigade had a similar experience.[25]

Fatigue was a key factor in the Army's disorganization. By twilight on April 6, Beauregard's men were simply physically exhausted. Inexperienced troops had marched under the worst of conditions for three days, and then had fought a thirteen-hour battle. Some commands had not slept since April 4. Others were weak with hunger, as some outfits had run out of food by April 5. Although he later criticized Beauregard's halting the attack, even Bragg admitted that as early as the night of April 5 his corps was "hungry and destitute," [26] and that by nightfall of the sixth his men were greatly exhausted.[27]

After the war, the condition of the Army at twilight on the sixth would be ignored by Beauregard's critics. His most severe critic was Johnston's son, William Preston Johnston. In a biography of his father, he argued that when Beauregard halted the attack the Rebels were on the brink of victory. Johnston claimed that at 6 P.M. the Army was in good condition, there was an hour of daylight remaining, and the fire from the enemy gunboats was harmless. He especially relied upon statements furnished to him by Bragg some ten years after the war. In these statements, made long after friendly relations between Beauregard and Bragg had eroded, the latter managed to assume the post of a thwarted warrior who had violently protested Beauregard's order. He charged that another assault would have captured Grant's force, and that the gunboat fire was actually harmless to the men on the front lines because the shells passed over them to the rear.[28] Colonel S. H. Lockett came up with a postwar account of how Bragg, when he received Beauregard's order, threatened to disobey the order and cried, "My God, was a victory ever sufficiently complete?" [29]

Yet Bragg had two versions of the story. When he wrote his wife on April 8, 1862, he stated that as the Army approached the river landing, it came under a heavy fire from the gunboats. Bragg described the Confederates as "disorganized, demoralized, and exhausted." [30] Bragg also

---

25 *Official Records*, X, Pt. 1, pp. 423, 417, 517–18, 521, 583, 489, 616, 526, 598.

26 Bragg's Report, Western Reserve.

27 *Ibid*. See also Hardee's Report, Chicago; Johnston, *Life of Johnston*, 567–68.

28 Johnston, "Albert Sidney Johnston at Shiloh," 567; Johnston, *Life of Johnston*, 633; Bragg to W. P. Johnston, December 16, 1874, in Barret Collection, Tulane.

29 Lockett, "Surprise and Withdrawal at Shiloh," 605.

30 Bragg to his wife, April 8, 1862, in William K. Bixby Collection of Braxton Bragg Papers, Missouri Historical Society, St. Louis, hereinafter cited as Bragg Papers, Missouri.

admitted to his wife that on the night of April 6 he was confident that Grant would be beaten the following morning. On April 30, in his official report, Bragg added that by sunset the Army was hungry and exhausted, and that commanders found it impossible to regroup their troops on the night of April 6. [31] There is even some contradictory evidence on Bragg's alleged shock at the news of Beauregard's order. Captain Clifton Smith, a Beauregard aide who bore the order to Bragg, later stated that Bragg took the news without a comment. Bragg's medical director, Dr. J. C. Nott, stated that he also heard Bragg raise no protests after he received the order. When Bragg rode to Beauregard's headquarters after dark, a witness to the meeting, Colonel Jacob Thompson, later reported that the conversation centered on the exhaustion of the troops, the large number of stragglers, and other problems.[32]

Johnston also quoted excerpts from battle reports of other officers in his indictment of Beauregard. He quoted a portion of Hardee's battle report which stated that Beauregard halted the attack when the Rebel advance was within a few hundred yards of a confused and demoralized enemy. Yet Johnston omitted that section of Hardee's report which described the Army at 6 P.M. as being exhausted, hungry, and "scattered and disordered." [33] Polk's report was also quoted to the effect that an hour of daylight remained, and nothing prevented a victory save Beauregard's order. Yet on April 10, 1862, Polk wrote his wife that the victory would have been complete if only they had had another hour of daylight. Some of Polk's own subordinates refuted the bishop's claim that both time and fresh men remained for a victory.[34]

Despite the clamor of Beauregard's critics, it is evident that the Army did fight until nightfall. Withers' division, closest to the river, repeatedly charged the steep bluffs, only to be pounded repeatedly by artillery and gunboat fire. Withers fought until darkness and fatigue compelled a halt. In fact, Jackson's brigade, having exhausted its ammunition, fought most of this last action with only bayonets as weapons. Beauregard's accusers have also charged that other units, released for service when Prentiss surrendered, were en route to the river landing when the battle was halted. Actually, most division and brigade commanders, including Ruggles, Cheatham, Stewart, Cleburne, Anderson, and others, and a large number of regimental commanders as well, reported a different situation in their battle accounts. These units were moving to aid Withers, but

31 Bragg's Report, Western Reserve.
32 Roman, *Beauregard Military Operations*, I, 538, 535; Jacob Thompson to A. T. Beauregard, April 17, 1863, in P. G. T. Beauregard Papers, National Archives.
33 Hardee's Report, Chicago.
34 Polk, *Leonidas Polk, Bishop and General*, II, 115; *Official Records*, X, Pt. 1, 410.

were halted for a variety of reasons, which included darkness, exhaustion, ammunition shortages, and a fierce barrage from the gunboats.[35]

Actually, Beauregard's order came not a moment too soon, for by nightfall the Army was rapidly melting away. Some commands slept on the field without trying to find their brigades or divisions. Other units stumbled to the rear in the rainy, murky night, and groped for the remainder of their commands. Some brigades found they had gone too far in advance of the remainder of the Army. Other units, such as Anderson's brigade, became badly separated while attempting to rejoin their division. The brigades of Withers' division became lost from one another. Cheatham's entire division appeared to vanish from the field. Polk had marched it back to Hardee's old encampment of the night of April 5. Many regiments and brigades went back to the rear and conducted frenzied searches of the Yankee camps for plunder. Bragg's chief aide, Colonel Urquhart, complained to Bragg that over a third of the Army was engaged in such looting.[36]

Frantic staff officers rode through the darkness in futile efforts to reorganize the Army. A terrible wind, thunderstorm, and rain descended upon the miserable troops. A continual barrage through the night by the Yankee gunboats also increased confusion. Matters were so disorganized that the high command was not exactly sure where the Army was on the night of April 6. Hasty revisions which were made in the command system indicated the extent of the turmoil. Hardee, formerly commanding on the far left, was now assigned to the far right. Bragg was moved from the right to the left, and Breckinridge from the right to the far left flank.[37]

If Beauregard is to be criticized, it should be for his overconfidence. When he halted the attack, he believed that either Grant could easily be defeated on the following morning or else the Federals would retreat across the Tennessee River. That night Beauregard telegraphed Richmond that the Confederates had gained "a complete victory, driving the enemy from every position." [38] He was not alone in his confidence. Bragg wrote his wife that on the night of the sixth the high command was confident of a Union rout the next morning, provided the Yankees did not escape across the river. One soldier in Russell's brigade observed

[35] Official Records, X, Pt. 1, pp. 532, 550–51, 555, 472, 440, 428, 582, 499, 577–78, 586, 599, 601, 616, 603, 559, 522, 509, 538, 546.

[36] Roman, Beauregard Military Operations, I, 551, 313; Official Records, X, Pt. 1, pp. 534, 448, 493, 499, 506, 428; Bragg's Report, Western Reserve.

[37] Merrill, "Nothing to Eat But Raw Bacon," 145; Beauregard, "Campaign of Shiloh," 591.

[38] Official Records, X, Pt. 1, p. 384.

that "every officer and soldier went to sleep serenaded by the guns from the river, and thought that the battle was won, that the victory was ours. . . ." [39]

Part of this feeling of confidence was based upon the information, or lack of it, which the Rebel command had of the whereabouts of Buell's army. Exactly what Beauregard knew and believed of Buell's location is difficult to describe because of contradictory evidence. Prior to leaving Corinth, the Confederates had information from scouts that Buell's army was pushing through the Duck River country south of Nashville, en route to join Grant. On April 5, the fear that Buell would reach Grant before the Confederates could reach Pittsburg Landing was a factor in Beauregard's proposal that the Army retreat to Corinth. Beauregard later wrote that Johnston assured him that Buell could not possibly join Grant before the night of April 7 or the morning of the eighth. [40]

On the afternoon of April 6, Jordan was handed a dispatch relayed from Corinth, addressed to Johnston. The dispatch, sent from Colonel Ben Hardin Helm in northern Alabama, reported that Buell was not moving to join Grant, but was pushing instead towards Decatur. That evening, after the attack had already ceased, Jordan handed Beauregard the dispatch. In his report of the battle, Beauregard indicated that at some hour on the sixth he received a second note, stating that Buell was moving to join Grant but would not arrive in time to aid Grant the following day. Prentiss, who shared a tent with some of his captors on the night of the sixth, foolishly boasted to Jordan and Thompson that their information was incorrect, and that Buell would arrive that night. Jordan even showed Prentiss the dispatch from Helm, but Prentiss again foolishly insisted that it was a mistake. [41]

Later, when Prentiss was proved to be correct, Beauregard changed his story. In 1862, when an article in a Savannah newspaper implied that Beauregard had been fooled as to Buell's whereabouts, Beauregard immediately began to assert that he knew all along that Buell's army and General Lew Wallace's division were reinforcing Grant on the night of the sixth. Beauregard's close friend Jordan wrote a fiery reply to the article in which he argued that Beauregard knew from prisoners and scouts interviewed on April 6 that Buell's arrival was expected. [42]

[39] "Reminiscences of Thomas Firth, Thirteenth Tennessee Infantry" (MS in Confederate Collection, Tennessee Archives).
[40] "Claiborne Sketch," UNC; Beauregard, "Campaign of Shiloh," 583; Beauregard to Thomas Jordan, August 8, 1862, in P. G. T. Beauregard Papers, Library of Congress.
[41] Jordan, "Shiloh Notes," 602–603; Official Records, X, Pt. 1, p. 387.
[42] Thomas Jordan, "The Lost Opportunity at Shiloh" (MS in Claiborne Papers, UNC).

On July 17, 1862, Beauregard wrote Jordan that he had halted the battle because he "expected the next morning to have to fight the fresh troops of Buell & Wallace which he had every reason to believe would reach the field of battle during the night. . . . "[43] In August, 1862, angered by other printed accounts which implied he had been misled as to Buell's arrival, Beauregard reiterated his earlier claim that his knowledge of the presence of Buell and Wallace motivated his decision to halt the battle. In this letter he admitted, however, that his recollections were "not however very distinct—for I was so unwell up to the time of assuming command, after the fall of Johnston, that my memory may betray me in certain particulars."[44]

Probably these later denials by Beauregard were merely an attempt by that somewhat vain officer to save face, and not to appear as though he had been misled as to Buell's presence. The evidence appears that Beauregard at least expected that Buell could not arrive in time to aid Grant on the seventh, and that this sentiment was shared by others in the high command. On the night of April 6, Colonel Jacob Thompson reportedly heard Beauregard remark that if Buell's army did not arrive during the night, the Confederates would surely capture Wallace's division on the next day.[45]

One such officer who appeared confident was Hardee. During the midnight hours of the sixth, the ever watchful cavalryman Bedford Forrest dispatched scouts dressed in blue overcoats to the river landing. The troopers returned and reported that heavy reinforcements were being unloaded at the landing. Forrest sought out Hardee with the news, but the disinterested general merely told him to go find Beauregard and tell him. Unable to find Beauregard in the darkness, Forrest again sent out scouts. They returned about 2 A.M. and again reported that steamboats were bringing reinforcements. Again Forrest went to Hardee. Instead of making any attempt to reach Beauregard, Hardee merely told the fretting officer to return to his command, keep a vigilant watch, and report all movements. For a general who later claimed that Beauregard had halted the attack when confronted only by a huddled mass of Federals, Hardee did not appear too concerned by Forrest's report.[46]

The master plan conceived at Corinth fell through on April 7. Unexpectedly, the Federals launched a vicious counterattack at dawn against the unready Confederates. The first blow struck Forrest, who

[43] Beauregard to Jordan, July 17, 1862, in Beauregard Papers, Library of Congress.
[44] Beauregard to Jordan, August 8, 1862, in *ibid.*
[45] Jacob Thompson to A. T. Beauregard, April 17, 1863, in Beauregard Papers, National Archives.
[46] Jordan and Pryor, *Forrest,* 135–37.

guarded Hardee's flank on the far right. Fresh Union troops threw back Forrest and smashed into Jackson and Chalmers. Bragg on the left and Breckinridge in the center were also soon under attack. Repeatedly the Federals slashed at the thin lines and gradually forced the Confederates back across the old battleground.

The Rebel left center was especially hard pressed. The absence of Cheatham's division, which Polk had marched to the rear on the previous night, created a gap in the line. By 10 A.M. the Federals were threatening to sever Beauregard's army in half. When the Federals first attacked, Beauregard had not even known where Polk and Cheatham were. He learned that the missing division was in the rear, and a courier was rushed to bring Polk. About 10:30 A.M. Beauregard was relieved to see Cheatham's men hurrying forward to stem the assault in the center.[47]

The check was only temporary. About 1 P.M. the Federals launched a new attack against Bragg's wing. By two o'clock the blue line had swept past the Hornet's Nest. Bragg was shoved back towards Shiloh Church and the Federals were threatening to seize the Corinth–Pittsburg road.

By early afternoon Beauregard knew the battle was lost. He could hardly muster twenty thousand men against the mass of fresh Union reserves. The severity of the attack had convinced him that Buell was here, as well as Wallace's division. Beauregard had no reserves. He had held a faint hope that he might be reinforced in time by Van Dorn's troops from Arkansas. Ironically, even after his death Albert Sidney Johnston cast a shadow of command weakness across the Army. Although Van Dorn's twenty thousand Arkansans had been under Johnston's supervision, Johnston had been slow to order Van Dorn to cross the Mississippi. Armed with his own dreams of glory, Van Dorn had refused all suggestions that he reinforce Johnston, and eventually was defeated on March 6 at the battle of Elkhorn Tavern. Only after Johnston arrived at Corinth and conferred with Beauregard did he take decisive action and order Van Dorn to join him. Unmindful that Van Dorn was experiencing transportation delays, Beauregard expected him daily at Corinth, and on April 7 dispatched couriers to hasten him to the field. By the afternoon of the seventh, messengers from Corinth indicated to Van Dorn that Beauregard's hopes were shattered. Van Dorn had not yet even arrived at Corinth.[48]

Faced with the danger of losing his entire force, Beauregard hastily conferred with his confidant, Colonel Jordan. Jordan had already spoken

[47] Roman, *Beauregard Military Operations,* I, 308–13.
[48] Roland, *Johnston,* 309–11; Roman, *Beauregard Military Operations,* I, 319–20; Bragg's Report, Western Reserve; Hardee's Report, Chicago.

with Governor Harris and both had agreed on the need for a retreat.
Jordan warned Beauregard that the Army was rapidly melting away. The
latter agreed, and orders went out for a retreat. Jordan gathered scattered
commands and formed a rearguard line near Shiloh Church. By 4 P.M.
the last of the Army was on the road to Corinth. Blinded by a cold rain,
sleet, and hail, the miserable column stretched eight miles over the muddy roads. Breckinridge's corps hovered at Mickey's for a few days, but
there was only token pursuit by Grant, who probably was grateful enough
to win the battle.[49]

More than a battle was lost. Beginning with the retreat to Corinth,
Beauregard's influence began to decline, and the Army of Tennessee again
suffered the pangs of command confusion. Since his arrival in the West,
he had preached a dual strategy—concentrate for a lightning offensive
and give priority to Mississippi Valley defense. Yet both ideas failed.
When the concentration scheme failed at Shiloh, an undaunted Beauregard drew back to Corinth and talked of another offensive. General
Henry W. Halleck, who assumed command of the combined Federal
armies at Pittsburg Landing, steadily inched his way toward Corinth
during April and May. Beauregard sent calls for aid to Richmond and
neighboring departments. He also urged the dawdling Van Dorn to hurry
his force to Corinth, luring him with promises of another offensive.[50]

But Van Dorn's arrival during the second week in April proved a disappointment. Though the blustery Van Dorn arrived boasting that he
felt like a wolf, he brought only fourteen thousand badly armed men.
Beauregard's combined force now numbered scarcely fifty thousand men,
while intelligence placed the Federals somewhere between eighty-five
thousand and a hundred thousand strong. Still, Beauregard clung to his
offensive hopes during April. He placed Polk's, Hardee's, and Bragg's

---

[49] Jordan, "Shiloh Notes," 603. Don Carlos Buell's army had left Columbia, Tennessee, on the evening of April 3, and had arrived at Savannah on the evening of the
fifth. On April 6, after hearing the noise of the battle, Buell went to Grant's headquarters where he received orders to march General William Nelson's division to the
bank opposite Pittsburg Landing and to ferry it across. General Thomas L. Crittenden's division would come by steamboat from Savannah to the landing. By 5 P.M. the
advance of Nelson's column had reached the landing and participated in the repulse
of Beauregard's last attack. By 9 A.M., Nelson's entire division was across; Crittenden's
division was in position by 5 A.M. the next day. General Alexander McCook's division
arrived at Pittsburg Landing at 5 A.M. on the eighth. Buell's other two divisions did
not reach the field in time for the battle. Buell's total reinforcement consisted of some
20,000 men. General Lew Wallace's division, some 5,000 strong, was delayed by a
confusion over routes of march, and did not reach the field until 1 A.M. of April 7.
Grant's total loss at Shiloh was reported as 13,047. See "The Opposing Forces at Shiloh,"
Battles and Leaders, I, 539–40; *Official Records*, X, Pt. 1, pp. 291–93, 354–55, 323–24,
303, 170.

[50] *Official Records*, X, Pt. 2, pp. 403, 405, 407, 414.

corps in a semicircular line three miles north of Corinth. Van Dorn guarded the east flank, while Breckinridge's corps was held in reserve. Beauregard sensed Halleck's strength and feared the Confederates might easily be flanked out of Corinth. His plan was to wait on the defensive until Halleck extended an exposed tentacle of his force toward Corinth. Then the Confederates would concentrate and strike.

Twice in May, Beauregard saw his opportunity when Halleck extended a division toward Farmington, four miles east of Corinth. Both times the Rebels mobilized, with essentially the same plan each time. While Bragg attacked from the front, Van Dorn would strike on the flank. Both times Van Dorn was slow to move, and the Federals escaped.[51]

These failures, combined with the tedium of awaiting Halleck's approach, grated on Beauregard's nerves. Almost daily, reports warned that a Federal attack was imminent somewhere on the line. Federals were reported to the north, to the southeast, and even in Beauregard's rear at Tupelo. The Tupelo reports especially worried the general, for he feared that Halleck would outflank Corinth on the west and seize the Mobile and Ohio south of the town. Even while Van Dorn was stalking the Federals at Farmington on May 9, Beauregard urged his commanders to hurry back into position lest Halleck try a flank move.

By late May, Beauregard was totally discouraged with his offensive prospects. Halleck loomed agonizingly close, halting each night to dig entrenchments. Every attempt to trap the Yankees had produced only wasted logistics, due to the constant marching and countermarching. Worse, Beauregard knew that Halleck had an accurate picture of Confederate strength. Halleck's spies had intercepted a Beauregard telegram to Richmond which listed Rebel strength at fifty thousand men. To Beauregard's chagrin, the note was printed in the New York *Herald* and was read by Beauregard's old enemies in Richmond.[52]

On May 25, Beauregard called a council of his corps leaders to discuss the situation. He had already admitted as early as May 9 that an offensive was now impossible. Halleck was closing in too tightly to allow any more attacks against isolated Federal positions. Yet Beauregard sought the assurances of his commanders. The council discussed the alternatives. To attack Halleck's entrenchments would be suicidal. To remain in Corinth and withstand a siege would be hazardous. Unsanitary conditions had already put at least twenty thousand men on the sick list. Water was scarce, and many men were forced to drink out of pools so

51 Roman, *Beauregard Military Operations*, I, 382, 386–87; *Official Records*, X, Pt. 2, pp. 403, 423, 440, 463, 465, 487, 516–17, 524, 538.

52 Roman, *Beauregard Military Operations*, I, 386–88; *Official Records*, X, Pt. 2, pp. 436, 463, 440, 487, 498, 562–63, 506–507, 516–17, 520, 552, 540.

contaminated that they held their noses when they drank. Halleck could easily flank the town, or could bring up his artillery and pound the defenses. Once a bombardment began, a retreat would be almost impossible. The only alternative was to abandon Corinth now. The corps commanders agreed, and Beauregard issued orders that night for the retreat. He felt the best line of retreat was south toward Baldwyn, along the Mobile and Ohio. Evidently Beauregard planned to form a defensive line at Baldwyn if good water and terrain permitted.

On May 30 the Army began slipping out of Corinth. The retreat was a masterpiece of trickery. To prevent Halleck from attacking while he retreated, Beauregard employed a series of ruses which left the impression that Corinth was being strengthened. Empty trains were run to the front lines, and designated bands of soldiers cheered each as if it held reinforcements. A regimental band wandered along the front lines playing to empty camps, and wooden "Quaker" guns bristled from the works. "Deserters" were sent to Halleck's camp with information of great Rebel strength. The ruse was so effective that the entire force had left Corinth before Halleck discovered the trick.[53]

South of Corinth, Beauregard's hopes of reviving his offensive plans flickered and died. Twice before he reached Baldwyn, at the Tuscumbia River and near Rienzi, he halted to give battle if pursued. There was no pursuit save by scattered cavalry forces. Harassed by Yankee troopers and short of water, the Army trudged through Baldwyn and formed a line on the south bank of Twenty Mile Creek. Again Beauregard's hopes were foiled. The barren country around Baldwyn also suffered from drought. Scouts reported Yankee cavalry to the south near Saltillo. Beauregard hoped a line could be formed at Saltillo, but again found poor water. More encouraging reports came from Tupelo, fifty-two miles south of Corinth. Though a move to Tupelo would take Beauregard probably much farther into Mississippi than intended, the position was a good one. Good water was bountiful, and a strong line could be formed on a range of sandy ridges fronted by Tupelo swamp. By June 9 the Army held the new line, and Beauregard awaited enemy developments.[54]

A defensive line at Tupelo seemed a long retreat from the Napoleonic plans Beauregard devised for Shiloh. The limitations of the offensive strategy had been demonstrated. Concentrated strikes at a superior force demanded a well-equipped and well-trained army, and a coordinated

53 *Official Records*, X, Pt. 2, pp. 545, 552–53, 555–58, 560; Roman, *Beauregard Military Operations*, I, 383–84, 389–92.

54 George Thompson Blakemore Diary (MS in Confederate Collection, Tennessee Archives), June 2, 1862; *Official Records*, X, Pt. 1, pp. 668–69, 861–66, 868–70, Pt. 2, pp. 556, 569–70, 574–76, 581, 586–88, 604; Roman, *Beauregard Military Operations*, I, 390–91.

high command. The Shiloh force had neither. The complex marching and battle orders were probably too involved for the hastily assembled force. The high command at Shiloh had never worked together before. At Corinth, Beauregard was new as commander, and men like the unsteady Van Dorn and the stubborn Polk could hardly be called a well-integrated command.

Beauregard's strategy of defending the Mississippi Valley had also failed. He had talked of little else since coming to the West. He had persuaded Johnston to leave the Heartland, and had even suggested that Charleston and Savannah might be given up to save the valley. At Tupelo, his plan seemed a failure on the map. His new line rested some 160 miles south of the Columbus line. The entire Mississippi Valley in Tennessee and a large portion in Mississippi was in Yankee hands. Since Shiloh, Beauregard had lost almost 15,000 square miles of territory.

Much of this lost area was in northern Alabama. Like Johnston, Beauregard had not provided for the area's defense. On April 10, a mere 150 Union cavalry seized Huntsville, cut the Memphis and Charleston Railroad, and captured fifteen locomotives and vast rolling stock. Within a week, the Federals held the railroad from near Chattanooga to the Mississippi line. Two new supply lines were open to the Federals from Nashville to Chattanooga—the Nashville and Decatur, and Nashville and Chattanooga Railroads.

At Corinth, Beauregard made no gesture to drive the Federals from northern Alabama and recover the railroad. In May he admitted that if Corinth fell, the Federals would have the long desired communication link from Paducah to Chattanooga. Though he felt as early as April 9 that Corinth might eventually be lost, Beauregard did nothing to protect northern Alabama. He felt that a retreat along the Mobile and Ohio would protect the munitions area of central and southern Alabama. Yet holding the Mobile and Ohio did not help northern Alabama, and did not guarantee the Federals would not move overland from the Memphis and Charleston Railroad on central Alabama.[55]

Had Beauregard been able to hold the Mississippi Valley, the Heartland losses would have been more forgettable. But he lost both areas. Even before he reached Tupelo, the chain of Mississippi River forts had been swept away, and the river was open almost all the way to New Orleans. On March 13, New Madrid was abandoned by a Beauregard appointee, General John P. McCown. Then Island Number Ten, the strongest fort on the river, was surrendered by General W. W. Mackall.

[55] *Official Records*, X, Pt. 1, pp. 641–45, 653–60, 867–70, Pt. 2, pp. 416–17, 420, 429–31, 441–42, 581.

Mackall, who boasted that he was a general made by Beauregard, surrendered seven thousand men on April 7. On June 1, Fort Pillow, the
next defensive link, was abandoned by another Beauregard appointee,
General John B. Villepigue. Five days later Memphis fell after Fort Randolph was abandoned and the Rebel fleet destroyed. Five key positions
had been surrendered or abandoned—all by Beauregard's lieutenants.[56]

More than Beauregard's strategy had failed. By early June his prestige
with the public and the government had dimmed. The populace hooted
at his attempts to paint Shiloh as a victory. Though he boasted of a
complete victory, the public was unconvinced. Rumor circulated that
the general had been insane at Shiloh, hiding in his tent or clutching
a pet bird. His strongest area of support had been the old Mississippi
River bloc, but much of that group was now under Yankee rule.[57]

The retreat to Tupelo also provoked an ugly quarrel between the
general and Richmond which further injured the Army's command structure. The trouble was caused by the old specters of personality conflict
and poor communication in the high command. Davis and Beauregard
had not been on speaking terms since First Manassas. Some felt that
Davis had duped Beauregard into accepting a sub-command in the West
to be rid of him in Virginia. Now Johnston was dead. By default, Beauregard, an avowed member of the anti-Davis faction in the Army and Congress, commanded the second most powerful Confederate army.

Had Beauregard tried to maintain good relations with Richmond, the
old differences might have been laid aside. Instead, from Shiloh to Tupelo, the general infuriated Davis by refusing to divulge his plans and by
sending contradictory reports when he did communicate. The result was
that Richmond received a false impression that affairs were going well in
Mississippi, an impression which was to be shaken by Beauregard's retreat to Tupelo.

The first misunderstanding arose over the outcome of Shiloh. When
Beauregard reported on April 6 that a total victory had been won, a
jubilant Davis reported the news to Congress on April 8. Congress
promptly gave the Army a vote of thanks for a brilliant victory. Davis
and the Congress did not know the Army had been defeated on April 7.
Beauregard did not report this until April 11. Even then, he played
down the disasters of the seventh, still spoke of Shiloh as a victory, and
even boasted that Halleck's army was so badly defeated and crippled that

56 Beauregard to Johnston, February 26, 1862, in Barret Collection, Tulane; Beauregard to McCown, March 10, 1862, in Beauregard Papers, Duke; Roman, *Beauregard
Military Operations*, I, 552–65, 352–75.
57 *Official Records*, X, Pt. 2, pp. 405, 407; Williams, *Beauregard*, 148.

it could not move on Corinth. In late May, both Davis and Lee still spoke of a Shiloh victory.[58]

But Beauregard's reports soon changed in tone. As early as April 9 he reported that Halleck, supposedly pulverized, was moving in great strength on Corinth. Throughout late April and May he corresponded with Richmond on several matters, but did not explain what he planned to do at Corinth. On May 19 he sent the government a confusing note filled with reasons why Corinth should be held. Yet the letter ended with a long argument for the use of the Mobile and Ohio Railroad as a line of retreat should the town be abandoned. On May 26 the government replied through Robert E. Lee. Lee approved the Mobile and Ohio Railroad as a possible line of retreat, but hoped a retreat would not be needed. He reminded Beauregard that the government had expected him to move north after the Shiloh victory.

Hence Davis and his advisers were probably shocked and angered by the crisp telegram Beauregard sent on May 28. In his first dispatch on the subject since the nineteenth, he simply announced that he was abandoning Corinth for reasons to be explained later.

Six days passed before Beauregard again reported to Richmond. Again he gave no reasons for the evacuation, and offered no hint of his destination. On June 12, Adjutant General Cooper wired Beauregard that Davis wanted an explanation for the retreat. Beauregard, almost as if deliberately provoking Davis, replied that there had been no time for a report, but that he would write soon. The next day he drafted his report. But it was too late—Davis had begun to move against him. Davis' chance came when he learned that Beauregard was in bad health. Governor F. W. Pickens of South Carolina wanted Bragg as commander of coastal defenses. Beauregard objected to Davis that his health would not allow Bragg to be spared. Armed with this news, Davis suggested to Pickens that he invite Beauregard to leave the West and restore his health commanding in the ocean climate. Beauregard refused the post, and said he was needed at Tupelo.[59]

By June 13, Davis seemed determined to be rid of Beauregard. He confided to his wife that Beauregard had been placed too high for his mental capabilities. On June 14, Davis sent Colonel William Preston Johnston to Tupelo. Johnston was to report on the Army's condition

[58] *Official Records*, X, Pt. 1, pp. 384–92, Pt. 2, pp. 405, 407, 414, 546, 529–30; Rowland (ed.), *Davis*, V, 249; James D. Richardson (ed.), *A Compilation of the Messages and Papers of the Confederacy, Including the Diplomatic Correspondence, 1861–1865* (Nashville, 1905), I, 208, 231.

[59]*Official Records*, X, Pt. 2, pp. 403, 529–30, 546, Roman, *Beauregard Military Operations*, I, 395–96, 591; Rowland (ed.), *Davis*, V, 274–75.

This contemporary drawing from *Harper's Weekly*, captioned "A Thrilling Scene in East Tennessee," shows Union sympathizers swearing allegiance to the United States flag at the outbreak of the Civil War.

On these two pages are pictured the men who commanded the Army of Tennessee during the first two years of the war. Top left is Isham Harris, who built the nucleus of the force while governor. General Leonidas Polk, top right, commanded the Mississippi River defenses of the Second Department. He was succeeded by General Albert Sidney Johnston, bottom left, who assumed control of the Army in September, 1861.

The Louisiana General P. G. T. Beauregard, shown at top left, took command of the Army of Tennessee at Johnston's death. Top right is Beauregard's successor, General Braxton Bragg, who led the invasion of Kentucky in the fall of 1862. Another major figure in the invasion was General Edmund Kirby Smith, bottom right, who commanded the District of East Tennessee in 1862.

A view of Nashville, Tennessee, during the Civil War. *Courtesy Tennessee State Library*

The Nashville and Chattanooga Railroad depot in Nashville, where many of the Army of Tennessee's food and munitions supplies were stored. A United States Army Signal Corps photograph. *Courtesy Tennessee State Library*

Union troops under U. S. Grant attack the Confederate position at Fort Donelson on the Cumberland River. *Harper's Weekly*

Bragg's Kentucky campaign came to a close with the defeat of his Confederate forces October 8, 1862, at the battle of Perryville, shown here in a drawing from *Harper's*.

Rebel soldiers charge through Union defenses near the Green River fortifications September 14, 1862, during the battle of Munfordville, Kentucky. *Leslies Illustrated Newspaper*

THE ATTACK ON FORT HENRY.

This contemporary sketch from *Harper's Weekly* depicts the capture of Fort Henry on the lower Tennessee River by Federal gunboats February 6, 1862.

A single sentinel guards the East Tennessee and Virginia Railroad bridge at Strawberry Plains, Tennessee. This bridge spanning the Holston River was repeatedly attacked by Unionists in the fall of 1861.

and was to obtain answers from Beauregard to a list of prepared questions which Davis sent along. The irritating questions ranged in topic from what measures were used to defend the Mississippi after Island Number Ten fell, to what were the reasons for evacuating Corinth.

That same day Davis bypassed Beauregard and wired Bragg. Bragg was ordered to go to Jackson, Mississippi, and temporarily assume command of General Mansfield Lovell's department. Since he had known by June 12 that Beauregard wanted Bragg to stay at Tupelo, Davis may have been provoking a fight. Whether provoked or not, a dispute ensued. By chance, Davis' note arrived the same day that Beauregard was making arrangements to leave Bragg in command while he took a sick leave. Hampered by a nasty throat infection, Beauregard secured a certificate of disability from his doctors. Bragg relayed Davis' note to Beauregard and innocently asked for the proper orders so that he could leave for Jackson. Instead, Beauregard refused to allow him to go. He explained to Bragg that he planned to leave on June 15 for Bladen Springs, Alabama, to recuperate, and would leave Bragg in charge.

Again Beauregard failed to keep Richmond informed. On June 14 he telegraphed General Samuel Cooper that he was leaving Bragg in command while he took a sick leave. He did not request permission for the leave, nor did he say where he was going or how long he would stay. When Beauregard did not receive a reply, he sent an explanation of his actions to Cooper on June 15. Instead of sending the explanation by wire, however, he chose to write a letter. He told Cooper his destination, and said he would be there a week or ten days, or long enough to restore his health. Still Beauregard did not ask permission to leave, and did not even await Cooper's answer. On June 17 he left for Bladen Springs.

By his aloof manner, the general had played into Davis' hands. His June 14 telegram to Cooper evidently reached Richmond on the fifteenth, and Cooper probably could have halted the trip if he had tried. Davis may have not known of Beauregard's intentions until June 18, but with a little effort could have intercepted the general at Mobile. Evidently the government stood by and let Beauregard leave, perhaps so he could be snared in the technicality of leaving his post without permission. Whether intended or not, the device succeeded. On June 19 Davis wired Bragg for an explanation of why he had not gone to Jackson. Bragg honestly replied that Beauregard was gone, leaving him in command. The next day, Davis removed Beauregard as department commander and appointed Bragg to the post. The president's explanation was that Beauregard had left his post without authorization.

Davis may have simply grasped at the first available means to oust his old enemy, for he did not even wait until Johnston filed his report. Beauregard did not see the list of questions until June 20, and did not file an answer until June 22. He gave Johnston detailed replies to the questions. Johnston praised the general's cooperation in answering the questions, and pronounced the Army in good shape. On July 15, Johnston filed his report—twenty-five days after Beauregard's removal.[60]

Beauregard's influence on the Army had been a mixed blessing. He had provided organizational talents which Albert Sidney Johnston lacked, and had welded the Army into more compact divisions and corps. Beauregard had been more successful than Johnston in stating the Army's case to the rest of the Confederacy. The public and the government had been roused to his pleas for aid, though Johnston had had little success in his efforts. Yet there was too fine a line between Beauregard's duties in the West and his desire to restore his standing in Richmond. His dreams of glory led him to propose grand invasion schemes which were unrealistic. He advocated a concentration, but once concentrated, the high command never seemed to attain cohesion. His complex preparations for Shiloh were too idealistic for the disorganized Corinth force.

When he left the Army, the old dual problem remained—lack of *esprit* for the leaders, and conflict within the high command. The Army still lacked a corps *esprit* and devotion to a commander-in-chief. The rapid turnover among the high command had frustrated these, and also had prevented coordination between the commander and corps leaders so vital for Beauregard's complex plans. In fact, Beauregard had added to the command problem by his break with Richmond. For the first time a quarrel had developed between Richmond and a commander of the Army of Tennessee. For the first time a commander of the Army had been removed. The personal element involved in Beauregard's removal was to have its own effect. Davis had replaced an old enemy, Beauregard, with an old friend, Bragg. Now Davis' prestige would be challenged in any dispute over Bragg's generalship. A censure of Bragg would be a censure of Davis as well. Beauregard's once cordial relations with Bragg would now be strained, and after the war there would be deep resentment between the two officers.

[60] Roman, *Beauregard Military Operations*, I, 396–99, 403–11; "Answers to Interrogatories Contained in a Letter of Instructions from President Davis to Colonel W. P. Johnston" (MS in Claiborne Papers, UNC); Bragg to William Browne, February 19, 1872, Davis to Bragg, June 14, 1862, Beauregard to Bragg, June 14, 1862, R. L. Brodie and Sam Choppin to Beauregard, June 14, 1862, all in Bragg Papers, Western Reserve; Rowland (ed.), *Davis*, V, 277.

The bitterness of the removal continued throughout the summer. Beauregard spent the rest of the summer in Alabama fanning any available flames of resentment against Davis. He corresponded with sympathizers in and out of the Army. His chief apostle in the Army, Colonel Thomas Jordan, busied himself composing articles in the general's defense. Beauregard utilized anti-Davis newspapers to plead his case. The newspapers in turn used Beauregard's misfortune as another excuse to slap at Davis.

Still hoping to retain a command somewhere in the West, Beauregard wrote Bragg several long letters during the summer. In true Beauregard style, he advised grand offensive plans in Tennessee, Kentucky, and Ohio. There is no doubt that Bragg appreciated the suggestions, for he had solicited Beauregard's advice in a letter of July 14. But Beauregard's influence had waned. Even before his reply to Bragg's letter reached Tupelo, Bragg had left. He was en route with the Army to Chattanooga, for a unique rendezvous with a young general named Edmund Kirby Smith.[61]

[61] Beauregard to Bragg, July 28, 1862, in Buell Papers, Rice; Beauregard to Bragg, September 2, 1862, in Bragg Papers, Western Reserve; Beauregard to Jordan, July 13, 1862, in Beauregard Papers, Duke; Roman, *Beauregard Military Operations*, I, 411–19.

PART V

the bragg–kirby smith influence

ten

"All Well in Dixie"

EDMUND KIRBY SMITH NEEDED A REST. ILL FROM TYPHOID FEVER AND WORRIED about his wife's first pregnancy, the young major general retired to Montvale Springs, Tennessee, in July of 1862 to ponder his unhappy situation. In February he had been called from enjoying his laurels won at First Manassas to head the difficult Department of East Tennessee, where his troubles began immediately. The department was an offspring of the old Western or Second Department commanded by Albert Sidney Johnston and Confederate departmental command theory. Jefferson Davis and his advisers believed that the more departments there were in existence, the more attention could be given to local problems—and East Tennessee was full of problems. So Kirby Smith was sent to Tennessee, in hopes that his presence there would counteract the strong Unionist element operating in the territory between the Tennessee River and the Appalachian Mountains.[1]

But everything went wrong. When he arrived he had some difficulty finding his department. In fact, he did not know whether his was to be another department or a district of the Second Department, and was surprised when the latter department's Adjutant General referred to Kirby Smith's command as separate. Kirby Smith had understood his assignment to be the District of East Tennessee in Johnston's department and now wrote Richmond for clarification. On July 18 his command was finally defined as a separate department composed of East Tennessee, that part

[1] Kirby Smith to A. S. Johnston, March 2, 1862, and Kirby Smith to Samuel Cooper, March 13, 1862, in Ch. II, Vol. 52, National Archives; *Official Records*, VII, 849.

of North Carolina west of the Blue Ridge Mountains, and the part of Georgia north of the railroad from Augusta via Atlanta to West Point.[2]

Now came another problem. On June 25 Braxton Bragg, new commander of the Second Department, was also notified of some changes. At his suggestion, his department was combined with Lovell's old Department Number One, so that the new command embraced eastern Louisiana, Mississippi, Alabama, and that part of Georgia west of the railroad from West Point to Chattanooga via Atlanta. Three weeks later, Bragg was consequently confused when he read orders which gave Kirby Smith territory in northern Georgia which had already been designated as part of his own department. On July 20 Bragg asked Kirby Smith whether he operated independently or was still under the jurisdiction of the Western Department. His pride hurt, Kirby Smith snapped back that his was a strictly independent command which reported directly to the War Department.[3]

Perhaps Kirby Smith had reason to be unhappy. For four months he had been defending one of the most difficult positions in the Confederacy with a piecemeal force of some nine thousand troops. On March 31 Lee had written him that his first duty was to hold the line of the East Tennessee and Virginia, and East Tennessee and Georgia Railroads, a link in the Confederacy's main line from Vicksburg to Richmond via Mobile, Atlanta, Chattanooga, Knoxville, and Lynchburg. If this fell, communication between the western and eastern theaters would be pushed back to a secondary and inferior line running from Richmond to Atlanta via Wilmington, North Carolina. The railroad through Kirby Smith's department was the soft underbelly of the entire system, for it was exposed along two hundred miles to Halleck's Union armies on the west and to guerrilla tactics by Union elements in the East Tennessee mountains.[4]

To guard this vital spot Kirby Smith had to disperse his troops on a line 180 miles long facing west, with his right flank anchored at Cumberland Gap and his left lapped around the Cumberland Mountains at Chattanooga. It would have been a difficult position to hold even

[2] Kirby Smith to W. W. Mackall, March 14, 1862, and Hugh L. Clay to J. A. McDowell, June 7, 1862, in Ch. II, Vol. 52, National Archives; General Order No. 50, Adjutant and Inspector General's Office, July 18, 1862, in Orders, Army of Mississippi, Western Department No. 2, and Army of Tennessee, 1862–1863, Ch. VIII, Vol. 342, National Archives, hereinafter cited as Ch. VIII, Vol. 342, National Archives.

[3] *Official Records*, XVII, Pt. 2, pp. 619, 624, 627, 649, 651–52; Kirby Smith to Braxton Bragg, July 24, 1862, in Ch. II, Vol. 51, National Archives.

[4] *Official Records*, X, Pt. 2, pp. 376–77; Kirby Smith to Jefferson Davis, March 10, 1862, in Ch. II, Vol. 52, National Archives; Black, *Railroads of the Confederacy*, 5–7; Charles W. Ramsdell, "The Confederate Government and the Railroads," *American Historical Review*, XXIII (July, 1917), 798.

with twice the number of men he had. He had tried to defend the gap with General Carter L. Stevenson's division of four thousand good troops against an expected advance of General George W. Morgan's Federal division. With twenty guns and an impressive array of earthworks Stevenson could have held out against an army had Morgan not easily crossed the mountains at Rogers' and Big Creek Gaps, eighteen and thirty-five miles southwest of his position. To avoid being outflanked by a move into Powell's Valley at his rear, Kirby Smith wisely ordered Stevenson to fall back on June 18 to Morristown, and prepare to make a stand to hold the railroad.[5]

Though the northern press would hail the withdrawal of his right flank as a great achievement, Kirby Smith could breathe a sigh of relief. Since his arrival in East Tennessee he had been forced to shuttle his six small brigades back and forth between Cumberland Gap and Chattanooga, and had experienced great frustration. Buell's Army of the Ohio was pushing slowly across northern Alabama toward his left flank at Chattanooga while another of Buell's divisions was biding its time until its leader arrived by harassing the unfortunate commander of the Chattanooga post, Brigadier General Danville Leadbetter. While Buell's column moved up the Memphis and Charleston Railroad, Morgan's division was applying pressure from the north. Kirby Smith was constantly drawn to one end of the 180-mile line only to find that pressure was being applied at the other end. Embarrassed and frustrated, he complained to Adjutant General Samuel Cooper, "My command has been almost broken down by constantly moving from one end to the other of the line. Communicating by telegraph and acting in concert from behind natural defenses of great strength they (the Federals) have foiled every effort made by me." [6]

He had good reason to complain. In May, news that 18,000 Federals were threatening Cumberland Gap while 11,000 were advancing on the railroad via Kingston forced him to throw most of his 8,600 men north to hold the right flank. No sooner had he arrived than the Federals moved to seize the bridge over the Tennessee River at Chattanooga. Surprised, Leadbetter failed to destroy the bridge, fell back into the town, and prepared to observe the enemy from that vantage point and await reinforcements. Nothing further developed and Kirby Smith

5 Kirby Smith to W. W. Mackall, March 14, 1862, and Kirby Smith to Jefferson Davis, March 10, 1862, in Ch. II, Vol. 52, National Archives; *Official Records,* X, Pt. 2, pp. 596–97, and XVI, Pt. 2, p. 691.

6 *Official Records,* XVI, Pt. 2, p. 685. Buell's total force numbered 63,102; of these, 7,235 were in Morgan's division and 44,172 were in the field with Buell present for duty. *Ibid.,* 193. For evidence Kirby Smith saw the Federal plan, see *ibid.,* pp. 683–85.

had sent his force back to the north end of the line when he received word that another heavy force was striking at Chattanooga. Kirby Smith raced to Chattanooga on June 7 to find Leadbetter's 3,000 troops enduring a terrific bombardment from a Federal force across the Tennessee. After shelling the town, the Federals retired down the river. Kirby Smith wired Beauregard for reinforcements and rushed north to meet Morgan's division which was pouring into Powell's Valley and flanking Stevenson at Cumberland Gap. Kirby Smith sent two brigades to Tazewell to stop Morgan from moving up the valley. Scarcely had this been done when Leadbetter nervously reported that Federals were moving into position near Jasper, Tennessee, for a full-fledged threat against Chattanooga. A hasty decision must be made, and Kirby Smith elected to hold the Georgia flank. So it was that Carter Stevenson spiked his guns, buried tons of shot and shell in the mountain ravines, and retreated back down Clinch Valley, demonstrating the vulnerability of Cumberland Gap.[7]

It was a wise decision, for Chattanooga was a more vital position than the gap. The town lay sheltered on the eastern slopes of the Cumberland Mountains at the point where the Tennessee River, fed by the Little Tennessee, the Clinch, and the Hiwassee, left the long trough between the Cumberland and Appalachian Mountain ranges, and instead pushed west through the treacherous gorge between Walden's Ridge and Raccoon Mountain into the cotton plains of northern Alabama. If Kirby Smith lost the town, the precious rail artery to Virginia would be cut and the road would be open to Atlanta, the most important rail hub in the Deep South. Should Atlanta fall, both trunk lines connecting Lee and Bragg would be severed.[8]

If Chattanooga fell, more of the Heartland's munitions and raw materials area would be vulnerable to invasion. Four of the South's eight arsenals—Atlanta, Augusta, Macon, and Columbus—all supplying Bragg, would be threatened if Buell seized the Chattanooga railhead. Atlanta, especially vulnerable, ranked third in November, 1862, in the production of Confederate small arms ammunition and second in the production of field ammunition. The Augusta arsenal ranked second in both areas, and Columbus and Macon were not far behind. Twenty-three miles south of Chattanooga at Dalton, Georgia, Bragg had ordered his chief

7 *Official Records*, X, Pt. 2, pp. 496, 504; Kirby Smith to Jefferson Davis, March 10, 1862, Kirby Smith to Danville Leadbetter, June 6, 1862, Kirby Smith to Robert E. Lee, June 6, 1862, all in Ch. II, Vol. 52, National Archives; *Official Records*, X, Pt. 2, pp. 496, 504, Pt. 1, pp. 656–59, and XVI, Pt. 2, pp. 677–79, 682–86, 693; Gilbert E. Govan and James W. Livingood, *Chattanooga Country, 1540–1951: From Tomahawks to TVA* (New York, 1952) , 200.

8 Buell, *Statement of Major General Buell,* 30; Black, *Railroads of the Confederacy,* 180–81.

ordnance officer, Colonel Hypolite Oladowski, to deposit supplies for sixty thousand infantry and six thousand cavalry, as well as a hundred pieces of field artillery. Stores were already accumulating. Rich coal, copper, and saltpeter deposits in northern Georgia and Tennessee would also be lost if Chattanooga fell.[9]

The situation was complicated by affairs in Virginia. Lee faced McClellan on the peninsula, and Stonewall Jackson was dazzling friend and foe in the Shenandoah country. Most of Richmond's time and material was absorbed on the Virginia line. In the West, Halleck with an estimated hundred thousand men faced Bragg's forty-five thousand troops. Halleck had taken advantage of the pressure on the Virginia front to detach Buell's Army of the Ohio to move along the Memphis and Charleston Railroad toward Chattanooga. By June 29 the Federal army was at Huntsville. Another detachment was at Battle Creek below Chattanooga, guarding engineers who were building pontoon bridges at Stevenson and Bridgeport, Alabama. It was evident that Buell planned to move to the south bank of the Tennessee and advance on Chattanooga. Buell moved slowly. His force was scattered from the Georgia line to Eastport, Mississippi, guarding the railroad, supply depots, and bridges.[10]

Slow or fast, Buell seemed an unstoppable threat to Chattanooga. Beauregard and then Bragg had refused Kirby Smith reinforcements because each planned his own offensive thrust. Kirby Smith then turned to Richmond. Although his argument—that either the East Tennessee railroad or Chattanooga would have to be abandoned if help were not sent—was sound, Richmond remained apathetic. After McClellan was forced to withdraw from the peninsula, Lee moved against a threat by John Pope in northeastern Virginia, and Richmond's attention was absorbed there. Randolph wrote Bragg on June 23 that he could attempt any plan he desired, and, instead of ordering Bragg to reinforce Tennessee, merely asked him to help Kirby Smith if he could. Jefferson Davis also offered no suggestions but merely expressed confidence that Bragg would aid Kirby Smith if he could. This inattention characterized the government's attitude in relation to Bragg and Kirby Smith. Davis and Randolph only expressed approval of plans already made or hopes for cooperation between the departments. It was on his own initiative, and not on orders from Richmond, that Bragg ordered McCown's division to Chattanooga on June 27 to help hold the Tennessee River line.[11]

9 Vandiver, *Ploughshares into Swords*, 148 n., 121–22; *Official Records*, XVI, Pt. 2, pp. 740–41.

10 Buell, *Statement of Major General Buell*, 1–16.

11 Kirby Smith to Samuel Cooper, July 2, 1862, Kirby Smith to George W. Randolph, July 4, 1862, Kirby Smith to Bragg, July 4, 6, 1862, all in Ch. II, Vol. 52, National Archives; *Official Records*, XVI, Pt. 2, pp. 701–702, 706, 696, 710.

McCown and three thousand troops arrived at Chattanooga on July 3. McCown did not come highly recommended to the new department. Bragg blamed him for the loss of New Madrid. Bragg warned Kirby Smith that McCown lacked nerve and a capacity to command and should not be trusted with an important position. Kirby Smith immediately showed his regard for Bragg's advice by making McCown commander of the Chattanooga flank, and then took advantage of Federal inactivity to reorganize his command into three divisions. The able Carter Stevenson commanded the pride of the department, nine thousand well-organized troops, who held the north flank near Clinch Mountain. Brigadier General Harry Heth, recently transferred from the Department of Western Virginia, commanded six thousand troops which, together with McCown's three thousand men, formed the only opposition to Buell's advance on Chattanooga. Satisfied with the new arrangement, Kirby Smith left the sultry Knoxville heat on July 7 to regain his strength at Montvale Springs and to contemplate the fate of a department he never wanted to command.[12]

As he tramped the rugged trails in the Smoky Mountains and surveyed the Tennessee Valley at his feet, he began to change his mind about the possibilities of his department. He had been unhappy to leave the halcyon days of his service on the Virginia front to take command of a weak defensive department, short on recognition and long on problems. He had wanted to take the offensive against Nashville in April when the Federals were diverted at Shiloh, and had even secured Lee's approval, but a lack of troops forced him to abandon the idea. Now that he was reinforced by McCown and a few scattered Florida and Georgia regiments, he again grew impatient with the defensive, and desired to launch an offensive campaign.[13]

There were several reasons for the change of attitude, and Kirby Smith's personality was probably the chief factor. When serving in Virginia, he had been hailed as the "Blucher of Manassas" for his timely

[12] *Official Records*, XVII, Pt. 2, p. 651. Grady McWhiney, in "Controversy in Kentucky: Braxton Bragg's Campaign of 1862," *Civil War History*, VI (March, 1960), 9–10, said that McCown was sent to Chattanooga to test the practicability of sending a larger part of Bragg's army there by rail. However, Bragg did not depart from his plan to move north on Nashville from Tupelo until mid-July. After a conversation with Bragg, Isham Harris reported on July 28 that the Army would probably cross the Tennessee at Florence or Tuscumbia. Harris to Andrew Ewing, July 28, 1862, in Buell Papers, Rice. See also *Official Records*, XVII, Pt. 2, p. 651, and XVI, Pt. 2, p. 734.

[13] *Official Records*, X, Pt. 2, pp. 422, 424–25, 417. Kirby Smith wanted to go to Mississippi with Albert Sidney Johnston. See Kirby Smith to Mackall, March 14, 1862, in Ch. II, Vol. 52, National Archives. See also Kirby Smith to his wife, August 6, 1862, in Edmund Kirby Smith Papers, UNC; Joseph Howard Parks, *General Edmund Kirby Smith, C.S.A.* (Baton Rouge, 1954), 156.

—some said lucky—arrival on the field at a crucial moment. Seriously wounded at Manassas, Kirby Smith recovered in Richmond amidst great popularity in social and government circles. Davis credited him with saving the day at Manassas, Lee called him one of his best officers, and when Kirby Smith later married, his wife was styled "The Bride of the Confederacy." Perhaps it had been too much and too soon for the young general. Modest at first, he had given credit for his achievements to "God in His mercy" who "spread a panic through their hosts," but soon was telling friends that it had been the arrival of his own troops that caused the Union panic.[14]

Kirby Smith had personality traits which could only be revealed when cooperation and self-sacrifice were needed. He was a good leader, but not a follower; he could command, but not cooperate. Mark it off to age, to inexperience, to ambition, the fact remains there were two sides to Kirby Smith. To his fellow officers he was their humble and cooperative servant, but privately he burned with a mystical desire to redeem, to conquer. On occasion he fancied himself as Cortez burning his ships behind him, and as Moses leading the Israelites from Egypt. His was a quiet ambition and a quiet conceit, and since his transfer to East Tennessee he had bided his time until he could again be the talk of Richmond.[15]

By early July, Kirby Smith was seeking a chance for new glory. He was already losing interest in the dull task of protecting Chattanooga from Buell's advance, which was rightfully his main objective, and was setting his sights elsewhere. Someone else, perhaps Bragg, could take care of Buell. On July 6 he wrote Bragg that he was mobilizing his command for a movement on Morgan at Cumberland Gap or on Middle Tennessee. Yet four days earlier Kirby Smith had written Samuel Cooper that the Federals were preparing to cross twenty miles below Chattanooga and the reinforcements were needed there. On July 7, Kirby Smith sent a confidential letter to Stevenson in which he outlined a plan to outflank General George Morgan at Cumberland Gap and drive into the Kentucky River country. On July 10 he wrote him again that this proposed expedition would depend upon the state of affairs at Chattanooga, where Kirby Smith knew at least thirty thousand Federals were threat-

14 *Official Records*, XIX, Pt. 2, p. 643; Rowland (ed.) , *Davis*, VI, 493; Parks, *Kirby Smith*, 196–97.

15 Kirby Smith's letters to his wife reveal his intense ambition. He compared himself to Cortez (August 24, 1862, in Kirby Smith Papers, UNC) , and his army to the Israelites moving out of Egypt (August 25, 1862, in *ibid.*) . He predicted that his campaign, if successful, would be considered "a stroke of inspiration and genius" (August 24, 1862, in *ibid.*) ; and after the campaign he wrote her, "I see the papers will keep my name in their columns" (November 18, 1862, in *ibid.*) .

ening. Yet this was not quite what he wrote Jefferson Davis on July 14, when he suggested that Bragg's cooperation would be needed to stop the Federal advance on Chattanooga, with no mention of his own private plan to leave Buell to someone else while his own East Tennessee army invaded Kentucky. In all justice, it appears that the reason Kirby Smith wanted Bragg to move to Tennessee was that this would free him of his obligation to meet Buell and enable him to move into Kentucky.[16]

Kirby Smith had several reasons for wanting to invade Kentucky other than just a desire to lead an expedition. The Yankee commander at Cumberland Gap, George Morgan, was an old friend from before the war. He and Kirby Smith had been carrying on a friendly duel by correspondence for several months. Kirby Smith's pride was definitely hurt by Morgan's success in forcing him out of the gap, and he wanted revenge. More important, the time seemed ripe for a move on Kentucky. On July 4, Kirby Smith had sent John Morgan on a long raid into Kentucky. It was Morgan's first raid into the Bluegrass, and he intended to destroy Federal supply depots, recruit for his own command, and strike at the communication line between Nashville and Louisville. The raid was a dazzling exhibition of Morgan's ability to strike quickly, to confuse the enemy, and to evade superior forces. Tompkinsville and a half million dollars in stores fell on July 8, and Glasgow, Springfield, and Harrodsburg were taken. By July 14, after having driven half way across the state and two hundred miles behind the lines in less than a week, Morgan's troopers were at Lawrenceburg, only fourteen miles from Frankfort, the capital.[17]

Unionists cursed and supporters of the gray cheered as Morgan drove northeast between Frankfort and Lexington to Cynthiana, almost to the Licking River, defeated all pursuers, and then retired from the state via Richmond and the old battleground at Mill Springs. It was an emotional experience for both sides: martial law was declared in Lexington, General Jeremiah Boyle at Louisville panicked and reported Morgan's force of nine hundred as five thousand, and a disgusted Abraham Lincoln wired Halleck at Corinth, "They are having a stampede in Kentucky. Please look to it." [18] Morgan became intrigued with the idea of arousing Kentuckians to the Southern cause, and urged them to rise and strike for their altars, their fires, the green graves of their sires,

[16] Kirby Smith to Bragg, July 6, 1862, Kirby Smith to Samuel Cooper, July 2, 1862, Kirby Smith to Carter Stevenson, July 7, 1862, Kirby Smith to Jefferson Davis, July 14, 1862, all in Ch. II, Vol. 52, National Archives; *Official Records*, XVI, Pt. 2, p. 725.

[17] Kirby Smith to Cooper, July 5, 1862, in Ch. II, Vol. 52, National Archives; *Official Records*, XVI, Pt. 1, pp. 731–84.

[18] *Official Records*, XVI, Pt. 1, p. 738.

God, and their native land. Kentuckians, especially women, were electrified by the exploits of the wild-looking crew dressed in sombreros, high cavalry boots, and large clanking spurs, who carried every conceivable weapon from long Enfields to shotguns.[19]

These Rebels were fabulous, men cast in heroic mold, who raged larger than life and compelled admiration. There were Morgan's adjutant, George St. Leger Grenfell, former British officer and French cavalryman, who claimed to have fought with the Moors against the French, battled the Riff pirates, and been with Garibaldi; Tom Quirk from Ireland, Morgan's excellent scout; D. Howard Smith of the 5th Kentucky with waistlong, flowing beard; and "Old Lightning" Ellsworth, telegrapher and buffoon extraordinary. Kentucky people seemed fascinated, or fearful, of the improbable aggregation led by the dark, bearded Lexington merchant. Exuberant with his achievements, Morgan telegraphed Kirby Smith from Georgetown: "I am here with a force sufficient to hold all the country outside of Lexington and Frankfort. These places are garrisoned chiefly with Home Guards. The bridges between Cincinnati and Lexington have been destroyed. The whole country can be secured and 25,000 or 30,000 men will join you at once." [20] It was a misleading report, for while Morgan and his men might have won the hearts of the Kentucky people, they had not won men. No more than three hundred volunteered, and Morgan was unable to hold the country outside Lexington and Frankfort the day after he wrote his dispatch. Failing to discern the difference between sentiment for the Confederacy and popular feeling for himself and his fellow Kentuckians, Morgan urged Kirby Smith to join him.[21]

Elated by Morgan's false news, Kirby Smith forwarded it to General Samuel Cooper in Richmond on July 24. That same day, he also sent Stevenson an almost incredible message that indicated the intensity of his desire to move into Kentucky. Stevenson was informed of Morgan's note, and was told that if Morgan at Cumberland Gap detached part of his command to pursue the raiders, the move would give Stevenson "the most favorable opportunity of pushing forward your operations, and probably enable you to enter Kentucky." [22] No doubt Kirby Smith was worried about conditions at Chattanooga, but the evidence is clear that he was more interested in getting his own expedition under way and leaving someone else to cope with Buell. Even his troop dispositions re-

19 Cecil Fletcher Holland, *Morgan and His Raiders* (New York, 1943) , 118.
20 *Official Records,* XVI, P. 2, pp. 733–34.
21 Holland, *Morgan and His Raiders,* 126–27; Kirby Smith to Cooper, July 26, 1862, in Ch. II, Vol. 51, National Archives; *Official Records,* XVI, Pt. 2, pp. 733–34, 741.
22 *Official Records,* XVI, Pt. 2, p. 734.

vealed this. He stationed Stevenson's division of nine thousand men to face Morgan, whom Kirby Smith believed to have ten thousand troops. Heth and McCown at Chattanooga were to oppose Buell, whom Kirby Smith believed to have at least thirty thousand men, with the most ill-armed and ill-trained nine thousand troops in the department. It appears strange that four days before Kirby Smith urged Stevenson to move into Kentucky with half the department's troops if he saw the chance, he had notified Bragg that Buell was preparing to cross the river at Bridgeport. And on July 4 he had written Bragg that Buell's whole force was across the Tennessee River and in considerable force twenty miles below Chattanooga. Again on July 19, five days before his note to Stevenson, Kirby Smith had telegraphed Bragg that "Buell with his whole force, is opposite Chattanooga, which he is momentarily expected to attack." Then he had urged Bragg to hasten to his department for "the successful holding of Chattanooga depends upon your co-operation." [23]

Kirby Smith was playing a hazardous game. While his responsibility as department commander necessitated the holding of Chattanooga, he was quite willing to allow half of his force to move over the Cumberland Mountains into Kentucky while the weaker half waited 180 miles south for an attack momentarily expected. Moreover, his game was succeeding. On July 20, Kirby Smith telegraphed Bragg that Buell was expected to cross the Tennessee River at Bridgeport hourly and added: "Your co-operation is much needed. It is your time to strike at Middle Tennessee." [24] Bragg, who had been planning to strike Buell's rear in Middle Tennessee, notified Davis on July 21 that he would move immediately to Chattanooga and advance from there. On July 22 he added that "obstacles in front connected with danger to Chattanooga induce a change of base." [25] Even before the campaign had been planned, a difference in objective was apparent. For Kirby Smith it was Kentucky; for Bragg it seemed to be Buell.

Bragg had been slow in making his decision, for he also had a host of departmental problems. After having finally ascertained the limits of his department in an embarrassing fashion, he revamped Beauregard's disorganized force. He created the District of the Gulf under General John H. Forney, who with nine thousand troops was to defend Mobile. Van Dorn, who suddenly found his Department of South Mississippi and East Louisiana merged into Bragg's, was reduced to commander of the District of the Mississippi, and his fourteen thousand men were assigned

23 *Ibid.*, 730–31. See also Kirby Smith to Bragg, July 4, 20, 1862, and Kirby Smith to Jefferson Davis, July 14, 1862, in Ch. II, Vol. 52, National Archives.

24 Kirby Smith to Bragg, July 20, 1862, in Ch. II, Vol. 52, National Archives.

25 *Official Records*, LII, Pt. 2, p. 330.

responsibility for Vicksburg. General Sterling Price was given eleven thousand men and the newly formed District of the Tennessee. He was ordered to prevent a Federal advance along the northern border of Mississippi. The command of Bragg's main force, the Army of the Mississippi, thirty-one thousand strong, was temporarily given to Hardee. Leonidas Polk was given the dubious title of "second in command of the forces." [26]

During June and early July, Bragg hesitated to send troops to Kirby Smith. Planning a drive into Middle Tennessee from his Tupelo base, he feared that if he detached heavily, his force would be too weak to be effective. On June 22 he asked Cooper in Richmond if Kirby Smith could not be aided more effectively from scattered regiments in Georgia, as he planned to strike the Federal center with his own army. The same day he wrote Kirby Smith that in the proposed move he would need every man. Yet Kirby Smith, a specialist at persuasion, continued to hammer at Richmond on the need for Bragg's assistance, and played down his own desire to take on the offensive, until he was reasonably sure of assistance. On July 20, Kirby Smith reminded Bragg that it was his time to strike at Middle Tennessee,[27] but it was not until July 24, after Bragg had written that Middle Tennessee could not be reached from Tupelo, that the East Tennessee commander laid out his cards. He proposed that Bragg move to Chattanooga and open an offensive campaign "with every prospect of regaining possession of Middle Tennessee and possibly Kentucky." [28]

By the time Bragg received this dispatch, he was already at Montgomery, en route with his army to Chattanooga. The decision to move was motivated by a combination of pressures. The idea of assuming the offensive appealed to all, including Bragg. John Morgan's information from Kentucky was evidently accepted by all concerned. Lee himself would write Jefferson Davis on July 26 that if the impression made by Morgan in Kentucky were confirmed by a strong infantry force, it would have "the happiest effect," adding that "if Bragg could make a move, or with E. K. Smith & Loring, it would produce a great effect." [29] The pressure was strong in Bragg's own camp for him to regain Tennessee and Kentucky. During June his headquarters resembled a legislative lobby as prominent Kentuckians dropped by to assure him that the state

26 *Ibid.*, XVII, Pt. 2, pp. 636, 639, 656–57.

27 *Ibid.*, XVI, Pt. 2, pp. 701–702, 730.

28 Kirby Smith to Bragg, July 24, 1862, in Ch. II, Vol. 51, National Archives.

29 Douglas S. Freeman, *Lee's Dispatches; Unpublished Letters of General Robert E. Lee, C.S.A., to Jefferson Davis and the War Department of the Confederate States of America, 1862–65* (New York, 1915) , 39–40.

would respond favorably to a Confederate invasion. Such pressure had a strong effect. The Tennessee delegation was headed by the exiled governor and persistent camp follower Isham Harris, who wrote his fellow Tennessean, Andrew Ewing, on July 28 that Bragg had assured him that he would carry him to Nashville before the last of August. The pressures were not always consistent—some visitors wanted Bragg to move toward the Bluegrass, some toward the Middle Tennessee basin—but the result was the same. Bragg decided great things were in store north of Mississippi.[30]

There were other reasons for going to Chattanooga. Bragg decided he could not operate north against Halleck from his Tupelo base. Bragg's army had dwindled to thirty-one thousand. He believed that any further reinforcements to Chattanooga, which must be held, would make impossible an advance against Halleck, who supposedly had sixty thousand men. Equally important, the country north of Tupelo was barren of supplies and the creeks were dry in the summer drought. Bragg's wagon transportation was deficient, his commissary depleted by the loss of the rail hub at Corinth, and the railroad between Meridian, Mississippi, and Selma, Alabama, which would have helped sustain his forces, remained unconstructed. A move east would exhibit the fine points of the Confederate defensive-offensive strategy—to remain on the defensive and receive attack until certain objectives could be attained by a counterthrust. These objectives, diplomatic, logistical, geographical, and political, were to be important in Bragg's decision for the move and Davis' silent encouragement of it.[31]

A move to regain Nashville or even drive to the Ohio River could be a vital factor in influencing England and France to recognize the Confederate States. During the summer of 1862 the gray fortunes rode high as Lee turned McClellan back on the James River line, Jackson frustrated his opponents in the Shenandoah, and Pope came to grief at Second Manassas. The London *Times* appeared to be whipping up sentiment for recognition. Confederate diplomat James L. Mason reported from London in the spring that all the intelligent classes in England were in complete sympathy with the South. The English cotton reserve had slipped to an alarming twenty thousand bales, so England might listen sympathetically to pleas for recognition. A smashing blow at Nashville, Louisville, Cincinnati, or even the Northwest might bring English support. The redemption of Kentucky would bolster the ranks of the

30 Isham Harris to Andrew Ewing, July 28, 1862, in Buell Papers, Rice; David Urquhart, "Bragg's Advance and Retreat," *Battles and Leaders*, III, 600.

31 *Official Records*, XVII, Pt. 2, pp. 624–25, 627–28; Black, *Railroads of the Confederacy*, 156–57; Vandiver, "Jefferson Davis and Confederate Strategy," 20–21.

slave states and add to the Confederacy's prestige abroad by presenting a more united front of the slave powers.[32]

There were also strong logistical reasons for Bragg's shift in plan. An offensive from Chattanooga might regain the Middle Tennessee and northern Alabama Heartland. Louisville and Lexington were reported by Morgan as filled with stores, and Tennessee and Kentucky were supposedly rich in eager recruits. Since Buell's supply line stretched from northern Alabama to the Ohio River, a dash into Buell's rear, even if there were no Confederate occupation or seizure of supply depots, could force him to abandon the advance on Chattanooga. No less important was the desire to keep the war out of East Tennessee. Kirby Smith had tried everything from proclamations of amnesty to declarations of martial law, but Unionist sentiment continued rampant. Twenty-four-hour watches were required to save the railroad from destruction. Kirby Smith could not get the militia to assemble and could not have trusted it if it came. On March 23 he wrote Cooper that no Confederate recruits were to be had while at least twenty thousand potential Union recruits were waiting for a successful Federal invasion of East Tennessee. Buell obviously had to be kept out of that area, and perhaps the solution was to force him to defend his own bases.[33]

Geographical factors also motivated Bragg's decisions. The rich Tennessee Valley, the railroad, and the Chattanooga bastion were endangered by Buell's move along the Memphis and Charleston Railroad. And from what better place than Chattanooga could a Confederate army start an offensive campaign? Bragg and Kirby Smith would have a choice of five possible routes of invasion: west to Jasper and then southward into North Alabama; west to Jasper and then north into the Middle Tennessee basin; north from Chattanooga through the Sequatchie Valley, shielded on the left by the Cumberland Mountains and on the right by Walden's Ridge; northeast along the eastern slope of Walden's Ridge to Crossville, where a move could be made west against Nashville or north against Kentucky; and northeast on the East Tennessee and Georgia Railroad, shielded on the left flank by the Tennessee River, and thence into Kentucky through Rogers' and Big Creek Gaps. Like fingers on

[32] Richardson, *Messages and Papers*, II, 172–74, 251, 198–99, 328, 321–22, 324–25; Frank L. Owsley, *King Cotton Diplomacy: Foreign Relations of the Confederate States of America* (Chicago, 1931), 337. Douglas S. Freeman, *R. E. Lee: A Biography* (New York, 1934–35), II, 350–414 gives Lee's reasons for invading Maryland, which must have resembled those of Bragg in Kentucky.

[33] *Official Records*, XVI, Pt, 2, p. 741, X Pt. 2, pp. 355–56; Kirby Smith to Bragg, July 24, 1862, and Kirby Smith to Davis, July 24, 1862, in Ch. II, Vol. 51, National Archives; Kirby Smith to Mackall, March 14, 1862, and Kirby Smith to Cooper, March 13, 1862, in Ch. II, Vol. 52, National Archives; Parks, *Kirby Smith*, 165–74.

a hand these five routes spread out from Chattanooga, and it would be impossible for the enemy to discern the objective until the move had begun, and even the destination could not be known for certain.[34]

But the political opportunities of a western offensive seemed most important to Richmond and perhaps to Bragg also. It had been a great blow to Southern hopes when Kentucky refused to secede, and when Confederates were forced out of the state, they were robbed of the natural defensive line of the Ohio River. Davis, Bragg, and others believed that Kentucky would rise to the Southern cause if given the chance. General Simon B. Buckner had tried to arouse support in the fall of 1861, but his two proclamations inviting Kentucky to throw off the Union yoke had produced little effect. After Johnston took command in the West, he issued another proclamation written by Davis, expressing the president's policy. The South invaded Kentucky in self-defense; if the Kentuckians desired neutrality Johnston would drive the Federals out and retire himself, but if they wanted to join the Confederacy they would be welcome home. But again the results were disappointing. John C. Breckinridge, who had left his Senate seat to fight for the South, issued a similar proclamation in October, Felix Zollicoffer in December, and George B. Crittenden, himself a Kentuckian, in January of 1862—but the results were negligible.[35]

The conviction that Kentucky's heart was with the South still persisted. A provisional government was established in November, 1861, at Russellville, Kentucky. George W. Johnson was elected governor, Kentucky congressmen were accepted at Richmond, and another star went up on the flag. Perhaps rationalization led Sidney Johnston to explain to Davis that a lack of concerted action and not a lack of will had held Kentucky back. Yet a genuine feeling prevailed among the Kentucky generals such as Breckinridge, Buckner, and Humphrey Marshall, that Kentucky had been kept in the Union against her will.[36]

There was more basis than cavalry reports and vague sentiment for the Confederate government's policy. The summer of 1862 saw rising discontent in Kentucky against Union military interference with courts and popular elections. The Union home guard and provost marshals were arresting everyone in sight, there was no uniformity in the methods of treating runaway slaves, and General Jeremiah Boyle, military commander of the state during the all-important summer, had become vast-

[34] Buell, *Statement of Major General Buell,* 21–24, 28.

[35] Rowland (ed.), *Davis,* V, 356, 313, VI, 156–57; *Official Records,* XVI, Pt. 1, p. 1088, IV, 420–21, VII, 787, LII, Pt. 2, pp. 250–52; Moore (ed.), *Rebellion Record,* III, 127–29, 256–57, IV, 17–18.

[36] Coulter, *Civil War and Readjustment,* 135–39.

ly unpopular among Confederate circles because of his treatment of Confederate sympathizers. Lincoln's suggestion in July of emancipating Kentucky's slaves had brought protest even from the Unionist state legislature. There was no doubt that Federal popularity had reached a low ebb in June, 1862, and John Morgan and others probably took cognizance of this in urging the Confederate army to enter the state. But the Confederates did not know—and could not know without an invasion—whether the Kentucky feeling was just resentment against Federal mishandling of the occupation of Kentucky or genuine sympathy for the Confederate cause.[37]

The time was ripe for such an invasion because the Confederates had gained the initiative when Buell's expected advance had bogged down unceremoniously. During July, Buell moved slowly from his Corinth supply base, along the Memphis and Charleston Railroad, which he was forced to repair as he went. As his supply line was extended, Rebel cavalry struck. General Frank Armstrong's troopers were sent by Bragg from Mississippi to strike the vulnerable line of track which stretched over 150 miles from Corinth to Stevenson. Buell was forced to divert so many troops to repair and guard the Memphis and Charleston Railroad that he did not have enough left for an offensive.[38]

Buell was also forced to shift his supply bases to Nashville and Louisville. He attempted to establish a supply line on the Nashville and Decatur and the Nashville and Chattanooga lines, but experienced more delays. Attempts to forage the country along the Memphis and Charleston Railroad proved useless, for the fertile territory west of Huntsville was planted mainly in cotton and a severe drought took care of what little food was available. The railroad lines to Nashville had been torn up during the Confederate retreat from Middle Tennessee, were damaged by heavy spring rains, and badly needed repair. Before any further advance, repairs must be made, and Buell put his army to work patching the supply line.[39]

By July 12 the Nashville and Chattanooga line was repaired, and the Federals were again in a position to move on Chattanooga. But the Confederate cavalry had located the weak spot in Buell's advance—the supply line that stretched almost three hundred miles from Stevenson to Louisville. On July 13 Forrest with 1,000 troopers swooped down from the

[37] *Ibid.*, 145–65; Shaler, *Kentucky*, 331–37.
[38] Buell to Halleck, June 21, 1862, and Halleck to Buell, June 25, 30, 1862, in Buell Papers, Rice; Buell, *Statement of Major General Buell*, 17–18; *Official Records*, XVI, Pt. 1, pp. 826–29; Don Carlos Buell, "East Tennessee and the Campaign of Perryville," *Battles and Leaders*, III, 35.
[39] Buell, *Statement of Major General Buell*, 13–16.

Cumberland Plateau into Murfreesboro, Buell's largest and most important garrison on the Nashville and Chattanooga Railroad. Forrest took 1,200 prisoners, including the post commandant, Brigadier General T. T. Crittenden, and perhaps a quarter of a million dollars' worth of stores. More important, the Rebel troopers burned the railroad bridges over Stone's River, and delayed the Federals for two more weeks.[40]

Forrest had done more. His raid, combined with Morgan's Kentucky expedition, forced Buell to take the first of several steps which would throw his force on the defensive. Unknown to the Confederates, Halleck ordered Buell to do everything in his power to put down the cavalry raids, even if the Chattanooga move were delayed. Buell sent a division to Murfreesboro and another to Shelbyville, Tennessee, to guard the Elk River bridges. By July 28 the Nashville and Chattanooga was repaired, and three days later the Nashville and Decatur Railroad was open to traffic. Supplies were pushed forward to the Stevenson depot, pontoons were readied, and the threat to Chattanooga again looked ominous.[41]

Again the Rebel horsemen stalled the advance. There simply were not enough Federals to concentrate for such a move and hold the 300-mile line to Louisville at the same time. While Frank Armstrong pressed Buell in northern Alabama, John Morgan delayed the Federals further. On August 12 his troopers slipped into Gallatin, Tennessee, captured the outpost, burned the depot, tore up the Louisville and Nashville track on both sides of town, destroyed the trestle bridges north toward Bowling Green, and then went to work on the 800-foot tunnel seven miles north of Gallatin. Burning cars were run in, the timbers collapsed, and the route to Louisville was closed for months. The only alternate route would be up the Cumberland River from the Ohio, and the drought-induced low water had already rendered this useless.[42]

By mid-August, Bragg's cavalry had forced Buell to abandon the offensive. Morgan's and Forrest's raids forced the Federals to detach more troops to guard the Louisville railroad link and the Federal supply depot at Nashville. His offensive bogged, Buell played his last card. The Federal army's cavalry was massed under Brigadier General R. W. Johnson to drive Morgan out of Middle Tennessee. The Federals, seven hundred strong, moved through Hartsville, Tennessee, in search of Morgan. John-

40 *Ibid.*, 17; *Official Records*, XVI, Pt. 1, pp. 810–11.
41 Buell, *Statement of Major General Buell,* 17–18; *Official Records*, XVI, Pt. 2, p. 143; Report of James St. Clair Morton, Chief Engineer, Army of the Ohio, July 26, 1862 (MS in Buell Papers, Rice).
42 Jere Boyle to Buell, August 16, 1862; Buell to Halleck, August 15, 1862, Buell Papers, Rice; Buell, *Statement of Major General Buell,* 17–20; *Official Records*, XVI, Pt. 1, pp. 158, 843–57.

son was confident as he passed through the town, and reportedly boasted to civilians he would bring Morgan back in a bandbox. Morgan, though weary from raiding the Louisville and Nashville Railroad, moved his 800-man column eastward and fell on Johnson's troops east of Castalian Springs. After he had been driven back all morning, Johnson decided a retreat would be in order. Thence began the famed "Hartsville Races," with Johnson racing for the Cumberland River and Morgan racing to cut him off. Early in the afternoon Morgan flanked him on both sides, the Federal column was routed, Johnson and his staff surrendered, and the remnant of the cavalry of the Army of the Ohio made its way through the high corn and woods to the Cumberland River. By mid-August, after Bragg and Kirby Smith had united forces at Chattanooga, it was obvious that Buell had abandoned his plans for that city. Bragg's cavalry and his move to Chattanooga had halted the Yankee drive. Instead the Federals were observed abandoning their North Alabama supply depots and concentrating in Middle Tennessee, with a new base at Decherd.[43]

On July 23, three days after Kirby Smith had written that Buell's crossing of the river was expected hourly, the first trainload of Bragg's army pulled out of Tupelo en route for Chattanooga. It was a tremendous task to move an army of almost thirty-five thousand men eight hundred miles across four states. The cavalry, artillery, and wagon trains went overland through Aberdeen and Tuscaloosa, across the Black Warrior River, through Jones Valley in the searing summer heat, across the Coosa River, and through Will's Valley to Rome, Georgia. The infantry, in the finest hour of Confederate railroads, went by rail to Mobile, by ferry across Mobile Bay, then by steamboat and rail to Montgomery, by rail to West Point and Atlanta, where the troops boarded the Western and Atlantic line for Chattanooga. The movement had been well planned on short notice. Each man received seven days' rations as he boarded at Tupelo, and commissary officers waited on station platforms along the way to hand out more. Discipline was exceptional, and even the

---

[43] Buell admitted that the cavalry raids forced him to abandon the offensive. He wrote "we must abandon our extensive lines. . . . Our communications are interrupted almost daily. . . ." (Buell to Halleck, August 29, 1862, in Buell Papers, Rice). ". . . no permanent advance into East Tennessee can be attempted without a much larger force. . . ." (Buell to Halleck, August 26, 1862, in *ibid*). Buell explained the withdrawal from advancing along the Memphis and Charleston Railroad ". . . became necessary both to accumulate from our extended lines a force sufficient to meet the enemy and to open our communications now effectually closed." (Buell to Halleck, September 2, 1862, in *ibid*.). See also Buell to Halleck, August 7, June 21, 1862, and W. H. Liddell to Colonel Fry, August 16, 1862, in *ibid*.; *Official Records*, XVI, Pt. 1, pp. 158, 110; Buell, *Statement of Major General Buell*, 20–21. Buell put his center at Decherd, his left at McMinnville, and his right at Battle Creek. He expected an advance on Nashville. Buell, *Statement of Major General Buell*, 21–24, 28.

swap of several regiments and batteries between Hardee and Forney at
Mobile went smoothly. On July 27, two days before General Sam Jones'
division boarded the last train at Tupelo, Bragg's advance regiments rolled
into Chattanooga.[44]

It was a long ride from Tupelo, but the strange new spirit which
seized the troops compensated for the hardships. Veterans knew that an
attempt would be made to regain the Heartland, and the trains that
rolled across Alabama and Georgia resembled one vast picnic. Rebels
stole apples and flirted with girls, and at every station they were showered
with fruits, flowers, and messages of ardent admirers. The Georgia countryside rolled by as the rickety trains puffed around Kennesaw Mountain,
roared through the pass at Allatoona, and whistled through mile-long
Tunnel Hill. The trains rattled across the Chickamauga bridges and at
last ground slowly around the north end of Missionary Ridge into Chattanooga.[45]

Bragg had numerous problems to occupy his mind as the rails clicked
off the long miles. He had grappled with the problem of whether he
should leave his department. Now that was settled, but there were other
problems to solve—who would command the proposed expedition, where
would it go, and what would be its purpose? None of these questions
had been worked out, and answers must await his meeting with Kirby
Smith. Only then would there perhaps be truth in John Morgan's dispatch to a Louisville editor as his cavalry thundered through Kentucky,
"All well in Dixie." [46]

[44] Special Orders No. 4, July 21, 1862, No. 133, July 26, 1862, No. 134, July 27, 1862,
No. 6, July 23, 1862, No. 131, July 24, 1862, all in Special Orders, Army of the Mississippi, Department No. 2 and Department and Army of Tennessee, 1862–1864, Ch. II,
Vol. 221, National Archives, hereinafter cited as Ch. II, Vol. 221, National Archives;
Diary of Major George Winchester (MS in Confederate Collection of Tennessee
Archives), July 25, 31, August 1–8, 1862, hereinafter cited as Winchester Diary, Tennessee Archives; Black, Railroads of the Confederacy, 182–84; Official Records, XVII, Pt.
2, p. 659.
[45] Winchester Diary, Tennessee Archives, July 24, August 26, 31, 1862; William
Vaught to Mary, August 9, 1862, in letters in possession of Mrs. Julian Fertitta, Beaumont, Texas.
[46] Official Records, XVI, Pt. 1, p. 780.

eleven

"I Am Not Ambitious"

IT WAS AN AWKWARD MEETING ON THE AFTERNOON OF JULY 31, 1862, when Kirby Smith arrived at Bragg's headquarters at Chattanooga. The two generals talked far into the night while a lamp flickered on a large map of Tennessee and Kentucky that Bragg had hung on the wall. It was a strange combination: Kirby Smith, who had trouble listening to people, and Braxton Bragg, who had never learned how to communicate with anyone.

Although only in his forties Bragg, stooped, thin, and haggard, had suffered for years from a collection of ailments ranging from dyspepsia to severe migraine headaches. These had colored his personality, and now he had a dullness and sourness which often made him quarrelsome. Even when he had been in the old army, out on the Texas plains and in Mexico, Bragg had always looked for infringements of his prerogatives by his superiors and for infractions of rules by his subordinates. Although his officers and men respected him for his abilities to organize and drill an army, many feared him, some disliked him, and others even hated him.[1]

It may have been that Bragg's harsh discipline and aloofness cloaked weaknesses he knew he had. He lacked the daring of a Morgan or a Forrest, and he lost great opportunities by wavering from attack at the crucial moment to busy himself with transitory details. Some would

[1] Kirby Smith to his wife, August 1, 1862, in Kirby Smith Papers, UNC; William H. Russell, *My Diary North and South* (Boston, 1863), 207; Richard Taylor, *Destruction and Reconstruction; Personal Experiences of the Late War* (New York, 1879), 100; *Official Records*, XVI, Pt. 2, pp. 745–46.

call him a pessimist, others a realist. With a mind too moody to dare and too administrative to deliver a lightning blow, Bragg was a brave soldier and a good provider—but he was not a fighter. When the pressure developed he would become pensive and fretful, would sulk, lose his sense of balance—and his opportunity. Somewhere in his career, Braxton Bragg, organizer and competent strategist that he was, had lost his nerve, and the ability to see a battle to the end had slipped from his grasp.[2]

His worst fault as a leader was probably his constant fear of making a mistake, and his consequent hesitation in committing his troops. He could drill, but he could not engage; he could plan, but he could easily change his mind. His weaknesses had not shown up in his previous career because he had been in situations where the final responsibility was not his—a captain in Zachary Taylor's army, a chief of staff to Beauregard, a corps commander, a second-in-command. But now he had full responsibility; for though Jefferson Davis, a little too busy on the eastern front, gave much encouragement and some advice, he gave few orders. Bragg would have to rise above his weaknesses now, and could no longer compensate for his dilatory mind by being stern.[3]

Their contrasting personalities and past friction over department boundaries did not promise a pleasing setting in which Bragg and Kirby Smith could settle the problems of command, objective, and overall purpose in the campaign. Although Bragg was senior officer, he was out of his department and somewhat embarrassed at the transfer. Kirby Smith had little desire to be placed under his control, and so the matter of authority was not pressed. Instead, the decision of the Chattanooga meeting was, as Bragg termed it, one of "mutual support and effective co-operation."[4] Kirby Smith only too willingly agreed and labeled the expedition as "a movement in co-operation with General Bragg."[5] Evidently a tacit agreement was reached that the commanders would operate independently until the columns united at their objective. Only after they united would Bragg command both forces. This seems to have been initiated by Kirby Smith. Bragg, conscious of being a man without a department, acquiesced, made no attempts to clarify his position with Richmond, and avoided further mention to Kirby Smith of the matter of who should command. Davis only muddled affairs when

2 Basil Duke, *Reminiscences of General Basil W. Duke, C.S.A.* (Garden City, N.Y., 1911), 298 n.; Thomas R. Hay, "Braxton Bragg and the Southern Confederacy," *Georgia Historical Quarterly*, IX (December, 1925), 294–95, 302 n.

3 Horn, *Army of Tennessee*, 113–14; Duke, *Reminiscences*, 297–98; Rowland (ed.), *Davis*, V, 356; Davis to Kirby Smith, October 29, 1862, in Kirby Smith Papers, UNC.

4 *Official Records*, XVI, Pt. 2, p. 741.

5 *Ibid.*, 742. See also Kirby Smith to Bragg, August 11, 1862, in Ch. II, Vol. 51, National Archives.

on August 5 he wrote Bragg that he would confidently rely on Bragg's and Kirby Smith's "cordial co-operation" [6] and on September 7 when he issued a triple letter to Bragg, Kirby Smith, and Robert E. Lee, each addressed as a commanding officer.[7]

Confusion also developed over the question of the immediate objective, for here again the two generals failed to arrive at a definite plan. The proposed strategy was to be highly tentative. Kirby Smith would move against Cumberland Gap and attempt to force the Federals out of the position. If successful, he would then join Bragg in a move against Buell in Middle Tennessee and perhaps into Kentucky. But the joint thrust at the Army of the Ohio that lurked beyond the Cumberlands depended upon precise timing. The absence of Bragg's wagon trains would delay him ten days or two weeks. During this interval, Bragg hoped that Kirby Smith could invest the gap. If the arrival of the trains timed correctly with Kirby Smith's move on Cumberland Gap, the two armies might expel Buell from Middle Tennessee and enter Kentucky; if not, the two forces might be wasted in piecemeal assaults.

The problem of timing became even more involved when Bragg elected to include two other armies in the campaign. Bragg wanted two of his sub-commanders, Earl Van Dorn and Sterling Price, to prevent the Federal armies of General William S. Rosecrans and Grant in West Tennessee and northern Mississippi from aiding Buell. Bragg also hoped Van Dorn and Price could later move to reinforce his own force. Yet Bragg gave his two lieutenants no specific orders or instructions, only suggesting that they prepare for a joint move. Nor did he clarify who was to command, except to tell Van Dorn that his rank was to give him the command whenever he joined Price.

Timing also became a problem on the right flank. By August 9 Kirby Smith had found another force to join the campaign. He secured the aid of Humphrey Marshall, who commanded three thousand men in the Western Virginia Department. Marshall, a nephew of antislaver James G. Birney, was a prominent Kentuckian who had fled the state under a treason indictment. Shortly after Kirby Smith returned to Knoxville from his meeting with Bragg, he met with Marshall. The two agreed that Marshall's troops would be held in readiness to move on the northern entrance to Cumberland Gap when Kirby Smith gave the word. It would be essential that Marshall move swiftly when the time came, should Morgan abandon the gap and attempt to reach the Ohio River.

Not to be outdone, Bragg was busily scraping up another force. He

6 *Official Records,* LII, Pt. 2, p. 335.
7 Rowland (ed.) , *Davis,* V, 338–39.

sent an envoy to the popular Kentucky general John C. Breckinridge, then serving as a division commander under Van Dorn, with an invitation to join the ever-growing throng. On August 25 Breckinridge became the last of the expeditioners to promise support, and the invasion column appeared complete. It would be a unique attempt at cooperation, with three departments represented by six armies. But it was poorly organized at the high command level. The ranking general, Bragg, was in another commander's department. Kirby Smith was responsible to Davis, not Bragg. Humphrey Marshall reported to Kirby Smith, Van Dorn and Price reported to Bragg, and Breckinridge remained under the immediate command of Van Dorn. Little bound this loosely organized group together save promises of support and the simple Confederate faith in a fellow officer's pledge to fulfill a task.[8]

Nor was the overall purpose of the campaign definitely established. Davis did inform Bragg vaguely of what he considered the objective, but gave little advice besides his hopes for cooperation among the generals. On August 5 he suggested that Bragg and Kirby Smith first defeat Buell and then, as they had already contemplated, move north and liberate Kentucky. The Confederate high command was anxious to reestablish the civil government on Kentucky soil, and Richard C. Hawes, former lieutenant governor of the defunct Russellville government which had supposedly brought the state into the Confederacy, was standing in the wings at Richmond. Should Bragg and Kirby Smith reach the Bloody Ground, Davis desired that Hawes be installed as governor of Kentucky.[9]

Davis left Bragg and Kirby Smith to resolve the problem as to what political policy was to be adopted in Kentucky. The only hint he gave them was a sample proclamation that Davis sent to Kirby Smith, Bragg, and Robert E. Lee, designed to explain the purpose of the invasions of Kentucky and Maryland. Upon entering a state, the generals

---

[8] After the October 2 reunion with Bragg at Lexington, Kirby Smith wrote, "Gen. Bragg is in command. I am no longer at head of affairs but have only to obey orders." (Kirby Smith to his wife, October 5, 1862, in Kirby Smith Papers, UNC) Kirby Smith's staff physician wrote that "Gen. Bragg . . . assumed command of all the forces as soon as he arrived in Lexington." (S. A. Smith to Mrs. Smith, October 22, 1862, in *ibid.*) Kirby Smith wrote that "Bragg's movements since taking command in Ky. have been most singular and unfortunate." (Kirby Smith to his wife, October 20, 1862, in *ibid.*) He later wrote that he moved into Kentucky on his own responsibility as department commander. See Kirby Smith to J. Stoddard Johnston, October 31, 1866, in J. Stoddard Johnston Military Papers, Filson Club Historical Society, Louisville. See also Diary of J. Stoddard Johnston (MS in Bragg Papers, Western Reserve), October 2, 1862; Kirby Smith, "The Kentucky Campaign" (MS in Kirby Smith Papers, UNC); *Official Records*, XVI, Pt. 2, pp. 741–42, 995, XVII, Pt. 2, p. 677, Pt. 3, p. 927.

[9] Rowland (ed.), *Davis*, V, 334; *Official Records*, LII, Pt. 2, p. 342.

were to convince the inhabitants that the Confederates were fighting only for peace, and that now, even though the gray armies had won new success in the summer, the same moderate plea of the days of Fort Donelson and Shiloh would be repeated—that the Confederacy simply wanted to be left alone. As the North had refused entreaties for peace, the South would now carry the war to enemy territory in hopes that the people might even conclude a separate peace with the Confederate States.[10] And Davis threw in for good measure a promise of free navigation of the Mississippi and its tributaries. It is doubtful if the sample proclamation helped clear the uncertainty surrounding what was to be done if Kentucky were reached. Davis' note of August 5 suggesting an early defeat of Buell was suggestive, not peremptory; though he evidently intended the proclamation for use on Kentucky soil, its reference to enemy territory was incongruous with the Confederate belief that Kentucky was a lost sheep out of the fold. Hence, another problem of the invasion remained unsettled.[11]

The Chattanooga agreement with its absence of unified command and vagueness of objective soon exhibited its weakness. On August 9 Kirby Smith prepared to lobby for an independent move into the Bluegrass. He had some bargaining power now, for on August 5 Bragg had sent him two of his best brigades, Patrick Cleburne's and Preston Smith's. Bragg now had only twenty-seven thousand troops to confront Buell on the Chattanooga line, while Kirby Smith had nineteen thousand to oppose George Morgan's lone division. Kirby Smith garnered more support for his case when he received information that Morgan had a month's rations at the gap. Armed with this news, he immediately suggested to Bragg that if the reduction of the gap proved to be impractical, the East Tennessee troops should move on Lexington. Of course Kirby Smith promised he would push into the state only if the experiment at Cumberland Gap proved slow and costly.[12]

Unwilling to breach the delicate command situation, Bragg could do little else but request that Kirby Smith not move too far into Kentucky before his own army could get in motion. Kirby Smith joyfully received this news on August 11 and immediately promised Bragg that his troops would remain on the north side of the gap until Bragg thought a thrust on Lexington was feasible. Yet on the same day Kirby Smith outlined a slightly different plan to Jefferson Davis. Knowing that he had the president's ear, Kirby Smith proposed to leave Stevenson with nine thousand troops in the valley south of Cumberland Gap

10 Rowland (ed.), *Davis*, V, 338–39.
11 *Ibid.*, 338–39, 334.
12 Kirby Smith to Bragg, August 9, 1862, in Ch. II, Vol. 51, National Archives.

and march the remainder of his command around the position to Barboursville, Kentucky, twenty-nine miles north of the gap on the road to Lexington. Should Morgan attempt to flee, he would be pursued; but if the enemy held the gap, Kirby Smith's next move would become a question of supply. Thus he proposed two alternatives to Davis: the gap must be assaulted or, if it were learned that Morgan had an abundance of supplies, Kirby Smith would have to move further north into Kentucky where he could obtain subsistence for his own troops. He pressed hard for permission to move on Lexington, labeled it the "true policy," and warned Davis that further delay would find "a large army between us and the waters of the Ohio." [13] But Kirby Smith omitted two details from his letter to the president which he knew and should have mentioned—that already a large army faced Bragg and that Morgan had thirty days' rations at Cumberland Gap.[14]

Two days later and unknown to Bragg, Kirby Smith privately abandoned any intention of bringing his army to unite against Buell. His desire for an independent expedition was stronger than his will to cooperate, and, in the bustle of preparations to take the field, he penned his wife a hasty note: "After crossing the mountains my advance on Kentucky will be depended on Gen. Bragg's movement and as we act in concert can only be made when he is prepared to advance on Buell." [15]

But supposing Morgan chose to defend the gap, would Kirby Smith keep his promise to Bragg not to move further until the time seemed right? That afternoon he impatiently inquired of Bragg as to just how long he would have to remain at Barboursville before Bragg was ready to move. Yet the same day he sent Carter Stevenson a curious and quite different message. Stevenson was ordered to pursue, should Morgan abandon the gap, and J. W. Stone, Kirby Smith's adjutant, added that "the general would prefer that Morgan should abandon the gap before he reaches his rear . . ." as "this would afford the only opportunity of moving direct upon Lexington." [16]

The evidence is strong that Kirby Smith did not plan to hold his position at Barboursville until Bragg could move, if the opportunity to follow Morgan into the Bluegrass presented itself. On August 10 Bragg had agreed to Kirby Smith's designs on Lexington with two stipulations: that it not be commenced while Morgan's force remained intact at the gap and that Bragg must first move his own army forward.

13 Kirby Smith to Davis, August 11, 1862, in *ibid.*

14 Kirby Smith to Bragg, August 11, 1862, and Kirby Smith to Davis, August 11, 1862, in *ibid.*; *Official Records,* XVI, Pt. 2, pp. 748–49.

15 Kirby Smith to his wife, August 13, 1862, in Kirby Smith Papers, UNC.

16 J. W. Stone to Carter Stevenson, August 13, 1862, in Ch. II, Vol. 51, National Archives. See also *Official Records,* XVI, Pt. 2, p. 755.

Evidently Kirby Smith either misunderstood or discounted the second stipulation, and readied himself to drive across the Kentucky River on Lexington should Morgan evacuate the gap. Two days after his adjutant had reported to Stevenson Kirby Smith's desire that Morgan abandon the gap, Kirby Smith wrote Humphrey Marshall that if Morgan retreated, he would follow him into Kentucky.[17]

Bragg knew nothing of Kirby Smith's intention not to await his move from Chattanooga should Morgan abandon the gap first. By August 12 he had not only given Kirby Smith his blessing and two fifths of the troops for the revised Lexington plan, but something more important—the initiative. Bragg meekly wrote Kirby Smith that he did not desire to hold up the Lexington thrust any longer than "will enable me to get in motion to support you," [18] and three days later asked Kirby Smith for his suggestions for the Army of the Mississippi's own move. Embarrassed at being in Kirby Smith's department, unfamiliar with the field of operations, and with no authority to order Kirby Smith to do otherwise, Bragg allowed the command initiative to slip from his grasp. Kirby Smith had been quick to seize advantage of these hindrances—so quick that by the time he left Knoxville on August 14, the direction of campaign seemed to be his.[19]

The sun had already swung low over Crab Orchard Mountain as John Scott's cavalry filed out of Kingston on the night of August 13. The troopers were bound on a long 160-mile sweep across the mountain range to cut Morgan's supply line at London, Kentucky. To the east, Kirby Smith pushed his infantry forward at dawn of the next day to outflank Morgan and gain his rear on the Lexington road. While Stevenson moved up from Tazewell to feint against the south entrance of Cumberland Gap, the three remaining divisions of the Army of East Tennessee filed out of Knoxville and Clinton and converged at Big Creek Gap on the afternoon of August 15. Heth's division, three thousand strong, was to cross the rugged Cumberlands at Big Creek and move over the narrow mountain roads to Barboursville. Kirby Smith, with General Thomas J. Churchill's and Pat Cleburne's divisions, a total force of six thousand, would veer northeast, follow the narrow road up Powell's Valley, and cross the Rogers' Gap, only eighteen miles southwest of Morgan's position.[20]

[17] Kirby Smith to Humphrey Marshall, August 15, 1862, in Ch. II, Vol. 51, National Archives. See also *Official Records*, XVI, Pt. 2, pp. 748–49.

[18] *Official Records*, XVI, Pt. 2, pp. 754–55.

[19] *Ibid.*, 759.

[20] J. F. Belton to Carter Stevenson, August 14, 1862, in Ch. II, Vol. 51, National Archives; Kirby Smith to his wife, August 15, 1862, in Kirby Smith Papers, UNC; Paul F. Hammond, "Campaign of General E. Kirby Smith in Kentucky, in 1862," *Southern Historical Society Papers*, IX (1881), 229–33; *Official Records*, XVI, Pt. 1, p. 938.

On the afternoon of August 15, Heth's and Smith's columns rested; early the next morning they disappeared into the mountains, to reunite at Barboursville. It was a difficult climb over the Cumberlands, and a strange Cromwellian zeal seemed to come over the entire force. Many were ragged and barefoot, and the stony roads, heat, dust, thin rations, the day and night marching, and the strain of hauling field pieces and wagons along the horse trails molded an almost fanatical spirit. Kirby Smith's troops developed a fierce religious fervor so powerful that the march to Barboursville became almost a mass prayer meeting. Whole regiments prayed for their enemies, "that God may turn them from the error of their ways," [21] and the desire was intense to carry flag and cross to Lexington.

In sixty hours, Kirby Smith marched his troops over the Cumberland Mountain range, and on the morning of August 18 the gray column swooped down on Barboursville. The three hundred pro-Union citizens were stunned as Cleburne and Churchill poured into the village and seized a train of fifty supply wagons bound for Cumberland Gap. Rebels suddenly appeared everywhere. To the northwest, John Scott, riding 160 miles in seventy hours, stormed in on London on August 17, drove the 3rd Tennessee Union Infantry back to Cumberland Gap, and seized 150 wagons. To the southwest Heth, burdened with the main wagon trains and the artillery, toiled through Boston, Kentucky, and would not be expected to join Kirby Smith until August 22. In a lightning blow the Lexington road had been reached and Morgan surrounded.[22]

Kirby Smith fretted as he waited for Heth to arrive at Barboursville. News which reached him on August 18 that John Morgan had smashed the Louisville and Nashville tracks at Gallatin only whetted Kirby Smith's desire to move on Lexington. Yet it had become a question of just who was cornered, Morgan at Cumberland Gap or the Confederates. Kirby Smith had the proverbial tiger by the tail, for the Barboursville area was violently pro-Union; bushwhackers and partisans sniped at his detachments from every rock, and the Confederates were forced to scavenge the area for food. Foraging parties reported few results, Kirby Smith's wagons had not come, and there was a genuine danger that enemy Fabian tactics could wear away his small army.[23]

Although he may have encountered more trouble at Barboursville than he had expected, Kirby Smith had willfully placed himself in a situation in which he knew his only choice was to advance further north.

[21] Kirby Smith to his wife, August 21, 1862, in Kirby Smith Papers, UNC.
[22] Hammond, "Campaign," 247; *Official Records,* XVI, Pt. 1, p. 938, Pt. 2, pp. 766, 777.
[23] Kirby Smith to his wife, August 19, 20, 23, 1862, in Kirby Smith Papers, UNC.

On August 20 he informed Bragg of the problems of remaining longer at Barboursville, despite Bragg's request that he do so, and announced that he had decided to advance as soon as possible upon Lexington. But Kirby Smith had already contemplated this when he was at Knoxville. His proposal to Jefferson Davis that a move on Lexington would be necessary if Morgan had ample supplies was made when he had information the supplies were in existence, information which was confirmed on August 20 by a captured dispatch. Thus the decision announced to Bragg was not as sudden as Kirby Smith made it appear. He had placed his army in such a position that neither Davis nor Bragg could object to his proposal.[24]

The bonds of promised support and cooperation against Buell were now openly severed. Kirby Smith spoke of the Army of the Ohio as Bragg's own worry. He remarked to Bragg that his own force would prove an advantageous diversion for Bragg's movements against Buell, and boasted to Jefferson Davis on August 21 that "I have therefore nothing to fear from Buell. . . ." [25] There was something foreboding for Bragg's hopes in the independent and aloof manner Kirby Smith exerted. Reveling in his march from Knoxville, Kirby Smith compared it to a Herculean endeavor, and wrote his wife on August 24: "My expedition is something like Cortez. I have burnt my ships behind me and thrown myself boldly into the enemies country—the results may be brilliant and if successful will be considered a stroke of inspiration and genius." [26] And now, by his independent action, he had left Bragg to shift for himself. True, Kirby Smith had an imagination and boldness not unlike that of Stonewall Jackson—but Jackson would not have forgotten Lee.[27]

Amidst self-applause, Kirby Smith poised his force for the drive on Lexington. He ordered John Morgan to tear up the Louisville and Nashville line north of Gallatin and then join him in Lexington, where he hoped to be by September 2. Stevenson was to hurry forward Reynolds' brigade, Marshall was ordered to move across Pound Gap into Kentucky, and McCown went back to Knoxville to take temporary command of the department. Still Kirby Smith delayed, for he wished to hear from Bragg, and Heth and Reynolds had not yet arrived. While he fretted over his wife's illness, bushwhackers, and the green corn his men were forced to eat, bad news came in from John Scott. The Louisiana cavalryman, in

---

24 Kirby Smith to Davis, August 11, 1862, and Kirby Smith to Bragg, August 9, 1862, in Ch. II, Vol. 51, National Archives; *Official Records*, XVI, Pt. 2, p. 766; Kirby Smith to his wife, August 21, 1862, in Kirby Smith Papers, UNC.

25 *Official Records*, XVI, Pt. 2, p. 769.

26 Kirby Smith to his wife, August 24, 1862, in Kirby Smith Papers, UNC.

27 Kirby Smith to his wife, August 25, 29, 1862, in *ibid.*; *Official Records*, XVI, Pt. 2, pp. 766, 769.

advance on the Lexington pike, had run into his old enemy, the Union
3rd Tennessee, posted on a strong natural position at Big Hill on the
Lexington road. Scott, realizing the Federals blocked the advance on
Lexington, attacked and drove the Federals back to Richmond, Kentucky.
But during the chase he captured a dispatch from Lew Wallace, commanding at Lexington, that contained disturbing news of heavy Union
reinforcements expected in Richmond on August 23. [28]

A strong Federal column was gathering to regain strategic Big Hill,
where a single regiment and battery could probably hold off the whole
Confederate army. Scott warned that he was sorely pressed, his supplies
were low, and without swift support he would be forced to retreat.[29]

Kirby Smith had not bargained for Federal resistance so soon and now
he groped for a plan. In letters to Bragg and Cooper on August 24, he
sketched a hasty proposal of long-range strategy for the combined forces
that indicated he had given little thought to just what he would do once
he reached Lexington. In a style reminiscent of a John Morgan raid, he
suggested he push his twelve-thousand-man army north to Lexington,
his admitted objective, and gamble that the Kentuckians would join the
Confederacy. If they rose to his banner, he would remain; if not, he
would have to fall back. He was risking more than Kentucky's loyalty,
for, if he met strong resistance on the Lexington road, his troops would
be trapped with empty knapsacks between the force guarding the approach to the Kentucky River and Morgan's division at the gap. Kirby
Smith offered no sound plan of operations should he break through into
the Bluegrass region. Instead he suggested that Marshall forget about
Morgan at Cumberland Gap and join in a drive toward the Ohio River.
And what would Bragg do? Delivering the *coup de grace* to any plans
for meeting Buell's force, Kirby Smith bluntly invited Bragg to evade
Buell, cross the Cumberland River, and move into Kentucky, where "we
might hope to reach the Ohio." [30] A frustrated symbol of a defensive line
that might have been, the Ohio River was an old thorn in the flesh of
the Confederates. Until its banks were reached and Kentucky restored,
most Confederates could feel no satisfaction that they had redeemed all
that was their own. Kirby Smith shared the overwhelming desire to put
the Rebel line to the Ohio, but exactly what he would do when or if
he got there, the East Tennessee commander did not confide.

Kirby Smith hurried his preparations, and hoped to hear from Bragg.
On August 27 he received the latter's complete assurance that he fully

28 *Official Records*, XVI, Pt. 1, pp. 885–87.
29 *Ibid.*, 886–87; Kirby Smith to his wife, August 29, 1862, in Kirby Smith Papers,
UNC.
30 *Official Records*, XVI, Pt. 2, p. 775–76, 778.

concurred with Kirby Smith's decision. It was only a formality, for the column was already in motion when the letter arrived. A wiser leader might have reflected on the dangers of moving so far away from Bragg's army with such a small army through a barren mountain country. But Kirby Smith was too caught up with his missionary zeal to restore Kentucky to turn back. On August 25, he wrote to his wife of the awaiting Federals, "like the Egyptians of old he has hardened their hearts & blinded their eyes only to make their destruction the more complete." [31] But Kirby Smith was not yet a Moses, and green corn did not taste as good as milk and honey.

By the evening of August 29, the column had cleared Big Hill and streamed into the rolling country separating the Bluegrass from the mountains. Scott's troopers had fallen back that afternoon to report that seven Union regiments were posted nine miles north on the Lexington pike in position to block the Confederate advance. It was a tough dilemma which Kirby Smith faced. The 5,500 Confederates that he had brought from Barboursville were exhausted and short of supplies, but were also too tired to retreat a hundred miles back across the mountains. If a fight must be made, it was best to make it here. If the Federals had chosen to defend Lexington from the high bluffs overlooking the Kentucky River, the little Rebel army could scarcely have dislodged them. Then, too, intelligence reports from Scott indicated the Federals were raw levies that might be easy prey for a sudden attack. Determined to seize this advantage, Kirby Smith ordered forward Pat Cleburne, his hardest hitter, to launch the attack.[32]

At daylight on August 30, Cleburne moved toward Richmond and struck the Yankee line a half mile north of the small village of Kingston. The Federals stubbornly resisted his and Churchill's attacks at Mount Zion Church and White's Farm, but were steadily shoved back toward Richmond. By 3:30 P.M., the Union force re-formed on the outskirts of Richmond to make one final stand.

Kirby Smith's own force was in bad shape. The Confederates had been marching and fighting without water since daylight. Scouts reported that the Union general, William Nelson, had received reinforcements from Lexington. Kirby Smith knew he could expect no aid, for in the hasty march from Barboursville, Heth and Reynolds had been left far behind. Nor did the Federal position appear an easy mark. The Union line was posted on a ridge on the south edge of the town. The

[31] Kirby Smith to his wife, August 25, 1862, in Kirby Smith Papers, UNC; See also *Official Records,* XVI, Pt. 1, pp. 775, 782; Hammond, "Campaign," 248–49.

[32] *Official Records,* XVI, Pt. 1, p. 938; Hammond, "Campaign," 249–50; Kirby Smith to his wife, August 29, 1862, in Kirby Smith Papers, UNC.

left was anchored behind a stone wall in the Richmond cemetery, and the right flank held a thicket on the west side of the Lexington road.

Shortly before 5 P.M., as shadows spread across the surrounding dry fields, the Rebel skirmishers moved toward the ridge. Canister and grape-shot soon drowned the popping skirmish fire as Ben Hill's brigade stalked wearily up the slope and into the cemetery. Twilight and smoke cast an eerie pall over the hand-to-hand fighting among the tombstones. Preston Smith, who took command of the division when Cleburne was earlier wounded in the face, threw in reinforcements and the Union left crumpled into the town. On the left, Churchill drove the Union right from the thicket and onto the Lexington road.[33]

Nelson's army streamed north on the Lexington and Lancaster roads, only to be met by John Scott's cavalry. Scott had been sent by Kirby Smith earlier in the afternoon to cut off a retreat. When the main body of Federals came flying down the Lexington road, Scott opened up with his horse artillery, and half the Federal army surrendered. General Nelson was wounded and captured but escaped in the confusion and second-in-command Mahlon Manson and his staff were captured. When it was all over, out of a force of 6,500 Federals, 1,000 had been killed or wounded and 4,300 were captured along with the trains and artillery. What remained of the organized Union forces in Kentucky fell back to the Ohio River. The mayor of Lexington surrendered an empty town to Kirby Smith's advance on September 1. Two days later John Scott was raising the flag of the 1st Louisiana Cavalry over the statehouse at Frankfort.[34]

Although Kirby Smith jubilantly wrote his wife that the force now opposing him was utterly demoralized, he probably did not know just how unprepared his dash on Lexington had caught the Ohio line. Cincinnati, Newport, and Covington were near panic and under martial law. Lew Wallace was sent in to organize resistance. Business was suspended while the entire population dug trenches on the south side of the Ohio River at Covington Heights. Fire and church bells pealed

33 Hammond, "Campaign," 249–53; *Official Records,* XVI, Pt. 1, pp. 932, 934–35, 940–41, 945–47, 907–13, 951–52; Buck, *Cleburne,* 105–106. General William Nelson had not intended to fight at Richmond, but had sent General Mahlon Manson and two brigades, a force of about 6,500, to bolster the Federal cavalry there. On the afternoon of August 29, Manson notified him of Kirby Smith's approach. Nelson, under orders from the Ohio Department not to fight at Richmond unless sure of success, ordered Manson to retreat to Lexington. The latter received the order during the battle. Nelson hurried to Richmond in time to rally Manson's force for a last stand.

34 Hammond, "Campaign," 253–54; Memphis *Daily Appeal,* September 4, 1862, p. 2; Chattanooga *Daily Rebel,* September 18, 1862, p. 1; Kirby Smith, "Kentucky Campaign," UNC; *Official Records,* XVI, Pt. 1, pp. 935, 938–39, 941, 907, 909, 932–33, 936. Nelson lost 5,353 men; Kirby Smith lost 451.

alarm across southern Ohio, and local militia groups, like the Minute Men and Squirrel Hunters, poured into Cincinnati to help their city cousins hold the town. In the panic, Kirby Smith's force was rumored as thirty thousand strong, Bragg was feared to be moving on Burkesville, and Buckner was reported with another army near Tompkinsville. Abraham Lincoln grew nervous, asked where Buell was, and inquired if Bragg might not be in the Shenandoah Valley. Meanwhile the hodgepodge Cincinnati defense force continued to watch the slopes of Boone County, Kentucky, for Kirby Smith's gray hordes to appear.[35]

Kirby Smith knew little of this excitement as he happily wrote Bragg on September 3 of his victory and of his intention to push soon to the Ohio River. But something was wrong; for, since the battle at Richmond, Kirby Smith's statements were unsure, contradictory, and lacked his earlier dash. On September 6 he boasted to his wife that the remnant of the Federal army had fled broken to the Ohio. Yet in the same letter Kirby Smith spoke of remaining in Lexington and awaiting attack. He described the force at Cincinnati as thirty thousand demoralized and untrained levies, yet in the same note doubted he could hold Lexington unless Bragg came to his support. On September 3 he informed Bragg that twenty-five thousand Kentuckians were flocking to his army, but twelve days later he warned Bragg he might fall back from the Bluegrass unless supported.[36] Something had happened to the general who had termed his march one of the most remarkable of the age and unparalleled in his experiences of war, who had been proud that his army had abandoned its communications and had turned its back to the enemy, and who had stoutly declared, "I care not what the world may say, I am not ambitious." [37]

The lack of planning at Chattanooga and the faults of Kirby Smith's hastily revised strategy at Barboursville were beginning to tell. Kirby Smith now faltered, lost his sense of balance, and fell back on the defensive. His revised plan as presented to Cooper and Bragg on August 24 had had little success. Humphrey Marshall was late, so late that Kirby Smith was not sure that he had cleared Pound Gap. And from August 27 until after September 13 Kirby Smith was totally out of communica-

35 Kirby Smith to his wife, September 6, 1862, in Kirby Smith Papers, UNC; Cincinnati *Enquirer*, September 3, 5, 8, 10, 1862; Whitelaw Reid, *Ohio in the War: Her Statesmen, Generals, and Soldiers* (Columbus, 1893), I, 83–98; Lincoln to Buell, September 8, 1862, in Buell Papers, Rice; *Official Records*, XVI, Pt. 2, pp. 478–79, 486–88, 496, 509.

36 Kirby Smith to his wife, August 24, 29, September 6, 1862; Kirby Smith to H. L. Clay, August 29, 1862, all in Kirby Smith Papers, UNC; *Official Records*, XVI, Pt. 1, p. 932, Pt. 2, p. 830.

37 Kirby Smith to his wife, August 24, 1862, in Kirby Smith Papers, UNC.

tion with Bragg, and did not even know Bragg's whereabouts. Kirby
Smith was so confused that eighteen days after he entered Lexington he
still could not decide whether to try to support Bragg, watch Morgan
at Cumberland Gap, or move against Covington, Kentucky, on the Ohio
River opposite Cincinnati. Unsure of himself, he ordered Harry Heth,
who had been moved toward Covington, not to risk a battle with the
raw levies unless more support came.[38]

There were other reasons for Kirby Smith to adopt the defensive besides his indecision. A believer in Jefferson Davis' Jominian ideas of defense, he considered the occupation of territory more important than
concentration. Hence he scattered his troops to perform such relatively
menial tasks as dispersing home guards, recruiting, and performing
acts of good will to impress the citizenry. Kirby Smith was so dedicated
to the occupation of territory that by September 11 his army, now
augmented by John Morgan and John Scott to 12,500 troops, was ordered dispersed over a 200-mile line from near Cumberland Gap to
within thirty miles of the Ohio River. General Danville Leadbetter
and Colonel W. G. M. Davis were sent to hold the center at Frankfort
and Georgetown; Preston Smith held Cynthiana, some thirty-four miles
north of Lexington; Heth was sent still further north to Falmouth;
and John Morgan's 2nd Kentucky went far below London to watch
the gap. By September 15, Kirby Smith was bound so tightly to the
occupation of territory that, when Bragg advised he should retreat if
hard pressed, he replied it was now impossible to abandon the foraging
and recruiting undertaken in the Bluegrass without suffering severe
loss. Four days later, Kirby Smith refused a suggested concentration with
Bragg south of Louisville, for fear of losing the valuable supply area.[39]

Kirby Smith's decision to adopt the defensive was also a product of
his conception of the way to redeem Kentucky. In a proclamation issued from Lexington, he reiterated the statements made to Bragg and
Cooper from Barboursville—that his campaign was to test the sentiment of central Kentucky, and that if the people did not join him,
he considered there would be no further need to remain. But as he
ordered copies of his proclamation scattered far and wide, Kirby Smith
took a different approach from that suggested to Bragg by Jefferson
Davis. Instead of first defeating Buell's army and then liberating the
state as advised by Davis, Kirby Smith felt the Kentuckians must rise
first, and merit their independence by defending themselves. Time must

---

[38] Kirby Smith to his wife, September 20, 1872, in *ibid.; Official Records,* XVI, Pt. 2,
p. 807; Hammond, "Campaign," 293–94.

[39] *Official Records,* XVI, Pt. 2, pp. 804–807, 812, 830, 850; Hammond, "Campaign,"
294–95.

be allowed for Kentuckians to join the Rebel army, so Kirby Smith substituted an offensive move by recruiting and other devices designed to enlist the state's aid. And a good appearance could scarcely be presented to the citizenry if the army of gray redeemers were defeated in the offensive campaign. It remained to be seen which would entice Kentucky to throw off the supposed yoke—military success or political bargaining. But Kirby Smith, who considered any military action now as not worth the risk of losing political prestige, was staking his success on the ballot box.[40]

There was a personal element in Kirby Smith's decision to remain idle at Lexington. He felt he had done his part and that now it was Bragg's time to confront the enemy. This somewhat immature feeling was evident on August 20 when Kirby Smith spoke of his own campaign as a diversion for Bragg's move against Buell. After the battle at Richmond, Kirby Smith wrote his wife: "This move has relieved Tenn. Buell is evacuating and if Bragg pushes him and gains a victory we will have made the most brilliant campaign of the war." [41]

The feeling of aloofness toward Bragg's struggle with Buell continued to rise. On September 6, Kirby Smith wrote Samuel Cooper that "if Bragg occupies Buell we can have nothing to oppose us but raw levies." [42] And on September 27, Kirby Smith wrote his wife that his final dealings with Morgan provided the "finishing touch to our brilliant little campaign." [43]

Again too much had come too swiftly to the young general who considered his "bold and hazardous enterprise" as "crowned with success, even beyond my most sanguine expectations." "A perfect ovation," he termed it; "old and young have flocked to me." [44] The only interest he manifested in what Bragg was doing was what Bragg could do for him. Not only did he expect Bragg to contest Buell alone, but now he considered him as a supporting arm of his own operations. Kirby Smith had digressed alarmingly toward an attitude of complete independence. His description on August 20 of his move as a diversion for Bragg, though itself steeped in a desire for freedom, was mild compared to his September 6 declaration that "should Bragg come to my support in time the deliverance of the state will be insured." [45]

40 Copy of Kirby Smith's proclamation to Kentuckians (undated), in Kirby Smith Papers, UNC.

41 Kirby Smith to his wife, August 30, 1862, in *ibid.* See also *Official Records*, XVI, Pt. 2, p. 766.

42 *Official Records*, XVI, Pt. 1, p. 933.

43 Kirby Smith to his wife, September 27, 1862, in Kirby Smith Papers, UNC.

44 Kirby Smith to his wife, September 6, 1862, in *ibid.*

45 *Ibid.*

Thus when Kirby Smith learned of Bragg's approximate location, he offered little help. On September 11, when information placed Bragg and Buell as maneuvering for a battle south of Green River, Kirby Smith made no move except to send John Scott to see which one crossed the river first if they did not fight, and to give Kirby Smith "timely notice of Buell's approach." [46] The same day he ordered Heth to fall back from near Covington without firing a shot because Kirby Smith feared to risk a battle. Although Heth reportedly urged pressing the Covington line, Kirby Smith decided otherwise, and lost an opportunity to force reinforcements to be withheld from Buell. Four days later, after additional information had placed part of Buell's force moving north from Bowling Green, Kirby Smith still remained idle. He merely suggested that Scott burn some bridges north of Munfordville and observe Buell's movements. If there was a fight, Scott was to place himself in communication with Bragg—all the help Kirby Smith planned to send.[47]

Kirby Smith's aloof spirit even moved him to be not wholly honest with Bragg. On September 15, when he wrote Bragg of the reasons why he did not want to retreat from the Bluegrass, Kirby Smith magnified the obstacles on his own front. Though he believed the forces at Cincinnati were demoralized, he failed to mention this fact to Bragg. Instead he described the "largely superior force of the enemy concentrating at Cincinnati." [48] Nor did Kirby Smith even offer to help Bragg by some totally independent operation. After the war Kirby Smith wrote that his duties at Lexington included holding his command ready to join Bragg when requested, but he had dispersed his command by the time Bragg reached Kentucky. Nor did he wait for word to join Bragg. Instead, on August 24, September 3, and September 15, Kirby Smith requested that Bragg join him, and on September 19 objected to moving to join Bragg below Louisville because he was reluctant to leave the Lexington area.[49]

Kirby Smith had come a long way from the Chattanooga meeting that night of July 31, when courtesies and promises of cooperation had been given. So far there was little to show for the meeting, save for a daring raid behind the enemy lines. Perhaps there was time to salvage something of the agreement, when Bragg moved out, far across the Cumberlands to the south.

46 *Official Records*, XVI, Pt. 2, p. 812.

47 *Ibid.*, 811–12, 829; William R. Boggs, *Military Reminiscences of General Wm. R. Boggs, C.S.A.*, ed. William K. Boyd, (Durham, 1913), 42.

48 *Official Records*, XVI, Pt. 2, p. 830.

49 *Ibid.*, pp. 830, 776, 850, Pt. 1, p. 932; Kirby Smith to his wife, September 6, 1862, and Kirby Smith, "Kentucky Campaign," in Kirby Smith Papers, UNC.

twelve

A Strange Brand of Cooperation

On August 28, Bragg's army moved north from Chattanooga, bound for Kentucky. His decision to move into that state had involved a steady retreat from his earlier resolution to face Buell in Middle Tennessee. On the night of August 7, J. Stoddard Johnston, a prominent Kentuckian and later editor of the *Kentucky Yeoman,* made his way to Bragg's headquarters. He had slipped through the Federal lines in Kentucky, and urged Bragg to move into the state. Bragg eagerly pressed him for information on the possibilities of an invasion. Johnston's escape route, by way of Harrodsburg, Danville, and Albany to Sparta, Tennessee, appealed to Bragg. As early as August 8, he privately confided to Johnston his ambition to drive into Kentucky.[1]

Bragg kept silent on his new idea, for he was struggling to make a final commitment amidst conflicting advice. Jefferson Davis had suggested that Buell be defeated first before such a move, and Isham Harris continued to head a strong lobby for an assault on Nashville. Bragg's military conscience would not allow him to ignore Buell, and during the first two weeks of August he continued to toy with the idea of moving into Middle Tennessee by way of Stevenson or Murfreesboro. By August 12, he wavered, and wrote Kirby Smith that he favored a move on Lexington—but still spoke of a possible move on Nashville. As the end of

[1] Diary of J. Stoddard Johnston, June 26–September 9, 1862 (MS in J. Stoddard Johnston Papers, Filson Club), August 8, 1862; J. Stoddard Johnston, "Bragg's Campaign in Kentucky, by a Staff Officer, January, 1863" (MS in J. Stoddard Military Papers, Filson Club).

August neared, it was clear that Isham Harris must wait a little longer before he could again occupy the governor's chair. Kirby Smith would not let Bragg forget Kentucky, and on August 24 invited him to skirt Middle Tennessee and concentrate somewhere in the Great Meadow around Lexington. Bragg stiffened, abandoned Buell as his objective, and on August 27 wrote John C. Breckinridge that he planned to evade Buell and move into central Kentucky.[2]

Although Bragg would be criticized for bypassing Buell and choosing Stoddard Johnston's route to the Bluegrass, he really had little choice. When Kirby Smith bowed out of any design on Middle Tennessee, Bragg was left with only twenty-seven thousand infantry to face Buell. Also, information indicated that the Federals were entrenching at Nashville. Since he had privately resolved at Chattanooga not to risk his depleted force in an assault on an entrenched position, Bragg considered a move on Nashville suicidal. More important, he disliked the idea of Kirby Smith's moving so far away from his own army as to enhance the danger of Buell's moving between them. As he had no power to stop Kirby Smith, he decided on the only alternative that would keep the columns within supporting distance—to join his colleague. If Bragg advanced by the Sparta route, he could keep between Kirby Smith and Buell. If Buell did move north into Kentucky to hit Kirby Smith, the Federal column would have to march across Bragg's front and be liable to a flank attack.[3]

Historians would later write that Bragg moved north from Chattanooga aimlessly, and that he waited for news of Kirby Smith's or Buell's operations before he decided his own destination. This is incorrect. Conceived in his own desire to liberate Kentucky and nurtured by Kirby Smith's pressures for a northward move, Bragg's plan began to take shape. He would move into Kentucky, unite with Kirby Smith, and perhaps move on Cincinnati. The wisdom of this decision was debatable, for it remained to be seen which would secure Kentucky: an early defeat of Buell or an immediate concentration of Confederate strength in the Bluegrass. Moreover, Bragg's plan was too ambiguous. Like Kirby Smith, he had given little thought to exactly what he would do once he had reached the Bluegrass, whether he then would turn and face Buell, occupy Louisville, or definitely move on Cincinnati. The danger was not the lack of a destination but what Bragg would do once

2 Rowland (ed.), *Davis*, V, 313; *Official Records*, XVI, Pt. 2, pp. 741, 754–55, 758–59, 775, 996, XVII, Pt. 2, 897.

3 J. Stoddard Johnston, "Memoranda of Facts bearing on General Bragg's Kentucky Campaign, January 8, 1863" (MS in J. Stoddard Johnston Military Papers, Filson Club).

he arrived there. Once Bragg was committed to Kentucky invasion, he must move swiftly, for hesitation might cost time, supplies, or even the campaign.[4]

The command structure of Bragg's army was not in the best of condition for such a delicate move. He had abandoned the somewhat clumsy corps system which he inherited at Tupelo for a more compact wing command. Yet his two wing commanders, Polk and Hardee, had temperaments which might not harmonize with his own difficult personality in the midst of an arduous campaign. Polk had lost none of his stubborn, aloof manner which had plagued Albert Sidney Johnston, and a new factor had developed. Feelings between Polk and Bragg were anything but affectionate, due to Bragg's criticism of the lack of discipline in Polk's corps at Shiloh. A perfectionist at organization, Bragg considered the bishop a slovenly disciplinarian. Hardee, a superb tactician, was respected by Bragg but was a potential troublemaker. He tended to criticize his superiors, yet shirked responsibility. There was a disturbing similarity in the mannerisms of Polk and Hardee, an old-womanly air which could be easily united against Bragg.[5]

The division commanders included Generals Benjamin Cheatham and Jones M. Withers. Cheatham was a hard fighter, but possessed a crudeness which did not appeal to Bragg, who also considered him incompetent. Withers had won Bragg's praise for his conduct at Shiloh, but he was probably in too poor health for a strenuous campaign. Generals Patton J. Anderson and Simon B. Buckner commanded in Hardee's wing. Anderson, who had performed well at Pensacola under Bragg's eye, had succeeded General Sam Jones, who remained at Chattanooga as post commander to forward supplies and recruits. Buckner, recently released from Fort Warren prison, was immensely popular in his native Kentucky. Though he would be good for public relations in that state, Buckner was still untried at division rank, and there still hung over him the cloud of his surrender at Fort Donelson. Bragg's staff was equally inexperienced. His chief of staff, Colonel Thomas Jordan, had been sent to Mississippi to organize exchanged prisoners, and his successor, Colonel George G. Garner, had little experience at the post. Jordan thought that Bragg's chief quartermaster, Colonel L. W. O'Bannon, might do well as supply officer for a small post on the Texas frontier—but not for the Second Department's largest army. A mixture of inexperience and even quiet rebellion, this command aggregation could only be held together

4 Ibid.

5 Braxton Bragg to his wife, March 28, 1862, in Bragg Papers, Missouri; Lord, Fremantle Diary, 111; Roy, "Hardee's Sketch," Alabama Archives; Official Records, XVII, Pt. 2, p. 628.

by some *esprit* for Bragg's leadership. Here Bragg had failed. At Chattanooga he had openly made critical observations of his staff which did not help the officer corps' morale.[6]

Although Bragg may have had worries, his troops were exuberant as they marched away from the river. Hymns had vied with "Dixie" around flickering campfires as Bragg's troops, like Kirby Smith's, whipped themselves up with a militant religious fervor. Up over the southern slope of Walden's Ridge, Hardee's men toiled. Far below, the Tennessee raced through the gorge and Raccoon Mountain loomed in the west, but heat and dust were closer than the beauties of nature. Parched and grimed, Buckner's and Anderson's men struggled to haul their field pieces out of the valley of the Tennessee. Once over the ridge, the troops dropped into the Sequatchie Valley and followed the long trough between the Cumberland Plateau and Walden's Ridge north into Pikeville. Polk, slowed by the army's main wagon train, moved up the east side of Walden's Ridge, crossed high up opposite Pikeville, and joined Bragg on September 1.[7]

West from Pikeville, Bragg pushed to the summit of the Cumberland range. Here the road forked: west lay the last good road to Nashville via McMinnville, and north the route led through Cane Creek Valley into Sparta. There was no hestitation. On September 3, Cheatham's advance marched into Sparta.[8]

Bragg arrived the following day—and soon found he had to make a decision. By September 5 he had received Kirby Smith's report of the Richmond victory and plea that Bragg join him at Lexington. News had also been received that the planned route to Kentucky was devoid of forage and supplies, and could not sustain his troops. Bragg paused briefly at Sparta to devise another route. Kirby Smith was at the moment in no immediate danger from Union forces already in Kentucky. The problem was to find a road that would both feed the Army and take Bragg into central Kentucky.[9]

[6] "Cheatham's Military Record," B. F. Cheatham Papers, Tennessee Archives; Lord, *Fremantle Diary*, 116; Don Seitz, *Braxton Bragg, General of the Confederacy* (Columbia, S.C., 1924), 60, 79, 118–20; *Official Records*, XVI, Pt. 2, p. 762, XVII, Pt. 2, pp. 680, 669–70.

[7] Winchester Diary, Tennessee Archives, August 26, 31, 1862; General Orders No. 124, August 25, 1862, in Sterling A. Wood Papers, Alabama Archives; Polk to Bragg, August 29, 1862, Cheatham to Polk, August 27, 1862, Jones Withers to Polk, August 27, 1862, all in General Orders No. I, August 29, 1862, Ch. VIII, Vol. 342, National Archives; Johnston, "Bragg's Campaign," Military Papers, Filson Club; Marcus J. Wright, *Diary of Brigadier-General Marcus J. Wright, C.S.A. April 23, 1861–February 26, 1863* (n.p., n.d.), August 22–September 2, 1862.

[8] Johnston Diary, Filson Club, September 1, 2, 1862.

[9] *Ibid.*, September 5, 1862; *Official Records*, XVI, Pt. 1, p. 932; Johnston, "Bragg's Campaign," Military Papers, Filson Club.

The nature of Bragg's decision at Sparta would be overrated by historians. The receipt of Kirby Smith's note did not convince Bragg that he should move into Kentucky, for already at Chattanooga he had determined to bypass Buell and move into the Bluegrass. Nor did he pause at Sparta and debate an attack on Nashville. True, the Sparta camp contained a large pressure group headed by Harris, exiled governor and probably general nuisance, who still pressed him to attack Nashville. Bragg, however, had determined at Chattanooga not to hit Buell if he fortified at Nashville. On the road to Sparta, Bragg had received further news that Nashville was being fortified. Consequently, on the day he reached Sparta, Bragg wrote Sterling Price to move rapidly and capture the city, as he suspected Buell would follow him north. Nor did Bragg decide to push into Kentucky because he received news on September 7 that Buell was evacuating Nashville and falling back to Bowling Green. As early as September 2 he had sent an officer to establish forage depots on the roads from Sparta to Carthage and Gainesboro, where the Army would cross the Cumberland River. On September 5, two days before Forrest reported Buell's retreating into Kentucky, Bragg had ordered Polk to move his wing to the river crossing at Gainesboro.[10]

Probably the single decision Bragg made at Sparta was to change his route of march so that the Army would move through the general area around Glasgow, Kentucky. The Glasgow region, fed by the Green and Barren rivers, was represented to him as being a fertile section. It was also accessible from the Cumberland River crossings. From Carthage and Gainesboro, the roads led forty-seven and thirty-seven miles respectively to Tompkinsville, Kentucky. At Tompkinsville the road debouched from the Cumberland foothills into the Green River plain. The road at Tompkinsville would give Bragg a choice of two routes. The army could move the twenty-six miles to Glasgow and get on the fine Bardstown pike which would lead into the Bluegrass region, or it could veer to the east, miss Glasgow, and intersect the Bardstown pike at Clear

10 Johnston Diary, Filson Club, September 2–5, 1862; *Official Records*, XVII, Pt. 2, p. 698; Horn, *Army of Tennessee*, 167; Parks, *Kirby Smith*, 223–24; Johnston, "Bragg's Campaign," Military Papers, Filson Club. By August 30 Buell had abandoned attempting to discern Bragg's destination, and had fallen back to Murfreesboro. Yet he sent Andrew Johnson a secret letter on the thirtieth stating his plans to retreat to Nashville, where he hoped reinforcements would swell his force to fifty thousand. On September 1 Buell, already at Nashville, learned of Nelson's defeat at Richmond. Though still unsure of Bragg's destination, he informed Halleck on September 2 that he was leaving a defensive force at Nashville and was marching into Kentucky. He reported to Halleck that some information indicated that Bragg "is moving up the valley, with the object of going into Kentucky." Buell to Halleck, September 2, 1862, Buell to George Thomas, August 31, 1862, Thomas to Buell, September 2, 1862, all in Buell Papers, Rice; Buell, *Statement of Major General Buell*, 24.

Point. When Bragg ordered Polk to move out on the fifth, he evidently had not yet decided upon the exact route to take through the Glasgow region.[11]

News from Bedford Forrest gave Bragg his answer. On the morning of the seventh, the wiry cavalryman, who had ranged toward Nashville to observe Buell, reported the Federals rapidly evacuating the city. Bragg, who had lost three days at Sparta, pushed his columns toward the Cumberland River, although he still had not chosen his exact route. On September 9 Forrest sent in more disturbing news. Half of Buell's army was on the move north from Nashville on the seventy-one-mile march to Bowling Green, and the other half would soon follow. Bragg had committed the kind of tactical error that constantly plagued his generalship—he had underestimated his opponent. Although his troops were not unduly jaded when they reached Sparta, Bragg had rested them while he issued proclamations of congratulations for Kirby Smith's victory. The excellent time made between Chattanooga and Sparta now threatened to be lost. Should Buell win the race to the Louisville turnpike, which ran parallel to the Bardstown pike, Kirby Smith would be isolated and Bragg would face alone an army he believed twice his size.[12]

Bragg studied a map Hardee had sent him and pinpointed his route. Polk, already across the river at Gainesboro, was ordered to hasten by way of Tompkinsville to Glasgow, where Hardee would join him. It would be a close race; for, while Polk must march sixty-three miles from the river to Glasgow, Buell, supposedly already in motion, had only seventy-one miles to go to Bowling Green. If Polk reached Glasgow swiftly, he could move nine miles across to the Louisville pike, which curved northeast from Bowling Green. If Bragg seized this junction, the main highway to Louisville would be blocked, and the Rebels could march unopposed on the parallel Bardstown pike to join Kirby Smith. To reach the junction, Buell must move twenty-eight more miles from Bowling Green. Thanks to John Morgan, the railroad between Nashville and Bowling Green was wrecked, but what of the line north from Bowling Green? Bragg saw the danger and on September 10 ordered Polk to seize the railroad near the Cave City junction on the Louisville pike. Determined to keep the campaign moving, he wrote Kirby Smith and suggested he fall back from Lexington if hard pressed, and then hurried north with Hardee to Polk's aid.[13]

11 Johnston, "Bragg's Campaign," Military Papers, Filson Club.

12 "Johnston Memoranda," Military Papers, Filson Club; Official Records, XVI, Pt. 2, pp. 796, 799–800; Hardee to Bragg, September 9, 1862, and Bragg to Polk, September 9, 1862, in Bragg Papers, Western Reserve.

13 Bragg to Polk, September 9, 1862, in Bragg Papers, Western Reserve; Official Records, XVI, Pt. 2, pp. 806, 811. Ironically, both Bragg and Buell received information on the seventh that was incorrect yet spurred each general to hurry into Ken-

Bragg reached Glasgow on September 14 and found the situation disappointing. Polk had succeeded in cutting the railroad. General James R. Chalmers' brigade was across it at Cave City, and General J. K. Duncan's brigade held the road at the Glasgow road junction. But Glasgow was not the land of plenty Bragg had hoped for. His troops, already self-subsistent, were in the Barren River country, where only three counties in the region raised over a half million bushels of corn a year. Buell held two of them, Warren and Simpson. Bragg held Barren, of which Glasgow was the county seat, but it had long since been scoured by foragers from Bowling Green.

Bragg would later be criticized for not striking Buell from Glasgow. On September 10 Bragg did have a fleeting desire to deviate from his plan to join Kirby Smith and to strike at Bowling Green, but his desire was abandoned when he reached Glasgow. By September 14 Bragg had information that Rosecrans and part of his army were at Nashville and that the bulk of Buell's army was moving into Bowling Green—too much for Bragg's undersupplied twenty-seven thousand troops to handle. The Rebel supplies were practically exhausted, Bragg believed he was heavily outnumbered, and Kirby Smith was still two hundred miles to the northeast. It was imperative that Bragg push on and join Kirby Smith.[14]

But with Buell so close, Bragg felt a revision of strategy was necessary. Instead of marching to join Kirby Smith for a move on Cincinnati, Bragg now planned a joint assault with him on Louisville. That shining city of the Ohio, the supply depot of Buell's army, symbolized Yankee power in Kentucky. So far Bragg had seen little enthusiasm for the Confederates; perhaps if the gray line swept to the Falls of the Ohio, the people could not resist this Southern army. David Harris, Bragg's chief engineer, suggested a route which offered ample water in the fierce

---

tucky. A reconnaissance force reported to Buell that Bragg's destination was Bowling Green; that morning Bragg received a report that Buell was evacuating Nashville. Neither was entirely correct. Buell's five divisions totaling some 35,000 men were not concentrated at Bowling Green until September 14. He was not certain Bragg was moving into Kentucky until the night of the thirteenth after which he called up Thomas's division, 7,400, from Nashville as a reinforcement. Thomas did not join Buell until September 20 at Green River. Two divisions totaling some 13,418 were left to guard Nashville. *Official Records,* XVI, Pt. 2, pp. 493, 562–63, 988; Buell to Thomas, September 13, 1862, in Buell Papers, Rice.

14 Special Orders No. 17, September 12, 1862, in Special Orders, Commands of Generals Leonidas Polk, D. H. Maury, S. D. Lee, and Richard Taylor, 1862–64, Ch. II, Vol. 15, National Archives; George Williamson to J. J. Walker, September 15, 1862, in Letters sent, General Leonidas Polk's Command, 1862–64, Ch. II, Vol. 13, National Archives, hereinafter cited as Ch. II, Vol. 13, National Archives; *Official Records,* XVI, Pt. 2, pp. 806, 811, 818, 825–26; Bragg to Kirby Smith, September 23, 1862, in Bragg Papers, Western Reserve; U.S. Bureau of the Census, *Agriculture of the United States in 1860,* 58–59, 62–63.

drought: north by way of New Haven on the gravel pike to Bardstown, from whence several roads led northwest to Louisville. Bragg liked the plan and wrote Kirby Smith for aid.

The difficulties of cooperative command were now to be augmented, for Bragg would stake all on two distant armies. On September 12 he had reiterated his order to Price, far south at Iuka, to sweep into Middle Tennessee. And now on September 15 Bragg requested Kirby Smith to hold his force in readiness for a combined thrust on Louisville by September 23. Bragg also asked that Cleburne's and Preston Smith's brigades be moved to Shelbyville forty-six miles west of Lexington, where they would be in position to join Bragg. Again the spirit of cooperation would be strained. Bragg, who expected a commander to accomplish a task about which the commander had received no exact orders, now counted heavily on Kirby Smith. Yet Bragg knew little of Kirby Smith's position, nor did the East Tennessee commander's past record in the campaign promise swift cooperation.[15]

The plan to join Kirby Smith suffered an early setback. Chalmers had marched his brigade north from Cave City to Munfordville and had attacked the Federal garrison guarding the Green River bridge. The unauthorized attack had been costly. Chalmers had been sharply repulsed by the 4,000-man post and had retreated to Cave City. He had lost only 285 men, but the defeat jolted Bragg and touched sore spots in his strategical ability. Bragg became easily upset when obstacles seemed to jeopardize his plans, and he tended to magnify problems out of proportion. Chalmers' loss was small—but it was Bragg's first as Second Department commander, and the first of the campaign. In the early hours of the fifteenth, the chagrin of defeat outweighed the geographical and logistical problems involved in moving the army over to the Louisville pike—and Bragg decided to march to Munfordville. He considered it a mere detour, for his request for Kirby Smith to prepare for a meeting was written *after* Bragg issued orders to march to Munfordville. But Bragg would have to pay a heavy price for the satisfaction to be gained in overpowering the garrison. Time, supplies, and the advantage of moving on the Bardstown pike would be sacrificed, and the all-important junction with Kirby Smith would be delayed.[16]

[15] Johnston "Bragg's Campaign," Military Papers, Filson Club; Seitz, *Braxton Bragg,* 173–74; David Harris to Bragg, September 15, 1862, in David Harris Papers, Duke; *Official Records,* XVII, Pt. 2, p. 706.

[16] *Official Records,* XVI, Pt. 2, 825. Buell did not expect Bragg to move from Glasgow to Munfordville, and so on September 16 prepared to move against Bragg at Glasgow. Buell to Halleck, September 14, 1862, Buell to H. G. Wright, September 14, 1862, Testimony of General A. M. McCook (MS), all in Buell Papers, Rice; Buell, *Statement of Major General Buell,* 31, 34.

Bragg now hurried to Munfordville, as Buell was reported assembling his army at Bowling Green, only forty miles southwest of the garrison. Polk scooped up what meager stores he had on hand, left his empty trains behind, swung east of Munfordville, crossed Green River, and came up behind the garrison. Hardee, with Bragg riding in the van, moved up the Louisville pike, and by the morning of September 16 was in position on the hills south of Green River. Bragg and his staff pushed forward to reconnoiter the fortifications. The garrison lay on the south bank of the river opposite the village of Munfordville. Any expectations Bragg may have entertained of a hasty seizure were dismissed when he observed the extensive rifle pits, stockades, and earthworks that guarded the bridge. As Hardee's skirmishers fanned out into the river bottom, the field pieces that bristled from behind the Yankee works flashed, and shells shrieked over Bragg's head. The capture of the garrison promised to be a difficult task, and he had little time to spare. He rushed a staff officer to Polk. Bragg would attack at daylight if his surrender demands were refused; Polk was to notify him when his wing was in position.[17]

Bragg sent the blue garrison a note, asking surrender; Colonel Cyrus Dunham replied he would defend to the last. The war of words was on. Surprised at the rebuff, Bragg moved his twenty-seven thousand in closer, unlimbered his artillery, and glanced nervously over his shoulder at Bowling Green. Eventually Dunham sent a request for a truce to consider Bragg's proposal. Bragg magnanimously agreed to hold his fire until 9 P.M.—as he did not plan to attack until dawn anyway. The afternoon wore into evening, and five note exchanges later, Colonel John T. Wilder was in command of the garrison. Wilder stalled for time by engaging Bragg in a discussion as to whether the rules of honorable warfare permitted Bragg to move his batteries into position while the truce flag was up. Then Wilder agreed to surrender if given ample proof of Bragg's strength. Bragg mustered his most militant language and promised the only proof Wilder would receive would be the use of his force—but agreed to another hour's truce. But Simon Buckner, the local boy from Hart County, came down to the river and took Wilder on a tour through Hardee's lines. Wilder counted some forty-five cannons, and decided a surrender would be honorable enough.[18]

17 George Williamson to Jones Withers, September 15, 1862, in Ch. II, Vol. 13, National Archives; Johnston, "Bragg's Campaign," Military Papers, Filson Club; Winchester Diary, Tennessee Archives, September 17–19, 1862; Official Records, XVI, Pt. 2, pp. 825–28, 833.

18 Johnston, "Bragg's Campaign," Military Papers, Filson Club; John T. Wilder, "The Siege of Munfordville," in Samuel Cole Williams, General John T. Wilder, Commander of the Lightning Brigade (Bloomington, 1936), 61–63; Official Records, XVI, Pt. 1, pp. 968–71.

But the night wore on and Wilder was not through stalling. Buckner brought him into Bragg's headquarters about midnight. Then the commander of the Munfordville garrison and the head of the Second Department bickered for two more hours over the semantics of the term "unconditional surrender." After a rousing debate over whether Bragg would march in or Wilder would march out, Wilder won. The surrender was signed, and the Federal chief agreed to move out at 6 A.M. and stack arms.[19]

Two precious days had been consumed, but Bragg, like Kirby Smith, was relishing his first victory as department commander, and was determined to act in grand style. Polk brought his troops across the river for the festivities, and the wing and division commanders joined Bragg and his cavalry escort in the reception line. Wilder was two hours late as his column approached the awaiting Confederates at Rowlett's Station. Buckner waited in the road, received Wilder's sword, and promptly handed it back, to the pleasure of onlookers. Then the Yankees stacked arms and marched off to be paroled while Bragg and his generals enjoyed themselves inspecting the fortifications.[20]

And now Bragg wavered at a crucial time. There was no change of plan—the march on Louisville with Kirby Smith would still be made—but he had lost his sense of urgency. Still elated by the first fruits of his campaign, Bragg probably was again underestimating his opponent. He expected Buell to be still at Bowling Green, and even boasted to Cooper on the seventeenth that Buell would not dare attack him at Green River. Lulled by his success, he set aside September 18 as a day of thanksgiving and prayer for his army. Had he planned to await Buell or had there been no force to the north to oppose his Louisville thrust, the delay might have been less serious. But on the seventeenth Bragg had informed Cooper that he would soon move to join Kirby Smith and reminded that commander to be ready for a concentration. If Louisville and the meeting with Kirby Smith were his objectives, he should have moved out swiftly. On the seventeenth he had information that a strong force was digging in at Louisville to oppose his advance. To capture the city before Buell came up from the south would be difficult enough, and the day of thanksgiving and prayer brought the blue defenders more time.[21]

19 Wilder, "Siege of Munfordville," 62–63.

20 *Official Records*, XVI, Pt. 2, p. 837; Winchester Diary, Tennessee Archives, September 17–18, 1862; Johnston, "Bragg's Campaign," Military Papers, Filson Club.

21 *Official Records*, XVI, Pt. 1, p. 968, Pt. 2, pp. 850, 858; General Orders No. 7, Army of the Mississippi, September 18, 1862, Ch. II, Vol. 342, National Archives; Johnston, "Bragg's Campaign," Military Papers, Filson Club.

On the night of the seventeenth, tension suddenly mounted at Green River as Bragg realized he had misjudged Buell. Spy and scout reports indicated Buell was not behind his Bowling Green entrenchments as Bragg had supposed. Instead the Yankees were swinging west of the main Louisville pike, and were reported moving through Leitchfield, Hawesville, Brownsville, and even Owensboro, to skirt Bragg and get into Louisville. Bragg, realizing his error, moved Cheatham's division north toward Beaver Dam Creek, and ordered the entire force to march at daylight on September 19 to join Kirby Smith.[22]

Bragg's inability to make a final commitment now began to tell. Early on the morning of September 18, in the midst of a drizzling rain, Wheeler's exhausted troopers staggered in from near Bowling Green. At a critical time Wheeler had failed to pinpoint Buell's location. He reported a heavy Union force was crossing Big Barren and moving north around Bragg. But another force of infantry in division strength had loomed up in Bragg's front on the Munfordville pike. Wheeler had been pushed back, his picket at Merry Oaks had collapsed, and he could tell Bragg little of the mysterious force approaching Green River. Bragg hesitated, ordered Polk to halt his column, and sent Wheeler back to Cave City to feel out the Yankee advance.

Had Bragg planned to remain and fight, should the force prove to be Buell's army, his hesitation might seem justified. But he was still committed to his junction with Kirby Smith, so committed that he sent Stoddard Johnston to Lexington on September 18 to arrange it. Johnston was to deliver an important verbal request—one which might easily be misconstrued. Would Kirby Smith do three things: send a heavy train of provisions to Bardstown to meet Bragg's column, move with all available forces to Bardstown to prepare for the Louisville attack, and keep a sharp eye on Morgan at Cumberland Gap? The request was a poor substitute for an order, but was all Bragg could do—the rest was up to Kirby Smith. Bragg wanted to hasten the junction and fulfill the ambition expressed to his wife on the eighteenth: "Tomorrow we march— full of hope and zeal. Cincinnati must fall for the redemption of New Orleans." [23] He could not bring himself, however, to move his army—but waited for news from Wheeler.[24]

On September 19 Bragg lost his nerve—and another day's supplies. Couriers from Wheeler had sloshed through the pouring rain on the

22 Johnston, "Bragg's Campaign," Military Papers, Filson Club; Wright, *Diary*, September 16–17, 1862; *Official Records*, XVI, Pt. 1, p. 894, Pt. 2, p. 843.

23 Bragg to his wife, September 18, 1862, in Bragg Papers, Missouri.

24 Johnston, "Bragg's Campaign," Military Papers, Filson Club; Wright, *Diary*, September 18–19, 1862; *Official Records*, XVI, Pt. 1, p. 894, Pt. 2, p. 843.

night of the eighteenth to bring news at last. Blue columns were massing at Cave City, and light skirmishing had already begun. Bragg had not expected a Federal move which might interfere with his strategy, and he was unprepared for it. At 1 A.M. on September 19, he panicked and decided Buell's whole army was moving through the cave country toward Green River. Although the paucity of Wheeler's information did not warrant it, Bragg halted temporarily plans to move north, and Bedford Forrest was called in from his position north near Elizabethtown. Out on the Louisville pike Cheatham's marching orders were an indication of Bragg's momentary breakdown—first toward Bardstown, then back toward Munfordville, then halted, and now back to Green River. Bragg, whose loss of balance was probably caused by a lack of sleep, waited for further word from Wheeler.[25]

By the afternoon of the nineteenth Bragg had recovered his determination to join Kirby Smith. Nothing more was reported from Wheeler except a continuation of skirmish fire. Impatient to uncover Buell's location, Bragg sent Buckner's division to the front to feel out the enemy. Some historians would later contend that he sent Buckner to draw Buell into battle, but this is probably wrong. Buckner was sent to ascertain if the force in Wheeler's front was merely covering the Yankee flank move that Bragg feared. Nor is there evidence Bragg would have remained to fight Buell should Buckner uncover the Union army, for his announcement of Buckner's move added that "we march at daylight tomorrow to effect a junction with General Kirby Smith." [26]

Buckner reported nothing of importance on his front, and Bragg continued plans for the junction. The trains were sent to Bardstown and early on the morning of September 20, the Army of the Mississippi moved north to Nolin and veered off the Louisville pike onto the Bardstown road. But the hesitation had been costly—three days had been lost, and the army had only three days' meager rations.[27]

Bragg knew only what was reported, and reports had pointed to a flanking move. Wheeler would later admit he considered the Federals might be moving north around Bragg, and so reported to the general. When Bragg conferred with his officers on the seventeenth, all agreed Buell would not move on Green River but would flank via Owensboro

25 *Official Records*, Pt. 1, p. 894, Pt. 2, p. 848; Polk to Cheatham, September 19, 1862, Polk to N. B. Forrest, September 19 (1:30 A.M.) , 1862, Ch. II, Vol. 13, National Archives; Johnston, "Bragg's Campaign," Military Papers, Filson Club.

26 *Official Records*, XVI, Pt. 2, p. 849.

27 George Williamson to N. B. Forrest, September 20, 1862, Ch. II, Vol. 13, National Archives; *Official Records*, XVI, Pt. 2, p. 849.

or Hawesville. And Bragg's own spies had reported that Buell was flanking the Confederates. If Buell had moved around Bragg, the Federals could move into Louisville or take a position in Bragg's rear at Elizabethtown, thirty-five miles north of Munfordville. Such a position at Elizabethtown would have effectually cut Bragg off from Kirby Smith, and also have stopped the planned move north. And on September 19, after Bragg recovered from his early morning consternation, his chief apprehension was a Federal flanking attempt—not a move toward Green River.[28]

Bragg would be maligned for seemingly turning away from Buell and marching off the Louisville road, and the "Munfordville Myth" would persist that at Green River Bragg blocked Buell's advance. However, Bragg realized that he did not have Buell cut off from Louisville, as there were a half dozen other routes by which the Federals could reach the city. Nor was the railroad bridge at Green River vital, for Chalmers reported on September 19 that John Scott had already cut the line north near Rolling Fork. And if Bragg had desired to fight at Green River, he would have placed his force in danger. Kirby Smith could not be ordered to Munfordville, and Bragg's own twenty-seven thousand infantry, with three days' poor rations, would have faced an army Bragg believed twice the size of his own—provided that army moved out to fight him. To remain at Munfordville would also pass the offensive to Buell. The Federals had three choices. They could flank Bragg out of his position, which move he feared. Or Buell could remain in the strong defensive works at Bowling Green which Bragg and his officers agreed were too strong to carry. Or, finally, Buell could attack Bragg at Green River. With short rations in the parched and barren Munfordville section, Bragg's small army would then be squeezed between Buell's army and the rapidly accumulating force at Louisville.

Bragg had good reason to fear losing his army. Jefferson Davis had given him private instructions not to risk his army where a defeat might be suffered. Self-confidence was never one of Bragg's virtues, and the admonition from Davis only moved him to be more cautious and fearful of making an error. To the south lay his own department. If his army were smashed, there would be nothing on Van Dorn's and Price's right flank to resist a Union drive into the Deep South.

[28] Bragg's own spies brought news of the flank move on the night of the seventeenth (Johnston, "Bragg's Campaign," Military Papers, Filson Club). Wheeler admitted he mistook Buell's empty wagon train, sent by Buell north around Bragg via Leitchfield, for Buell's army. *Official Records*, XVI, Pt. 1, p. 894. See also *ibid.*, p. 1090, Pt. 2, pp. 849, 876.

The burden of responsibility—which Bragg disliked—lay heavily on his shoulders.[29]

Considering what he planned to do, Bragg's mistake was not in abandoning Munfordville but in going there in the first place. The move had shown his consistent lack of appreciation for geography. He had thrown his army off the fine New Haven pike that ran north to Bardstown, and thus delayed his junction with Kirby Smith. At Green River, Bragg had placed his small force between Buell and the army at Louisville. Already he was separated from Kirby Smith by the Muldraugh's Hill range northeast of Munfordville, and a defeat at Green River would have driven Bragg into an angle between the Ohio and Salt Rivers. The Green River adventure may have slightly boosted morale, but it had proved detrimental in time, position, and supplies. That Bragg fully realized his danger is uncertain, but he understood enough to abandon Green River for the belated junction at Bardstown.[30]

But the Bardstown meeting never came. On September 22, Bragg arrived at Bardstown only to make probably the most signal decision of the campaign—to abandon the offensive. It came suddenly, a far cry from his resolutions to sweep to the Ohio, avenge New Orleans, and strike at Louisville. Bragg would later blame Kirby Smith for the abandonment of the Louisville design. Kirby Smith, enjoying his independence, had not responded to Bragg's letter of September 15 or to his personal emissary. Instead he held the bulk of his army at Georgetown and Paris, near Lexington. On September 21 he wrote Bragg, "With the enemy advancing from Covington and the Gap, and Marshall not in supporting distance, a junction with you below Louisville both loses us the valuable stores and supplies captured here and checks the organization of the new levies now in fair progress." [31] Moreover, Kirby

29 *Official Records*, XVI, Pt. 1, pp. 894, 1090, Pt. 2, p. 876; Johnston, "Bragg's Campaign," Military Papers, Filson Club; Buell, *Statement of Major General Buell*, 31; Wilder, "Siege of Munfordville," 57; Parks, *Kirby Smith*, 225–26; Duke, *Reminiscences*, 307–17. General McCook said there was no place between Munfordville and the mouth of Salt River where an army could get supplies. *Official Records*, XVI, Pt. 1, p. 113; "Johnston Memoranda," Military Papers, Filson Club.

30 "Johnston Memoranda," Military Papers, Filson Club. Buell said Munfordville was not "essential to Bragg's army in a strategical point of view." Buell, *Statement of Major General Buell*, 32–33. On the seventeenth Buell learned of Munfordville's surrender, and pushed to Green River, expecting Bragg to fight. He hesitated to attack Bragg until Thomas arrived, and so did not advance until the twentieth, as he thought Bragg had at least thirty-five thousand men, independent of Kirby Smith. On the 21st, Buell learned Bragg had left Munfordville. See Thomas B. Van Horne, *History of the Army of the Cumberland, Its Organization, Campaigns, and Battles* (Cincinnati, 1875), I, 173; *Official Records*, XVI, Pt. 1, pp. 47–48, Pt. 2, p. 527; Buell to C. C. Gilbert, September 21, 1862, in Buell Papers, Rice.

31 *Official Records*, XVI, Pt. 2, p. 861.

Smith had halted, until further orders came from Bragg, Cleburne's and Preston Smith's brigades, which had been promised at Shelbyville by September 23. Bragg would later criticize the abandonment of the Louisville plan, and in May, 1863, he wrote Cooper that Kirby Smith's action "prevented a junction of our forces, and enabled General Buell to reach Louisville before the assault could be made upon that city." [32] But Kirby Smith had not disrupted Bragg's designs on Louisville. On September 23 Bragg expressed no criticism to Kirby Smith for his actions. Indeed, he termed the halt of Cleburne and Preston Smith as "a very judicious move—and fully approved." [33] Bragg added that he did not move directly on Louisville because of a lack of supplies, and noted that his troops were so jaded that they could not move anywhere for several days.

Instead Bragg decided to fall back on a defensive line in the Kentucky River region. He had changed his attitude suddenly, and had become despondent and discouraged over future prospects in Kentucky. By September 23 he was convinced that the Confederates could not successfully compete with the force gathered at Louisville. He suggested to Kirby Smith that the two armies might draw back to Danville, forty-five miles east of Bardstown and near the confluence of the Kentucky and Dick's rivers, "if obliged to retire." [34] Two days later, Bragg gloomily wrote Samuel Cooper that "the garden spot of Kentucky" might have to be abandoned, and discussed the losses that would occur "should we have to retire." [35] On September 27 Bragg carried his mental retreat further. He informed Kirby Smith that a depot was to be established at Bryantsville, fifty-five miles east of Bardstown and across Dick's River. The depot would serve as "a rallying point for us in case of necessity." He also directed a depot to be established on the road to Cumberland Gap. He explained to Kirby Smith that this was necessary "so that in case of absolute necessity we could make the gap with our haversacks. . . ." [36]

What caused Bragg's despondency and his decision to fall back into the Bluegrass on a defensive line? His personality and strategical concepts were important factors. When he started north through Tennessee, he had devised a loose but large plan with several interdependent components. Kirby Smith would cooperate with him, and the two would carry their banners to the Indiana or Ohio shore. Price and Van Dorn must

[32] *Ibid.*, Pt. 1, p. 1091.
[33] Bragg to Kirby Smith, September 23, 1862, in Bragg Papers, Western Reserve.
[34] *Ibid.*
[35] *Official Records*, XVI, Pt. 2, p. 876.
[36] Bragg to Kirby Smith, September 27, 1862, in Bragg Papers, Western Reserve.

press Grant and Rosecrans to prevent their reinforcing Buell, and then must sweep into Middle Tennessee. Breckinridge, the popular hero, must hasten reinforcements. And most important, Kentuckians must rise to defend themselves. The plan was difficult as it would require clear instructions and perfect timing. Bragg, until then recognized chiefly as an able disciplinarian, went into the campaign inexperienced in the planning of long-range moves. When he reached Bardstown, it was evident to him that his strategy was falling apart. An inability to give specific orders meant that the separate forces, instead of being coordinated, must rely on each commander's personal discretion. The plan of concerted action with Kirby Smith had tied Bragg's hands. Bragg lacked the air of one who could command respect, and was unable to assume the initiative which might have brought Kirby Smith into closer cooperation. Nor could he bring himself to give specific orders to those he could command—Price, Van Dorn, and Breckinridge. He gave them little personal attention, allowed them discretion to formulate much of their own plan—although he counted heavily on the results. His inability to commit an order now hurt, for the grand plan of invasion had broken apart. Seldom able to readjust a rigid scheme, he now became confused, lost his sense of timing—and surrendered the initiative to Buell.[37]

The first failure of the strategy came in the Bluegrass. Kirby Smith could have aided Bragg in several ways, but he failed to attempt any of them. While Bragg moved through Tennessee and into Kentucky, Kirby Smith could have threatened Cincinnati and relieved pressure on the Louisville line. Instead, he dispersed his force to perform numerous duties, considered his military objective to have terminated at Lexington, and waited for Bragg to finish with Buell. After the war he would write that he did not press Cincinnati because Bragg requested first he hold the command ready for a concentration. Yet Kirby Smith did not receive Bragg's request until September 18. In the first sixteen days of his Lexington sojourn, Kirby Smith had made only one halfhearted feint with Heth's division.[38]

Kirby Smith could have moved west to Bragg's support. But this he failed to do as he considered Buell to be Bragg's responsibility. In letters to Bragg on September 18–21, Kirby Smith advised that the former move on Louisville alone, since he was unwilling to leave the country around Lexington. He never took seriously Bragg's request for a concentration. Two days after he had received Bragg's note of the

---

37 Hay, "Braxton Bragg," 302 n., 304.

38 Kirby Smith to his wife, August 29, September 6, 1862, and Kirby Smith, "Kentucky Campaign," in Kirby Smith Papers, UNC; *Official Records*, XVI, Pt. 1, p. 933, Pt. 2, pp. 807, 812, 845–46.

fifteenth, Kirby Smith wrote his wife, "Bragg is moving on Louisville. Morgan is reported to have evacuated the Gap and my little command is posted so as to cooperate with Bragg, to concentrate against Morgan or the force from Cincinnati as circumstances may demand." [39]

Kirby Smith also took Bragg's personal emissary lightly. After the war Kirby Smith would assert that Bragg did not request a concentration *at* Bardstown but preparation *for* a concentration there. Thirty years after the war Stoddard Johnston could not remember exactly what he told Kirby Smith.[40] The latter seems to have taken advantage of Bragg's lack of authority to give him an order. After his meeting with Stoddard Johnston, Kirby Smith wrote Humphrey Marshall on September 21 that, although Bragg had requested aid for a Louisville attack, "I feel every confidence in the ability of General Bragg to take Louisville and in our ability to hold this section." [41] Then the young commander dashed off his note to Bragg informing him that there would be no concentration below Louisville.[42]

Kirby Smith could also have kept a sharp eye on George Morgan at Cumberland Gap. This he failed to do. Like Bragg, he was concerned with the possibility of Morgan's escape. He had counted heavily on Humphrey Marshall's force marching through Pound Gap to intercept Morgan should he retreat north. On September 18 Kirby Smith learned that Morgan had left the gap and was fleeing for the Ohio River. Six days later Morgan was reported sixty-eight miles southeast of Lexington and driving hard for the Ohio. Although Marshall had arrived at Mount Sterling, Kentucky, in position to block Morgan's path, Kirby Smith's old rivalry with Morgan and fears of losing prestige in Kentucky perhaps got the better of him. He marched his entire force to Mount Sterling to join Marshall. But Morgan veered to the east and escaped across Licking River with Colonel John Morgan's cavalry nipping at his heels. The failure to stop the retreating Yankees was less serious than the consequences of Kirby Smith's move—he was now 101 miles east of Bragg.[43]

The second failure of the grand strategy, Marshall's support in southeastern Kentucky, indicated something was seriously wrong with the scheme of cooperation. Marshall had arrived late partly because of a

39 Kirby Smith to his wife, September 20, 1862, in Kirby Smith Papers, UNC.

40 Kirby Smith to J. Stoddard Johnston, October 31, 1866, in Johnston Papers, Filson Club; "Bragg's Kentucky Campaign, 1895" (MS in Johnston, Military Papers, Filson Club). In his 1895 account Johnston changed from his 1863 version and said Kirby Smith was supposed to concentrate, but did not mention where.

41 *Official Records,* XVI, Pt. 2, p. 859.

42 *Ibid.,* 861. See also pp. 845–46, 850, 856.

43 *Ibid.,* 846, 859, 861, 866, 869–75.

long struggle among the Confederate high command as to whether he would be allowed to enter Kentucky. In March, Robert E. Lee had placed Marshall under Kirby Smith's direction should the latter desire to enter Kentucky. Kirby Smith, Bragg, and Marshall neglected to inform Richmond that Marshall was to be included in the Kentucky plan. After General W. W. Loring, commander of the Department of Western Virginia, complained of the proposed move, Jefferson Davis on August 6 refused to allow Marshall to leave the department. Davis, ignorant of Kirby Smith's meeting with Marshall, assumed that Marshall desired to raid Kentucky in conjunction with John Morgan. It was not until August 14 that Richmond gave evidence of knowing Marshall was to participate in the invasion.[44]

But Marshall's personality proved another problem. A prominent Kentuckian, Marshall had become embittered by his service in the rugged Department of Western Virginia, for he felt it was a long step down from what he merited by his reputation. He had become quarrelsome, quick to perceive an injustice, and fearful of losing authority. His near 300-pound frame caused him to move slowly in the mountains, and had he arrived sooner in East Kentucky he might have intercepted Morgan at some point south of Mount Sterling. But this unusual fellow, reportedly a devout believer in spiritual seances, failed to provide the necessary support on the right flank. And Bragg had needed a general there—not a spiritualist.[45]

Failure had also come on the left flank. Bragg had counted heavily on Van Dorn and Price to prevent Rosecrans from reinforcing Buell, and on September 4 and 12 had sent Price instructions to move on Nashville. But at Bardstown Bragg received news from Kirby Smith and other sources that indicated his lieutenants had failed him. The combined armies of Buell, Rosecrans, Grant, Curtis, and the new levies from Ohio and Indiana were reported at Louisville. Bragg was bitterly disappointed at the apparent failure to stop Grant and Rosecrans. Although he lashed out at Van Dorn as being self-willed and weak-minded, Bragg himself had made the error. He had not outlined for Richmond what he desired of his Mississippi command. Van Dorn, who disagreed with Bragg over moving into Middle Tennessee, wanted Price to join him in a move through West Tennessee and western Kentucky.

44 *Ibid.*, XII, Pt. 3, pp. 921–22, 927, XVI, Pt. 2, pp. 745, 759, 763–65, LII, Pt. 2, p. 341, X, Pt. 2, pp. 330–31.

45 Humphrey Marshall to Alexander Stephens, November 30, 1861, February 22, 1862, and Marshall to A. S. Johnston, December 17, 1861, in Humphrey Marshall Letters, Filson Club; Marshall to his wife, December 18, 1861, in Buell Papers, Rice; Duke, *Reminiscenes*, 142–46.

When Price refused, Van Dorn appealed to Richmond. Although Davis admitted he was ignorant of Bragg's plans for Van Dorn and Price, he placed Van Dorn in command of Price's column. Bragg had intended for Van Dorn to command Price only when the two were joined for a thrust into Middle Tennessee. Van Dorn now took advantage of his authority, stopped Price on the eve of a march on Nashville, and prepared to accomplish an old ambition—to attack Corinth, Mississippi. Not only did Bragg's left flank not threaten Middle Tennessee, it never crossed the Tennessee River.[46]

The failure of Breckinridge to arrive proved a fourth disappointment. Again Bragg had counted heavily on a commander to accomplish a task without providing sufficient orders to insure its execution. Bragg never ordered Breckinridge to come, nor did he order Van Dorn to allow the Kentuckian to leave his district. Confusion ensued on August 25 when Breckinridge notified Bragg he would come to Chattanooga. That same day, Bragg had wired Van Dorn to push with Sterling Price to cut off reinforcements reported moving from Corinth to Nashville. As Bragg had not authorized Breckinridge's departure, Van Dorn refused to let him leave. Instead Van Dorn wanted Breckinridge's support in his own move north. Van Dorn later relented, but Breckinridge had been seriously delayed. On October 2, at Lexington, Bragg would learn that Breckinridge had just arrived at Chattanooga and for all purposes was out of the invasion.[47]

And what had become of the planned attack on Louisville? The Louisville myth would be almost as persistent as that of Munfordville, and Bragg would later be maligned for not moving on a city defended mainly by levies. Such criticism fails to consider what Bragg knew of Louisville. At Munfordville he knew Louisville was defended by a rapidly accumulating force of undetermined origin. At Bardstown he received information from Kirby Smith and others that five armies, including Buell's, were massed at Louisville, and that the much desired supplies in Buell's depot were already being transferred to the Indiana shore. Bragg's mistake was not in abandoning his Louisville plan but in his intention to go there at all. Had he marched there from Green River, he would have been trapped in the angle of the Ohio and Salt Rivers, between Buell and the Louisville force, with three days' rations and the Federals in control of the opposite bank of

---

[46] Bragg to Davis, October 2, 1862, in Braxton Bragg Papers, United States Military Academy Library, West Point; *Official Records*, XVII, Pt. 2, pp. 675–77, 691–93, 696–700, 705–706; Horn, *Army of Tennessee*, 174.

[47] Bragg to Davis, October 2, 1862, in Bragg Papers, West Point; *Official Records*, XVI, Pt. 2, pp. 995–97, XVII, Pt. 2, p. 897, LII, Pt. 2, p. 350.

the Ohio River. And if he had moved from Bardstown, he would have stood little chance against the force he believed there, as his army was extremely worn. Bragg realized only part of the danger. On September 23, he wrote Kirby Smith that he had actually contemplated marching directly on Louisville from Green River and abandoned the idea only for lack of supplies. Yet at Bardstown he evidently sensed Louisville was a trap, for he wrote Kirby Smith that the combined Confederate forces, much less Bragg's own army, could not successfully compete with those at Louisville.[48]

Bragg was disappointed that a move could not be made on Louisville, but the failure of Kentucky to respond to his invasion was even a more bitter blow. Bragg had chosen the same policy as had Kirby Smith in his treatment of Kentucky. At Glasgow, Bragg proclaimed that Kentuckians must rise and earn their freedom; if they refused, "show it by your frowns and we shall return whence we came." [49] Yet Bragg's plea had fallen on deaf ears, and between Glasgow and Bardstown there was little visible support manifested for the gray column. Then Bragg received news that Kirby Smith had actually recruited scarcely a brigade, although he had boasted twenty-five thousand Kentuckians would enlist. And as for Bragg himself—he had received no recruits.[50]

A similar situation had arisen in April of 1861 which Bragg and Kirby

---

[48] *Ibid.*, XVI, Pt. 2, p. 876; Bragg to Kirby Smith, September 23, 1862, in Bragg Papers, Western Reserve. On September 23, two days before Buell's lead division reached the city, Louisville was manned by some thirty-seven thousand troops plus between four thousand and five thousand civilian volunteers. Bragg erred in stating that Grant, Rosecrans, and Curtis were there. Only five regiments under General Gordon Granger were sent from any of these armies. The Louisville entrenchments, manned by forty guns, were unfinished until September 28. Heavy guns were planted on the Indiana shore and gunboats were in the Ohio River. Apparently the Federal commanders hoped that Bragg would move on Louisville and fall into a trap. The post commander, General William Nelson, wanted to hold the city until Buell was close behind Bragg, then burn it and escape across the Ohio. Granger suggested abandoning the town, letting Bragg enter, joining Buell, and trapping the Rebels. He argued that everything valuable had already been taken out of the city. He also stated that it was hoped that Bragg and Kirby Smith would join and march on Louisville from Bardstown. Granger felt that the two Rebel armies could have been trapped in the angle of the Salt and Ohio rivers. By September 29, the last of Buell's forty-three thousand troops entered Louisville. An additional scrap of evidence that Louisville was not the Confederate prize as depicted (Vandiver, "Jefferson Davis and Confederate Strategy," 25; Horn, *Army of Tennessee*, 176; Parks, *Kirby Smith*, 226) was a note by Granger to Buell on the twenty-fourth. He wrote "I have thirty-five thousand men. I am entrenched and believe I can hold the city. . . . When you have brought Bragg to bay then I will attack him. Only let me know the route and time." Granger to Buell, September 24, 1862, in Buell Papers, Rice.

[49] *Official Records*, XVI, Pt. 2, p. 822.

[50] *Ibid.*, 876; Bragg to Davis, October 2, 1862, in Bragg Papers, West Point; Bragg to Kirby Smith, September 23, 1862, in Bragg Papers, Western Reserve.

Smith should have remembered. Governor Beriah Magoffin wanted to lead Kentucky out of the Union, but feared a retaliatory invasion from across the Ohio. Through the interposition of General Gideon Pillow, Magoffin tried to obtain arms from the Confederate government. Secretary of War Leroy P. Walker refused aid until Kentucky first joined the Confederacy, and so created a deadlock with the Southern Rights Party leaders in Kentucky who opposed a move out of the Union without Confederate protection. Fear of Union retaliation had proved stronger, and Magoffin's desires were frustrated.[51]

But even if Bragg had realized that a military victory might have to be won before Kentucky joined the Confederates, he had little choice but to adhere to the policy already established. There could be no victory now, Bragg believed, unless fifty thousand recruits from Tennessee and Kentucky joined his ranks. The information of the Yankee strength at Louisville was awesome, and Bragg felt he needed support if he were to hold his position. It had not come through pleas to the citizenry, so Bragg decided to adopt a harder line. Several Kentuckians had assured him that many wanted to join Bragg's army but feared confiscation of their property should the Confederates retreat. If Bragg proclaimed a conscription act, Kentuckians who joined the Rebels would stand less chance of punishment should the Federals return. This made sense to Bragg, and by October 2 he decided to speed the inauguration of Richard Hawes as governor so that the conscription act would appear completely legal. Bragg would later be criticized for abandoning his campaign to engage in "puppet government," but the reported Federal superiority gave him little choice. He reviewed the lethargy of the Kentucky people in a letter to Jefferson Davis, and added that "In this condition I see no hope but in the conscript act and I propose to enforce it immediately after installation of the provisional civil government on Saturday the 4th." [52] Bragg felt this was his last chance. If Kentucky failed him now, the state could no longer be held. To implement the civil government would necessitate a cessation of the campaign until the sorely needed recruits could be gathered. Thus Bragg must temporarily at least hold a defensive line in the Bluegrass.

Such a line appealed to Bragg, for he understood defensive warfare. Schooled in the Confederate doctrine of territorial defense, he like Kirby Smith had adopted the Jominian principles of defense. Fix the enemy's position, force him to commit his reserves, and then strike a hard

---

51 Coulter, *Civil War and Readjustment,* 84.

52 Bragg to Davis, October 2, 1862, Bragg Papers, West Point. See also *Official Records,* XVI, Pt. 2, p. 876.

and decisive blow. Awaiting Buell in the Bluegrass would be in accord with the defensive-offensive, which Jefferson Davis favored. An army could await the enemy on a prepared field, with the advantages of re-sources and terrain, and strike when an opportunity presented itself. That part of the Bluegrass east of Bardstown and west of the Kentucky River appeared an excellent place to utilize this strategy. Kirby Smith had accumulated ample stores at Lexington. Should Bragg be too hard pressed by Buell, the Confederates could move to the east bank of the Kentucky and Dick's rivers, and operate on the interior line between the Lexing-ton and Bryantsville depots.[53]

Bragg could scarcely be blamed for adopting the defensive. He needed time to revise his strategy if something were to be salvaged of the in-vasion. Yet Bragg's defensive plan threatened to carry the seeds of its own failure. The offensive had stumbled to a halt because the forces were not coordinated and had no single director. The failures of Van Dorn, Price, Breckinridge, and Kirby Smith should have taught Bragg a lesson—yet he had failed to mature as a leader with the cam-paign. His new strategy contained the same points which had brought him grief on the offensive. He still expected Van Dorn and Price to move into Middle Tennessee; on September 28, he wired Van Dorn to sweep into Middle Tennessee, capture Nashville, and push northward to join Bragg in the Ohio River country. Breckinridge was still ex-pected in Kentucky, and Kirby Smith was still trusted in good faith. Kentucky must yet join the gray ranks, and additional men and supplies must come from Tennessee. Each of these things had so far shown little promise. Yet Bragg, partly through necessity, partly because his rigid mind admitted few revisions, clung to these ideas as firm prerequisites to his remaining in Kentucky.[54] Could the piecemeal strategy hold Ken-tucky? As Bragg wrote Cooper, "A few weeks will decide the question." [55] If the strategy succeeded, Bragg and Kirby Smith might yet unite on the Ohio.

---

[53] J. D. Hittle (ed.), *Jomini and His Summary of the Art of War* (Harrisburg, Pa., 1952), 69, 101, 104; Vandiver, "Jefferson Davis and Confederate Strategy," 21 *n.*; Archer Jones, *Confederate Strategy from Shiloh to Vicksburg* (Baton Rouge, 1961), 18–23; Frank E. Vandiver, *Rebel Brass: The Confederate Command System* (Baton Rouge, 1956), 16–17; Bragg to Kirby Smith, September 23, 27, 1862, in Bragg Papers, Western Reserve.

[54] *Official Records*, XVI, Pt. 2, p. 876, XVII, Pt. 2, p. 713. By an error in transmission, Van Dorn did not receive Bragg's dispatch of September 28 until November 2; by the time Bragg wrote Cooper on September 25 that he hoped Price and Van Dorn could invade Middle Tennessee, they had been defeated at Corinth. See also Bragg to Davis, October 2, 1862, in Bragg Papers, West Point; Horn, *Army of Tennessee*, 174–75.

[55] *Official Records*, XVI, Pt. 2, p. 876.

thirteen

"Your Powerful Chief Magistrate"

THE NEW STRATEGY OF TERRITORIAL OCCUPATION MAY HAVE BEEN A political necessity, but it lost the Rebels the advantage of geography. Bragg never understood the Kentucky terrain. The disappointments of the proposed Albany route, of the lack of forage at Glasgow and Green River, and of the near trap at Louisville indicated he lacked respect for map and compass. And now Bragg made another error. After assuming command of Kirby Smith's army on October 2 at Lexington, he dispersed his forces in what amounted to a hollow square on the fertile plain between the Muldraugh's Hills and the Kentucky River. Polk with the bulk of the Army of the Mississippi held the southwest corner at Bardstown; Cleburne and Preston Smith the northwest corner at Shelbyville, forty-five miles north of Bardstown; Harry Heth the northeast corner, forty miles east of Shelbyville at Georgetown; and Carter Stevenson the southeast corner at Danville.[1]

Bragg's mistake was not in dispersing his troops but in the manner of dispersion. His troop dispositions would hamper any chance to anticipate Buell should he move out of Louisville. From that city a number of roads branched out into central Kentucky. Once Buell's force cleared the Muldraugh's Hill range it could easily maneuver and extend its lines in the Bluegrass plain. Buell's superior numbers would be less of a threat while moving on the narrow roads. If Bragg placed the bulk of his forces on the western edge of the Bluegrass, Buell's move could be contested before the Yankee lines were extended. A strong position along

[1] Hammond, "Campaign," 456–57; Polk, *Leonidas Polk, Bishop and General,* II, 135–36.

the Bardstown–Shelbyville line could perhaps anticipate his advance and compensate for Bragg's failure to learn his intentions. Gray spies had failed to learn which route Buell would take, should he move east to attack Bragg. Bragg's cavalry commands—Forrest's, Wharton's, and Wheeler's—had been operating loosely, with no unity of purpose. Bragg had sent Forrest back to Tennessee, and Wharton and Wheeler alone were unable to discern Buell's strength or intentions. There appeared no other way to prevent Buell from spreading his forces on the Bluegrass plain than to await the Federals on a line near Louisville.[2]

But Bragg hesitated to place a sufficient force on the Bardstown–Shelbyville line. Failing again to profit by past mistakes, he again underestimated what Buell could accomplish. He was confident the Yankees would remain in Louisville for several weeks. Had not Cleburne written on September 26 that no activity was observed west of Shelbyville? And Polk had written Bragg that news from Wharton's position at Mount Washington indicated great demoralization in Buell's army at Louisville. So confident was he that Buell would remain inactive that on September 28 he left Polk with the army at Bardstown and toured the Bluegrass.[3]

Bragg also refused to relocate his command because any line he drew would cost the Rebels some advantage. Confused, he advocated concentration at a half dozen places. On September 23 he suggested to Kirby Smith that Danville might be a rallying point; four days later he suggested the troops join at Bryantsville. To Stoddard Johnston he hinted a retreat into Tennessee, but he wrote to Jefferson Davis of advancing beyond the Ohio.[4]

Bragg's defensive strategy had placed him in a serious dilemma, and he stood to lose wherever he concentrated. If the line were drawn between Bardstown and Shelbyville, Buell's maneuverability would suffer—but he also would suffer. The force at Cincinnati, represented by Kirby Smith as formidable, would threaten the route of retreat through Cumberland Gap and Bragg's supply bases at Bryantsville and Lexington. He suggested to Kirby Smith they might await Buell along a line

2 Buell to Thomas, October 1, 1862, in Buell Papers, Rice; Johnston "Bragg's Campaign," Military Papers, Filson Club; Thomas R. Hay, "The Campaign and Battle of Chickamauga," *Georgia Historical Quarterly*, VII (September, 1923), 247–50; Polk, *Leonidas Polk, Bishop and General*, II, 136–37.

3 Cleburne to Bragg, September 26, 1862, in Bragg Papers, Western Reserve; *Official Records*, XVI, Pt. 2, p. 892; Johnston, "Bragg's Campaign," Military Papers, Filson Club.

4 Bragg to Kirby Smith, September 23, 27, 1862, in Bragg Papers, Western Reserve; Bragg to Davis, October 2, 1862, in Bragg Papers, West Point; "Johnston Memoranda," Military Papers, Filson Club.

from Frankfort south to Danville. True, this position would put Bragg near his supplies. Yet it would concede to Buell a strip forty-six miles wide between Bardstown and Danville in which to unlimber his heavy force. Also, Bragg and Kirby Smith would have the Kentucky and Dick's Rivers at their backs, and Buell in their front, capable of outflanking them or forcing them to weaken their lines by extension.

Bragg mused over another line—along the eastern bank of the Kentucky and Dick's Rivers, with headquarters at Bryantsville. He liked this position and had ordered Polk to withdraw there if severely attacked at Bardstown. The position was impressive enough. To the west Dick's River flowed north to join the Kentucky near Harrodsburg. Dick's River was fordable at only four places in the area—near Bryantsville, Danville, Lancaster, and Stanford. The eastern bank with its towering rock bluffs was an impregnable artillery position. Five miles north of Bryantsville the Kentucky River guarded the right flank. Fed by Troublesome, Laurel, and Hell-fer-Sartain, the river poured into a deep gorge west of Bryantsville, picked up Dick's River, and then veered north on its way to the Ohio. On the left flank lay the route of Bragg's escape, if escape became necessary, by the Lexington pike through Cumberland Gap.

But even this position had serious flaws. If Bragg chose to defend Lexington, an important supply depot, his army would be cut in two by the Kentucky River. The oncoming fall rains would swell the mountain streams which fed the Kentucky. Nor were the crossings of Dick's River totally secure. If the Yankees swung to the south and crossed, they would both flank Bragg and sever his line of retreat through the gap. Also, a stand there would concede Frankfort, capital and symbol of Rebel power in the Bluegrass. Such a loss might nullify any political gains achieved among the people.[5]

Unable to commit himself to a defensive position, Bragg decided to postpone the problem until after he had inaugurated Richard Hawes. On October 2 he met with Kirby Smith and Hawes at Lexington. The three agreed to hasten the event so that the conscription act might be proclaimed. Again Bragg failed to learn from old mistakes. He did little to guard against a surprise move by Buell while the high command was busy with erecting a civil government. The only disposition he made was halfhearted—he ordered Polk to move forward to hold an arc from Elizabethtown on the Bowling Green pike to Shelbyville on the Frankfort road. It was an important order, for such a move might anticipate

5 *Official Records*, XVI, Pt. 1, pp. 433–35, Pt. 2, p. 850; Bragg to Kirby Smith, September 27, 1862, in Bragg Papers, Western Reserve.

Buell's column should it move out of Louisville. Yet Bragg made it discretionary, not mandatory, subject to favorable reconnoitering of the ground in Polk's front.

The lack of vigor in the lone order issued to Polk indicated that perhaps Bragg was overcome with his new responsibilities as commander of the joint columns. Unfamiliar with directing such a large-scale operation, he was having trouble convincing himself he was in command. Though he had only contempt for the bishop's abilities, he now trusted Polk with a crucial discretionary order. Perhaps Bragg had again failed to grow as a leader during the campaign. He still magnified problems out of proportion to their importance. Hawes' inauguration was necessary, but should Buell slip by the thin Bardstown line there would be little need for a Confederate governor. Again underestimating the opposition, Bragg did not expect Buell to make a sudden move. And what if Buell did attack prematurely? Bragg still possessed that simple Confederate faith that a fellow soldier, even a personal enemy such as Polk, would accomplish an important task.[6]

But on October 2 Bragg received news at Lexington which indicated Polk had failed. Colonel W. G. M. Davis at Frankfort telegraphed that John Scott's cavalry had run into a large Yankee horse column west of Shelbyville. Davis reported the cavalry was believed to be the advance of a considerable infantry force, and that Cleburne was preparing to fall back from Shelbyville on Frankfort. At first Bragg took the message lightly, for he still doubted Buell could move so early. Polk was ordered to hold in readiness to strike the mysterious force on flank if he ascertained the column was large. Then came another telegram from Davis which struck home. The Federals had taken Shelbyville and were already within twenty-one miles of Frankfort, driving hard for the capital. Cleburne, the hard hitter of Shiloh who never jumped at shadows, was falling back swiftly. Already his lead column was within five miles of Frankfort. The situation was grave. If the Yankees broke through at Frankfort, Bragg's force would be cut in half, the depots would fall, and the road to Cumberland Gap would be cut.[7]

At the crucial hour Bragg shirked the responsibility that was rightfully his. Unwilling to depart from the rigid scheme devised at Bardstown, he decided that Hawes' inauguration must still receive his own first consideration. He left to his subordinates the task of repulsing the enemy force. While he busied himself with preparations for the festivities in

6 Johnston "Bragg's Campaign," Military Papers, Filson Club; *Official Records*, XVI, Pt. 2, pp. 891–92.

7 *Ibid.*, 896–97; W. G. M. Davis to Bragg, October 2, 1862, in Bragg Papers, Western Reserve.

Frankfort, he devised a hasty, ill-organized plan. Davis was ordered to pull in Heth, Stevenson, and Humphrey Marshall—who still had not arrived—and to hold fast at Frankfort. Polk would move north by way of the Bloomfield pike and strike the Yankees on the flank as they were strung along the road to Frankfort. The plan was bold and smacked of Lee and Jackson at Second Manassas. But it was unrealistic, for Bragg knew nothing of the situation on Polk's front, fifty-three miles to the west. Still he counted heavily on the bishop to execute another vague order. Bragg also gambled that Kirby Smith's forces could move into Frankfort and hold the town before the Federals drove through and isolated Polk. He gambled that the Union column would delay until Polk and Kirby Smith could swing into position. Yet he was unwilling to take the responsibility of making certain that the strategy would succeed. Instead, he proceeded to Frankfort to inaugurate Richard Hawes. Only after that would Bragg seek out the enemy.[8]

To the west, at Bardstown, the enemy was seeking out Bragg. On October 1 Polk had received Bragg's instructions to push his force forward. He never had the chance. Later that night Wharton reported from Mount Washington. His Texans had been hit hard at Wilsonville, Shepherdsville, and in front of Mount Washington. Polk's right flank was crumbling, and Wharton could not hold much longer. Surprised, Polk ordered Wharton to fall back to Bardstown. Wheeler was called in from near Elizabethtown, and Polk waited through the night to see whether the enemy intended to attack the Bardstown position or merely reconnoiter Polk's line.[9]

The Federal advance continued to develop. By 10 A.M. on October 2, the blue columns were reported in strong force on the three main routes to Bardstown, via Shepherdsville, Mount Washington, and Taylorsville. By early morning of the third, the situation was grave. Taylorsville and Shepherdsville had fallen. The Yankee advance on the Mount Washington road had driven to within twelve miles of Bardstown, and a heavy force in line of battle was pushing up the Shepherdsville road. A note from Cleburne reported the Rebel right at Shelbyville had been swept away.[10]

8 Bragg to W. G. M. Davis, October 2, 1862, Bragg to Polk, October 2, 1862, Johnston Diary, October 2–3, 1862, all in Bragg Papers, Western Reserve; Colonel George Brent's Diary (MS in Bragg Papers, Western Reserve), October 3, 1862. Brent recorded that on the third in Lexington "the impression strongly prevails that the great battle will be fought in this vicinity."

9 *Official Records*, XVI, Pt. 2, p. 897; Polk, *Leonidas Polk, Bishop and General*, II, 137–38.

10 Cleburne to Polk, October 1, 1862, and Polk to Bragg, October 2, 1862, in Bragg Papers, Western Reserve; *Official Records*, XVI, Pt. 2, pp. 900–903.

While the Bardstown line tottered, Polk received Bragg's order to make the flank attack. It was obvious that Bragg did not understand the situation. How could Polk move north via Bloomfield to strike the Yankees when the blue line lay squarely across the road at Taylorsville? Even if Polk tried to dislodge the Federals, the forces moving on the Shepherdsville and Mount Washington roads would get in his rear. Then he would be trapped between the Frankfort pike and Bardstown. Polk considered Bragg's request impossible, and called a council of war to bolster his position.[11]

The council was only a formality, for Polk went into the meeting determined to disobey the order. He read Bragg's letter to the wing and division commanders and insisted that Bragg could not have had the "lights" before him when the order was issued. Some dissension arose for fear that Kirby Smith would be endangered if Polk did not support him. Although unsure, Polk stated he did not think Kirby Smith would move until he heard from him. Then, determined to win his case, Polk asked the generals what would be done had Bragg not sent the order. The answer was unanimous—follow Bragg's original instructions and fall back to Bryantsville. Polk agreed, and hurriedly wrote Bragg that he was retreating.[12]

The importance of the Bardstown council would be greatly exaggerated. Polk's decision was a necessary one. His position at Bardstown was collapsing, and he certainly could not move north as requested. The bishop's mistake was in the way he reported the decision to Bragg. The problem was one which again indicated a command sickness in the army. Bragg and Polk did not know how to talk to each other. Bragg's order had been vague, and he had failed to specify what Kirby Smith would do while Polk struck the flank. Polk replied with an equally vague explanation of his disobedience at a time when Bragg needed to be apprised of the situation. The necessity for the disobedience was excusable, but Polk's and Hardee's aloof manner toward Bragg at this critical time had little excuse. Although they might not respect Bragg, he was still commander and deserved to know what had gone wrong. Polk did not tell him. Instead he wrote a clouded note stating, "The last twenty-four hours have developed a condition of things on my front and left flank which I shadowed forth in my last note to you, which makes compliance with this order not only eminently inexpedient but impracticable.

11 Polk, *Leonidas Polk, Bishop and General*, II, 138–40.
12 Patton Anderson to Bragg, April 15, 1863, S. A. M. Wood to Bragg, April 14, 1863, B. F. Cheatham to Bragg, April 20, 1863, Bragg to Anderson, April 21, 1863, St. John Liddell to Bragg, April 16, 1863, Bushrod Johnson to Bragg, April 17, 1863, all in Bragg Papers, Western Reserve; *Official Records*, XVI, Pt. 2, pp. 1101–103.

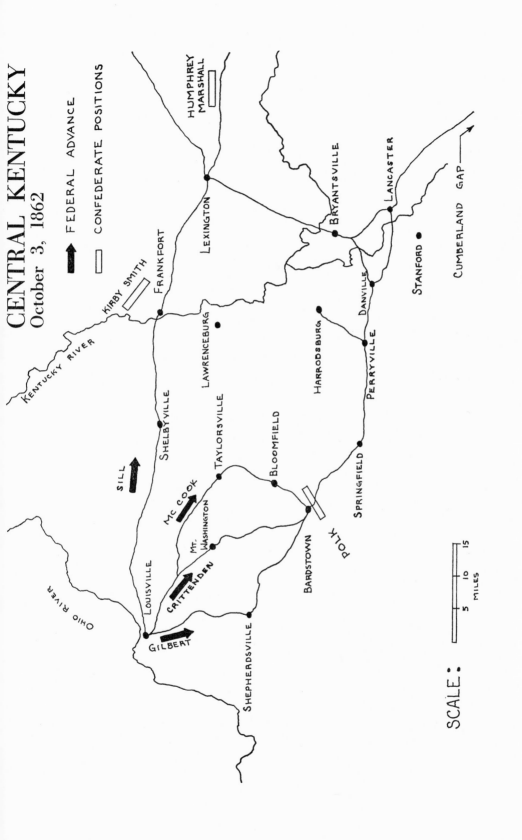

CENTRAL KENTUCKY
October 3, 1862

→ FEDERAL ADVANCE

▭ CONFEDERATE POSITIONS

OHIO RIVER

KENTUCKY RIVER

LOUISVILLE

SHEPHERDSVILLE

GILBERT

CRITTENDEN

Mt. WASHINGTON

McCOOK

SILL

SHELBYVILLE

TAYLORSVILLE

BLOOMFIELD

LAWRENCEBURG

FRANKFORT

KIRBY SMITH

LEXINGTON

HUMPHREY MARSHALL

BRYANTSVILLE

LANCASTER

CUMBERLAND GAP

STANFORD

DANVILLE

PERRYVILLE

HARRODSBURG

SPRINGFIELD

BARDSTOWN

POLK

SCALE:

5   10   15
MILES

I have called a council of wing and division commanders to whom I have submitted the matter, and find that they unanimously indorse my views of what is demanded." [13]

The only information Polk had supplied Bragg prior to this note was two notes he sent Bragg in the morning and evening of October 2, in which Polk reported an enemy advance on Bardstown. Even if this sketchy information were considered a fair appraisal of what was happening, Hardee included a confusing letter to Bragg giving his own views: "I believe the enemy is advancing in force on Lexington with the view, in its present defenseless condition, of capturing it. A demonstration will be made on this command, but the *real attack* may be expected on the other line." [14] The two commanders were being unfair to Bragg. Neither Polk nor Hardee explained the circumstances that forced a retreat from Bardstown. Bragg was left with only two bits of information on which to rely. Hardee warned that the main Federal force was probably threatening the right flank at Frankfort, and, for some reason not fully explained, Polk was in retreat.[15]

At Frankfort, Bragg seemed disinterested in all reports of a Federal advance. He tended to form an entire plan upon the basis of the latest rumor received, without careful investigation. When he arrived at Frankfort on the night of October 3, excitement had died down. He received Polk's note of the afternoon of October 2, which included Hardee's private letter warning of a move against Kirby Smith. But the Federal column between Frankfort and Shelbyville was inactive, and Kirby Smith's twenty thousand troops seemed enough protection. Bragg was lulled into a sense of security and countermanded the order for Polk's flank assault. On the morning of the fourth he received Polk's note advising of his retreat. Polk was not ordered to report at Frankfort or censured for disobedience but instead was simply ordered to concentrate his force at Harrodsburg. Later in the morning Bragg received Polk's note of the morning of October 2. He still did not take seriously the Federal advance on either Polk or Kirby Smith. Had not the reported move on Frankfort proved a feint? Clearly the Federal army had disappeared, and Bragg admitted to Polk on the fourth that he was unsure whether it was moving against Frankfort or against Polk's position. Yet Bragg seemed unworried. Perhaps it was again his old inability to deviate from his rigid policies. Hawes' inauguration, though

13 *Official Records,* XVI, Pt. 2, p. 901.
14 Hardee to Bragg, October 2, 1862, in Bragg Papers, Western Reserve.
15 Bragg to Patton Anderson, April 21, 1863, in *ibid.* Bragg wrote: "You will be surprised to learn I have a note from Gen. Hardee at Bardstown on the 2nd of October advising the very order given by me to Gen. Polk."

important, would be useless should the Rebels be defeated. But he had decided that nothing would stop the inauguration.[16]

A murky, drizzly rain almost hid the Confederate flag flying above the capitol on October 4. This was the day Bragg had waited for, and he was determined the inauguration should be done with grand style. A large crowd lined the streets to catch a glimpse of Bragg, Kirby Smith, and local boys like Buckner who had "made good" in the Southern ranks. Unfortunately, Humphrey Marshall, marching from Owingsville, had not arrived and was unable to visit the capital that once put a price on his head. Despite pouring rain, the crowd packed the hall of the House of Representatives and another waited in the rotunda to get a glimpse of the man who had come to be their governor. Shortly after noon, Bragg stepped to the podium and introduced Richard C. Hawes.[17]

Bragg began innocently enough. He explained that his mission was to install the provisional governor and to transfer the government to civil authorities. However, he did not mention his plans for the conscription act. Then he accused Lincoln's government of decreeing that Kentucky should join in a war for "the confiscation of property, the excitement of servile insurrections, and the desolation of your homes." Not so with the Confederates: "respecting the civil magistrate of this state, we wish only to support his rightful authority, and limit our own power." [18]

There was something pathetic, hopeful, and even amusing about Bragg's introductory remarks. He had summarized the whole Confederate philosophy of Kentucky. Kentucky had remained in the Union against her will, and now the Confederates had come to restore her to the cause for which she yearned. To insure the restoration, Bragg had brought along his own governor. It was a test case, and Bragg knew it. While his plans did not call for bayonet rule, he would give himself every benefit of doubt in deciding if Kentucky desired to join the Confederacy. "Irrespective of past opinions," [19] which probably meant the voting record on secession, Bragg proposed to "obtain the expression of the public will . . . on those points which have unfortunately divided the people." [20]

[16] Though Bragg charged that Polk's disobedience forced the evacuation of Frankfort and the loss of the Lexington supply depots, Bragg had actually countermanded his order to Polk the night before he learned of the latter's retreat. See Bragg to Anderson, April 13, 1862, in Bragg Papers, Western Reserve; *Official Records*, XVI, Pt. 1, p. 1091, Pt. 2, p. 903.

[17] Johnston Diary, October 4, 1862, and Brent Diary, October 4, 1862, in Bragg Papers, Western Reserve; Johnston, "Bragg's Campaign," Military Papers, Filson Club.

[18] MS of Bragg's address, in Bragg Papers, West Point.

[19] *Ibid.*

[20] *Ibid.*

Of course this could not be done immediately, but "as soon as greater tranquility is restored." [21] Meanwhile, he promised to respect private citizens' rights, yield deference to civil authorities, and "defend your honor and your territory." [22] Like it or not, Kentucky had a redeemer, and with a final flourish he introduced his prophet, "your powerful Chief Magistrate, His Excellency, Governor Hawes." [23]

The elderly Hawes made his way to the speakers' stand while the pro-Confederate crowd went wild. He slowly delivered his speech amidst more cheering. Outside, cannon began to boom, and the crowd continued to cheer. Hawes finished, and cries went up for more speeches. But there were to be no more. Couriers hastened through the crowd— the Federals were across the Kentucky in force and were shelling the town. Bragg now thought he had been tricked. Perhaps Cleburne and Hardee had been right—the main Federal column was approaching. His plans upset, Bragg lost his sense of balance. He should have reconnoitered the Yankee force but instead assumed it was too strong for him to resist by remaining in Frankfort. On the afternoon of October 4, Bragg hastily ordered the Kentucky River bridges destroyed and prepared to fall back to Harrodsburg for a junction with Polk.[24]

The hasty collapse of the Bardstown–Shelbyville line and the sudden fall of Frankfort showed the fragile nature of the Rebel strategy. Bragg had delayed too long in drawing a firm defense line. Buell had not been anticipated, and his destination was still unknown. The Rebel force was divided, almost completely out of communication, and threatened with destruction in detail. Bragg had hoped that Hawes' inauguration would gain civil support. Even this was now doubtful. Bragg had yet to quell the fears of the people by a show of force against the Yankees. Instead he was falling back, and the inauguration of a provisional governor was small compensation for the Rebels' loss of territory. The reaction was swift in Frankfort. Jubilation turned to despair among the pro-Confederates as flames licked at the river bridge west of town. Many

21 *Ibid.*
22 *Ibid.*
23 *Ibid.*
24 Hammond, "Campaign," 458–60; Johnston, "Bragg's Campaign," Military Papers, Filson Club; *Official Records,* XVI, Pt. 1, pp. 660, 1024, Pt. 2, p. 905; Buell to Halleck, October 3, 1862, Buell to Thomas, October 2, 1862, Buell to H. G. Wright, October 5, 1862, all in Buell Papers, Rice. On October 1, Buell moved out of Louisville, seeking to turn Bragg's left and seize the line of retreat to Cumberland Gap. Expecting Bragg to concentrate at Danville, Buell massed McCook's, Gilbert's, and Crittenden's corps on the right, fifty-eight thousand strong against Polk at Bardstown. Sill's eight-thousand-man division feinted against Frankfort on Bragg's right. Buell left forty-five thousand raw recruits in Louisville to be organized. He did not expect resistance until his three corps, marching on parallel roads, could concentrate near Danville.

wished their sentiments had been displayed with less passion, and Richard Hawes suddenly decided the best place for the Kentucky capital was the eastern part of the state. Meanwhile Bragg sought to gather his far-flung forces for a stand at Harrodsburg—if he could find them.[25]

To the south, Polk's army was blindly falling back toward Danville. Nothing seemed to go right for the bishop. Upon leaving Bardstown, he had neglected to inform John Wharton at Mount Washington that the town was being evacuated. Wharton was surrounded by Yankee cavalry, and only a courageous charge by the Texans saved the entire cavalry force of Polk's right wing. The column was slowed when Hardee, moving on the Glenville pike, found the road slippery and rocky. His wing was forced to detour to the Springfield pike and follow Polk toward Danville, while the Yankee cavalry pressed behind. On the fifth Polk finally received word from Bragg that he knew Polk was in retreat.

Although he promised to move to Harrodsburg as Bragg ordered instead of to Danville, Polk, perhaps a little stubborn, determined that at least part of his force would move toward Danville. On October 5 he sent Wharton's entire command to gather supplies at the small Lebanon depot, and picket the flank near Danville. Wharton reached Lebanon on the sixth, loaded his wagons, and started for Perryville, a small village on the road between Bardstown and Danville. Wharton had gone scarcely four miles when a private war began between Bragg and Polk over the place where Wharton should concentrate. Polk, overlooking the need for reconnaissance, ordered Wharton to remain at Lebanon until further orders. Wharton returned to Lebanon where he received a command from Bragg to move to Harrodsburg. Wharton, now confused, wrote Hardee for orders. The latter had none and referred the note to Bragg. Bragg set matters straight by ordering the Texan to report to Hardee at Perryville. But the damage was done, for Polk had ridden Wharton almost out of the campaign. Wharton would not arrive at Perryville until the night of October 7. In his absence, Wheeler was forced to double as rear guard and scout. The result was that on October 5–7 Bragg had no effective cavalry reconnaissance in the country west of Harrodsburg.[26]

Bragg, who arrived at Harrodsburg on the fifth, had the difficult

[25] Brent Diary, October 4–5, 1862, and Johnston Diary, October 4, 1862, in Bragg Papers, Western Reserve; Johnston, "Bragg's Campaign," Military Papers, Filson Club; Hammond, "Campaign," 459–60.

[26] John Wharton to Polk, October 6, 1862, Joseph Wheeler to T. B. Roy, October 6 (3 P.M., 4 P.M.) , 1862, Wharton to Polk, October 4, 1862, all in Bragg Papers, Western Reserve; R. F. Bunting, "Life of General John Wharton" (MS in John A. Wharton Papers, Rosenberg Library, Galveston, Texas) ; Official Records, XVI, Pt. 2, pp. 912–14, 900–902, 905–906, Pt. 1, p. 896.

problem of locating the Federal advance. He must rely on secondhand information from his generals, for Scott, Wheeler, and Wharton were reporting directly to Kirby Smith, Polk, and Hardee. Information pointed to a threat against Kirby Smith. Kirby Smith, who had planned to move to Harrodsburg, sent a note from Versailles, thirty miles north and across the Kentucky River. He admitted the retreat from Lexington was premature. A scout had informed him that the only force on the Louisville-Frankfort road was General Joshua Sill's division. But Kirby Smith reported a new threat. Rousseau was supposedly at Taylorsville and McCook was placed at some point between there and Shelbyville. A Yankee force at Taylorsville could move northeast on Frankfort or southeast on Harrodsburg. Kirby Smith implied the threat was against his sector. He requested Bragg to allow him to remain north of the Kentucky, and added that the moment he crossed the river, Lexington would be endangered.[27]

Bragg again leaned heavily on sparse intelligence. His mistake was not in believing Kirby Smith's report but in acting without further information. Although Polk had not reported from his front, Bragg revised his plan to concentrate at Harrodsburg. Instead, Kirby Smith would hold his divisions north of the Kentucky River: Stevenson with 11,000 men at Versailles; Heth and Churchill with 7,000 troops at McCown's Ferry on the Kentucky; and Marshall with 4,500 men at Lexington. Bragg would do more. He would uncover his base at Bryantsville and his line of retreat to Cumberland Gap and march north with Polk's army to meet the threat Kirby Smith had reported. With no word yet from Polk, Bragg was firmly dedicated to the new plan.[28] To Kirby Smith he wrote, "It is my intention to move on the enemy whether at Shelbyville or Frankfort as soon as my force arrives here." [29]

Intelligence from Kirby Smith on October 6 fortified Bragg's new strategy. Kirby Smith had sent several dispatches which Colonel George Brent of Bragg's staff termed as "announcing the concentration of enemy's forces, evidently with a design on Frankfort and Lexington, and begging for help." [30] But north of the Kentucky, Kirby Smith was giving Bragg little help. Although he was baffled as to the enemy's position, Kirby Smith was also determined to maintain some independence. His dispatches were so urgent that Bragg could scarcely ignore them. Yet they contained so little actual information that it was evident Kirby

27 Kirby Smith to Bragg, October 5 (10 A.M.), 1862, Brent Diary, October 5, 1862, Johnston Diary, October 5, 1862, all in Bragg Papers, Western Reserve.
28 Bragg to Kirby Smith, October 5, 1862, in *ibid.*; Hammond, "Campaign," 458–59.
29 Bragg to Kirby Smith, October 5, 1862, in Bragg Papers, Western Reserve.
30 Brent Diary, October 5–6, 1862, in *ibid.*

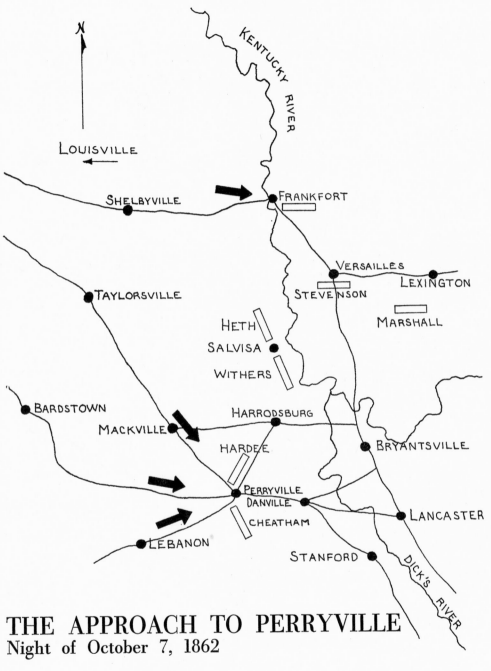

N

LOUISVILLE

SHELBYVILLE

FRANKFORT

KENTUCKY RIVER

VERSAILLES

LEXINGTON

STEVENSON

MARSHALL

TAYLORSVILLE

HETH

SALVISA

WITHERS

BARDSTOWN

HARRODSBURG

MACKVILLE

HARDEE

BRYANTSVILLE

PERRYVILLE

DANVILLE

LANCASTER

CHEATHAM

LEBANON

STANFORD

DICK'S RIVER

THE APPROACH TO PERRYVILLE
Night of October 7, 1862

CONFEDERATE POSITION

UNION ADVANCE

Smith had no clear knowledge of the situation. On the night of the fifth he reported again that the pressure against Frankfort had eased. But he warned Bragg that the position of Heth and Churchill, who had moved across the river to Salvisa, seemed rather critical. He feared that Stevenson, still at Versailles, would be cut off should the reported force at Taylorsville move east. By the night of the sixth Kirby Smith had found a new threat. John Scott, picketing at Frankfort, reported Yankees in heavy force were shelling the town. Kirby Smith relayed the news to Bragg and added that Stevenson would attack if the Yankees advanced across the river. Bragg, who still had received no definite news from Polk, was convinced that the information was correct. He ordered Withers, who had just arrived at Harrodsburg, to move his division to Kirby Smith's support. Cheatham would also be sent when his division arrived.[31]

On the night of October 6 Bragg's plan was sustained by news, or rather a lack of news, from Polk's army. Polk's own divisions, Withers' and Cheatham's, moved into Harrodsburg during the night. Hardee's wing lagged behind. Patton Anderson camped at Salt River between Perryville and Harrodsburg while Hardee with Buckner's division halted at Perryville. Hardee did not stop at Perryville because he was hard pressed and knew he must fight a battle. He halted there in order to obtain water, scarce in the summer drought. There was a little water in the bed of Doctor's Fork, a small stream that ran across the Springfield road two and a half miles west of Perryville. Buckner's division was halted at Perryville to use this supply, and Patton Anderson's division was sent ahead to Salt River. Hardee planned to continue his march to Harrodsburg the following day.[32]

On the night of October 6, Hardee was confused as to the force pursuing him. He had expected the main thrust to be against the Frankfort position, but the column on the Springfield road irritated him. Wheeler had found out little, and Wharton was still absent. Although he did not take the Yankee threat seriously, Hardee disliked the thought of marching north to Harrodsburg from Perryville with the blue column on his left flank. At 8 P.M. he requested Polk to send back Anderson's division and Cleburne's brigade. Hardee gave no reason. He merely suggested that if Anderson *did* come he should start early in the morn-

31 Kirby Smith to Bragg, October 5 ("sunset") , October 6, 1862, John Scott to Kirby Smith, October 5, 1862, Scott to Carter Stevenson, October 6 (4:45 P.M.) , 1862, all in *ibid.;* Johnston, "Bragg's Campaign," Military Papers, Filson Club; *Official Records,* XVI, Pt. 2, p. 918.

32 *Official Records,* XVI, Pt. 1, p. 1024, Pt. 2, p. 1109; Hambleton Tapp, "The Battle of Perryville, 1862," *Filson Club History Quarterly,* IX (July, 1935) , 164–65.

ing. Polk, who had offered little information, forwarded the note to
Bragg later that night.[33] He sent along a note of his own, with the only
statement of strength that Polk had or would give of the force on the
Perryville front. Of the force threatening Hardee, Polk wrote that he
"cannot think it large." [34]

Since Polk and Hardee had given no hint of a large Federal force on
their front, Bragg expressed his intention of moving to oppose the
Yankees on Kirby Smith's front. He believed the best place to oppose
the column threatening Frankfort would be at Versailles, thirty miles
north of Harrodsburg and thirteen miles west of Lexington. On the
morning of the seventh he completed his plan. Cheatham would move
that night to join Withers on the east bank of the Kentucky opposite
Salvisa. Both divisions would then march east to reinforce Stevenson
at Versailles. Kirby Smith would move on the inner line from McCown's
Ferry and come into Versailles from the south. Hardee would brush
away the annoying force at Perryville and follow "as circumstances
allow. . . ." [35] Based upon the intelligence sent from Kirby Smith,
Bragg's plan seemed foolproof. The Louisianian regained the offensive
spark, showed a map of the country to his staff, and remarked that
at Versailles would occur the great battle for Kentucky.[36]

During the afternoon of October 7, Bragg received more information to sustain his move. Colonel Benjamin Allston, reconnoitering
in advance of Lawrenceburg, supported Bragg's fears for the safety of
the right flank. He reported two Yankee divisions under Thomas and
Robert Mitchell were moving from Bardstown on the Lexington road.
A Federal column under Rousseau and McCook was moving from Taylorsville on Lawrenceburg, twenty-three miles west of Lexington. A
third column under T. L. Crittenden and Sill was advancing on Frankfort. Allston added that "from the nature of the information I think
it's highly probable that it is correct in the main." [37] This information
would jibe with what was already feared of the Taylorsville column
which lapped around Polk's right flank at Bardstown. The main Federal force was not moving southeast towards Perryville and Harrodsburg,
but east and northeast against Kirby Smith. If the Yankees crossed the
river at Lawrenceburg, the Confederates would be cut in half. Bragg's
fear that the Taylorsville force was the bulk of Buell's army was strength-

[33] Wheeler to T. B. Roy, October 6 (7 P.M.), 1862 (with endorsement, Hardee to
Polk—8 P.M.), Brent Diary, October 6–7, 1862, all in Bragg Papers, Western Reserve.
[34] *Official Records*, XVI, Pt. 1, p. 1095.
[35] *Ibid.*
[36] Johnston Diary, October 7, 1862, in Bragg Papers, Western Reserve.
[37] Benjamin Allston to George Brent, October 7 (12 noon), 1862, in *ibid.*

ened by more word from Kirby Smith. Scott had reported twenty thousand
infantry crossing at Frankfort. Already the Rebel pickets were being
pushed from the river. Marshall, still on his way to Lexington, was
ordered to hurry. Heth was to be rushed to aid Stevenson lest Versailles
fall and Lexington be lost. Kirby Smith, who had regained much of his
independence, outlined his plan. He would concentrate at Versailles, and
strike the force at Frankfort. If the Yankee threat proved another feint,
Kirby Smith would cross the Kentucky River and cut the enemy center
in the Taylorsville-Lawrenceburg area.[38]

On the seventh Polk and Hardee reported little that indicated a major
threat on their flank. At 9:30 A.M. Hardee did forward a dispatch from
Wheeler. Wheeler's troopers had fought all morning for the waterhole
at Doctor's Fork. The cavalryman reported long lines of Yankee infantry
with colors flying approaching Perryville. Prisoners boasted that Buell
commanded and that Rousseau led the van. Yet Hardee made no comment on the reliability of their statements save that he had not seen the
prisoners.[39] Moreover, Bragg had consistently received information that
Rousseau was advancing on Frankfort. The afternoon wore on. Finally
Hardee sent a dispatch at 3:20 P.M. that was later to be misunderstood.
After the campaign Hardee contended that he "informed General Bragg
. . . that the enemy was moving in heavy force against my position." and
that Hardee "urged the concentration of our whole army at Perryville." [40] Yet this is not what Hardee wrote. He reported Wheeler and
the enemy were engaged in a sharp cannonade, and that a fight could
be expected on October 8. But his note was not urgent. He gave no
estimate of the size of the Yankee column. Hardee only suggested that
Bragg should send reinforcements, take command in person, and wipe
the Federals out. But even this request was conditional. Hardee asked
for support only if Bragg were not "pressed in another direction. . . ." [41]
All reports had indicated Bragg was hard pressed on the Lexington line.

Yet the Yankee force near Perryville irritated Bragg, since it delayed
his plan of concentration. Determined to dispose of it, he ordered Polk
at 5:40 P.M. to move Cheatham's division back to Perryville, rout the
enemy immediately, and "then move to our support at Versailles." [42] Polk
had made no further statements about danger on his front, Hardee's

[38] Carter Stevenson to John Pegram, October 7, 1862, in *ibid.; Official Records*, XVI,
Pt. 2, p. 920.

[39] Wheeler to T. B. Roy, October 7 (1 A.M., with endorsement, Hardee to Polk—
9:30 A.M.) , in Bragg Papers, Western Reserve.

[40] *Official Records*, XVI, Pt. 1, p. 1120.

[41] Hardee to Bragg, October 7 (3:20 P.M.) , 1862, in Bragg Papers, Western Reserve.

[42] *Official Records*, XVI, Pt. 1, p. 1096.

letter had been noncommittal, and Kirby Smith pressed for aid on his front. Bragg then had reason to expect the battle on the right. Two hours after he sent Polk the order, he received more support for his move. A citizen of Cornishville, a village five miles northwest of Harrodsburg, came to Bragg's headquarters with an interesting tale. He reported McCook's corps was at Mackville, twenty-seven miles west of Harrodsburg. The Yankees were apparently marching from Taylorsville to the Kentucky River, moving north around Harrodsburg. Bragg hastily sent Stoddard Johnston with a patrol to confirm the report. Johnston probed at Cornishville and reported McCook was at Mackville. Moreover, the Yankee pickets pushed out on the Salvisa road to Cornishville had been withdrawn before the Rebel patrol arrived. Bragg was pleased. Stoddard Johnston's report had confirmed Kirby Smith's fears of an attempt to isolate the Rebel right.

Yet Bragg revealed his consistent lack of appreciation for geography. Earlier reports had placed McCook at Taylorsville and then farther south at Chaplaintown. Could it be that the Yankees were moving on the road that ran from Taylorsville to Harrodsburg and Perryville by way of Chaplaintown and Mackville? If Bragg feared such a move, he gave no indication. He was trusting that Kirby Smith's reports were correct, and that Polk and Hardee were reporting fully to their commander. Confident of success, he retired, after remarking that the great struggle for Kentucky would take place *north* on the Kentucky River. The following morning, he would move to join Kirby Smith.[43]

At dawn on the eighth, there was consternation among the high command at Perryville. Polk held a council of war with Hardee, Cheatham, and the division commanders. In the dim light he laid before them Bragg's order to give battle immediately. Polk and Hardee, like Bragg, had not taken the Perryville force seriously. But the blue columns were now swelling. Wheeler had come in the night before with disturbing news. His troopers had fought into the night out on the Springfield road for the precious water. Then a mass of blue infantry in division force smashed into the Rebel cavalry. Under the eerie moonlight Wheeler had

43 *Ibid.*, pp. 1024–25, 1038; Johnston, "Bragg's Campaign," Military Papers, Filson Club. The Cornishville affair was perhaps the most peculiar incident of the campaign. McCook actually was at Mackville, marching on Harrodsburg via the Taylorsville road. But at 7 P.M. the skirmishing at Perryville caused Buell to order a halt and concentrate. At 2:30 A.M. on the eighth, McCook turned south to Perryville; had Buell not stopped him, he unknowingly would have split Bragg's forces in half. Johnston thought McCook's advance picket was merely a flank guard thrown out. Buell planned to attack on the eighth, but delays in receipt of his orders among the corps caused him to postpone the attack until the next day. The same water shortage which prompted Hardee to halt at Perryville was also a cause in the delay of the Federal attack planned for the eighth. See James Fry to George Thomas, October 7, 1862, and Thomas to Buell, October 7, 1862, in Buell Papers, Rice.

seen more infantry coming up behind. Skirmish fire was now flaring
up south of Perryville on the Lebanon road. West of town St. John
Liddell's advance infantry brigade was in trouble. A wave of infantry
with reinforcements coming all the time pounded away at Liddell's
Arkansans. Cavalry hit Liddell on the flank, and canister raked the
Rebels until they were pushed back into Perryville. Polk and Hardee
were still unsure of the Yankee strength, but they determined to be
cautious. They agreed to adopt a defensive-offensive, and await the enemy from the ridge east of Chaplain's Fork, a small stream flowing
north on the west side of Perryville.[44]

Yet Hardee and Polk, just as at Bardstown, were not being fair with
Bragg. After the campaign Polk claimed the order to attack was dis-
obeyed because he considered a "great disparity . . ." [45] of numbers to
exist. Yet Hardee and Polk expressed no concern to Bragg over the
Perryville situation on the night of October 7 and the following morning. During the night Hardee had sent Bragg a private letter giving
his views of the situation. Hardee did not write that Buell was before
him. Nor did Hardee hint that he considered the Yankee force before
him any stronger than that before Kirby Smith. Hardee's was an appeal
to Bragg's military training. He urged Bragg not to divide the force
but to strike "the fractions of the enemy." [46] Hardee would later contend
he "earnestly urged upon General Bragg the necessity of massing his
forces on that important point." [47] But this is not what Hardee wrote on
the night of the seventh. Instead he suggested that, if Bragg desired to
move to Versailles, he should take the entire force there and strike. If
he wished to strike at Perryville, do it then "with a force which will
make success certain." [48] Hardee only advised striking first at Perryville
because the Bryantsville depot was nearby. He gave no intimation of a
superior force on the Perryville front. If Hardee thought Buell was near,
he was not telling Bragg.

Polk was again not confiding in his commander. After the council
of war Polk sent Bragg a dispatch which explained little of the situation. Polk expressed no alarm, asked for no reinforcements, and gave
no estimate of the Federal strength. Instead he only promised to give
the enemy battle vigorously and, if successful, to join Kirby Smith.
Nothing Polk wrote Bragg indicated he thought he was outnumbered.

44 *Official Records,* XVI, Pt. 1, pp. 897, 1110, 1120; Joseph Wheeler, "Bragg's Invasion
of Kentucky," *Battles and Leaders,* III, 15.
45 *Official Records,* XVI, Pt. 1, pp. 1110.
46 Hardee to Bragg, October 7 (7:30 P.M.) , 1862, in Bragg Papers, Western Reserve.
47 *Official Records,* XVI, Pt. 1, p. 1120.
48 Hardee to Bragg, October 7 (7:30 P.M.) , 1862, in Bragg Papers, Western Reserve.

Yet if he felt, as he later wrote, such a disparity[49] of numbers existed, why did he not tell Bragg? Bragg had ordered an attack, yet Polk did not even tell him the troops had gone on the defensive—nor even that a council of war had been called. The evidence appears that Polk was unsure of what was in his front. Yet he failed to inform Bragg of the things of which he *was* sure, such as the decision to adopt the defensive-offensive. Moreover, if Polk did believe the main Federal body was before him, as he later claimed, then his failure to inform Bragg was inexcusable.[50]

Polk's aloof attitude was another indication that the Confederates were beating themselves by failing to cooperate. Kirby Smith's independent move and subsequent indifference toward Bragg had frustrated a united effort. Polk's silence at Bardstown left his commander puzzled over the threat on the Confederate left. Hardee's letters from Perryville had not clarified the extent of danger on his front. Bragg was also at fault. His constant failure to give specific orders to his subordinates gave them freedom unmerited by personal relations and past experience. The result was that the cohesion of the high command in Kentucky had become dependent on respect for Bragg, but this seemed to be lacking among his subordinates. Kirby Smith had shown little respect for Bragg, even after Bragg took command of both columns. And now Polk's attitude had led him to hold back explanations for disobedience at Bardstown and Perryville, which jeopardized the safety of that army. This is not to say that Polk understood the situation that was developing on his front at Perryville. But Bragg had a right to know what Polk knew—and Polk had not been telling him.

[49] *Official Records,* XVI, Pt. 1, p. 1110.
[50] *Ibid.,* 1096, 1110.

fourteen

Some Truths Become Evident

ALTHOUGH BRAGG HAD PLANNED TO LEAVE ON OCTOBER 8 TO JOIN KIRBY Smith, he rode south to Perryville instead. He was irritated by information from Polk's front. He had received Hardee's letter during the night and decided the Yankee force at Perryville might require his personal attention. Early the following morning, when Polk's guns were not heard, Bragg rode south to dispose of the force that was delaying his master plan. When he reached Perryville he was surprised and angry to find Polk drawn back in a defensive line behind Chaplain's Fork. Anxious to crush the Federals and move north, he decided to attack. But to reach the Federal position the army must cross Chaplain's Fork, move across the rolling pasture to Doctor's Fork, and then ascend the bluffs on the west side. The Federals were on the ridge west of Doctor's Fork and were extending their line north to outflank Bragg's right. Although it would cause further delay, Bragg must adjust his front.[1]

He massed his troops to break the Union left and center north of the Springfield road. The Rebel army moved forward onto the rolling ground between the two creeks. On the far left only Wheeler's cavalry picketed the Danville and Lebanon pikes, as neither Bragg nor Polk expected serious trouble there. To Wheeler's right, two brigades of Anderson's division, Dan Adams' and Sam Powell's, were placed across the Springfield road. Buckner's division held the Rebel center between the Springfield and Old Mackville roads, while Cheatham held the line north

[1] Brent Diary, October 8, 1862, and Johnston Diary, October 8, 1862, in Bragg Papers, Western Reserve; William Hardee's official report of Perryville submitted to George Williamson, December 1, 1862 (MS in William Palmer Collection of Confederate Papers, Western Reserve), hereinafter cited as Hardee's Report, Western Reserve.

across the New Mackville pike. To insure a heavy blow on the Yankee left, Bragg threw in two brigades from Anderson's division and a reserve brigade from Buckner's to fill a small gap between Buckner and Cheatham.[2]

Shortly before noon the last of Cheatham's men filed into position, and Bragg outlined his plan of attack to Polk and Hardee. At 1 P.M., Polk, who would command the right, was to hurl Cheatham's division, in echelon from the right, against the ridge. Hardee, commanding the left and center, would press the assault when Cheatham's guns opened. At noon artillery opened on the right. Had Cheatham advanced so soon? Bragg investigated. A Federal battery on the ridge overlooking Doctor's Fork was dueling with Carnes's battery of smoothbores. Cheatham pushed up a battery of rifled guns in support, and the artillery thundered across the valley. By 1:30 P.M. the artillery duel ceased. The field was silent except for a strong wind that scattered twigs and dust into the waiting gray line. Why had Cheatham not attacked? Fretful, Bragg rode to the right and found Polk in conversation with Wharton, who was covering the flank. Polk had decided to postpone the attack until a Federal column, approaching on the New Mackville pike, was in position. Should he move now, the blue line would take him in flank. Bragg rode back to the rear and nervously waited.[3]

At last Cheatham moved forward, then dropped off into the hollow of Doctor's Fork and disappeared. Suddenly Donelson's brigade rose out of nowhere onto the steep bluffs across the creek and fell on a Union water detachment. Gray figures were everywhere scrambling out of the creek bed. They paused to adjust their lines, moved forward, and the battle for Kentucky was on. Yankee artillery atop the ridge found the range, and Donelson's brigade was cut to pieces. Still Donelson pushed on. The Federals were in position in a cornfield a half mile from the creek. Donelson's exhausted troops staggered into a small woods on the east side of the field to await reinforcements. A Yankee advance battery scarcely a hundred yards to the front raked the thicket with canister and grape, and Donelson lost a third of his command.[4]

Cheatham saw his plight and threw in Maney's brigade on the right. Maney's Tennesseans also reached the thicket but ran headlong into a

2 Benjamin F. Cheatham's official report of Perryville, submitted to Marcus Wright, November 18, 1862 (MS in Western Reserve), hereinafter cited as Cheatham's Report, Western Reserve; Brent's Diary, October 8, 1862, in Bragg Papers, Western Reserve; Johnston, "Bragg's Campaign," Military Papers, Filson Club.

3 Official Records, XVI, Pt. 1, p. 1110; Cheatham's Report, Western Reserve.

4 Tapp, "Battle of Perryville," 172 n.; Daniel Donelson's official report of Perryville, submitted to Marcus Wright, October 26, 1862 (MS in Western Reserve), hereinafter cited as Donelson's Report, Western Reserve; Cheatham's Report, Western Reserve.

high rail fence dividing the woods from the open ground. The Union advance battery of eight Napoleons seared the thicket. For the second time, Cheatham's attack threatened to collapse.[5]

Maney rode into the woods and ordered the line forward. With a cheer the Tennesseans climbed the fence and poured into the field. The advance battery fell, and Cheatham's men charged up the slope. The Yankee division defending the ridge broke and ran, leaving its commander, General James Jackson, dead on the field. A mile to the rear the Federals made another stand, but A. P. Stewart's brigade and Donelson's reserve regiments hurled the line back. By sunset the Yankees had re-formed on a ridge three-fourths of a mile west. Cheatham, his reserves all committed, was unable to break the line. The weary Rebels surged against the slope but were pushed back by a fresh Union brigade. Donelson was fought out, Stewart was out of ammunition, and Maney had suffered heavy losses. Still the Rebels kept up desultory skirmish fire until evening, then finally fell back several hundred yards. Bragg's plan to crush the Union left had succeeded. He had wrecked the Yankee left and had driven it back almost two miles.[6]

When Cheatham's guns opened, Hardee concentrated his attack in the center against the Federal line where it crossed the Old Mackville pike. Here the Federal line formed an obtuse angle which, if broken, would divide the Yankee left and center. Determined to gain the position, Hardee massed seven of his eight brigades on the left and center to break the line. The task would be difficult, for the Federals had a great advantage in terrain. As the Rebels advanced down the slope to Doctor's Fork, they would be in full view of the Union artillery on the ridge west of the creek. Blue patches of infantry could be seen behind rock and rail fences along both banks of the creek, around the

[5] Donelson's Report, Western Reserve; Cheatham's Report, Western Reserve; George Maney's official report of Perryville submitted to Marcus Wright, October 29, 1862 (MS in Bragg Papers, Western Reserve), hereinafter cited as Maney's Report, Western Reserve.

[6] The Union line that broke was the extreme left of McCook's corps which formed Buell's left. Cheatham attacked Terrill's brigade of Jackson's division. Brigadier General James Jackson was killed defending the first line, while Brigadier General William Terrill was killed defending a second line. Jackson's other brigade commander, Colonel George Webster, was killed in Hardee's attack on McCook's right. According to some reports, the night before the battle Jackson, Terrill, and Webster discussed the chances of being hit in battle and concluded the chances of any person being killed were so slim as not to concern them. See Charles C. Gilbert, "On the Field of Perryville," *Battles and Leaders*, III, 57 n.; *Official Records*, XVI, Pt. 1, pp. 1040–41, 1155–56, 1110–11. See also Tapp, "Battle of Perryville," 169, 172–73; Cheatham's and Donelson's Reports, Western Reserve; Maney's Report, Bragg Papers, Western Reserve; A. P. Stewart's official report of Perryville, submitted to Marcus Wright, October 28, 1862 (MS in Bragg Papers, Western Reserve).

Henry Bottom farmhouse on the west bank, and on the ridge slope beyond. Hardee ordered the key attack along the Old Mackville pike to be made by Bushrod Johnson and Pat Cleburne. When Cheatham's guns were heard, Johnson moved forward with Cleburne in support.[7]

For over an hour Johnson struggled to get a footing in the creek bottom, as the fight raged around the farmhouse. At last the Yankees were pushed back up the slope to a second line at the crest of the ridge. Cleburne took up the attack, moved up the slope in dress parade, and smashed into the Union line. The Federals fell back to open ground atop the ridge and with artillery attempted desperately to drive Cleburne back to the creek. Cleburne, John C. Brown, and Sterling Wood were wounded, and Buckner's division lost heavily. Then the Rebels brought up their own artillery from the creek bottom and pounded the Union position. The blue line disintegrated, and the fragments fell back to the rear of the Russell farmhouse.[8]

On Cleburne's right Sterling Wood's troops rushed past the farmhouse in an attempt to seize the vital junction of the Dicksville-Springfield and Perryville-Mackville roads. If this were taken, the Yankees opposing Cheatham and Buckner would be cut in half. The Federals massed infantry and artillery to hold the junction. Dusk fell as Wood's men came through the timber only to be thrown back by blue artillery firing point blank. Again and again the Rebels came through the woods. Although the Confederate dead and wounded were stacked before the cannon, the line held. Blue reserves came in from near the Springfield pike, and Wood's men fell back to join Cleburne, who had been stopped short of the Russell house.[9]

The last fragment of the Yankee left and center was thrown back shortly after dusk. Hardee sent St. John Liddell's brigade, his last reserve, with orders to go where the firing was most concentrated. Liddell, after a conference with Cheatham, smashed into an isolated strip of the Yankee line that Buckner and Cheatham had bypassed. The last of the Union line melted, and Liddell's men gathered up the spoils of the field —prisoners, arms, and colors. This routine scavenge also netted something that would greatly interest Braxton Bragg—the baggage and papers of Major General Alexander McCook, commanding First Corps, Army of Ohio.[10]

[7] Hardee's Report, Western Reserve; *Official Records*, XVI, Pt. 1, pp. 1125–26.

[8] *Official Records*, XVI, Pt. 1, pp. 1126–27, 1039–41; Tapp, "Battle of Perryville," 174–75; Buck, *Cleburne*, 112–14. Hardee attacked Lovell Rousseau's division, McCook's right flank.

[9] *Official Records*, XVI, Pt. 1, pp. 1041, 1080; Tapp, "Battle of Perryville," 176–77; Buck, *Cleburne*, 113–14. Wood attacked reserves from Gilbert's corps.

[10] Hardee's Report, Western Reserve; *Official Records*, XVI, Pt. pp. 1121, 1159–60.

That night Bragg, Polk, and Hardee at last learned that their fifteen thousand men were facing Buell's entire army. An indication of this had been the lack of Confederate success on the left flank. Bragg had expected no real opposition on the left. Only Wheeler's cavalry guarded the Danville and Lebanon pikes, and Dan Adams' and Sam Powell's brigades were the only Rebel infantry sent into action on the Springfield pike. But Adams and Powell ran into an entire Union corps. Bragg's left was so weak that a lone Yankee brigade had driven Powell back that evening and had fought its way through the Perryville streets before being driven out. Meanwhile a new threat arose on the far left. The Rebel cavalry reported a strong enemy column moving toward Perryville on the Lebanon road. Bragg had nothing to send to the left except Preston Smith's brigade, and this force would be insufficient should the unexpected Federal column attack. Prisoners assured Bragg that Buell's army lay in the darkness outside Perryville. Liddell had captured McCook's chief of artillery, as well as the general's papers, and Kirby Smith's cavalry had found that McCook was moving on Frankfort! Prisoners were taken from Rousseau's division—Rousseau was also supposedly moving on Frankfort. The prisoner list read like an organizational chart of Buell's army—captives from Gilbert's corps, Sheridan's division, Mitchell's division. And what of the column yet to arrive on the far left? It was rumored to be a fresh corps commanded by T. L. Crittenden.[11]

Bragg, Polk, and Hardee obviously could not stay at Perryville. Preliminary reports listed 30 per cent casualties for the force. The valley of Doctor's Fork was already a sea of bobbing lanterns as the wounded and dead were sought out. At Green River, Bragg had feared Buell's army was twice the size of his own. The disparity of numbers had been increased at Bardstown by heavy additions to the Yankee column. Bragg and his generals agreed that the small Rebel force could not survive an attack against such odds. The Army must be saved, and the solution appeared to be a retreat to Harrodsburg, where Bragg hoped a junc-

[11] Powell's brigade had attacked Gilbert's entire corps before being thrown back by part of Mitchell's division. See Tapp, "Battle of Perryville," 175–76. Earlier in the afternoon Bragg had received ominous rumors of a strong Federal force coming up on the extreme left and sent Preston Smith's brigade to hold the roads south of town. The force was T. L. Crittenden's corps commanded by General George H. Thomas. See Johnston Diary, October 8, 1862, in Bragg Papers, Western Reserve; Preston Smith's official report of Perryville submitted to Marcus Wright, October 23, 1862, in Western Reserve. Buell at his headquarters on the Springfield road did not even know a battle was in progress, for an "acoustical shadow" caused by wind and terrain obscured the sounds until about 4 P.M. See Gilbert, "On the Field of Perryville," 57–58. Interviews with prisoners convinced Bragg that he opposed Buell's main force. See Johnston Diary, October 8, 1862, in Bragg Papers, Western Reserve; Johnston, "Bragg's Campaign," Military Papers, Filson Club.

tion could be made with Withers and Kirby Smith. Orders were issued immediately, and early on the ninth, the victorious but battered Rebel army fell back to Harrodsburg.[12]

Historians would portray Bragg at Harrodsburg as undecided about future moves and would accuse him of losing his nerve for not remaining there and fighting Buell. Yet it is doubtful that Bragg ever intended to halt at that town. On the contrary, by the time he arrived there on the ninth, he had already issued orders for a retreat across Dick's River to Bryantsville.[13]

Bragg moved to Harrodsburg because he had little choice—not because he planned to fight Buell there. The only other line of retreat from Perryville to Bryantsville was by way of Danville. The Danville route would have required only an eighteen-mile march to strike the Cumberland Gap route road across Dick's River. Yet, if Bragg had chosen this route, he would have jeopardized his army's safety. Bragg's and Kirby Smith's armies were scattered throughout 320 square miles of Bluegrass from Perryville to near Lexington. If Bragg had moved east by way of Danville, Harrodsburg would have fallen to Buell, and the two Confederate forces would have been cut off from each other.[14]

Bragg's decision not to remain at Harrodsburg was wise, for he knew the position was a trap. On October 8 Wheeler reported that the Yankees had swung southeast of Perryville to outflank Bragg and cut him off from Cumberland Gap. He added that Mitchellsburg, only fourteen miles west of Danville, had already fallen. Federal cavalry were smashing Wheeler's advance near Danville. If Danville fell, the Yankees would be only eight miles from the Cumberland Gap road and only ten from Bragg's depot at Bryantsville. A loss there would leave Bragg without a base, since the necessary withdrawal of Kirby Smith from north of the Kentucky would surrender the Lexington depot. Moreover, Bragg's back would be to the Kentucky River and to the Federal column at Coving-

12 Brent Diary, October 9, 1862, and Johnston Diary, October 9, 1862, in Bragg Papers, Western Reserve; Johnston, "Bragg's Campaign," Military Papers, Filson Club; Polk, *Leonidas Polk, Bishop and General*, II, 159; *Official Records*, XVI, Pt. 1, p. 1083, 115–16. Bragg's retreat was wise. Buell had ordered an attack the next day for 6 A.M., expecting Bragg to fight and thinking Bragg's whole army was at Perryville. When he saw Bragg's army retreat, he mistook the move for a flank attack on McCook and ordered Thomas to attack. Thomas found an empty town. See Buell to Halleck, October 9, 1862, Buell to Thomas, March 2, 1864, James B. Fry to Thomas, October 9, 1862, C. C. Gilbert to Buell, October 9, 1862, all in Buell Papers, Rice.

13 Brent's Diary, October 8–9, 1862, Johnston's Diary, October 8–9, 1862, Kirby Smith to Bragg, October 9 (9 P.M.), 1862, all in Bragg Papers, Western Reserve; *Official Records*, XVI, Pt. 1, p. 898; Johnston, "Bragg's Campaign," Military Papers, Filson Club.

14 Hammond, "Campaign," X, 72–73.

ton and Cincinnati. Bragg, determined to avoid such perils, ordered Polk on October 9 to begin moving across Dick's River at King's Mill Ford, even before Kirby Smith had arrived at Harrodsburg.[15]

What then, is the basis for the criticism that Bragg first decided to fight at Harrodsburg and then panicked and retreated? On the morning of October 10, as the rear of Polk's column disappeared down the King's Mill road, Kirby Smith arrived at Harrodsburg, met Bragg, and the two conferred on future plans. Their conversation was interrupted by a message from Wharton, who was on the picket line south of Harrodsburg on the Perryville road. He reported the Federals were approaching. Bragg had little choice but to halt the rear of Polk's column and to move Kirby Smith's troops out to Salt River to form a strong battle line. If Wharton's message had gone unheeded and the Federals had attacked Harrodsburg, Bragg's column would have been cut in half. Hardee was already across Dick's River, and the rear of Kirby Smith's force had not yet reached the town. If the warning had been ignored, Kirby Smith's troops might have been struck on their right flank as they moved toward King's Mill Ford. Although he had not planned to fight, Bragg had little choice but to deploy a line of battle.[16]

On the tenth, however, Bragg received information which indicated that Harrodsburg was a far more dangerous trap than it had been on the ninth. After he placed Kirby Smith's troops in line south of Harrodsburg, there was no further Federal activity on the Perryville road. Bragg grew suspicious. On the night of the tenth, Wheeler sent a dispatch which said that the Federals had veered off the road to Harrodsburg and were moving on Danville. Wheeler's troopers had been driven back into the town by infantry in division strength, as well as by cavalry. The situation was grave. If Buell took Danville, he would be only eight miles from the Cumberland Gap road. From Harrodsburg Kirby Smith's troops would have to march fourteen miles to strike the gap road, and still would be five miles north of the point where Buell's column would intersect it.

Simultaneously, bad news came from the north. Dumont's Federal brigade was reported advancing southeast from Frankfort on the Versailles road, threatening to cross the Kentucky River in Bragg's rear. If Dumont seized the Kentucky River bridge on the Cumberland Gap road,

---

[15] Wheeler to Hardee, October 8, 1862, in Bragg Papers, Western Reserve; *Official Records,* XVI, Pt. 1, p. 898; Johnston, "Bragg's Campaign," Military Papers, Filson Club.

[16] Brent's Diary, October 10, 1862, and Johnston's Diary, October 10, 1862, in Bragg Papers, Western Reserve; Kirby Smith, "Kentucky Campaign," UNC; Hammond, "Campaign," X, 71–73.

Bragg's northern line of retreat would be cut. Moreover, Dumont could move south, block Kirby Smith from crossing Dick's River, and cut the Confederate army in two. If Bragg remained at Harrodsburg, his army would be caught in a pincer. Realizing his danger, he ordered Wheeler to hold Danville as long as possible, while Humphrey Marshall, still on his way from Lexington, was to hold the Kentucky River bridge. At daylight on October 11, Kirby Smith started moving his troops across Dick's River to Bryantsville.[17]

Kirby Smith contended later that he objected to retreating from Harrodsburg. After the war, he asserted that upon reaching Harrodsburg, he was surprised to find Bragg's column in retreat and urged that "for God's sake General, let us fight here." [18] Yet Kirby Smith knew as early as the night of the ninth that Bragg was not to stay at Harrodsburg. Nor did he object to the move but only remarked, "I will try to see you at Harrodsburg before you leave there in the morning." [19] Too, Kirby Smith planned his march from Salvisa so that only Stevenson's division would pass through Harrodsburg. Until the news was received from Wharton on the tenth, he did not intend for Withers and Heth even to pass through Harrodsburg. Instead, they were to swing east, cross the Kentucky River twice, and come into Bryantsville from the north—hardly a marching plan for a general determined to fight at Harrodsburg.[20]

Kirby Smith, by his criticism of Bragg's evacuation of Harrodsburg, seemed to be compensating for his own mistakes made north of the Kentucky River. It had been partly on his word that Bragg had thrown thirty thousand troops into the line to hold Lexington while leaving only fifteen thousand at Perryville. He appeared as misled as Bragg,

17 Wheeler to George Brent, October 11 ("before daylight"), 1862, George Brent to Humphrey Marshall, October 10 (7 P.M.), 1862, Johnston Diary, October 10–11, 1862, Brent Diary, October 10–11, 1862, all in Bragg Papers, Western Reserve; Johnston, "Bragg's Campaign," Military Papers, Filson Club; *Official Records*, XVI, Pt. 1, pp. 52–54, 152, 1028, 1036, 898, Pt. 2, p. 930; Polk, *Leonidas Polk, Bishop and General*, II, 169; Buell to Thomas, March 2, 1864, and Buell to Halleck, October 13, 1862, in Buell Papers, Rice. Buell did not actually try to cut Bragg off from the crossing of Dick's River until the morning of the twelfth. Buell had expected Bragg and Kirby Smith to fight at Harrodsburg and had stationed his force between that town and Perryville, awaiting reinforcements. The force that threatened Wheeler on the tenth was only an extension of Crittenden's corps; the next day a reconnaissance force sent to Danville by Buell drove Wheeler from the town while another force sent to Harrodsburg found it evacuated. Only when Buell learned Bragg had gone did he pivot his army on Danville to prevent Bragg's crossing of Dick's River; but on the twelfth Buell learned Bragg had escaped across Dick's River.

18 Kirby Smith, "Kentucky Campaign," UNC.

19 Kirby Smith to Bragg, October 9 (8 P.M.), 1862, in Bragg Papers, Western Reserve.

20 Kirby Smith, "Kentucky Campaign," UNC; Kirby Smith to Bragg, October 9 (8 P.M.), 1862, in Bragg Papers, Western Reserve.

Hardee, and Polk as to the whereabouts of Buell's main army. Not only did he send consistent pleas for aid on the three days before the fight at Perryville, but he still thought on October 8 that Buell was in his front. On that morning, after rushing his troops to Versailles to meet an advance from Frankfort, he had found that the force was not crossing the river at Frankfort but was moving down the west bank toward Lawrenceburg. It was not until that night, after he rushed back down the east bank of the river, that Kirby Smith discovered he was opposed by only Joshua Sill's ten-thousand-man brigade. Still Kirby Smith failed to employ his thirty thousand men with success. In the early morning of the ninth, he met Sill in the battle of Dog Walk, yet the latter slipped away and joined Buell.[21] The battle was an uninspiring finish to Kirby Smith's attempt at command in Kentucky. He had taken advantage of Bragg's hesitancy in giving him orders and had continued to maintain an independent position north of the Kentucky River.

The failures of the campaign lay heavily upon the camp at Bryantsville. On October 12 Bragg called a council of Kirby Smith, Polk, Cheatham, Hardee, and Marshall to discuss a retreat from Kentucky. When he revised his strategy at Bardstown, Bragg had set up several prerequisites to his remaining in Kentucky. At Bryantsville he was finally convinced that his plan had failed. He had expected Price and Van Dorn to provide support in Middle Tennessee, but now news trickled in that they had been crushed at Corinth. This defeat meant that Bragg's own army was the only strong force in the field between the Appalachians and the Mississippi to oppose a Yankee invasion into the Deep South. He now could not chance his army's defeat, and must look to the rear lest the Chattanooga base be overrun. He felt he was only doing what Jefferson Davis wanted—saving the army. Partly for this reason Bragg had chosen not to follow Buell to Nashville, had not pursued to Louisville, and had retreated from Harrodsburg. More self-conscious than most, he had an unusually strong fear of making a mistake. And now that Price and Van Dorn had failed, he felt the pressure of responsibility even more strongly.[22]

Bragg had also expected aid from John C. Breckinridge. The latter

[21] Kirby Smith to Bragg, October 8 (11:30 A.M.) , 1862, in Bragg Papers, Western Reserve; *Official Records*, XVI, Pt. 2, pp. 925, 927–28.

[22] Johnston Diary, October 11–12, 1862, and Brent Diary, October 11–12, 1862, in Bragg Papers, Western Reserve. When Bragg learned of the Corinth defeat, he immediately decided to retreat ("Johnston Memoranda," Military Papers, Filson Club) ; he privately told Kirby Smith before the council of war that his instructions from Davis did not allow risking the loss of the Army, and Bragg later reported this to the council. Kirby Smith to J. Stoddard Johnston, October 31, 1866, in Johnston, Military Papers, Filson Club; see also *Official Records*, XVI, Pt. 1, p. 1093.

had not arrived, and Bragg had learned that a conflict between his own request and Van Dorn's desire to retain Breckinridge had produced a fatal delay.[23] And what of the help Bragg expected from Tennessee? On September 23 he had written Samuel Cooper that it would take fifty thousand recruits to hold that state and Kentucky. When Bragg left Chattanooga, he put Sam Jones in charge of the Army's base, to send forward all men and supplies that he could assemble. The situation which occurred in Bragg's absence was an example of the faults of the interdepartmental scheme. Just as Kirby Smith was communicating directly with Richmond, so too, were the commanders that he and Bragg left behind.

McCown, whom Kirby Smith had left in command of the East Tennessee Department, was supposed to watch Morgan by maintaining Stevenson's division south of Cumberland Gap, send forward recruits, and guard the other mountain passes through which Kirby Smith had just passed. Instead of detaching part of Stevenson's oversized command to guard the passes, McCown went straight to Secretary of War George Randolph and asked him to countermand orders which both Kirby Smith and Bragg had sent requesting Colonel Sumner Smith's legion to move to Kentucky. On September 14 he asked the secretary also to countermand orders for some 1,800 convalescents and some 1,000 recruits which Kirby Smith had wanted in Kentucky. He even asked Randolph to order two or three regiments from Bragg's own department to aid in opening the gaps.[24]

It was not what McCown did that hurt Bragg (he failed to stop Smith's legion), but what he failed to do. He made no further effort to send Kirby Smith any reinforcements, nor did he reopen the gaps. Instead he wrote Bragg that his command had become "an Army of Observation" [25]—which meant it would sit and watch Morgan at Cumberland Gap. But McCown managed to keep busy in other areas. He started a feud with Sam Jones at Chattanooga over which department would conscript in East Tennessee and demanded that the latter halt conscription in the area until the two officers conferred. Then the two feuded over which department controlled

23 "Johnston Memoranda," Military Papers, Filson Club; Sam Jones to Bragg, September 10, 17, 20, 1862, in Letters and Telegrams Sent, Headquarters, Confederate Forces at Chattanooga and Department of Western Virginia, 1862–1863, Ch. II, Vol. 233, National Archives, hereinafter cited as Ch. II, Vol. 233, National Archives; Jones to Bragg, September 29, 1862, in Ch. II, Vol. 51, National Archives; Official Records, XVI, Pt. 2, pp. 995–1003.

24 McCown to Randolph, September 3, 14, 1862, McCown to Cooper, September 8, 12, 14, 1862, McCown to Stevenson, September 10, 1862, McCown to Sam Jones, September 10, 11, 1862, McCown to Bragg, September 14, 1862, all in Ch. II, Vol. 51, National Archives.

25 McCown to Bragg, September 14, 1862, in ibid.

the cornfields on the east side of the Hiwassee River, which Jones' quarter-master had impressed so that corn might be sent forward to Bragg.[26]

Bragg was as ignorant of this activity as he was of what would follow. On September 20, Jones received a telegram from Randolph that directed him to assume command of the Department of East Tennessee while McCown moved to join Kirby Smith. Not only was Bragg not informed that his base commander had been transferred, but no provisions were made for the sending of supplies and recruits to Bragg in Jones's absence. Ignorant of this change of command, Bragg assigned Jones to command the District of Middle Tennessee of Department Number Two, move his headquarters to Murfreesboro, forward all recruits and conscripts available, and try to capture Nashville. But by the time he had penned this order, McCown was on his way to Kirby Smith, and Jones was operating another department. No one in Richmond bothered to inform Bragg.[27]

Once Jones took over at Knoxville, the situation became ridiculous. Without informing Bragg, he wrote Samuel Cooper and asked that the District of Middle Tennessee in Department Number Two be added to his own department. This request was granted. Jones now went further. Bragg had wanted him to hurry Breckinridge's command, which included about two thousand exchanged prisoners, to Kentucky. But Jones became interested in keeping these in his new department and asked Cooper for authority to retain them. This he received, as well as authority to keep part of Breckinridge's division if necessary for operations in Middle Tennessee. Jones immediately ordered Breckinridge to send him the Tennessee regiment.[28] Not until October 12, sixteen days after Bragg assigned him to the Middle Tennessee command, did Jones inform him that Middle Tennessee was no longer in Bragg's department and that the Tennessee troops had been retained. If it were any solace, Jones added that Bragg could rely on his "most zealous support and co-operation." [29] Thus he bowed out of the scheme to reinforce Kentucky.

Bragg now realized that his plans to supply his army in Kentucky had failed. At Bardstown he had specified that ample stores must be gathered

[26] McCown to Jones, September 12, 1862, in *ibid.*

[27] McCown to Jones, September 20, 1862, Jones to Cooper, October 5, 1862, Jones to Bragg, October 12, 1862, all in *ibid.;* Jones to Bragg, September 20, 1862, in Ch. II, Vol. 233, National Archives; General Orders No. 130, Dept. No. 2, September 27, 1862, Ch. VIII, Vol. 342, National Archives.

[28] Jones to Cooper, October 10, 1862, and Jones to Breckinridge, October 11, 1862, in Ch. II, Vol. 51, National Archives.

[29] Jones to Bragg, October 12, 1862, in *ibid.*

if the army were to remain in the state, and had ordered that the supplies gathered at Lexington and Danville be moved to Bryantsville for safety. But the commissary officers were slow in moving the goods; the city fell when Kirby Smith moved to join Bragg, and his only supply of breadstuffs was lost. Now at Bryantsville the army was backed into a less fertile region with only four days' rations on hand.[30] A persistent myth would arise that Bragg's army departed from Kentucky with full stomachs; after the war Kirby Smith would say that his troops at Harrodsburg "had supplies and provisions."[31] Yet on October 22 he complained to Bragg from Cumberland Gap that ten thousand of his command were scattered over the country searching for "something upon which to live." [32] He described his command to his wife as being "famished, sick, worn out and exhausted." [33] Historians would contend that the army departed from Kentucky laden with a large wagon train filled with supplies. However, these were arms, not food. Bragg would bring from Kentucky the 20,000 rifles he had carried into the state to arm volunteers, as well as some 15,000 captured rifles.[34]

But what of the primary object of the campaign—to bring Kentucky back into the Southern fold? On October 12 at Bryantsville, Stoddard Johnston glumly commented that "the primary object of the invasion of Kentucky has failed." [35] Both Kirby Smith and Bragg had attempted to rationalize the lethargy of the state's citizens. When he first reached Lexington, Kirby Smith had boasted that Kentuckians were rising to the Southern banner. His chief of staff, Colonel John Pegram, added that "if the arms were here we could arm twenty thousand men in a few days." [36] The captured weapons from Richmond arrived, but Kentucky did not respond. Kirby Smith groped for reasons. If Breckinridge had come, "his regiments would have been filled up immediately." [37] Still they did not enlist, as "wealth, property and Yankee intercourse have had their corrupting influences." [38] And then, curiously, from the man who had been advocating territorial occupation before defeat-

30 *Official Records*, XVI, Pt. 2, p. 833; Bragg to Kirby Smith, September 27, 1862, in Bragg, Western Reserve; Hammond, "Campaign," X, 74.

31 Kirby Smith, "Kentucky Campaign," UNC.

32 *Official Records*, XVI, Pt. 2, p. 975.

33 Kirby Smith to his wife, October 25, 1862, in Kirby Smith Papers, UNC.

34 Tapp, "Battle of Perryville," 177; Report of Bryantsville Stores, October 7, 1862 (MS in Bragg Papers, Western Reserve) ; George Finnell to Buell, February 20, 1863, List of Property Captured at the State Arsenal, Frankfort, Kentucky, August, 1862 (MS in Buell Papers, Rice) .

35 Johnston Diary, October 12, 1862, in Bragg Papers, Western Reserve.

36 *Official Records*, XVI, Pt. 2, p. 797.

37 *Ibid.*, 846.

38 Kirby Smith to his wife, September 16, 1862, in Kirby Smith Papers, UNC.

ing the Federal army, "the defeat of Buell would rally the whole of Kentucky to our cause." [39]

Bragg, too, had been disappointed in Kentucky's response and had sought a reason. He saw no Confederate sympathy manifested until he reached Bardstown. Even then, the sympathy was restrained, and gave no evidence that Kentucky was flocking to the Rebel standard as Kirby Smith had promised. Although he had received no recruits, while Kirby Smith had netted only 1,500, Bragg at Bardstown rationalized that the Kentuckians feared to volunteer but would willingly be conscripted. He decided that his proposed conscription act would be the last call for Kentucky support. If the state did not respond, he would leave, for he wrote Kirby Smith that unless Kentuckians joined the ranks, it would be impossible for the Army to stay in Kentucky. The fortunes of the campaign did not give Bragg his opportunity to test the state's sentiment. Yet at Bryantsville he was convinced it would be useless to try. He had suffered some 4,200 casualties at Munfordville, Richmond, and Perryville, and by October 12 only 2,500 Kentuckians had volunteered to replace them.[40] Discouraged, Bragg wrote Cooper on October 1 that while the Kentucky people had been given every opportunity "to assert their independence," that "there is little or no disposition to avail of it." [41]

Even if Bragg had been given the opportunity of proclaiming a conscription act, it probably would not have succeeded. Kentuckians did not understand the reasoning that demanded they express Confederate sentiment before the Federals would be driven out. And Bragg, Kirby Smith, and Jefferson Davis did not understand Kentuckians. Kentucky sentiment was a curious mixture of intense support for state rights combined with a fierce devotion to the Union and the Constitution. State rights had come out of a time of frontier struggle, when Kentucky had borne the brunt of the Revolution and the War of 1812 west of the Alleghenies. The long period of almost standing alone had convinced these people that their destiny was their own. Although slavery, by the time of the war, was dying out in Kentucky (only seventy people owned over fifty slaves), the institution was defended even by non-slavers. They argued that a state should be allowed to exercise every power delegated by the Federal constitution. Yet Kentucky was strongly for a continued

[39] Kirby Smith to his wife, September 20, 1862, in *ibid.*

[40] Bragg to Kirby Smith, September 23, 1862, in Bragg Papers, Western Reserve; Bragg to Davis, October 2, 1862, in Bragg Papers, West Point. Bragg's casualties also included some two thousand sick, part of whom were captured at Harrodsburg, and some one thousand other losses from minor engagements. See *Official Records*, XVI, Pt. 1, pp. 1088, 936, 982, 1108; Hammond, "Campaign," X, 72 *n.*

[41] *Official Records*, XVI, Pt. 1, p. 1088.

Union. Populated by Southerners, the state also had a large immigrant influx and close ties of kinship with Illinois, Ohio, and Indiana.

When war broke out, Kentucky was in a dilemma—sentiment held with the South, but economics demanded a preservation of the Union, and the North stood for that preservation. By 1860 the North had weaned away the state's trade. Imports and exports were no longer moving along the Mississippi to New Orleans but over the Appalachians in the east, along the Ohio, or by the Great Lakes route. Southern railroad builders, content with linking seaboard and the Delta, had not foreseen this. On the eve of the war, the Louisville and Nashville was the only railroad connecting central Kentucky with the South. The only other railroad that ran South, the Mobile and Ohio, barely skirted the western edge of the state. But the East, realizing the South's advantage in geographical ties with Kentucky, sought to surmount its own trade barrier—the Appalachian Mountains. During the great railroad boom from 1840 to 1860 the East pushed twelve railroads to the north bank of the Ohio to draw Kentucky trade that could not overcome the mountain roads and unnavigable waters of the Appalachians. The state came to rely on the East for such commodities as salt, railroad iron, furniture, and hardware. The only important foreign product that was still procured from the Southern route was coffee. Kentucky could not afford to break her commercial ties with the East, or even with the South; therefore she strove to preserve—and then to restore—the Union.[42]

The Confederates also seemed unable to understand Kentuckians' border state complex. The latter were afraid of being caught in the middle and of being a buffer in a war. They feared a mass attack from across the Ohio should the state secede. Even in the Bluegrass, the stronghold of Southern support with over 50 per cent of the state's slaves, the river seemed too near for comfort; an invasion might sweep away the slave investment. Secession was not adequate compensation to them for a loss of the protection of the Fugitive Slave Law which turned runaways back from the promised land on the Ohio and Indiana shores.

Confederate sympathizers in the Bluegrass were also isolated from other Confederate areas. To the east lay the pro-Union mountain regions; to the north was the Ohio River; and to the southwest lay the Green and Barren River country, where slaves were few and where the pro-Union congressional candidates consistently swept the districts

42 Coulter, *Civil War and Readjustment*, 7–10, 160–63, 8, 12–17; Carl Russell Fish, "The Decision of the Ohio Valley," *American Historical Association, Annual Report, 1910* (Washington, 1912), 158–61; *Eighth Census*, III, cxliv–ix.

by margins of four and five to one. The only other slave areas of any size were fifty to a hundred miles to the southwest on the Cumberland and Tennessee rivers. Even if these people had been willing to support the Confederates openly, they were too few. The only large group still concerned with trade down the Mississippi were the tobacco growers—who were also the slaveholders. Even among these, Southern sympathy and secession were not the same, for there was too much to lose by leaving the Union.[43]

Kirby Smith, Bragg, and Davis had relied upon John Morgan's promise of 30,000 eager volunteers. But had not the Confederates misinterpreted popular sentiment for Morgan as desire to join the Confederacy? The 30,000 had not come—only 2,500, most of whom were youths wishing to be "Morgan's men." Bragg and Kirby Smith had counted heavily on John C. Breckinridge to whip up Confederate sentiment. Breckinridge was immensely popular in Kentucky, but this did not mean sentiment for the Confederacy. Even twenty-three of the most staunch Union counties in eastern Kentucky had voted for Breckinridge in 1860—but only one elected a secession candidate for Congress. He had carried fourteen Bluegrass counties while the secessionists had carried only four. And what of the general unrest John Morgan saw among the Kentucky people during the summer? There was widespread protest against the Federal army's control of elections and the judiciary, their wholesale arrests of suspected Southern loyalists, and intimidation at the polls. The unfavorable reaction, however, was not against the Constitution but against the infringement of rights Kentuckians felt were preserved by the Constitution.[44]

Even if the state had been willing to respond to the pleas of Bragg and Kirby Smith, the requirement that it must help earn its own freedom made a favorable reaction difficult. The Confederate leaders had not remembered the lesson of 1861, when Magoffin tried to lead his people into the Southern camp. The Federals had won a bout of psychological warfare in the Bluegrass. Confederate sympathizers were cowed, and feared Union reprisals if Rebel sentiment became overt. Bragg partially understood this fear, but failed to appreciate its deeper meaning when he wrote his wife on November 9: "Why then should I stay with my handful of brave Southern men to fight for cowards who sulked about in the dark to say to us 'We are with you; only whip these fellows out of our country, and let us see you can

43 Shaler, *Kentucky*, 255–56; Coulter, *Civil War and Readjustment*, 11–12; Fish, "Decision," 163; Speed, *Union Cause in Kentucky*, 173, 177.

44 *Official Records*, XVI, Pt. 2, pp. 733–34; Johnston, "Bragg's Campaign," Military Papers, Filson Club; Shaler, *Kentucky*, 333–37; Coulter, *Civil War and Readjustment*, 145–63; Fish, "Decision," 163.

protect us, and we will join you.' " [45] Their point was well taken. But Bragg continued to hold to the rigid standard that Kentuckians must first join him and then help earn their freedom.

Kirby Smith at first held this same philosophy, but by the end of September he apparently sensed that Kentucky could not be secured unless Buell's force was beaten. On September 23 he wrote Bragg, "I regard the defeat of Buell before he effects a junction with the force at Louisville as a military necessity, for Buell's army has always been the great bugbear to these people, and until defeated we cannot hope for much addition to our ranks from Kentucky." [46] Why then, did Kirby Smith not cooperate in an attack against Buell's army? After the war he admitted his move to Lexington was a violation of the Chattanooga agreement to march against Buell in Middle Tennessee.[47] He failed to send aid when Bragg and Buell were moving toward Green River, and made no attempt to keep the Louisville force occupied so it would not move out against Bragg while he was at Green River. After the war he attempted to explain his failure: "The occupation of Cincinnati or Louisville might have endangered our concentration—whilst our concentration effected Buell's defeat was certain and not only Louisville and Cincinnati but the North would be the fruits of victory." [48]

Yet Kirby Smith did not encourage a concentration. On the contrary, he worked against it. On September 19 he wrote Bragg that he felt his force should remain at Lexington. On September 21 he protested a meeting with Bragg below Louisville as injurious to recruiting and gathering of stores at Lexington.[49] And on September 23, in the same letter in which he said that Buell first must be defeated, he wrote Bragg that "I will be in supporting distance of you in your operations against Buell." [50] Although Kirby Smith seemed to realize what must be done to gain Kentucky support, he was unwilling to sacrifice independent command to make Buell's defeat a possibility.

Again the old command problem had troubled the Army. There had been little communication between Davis and his commanders on the Kentucky policy. Davis never clarified exactly whether the sample proclamation which he gave them was to apply to Kentucky. Bragg and Kirby Smith assumed it did not. In various proclamations which they issued in Kentucky, they did not speak of carrying the war to country occupied by the enemy. Instead they asked the Kentuckians for support and vowed

45 Seitz, *Braxton Bragg*, 207.
46 *Official Records*, XVI, Pt. 2, p. 866.
47 Kirby Smith, "Kentucky Campaign," in Kirby Smith Papers, UNC.
48 *Ibid.*
49 *Official Records*, XVI, Pt. 2, pp. 850, 861.
50 *Ibid.*, 866.

they would leave the area if help was not received.[51] The only use of Davis' document was at Bardstown. Bragg issued it vaguely "To the people of the Northwest," [52] with no mention of Kentucky.

Davis also never explained what he hoped for in strategy. When he suggested before the campaign that Buell be defeated first, he gave this as opinion, not as an order. Yet by September 4, he had evidently approved of the opposite plan. In a dispatch captured at Glasgow by the Federals, Davis, obviously speaking of Kirby Smith's independent move, told Bragg that he approved. Much of the absence of a policy for the campaign seems to be the responsibility of President Davis.[53]

Even if there had been a policy for Kentucky, the problem of inter-departmental command would have made it difficult to execute. From the July 31 Chattanooga meeting until the Lexington meeting on October 2, the campaign had two commanders. Kirby Smith had used his independence to launch his own moves and stifle cooperation. Thus when Bragg did assume command at Lexington, many of the campaign's mistakes had already been made—but Bragg was left to bear full responsibility.[54]

Jefferson Davis and his advisers had maintained a dualistic attitude toward this situation. Except for a blind hope for "cordial co-operation" between his generals, Davis did nothing to solve the problem. Yet Richmond attempted a halfway control of the campaign from behind the scenes. On September 19 Davis admitted that he did not know of Bragg's plans for Tennessee and was at a loss to know how to remedy problems. Bragg's supply and recruiting systems in Tennessee were damaged by Randolph's manipulations with McCown and Jones. In Mississippi, Davis and Randolph had meddled with Bragg's plans for Price and Van Dorn. The communication lag between Richmond and Bragg was such that the government did not even know that Van Dorn, Price, and Breckinridge were part of the invasion column. The fault was partly Bragg's, for he had not fully explained to Richmond the purpose of the Mississippi column.[55]

51 *Ibid.*, 822–23, LII, Pt. 2, pp. 363–65, 367–68; Kirby Smith's proclamation, undated (MS) , in Kirby Smith Papers, UNC.

52 *Official Records*, XVI, Pt. 2, p. 363.

53 Davis to Bragg, September 4, 1862, in Buell Papers, Rice.

54 Finally seeing the fault of the command structure, Kirby Smith wrote on November 23, "We need some one controlling mind who can direct operations over an extended sphere. . . ." Kirby Smith to his wife, November 23, 1862, in Kirby Smith Papers, UNC. After the dual command failed in Kentucky, Davis returned to the idea of broad theater command similar to that of A. S. Johnston, and sent Joseph E. Johnston to the West. See Rowland (ed.) , *Davis*, V, 356; Davis to Kirby Smith, October 29, 1862, in Kirby Smith Papers, UNC.

55 For evidence Richmond realized the mistake in reference to Price and Van Dorn, see *Official Records*, XVII, Pt. 2, p. 707. See also Horn, *Army of Tennessee*, 172–74.

At Bryantsville, it was clear that Bragg's defensive plan had been wrecked by the same lack of planning, cooperation, and timing which had brought grief to his earlier offensive. Though Bragg had seen his offensive strategy falling apart at Bardstown, he had clung to the same ideas for the new plan. Unable to revise, Bragg had expected too much of his piecemeal defensive hopes, and now was jolted severely when he realized he had failed. Van Dorn's rumored defeat, the absence of support from Tennessee, Breckinridge's absence, the lack of food sources around Dick's River, Kentucky's indifference—all left little to expect in the state.

Even if Bragg had desired to give Kentucky another chance, it was evident at Bryantsville that success could not be retrieved. Instead of plans for occupying Louisville, the generals must now talk of means to save their armies. The Dick's River line had become a trap. Wheeler's exhausted troops had already been driven from Danville, and the Federals were only eight miles from the Cumberland Gap road. Buell was reported everywhere—swinging south to cross Dick's River near Stanford and Lancaster to outflank Bragg, pushing directly through Danville to the gap road, and moving north to King's Mill Ford, where Kirby Smith's troops were still crossing. Dumont was still rumored as approaching from Frankfort, and news had been received of a third Federal force moving out of Cincinnati. If Buell did turn Bragg's left, the Confederates would be trapped between Buell and the force moving south to the Kentucky River.[56]

Bragg explained the situation to his generals. Only four days' rations were left, and the mills west of Dick's River were captured. The fall rains would soon make the road over Cumberland Gap impassable, and then a retreat would be impossible. Davis had above all urged Bragg to save the Army. Buell was reported swinging as far south as Crab Orchard to cut Bragg off from Cumberland Gap.

It was enough. Polk, Cheatham, Hardee, and Kirby Smith voted to retreat. Humphrey Marshall, who had just arrived after touring Kentucky with his troops, voted to remain in the Bluegrass and then retreat into Virginia. He was granted his request—Bragg's force would retreat south at daylight. Quickly the plans were made. Kirby Smith would

[56] Wheeler to Brent, October 1, 11 ("before daylight"), 12 (7:20 P.M.), 1862, in Bragg Papers, Western Reserve; *Official Records*, XVI, Pt. 1, p. 898, pp. 935–36; Johnston, "Bragg's Campaign," Military Papers, Filson Club. Bragg's fear of a flanking move was premature, but well founded. On the thirteenth Buell began to move south to try to cross Dick's River at the Stanford and Lancaster fords and cut Bragg's line of retreat. By 10:30 P.M. that day, he learned that Bragg had left Bryantsville. Buell pursued only as far as London, Kentucky, and halted for what he termed a lack of supplies and forage. His failure to pursue was probably a cause of his later being relieved of command. See Buell to Halleck, October 13, 1862, and Buell to Thomas, March 2, 1864, in Buell Papers, Rice; *Official Records*, XVI, Pt. 1, pp. 53–54, 1028–29.

take the left fork at Lancaster and move via Big Hill, and Bragg would move on the right fork via Crab Orchard. Joe Wheeler, newly appointed chief of cavalry of the Second Department, would command the rear guard. The meeting closed, and the generals went out into the murky night.[57]

Two years of the Army's fortunes had come to this. Another campaign had been lost, and now the potential fortunes of the Army of Tennessee were waning. The old problems remained which had beset the Army on the Bowling Green line, at the inland rivers, Mill Springs, Columbus, Corinth, and Shiloh. The command structure remained weak, understanding with Richmond was still feeble, and the burden of defending the Heartland was still heavy. Almost every conceivable type of command structure had been utilized since the Army's infancy in the Tennessee state force—Harris as war governor; Polk and Harris in a joint Confederate-state command; Johnston and Beauregard as department commanders; and now Bragg and Kirby Smith in interdepartmental command. All attempts had failed. Not that the Army had ever been strong—but it was getting weaker, and the enemy was stronger. Perhaps the Kentucky invasion had seen the Army's high tide, a peak it would never reach again. Never again would the gray infantry reach to the Ohio. Never again could the Army muster enough men, rations, and railroads for a long offensive campaign. Now that tide had ebbed into the bitterness of another retreat.

Seven days later Braxton Bragg stood on the summit of Cumberland Gap and watched Polk's lead column ascend the slope. Kirby Smith trailed far to the rear near London. Although Bragg had left Chattanooga fifty-four days earlier for a concentration with his colleague, the two forces were never together at the same place during the campaign.

The sun came out the next morning as Bragg urged his horse to the southern rim of Cumberland Gap. Below lay the valley of the Clinch River, and off to the southwest stretched the Cumberland Mountain range. Far over the mountains, too far to be seen from Cumberland Gap, lay the town of Murfreesboro. There the old Indian war trail stretched southward to Chattanooga, and across Chickamauga Creek to the military depot at Atlanta.

---

[57] Kirby Smith to Stoddard Johnston, October 31, 1866, in Military Papers, Filson Club; Johnston, "Bragg's Campaign," *ibid.;* "Johnston Memoranda," *ibid.; Official Records,* XVI, Pt. 2, pp. 940–41.

Bibliography

MANUSCRIPTS

Alabama State Department of Archives and History, Montgomery.
  Lieutenant General William Hardee Papers
  Governor John Gill Shorter Letters
  Sterling A. Wood Papers
  Earl Van Dorn Papers

Chicago Historical Society.
  John C. Breckinridge Papers
  Benjamin Franklin Cheatham Papers
  Nathan Bedford Forrest Papers
  William Hardee Papers
  John T. Morgan Papers
  Leonidas Polk Papers
  Joseph Wheeler Papers

Duke University Library, Durham, N. C.
  P. G. T. Beauregard Papers
  Braxton Bragg Papers
  John Buie Letters
  Confederate Archives: Army of the Mississippi Papers, 1861–65
  Confederate Archives: Miscellaneous Soldiers' and Officers' Letters
  Jefferson Davis Papers
  John B. Floyd Papers
  Nathan Bedford Forrest Papers
  David B. Harris Papers
  Edmund Kirby Smith Papers
  McKinney Family Papers
  Munford–Ellis Papers (G. W. Munford Division)
  Hypolite Oladowski Papers

Gideon Pillow Papers
Leonidas Polk Papers
C. T. Quintard Papers
Daniel Ruggles Papers
Tennessee Rolls and History, 3rd Tennessee Infantry Papers
C. B. Tompkins Papers

Mrs. Julian Fertitta, Beaumont, Texas.
Letters of William Vaught, Slocumb's Battery, Washington Artillery of New Orleans

Filson Club Historical Society, Louisville, Ky.
J. Stoddard Johnston Military Papers
J. Stoddard Johnston Papers
Alfred Pirtle Journal
Humphrey Marshall Letters

Houghton Library, Library of Harvard University, Cambridge, Mass.
Braxton Bragg Letters
John C. Breckinridge Letters
Simon Buckner Letters
William Joseph Hardee Letters
Joseph Eggleston Johnston Letters
Leonidas Polk Letters
Joseph Wheeler Letters

Henry E. Huntington Library, San Marino, Calif.
Simon Bolivar Buckner Papers, 1830–1912
Joseph Eggleston Johnston Papers, 1861–65

Library of Congress, Washington, D.C.
P. G. T. Beauregard Papers
Leonidas Polk Papers
Alfred Roman Papers
Louis Wigfall Papers

Department of Archives, Louisiana State University, Baton Rouge.
P. G. T. Beauregard Papers, 1860–66
Gras–Lauzin Family Papers
Charles James Johnson Family Papers
Liddell (St. John and Family) Papers

Missouri Historical Society, St. Louis.
William K. Bixby Collection of Braxton Bragg Papers

National Archives, Confederate Records Division, Washington, D.C.
P. G. T. Beauregard Papers
Correspondence of Brigadier General John B. Floyd, 1861–65
General T. C. Hindman Papers, 1861–64
General B. R. Johnson Papers, 1862–65
General St. John R. Liddell Papers
Correspondence of Brigadier General Gideon Pillow, 1861–65
General Leonidas Polk Papers, 1861–64

General Joseph Wheeler Papers, 1863–64

Letters and Telegrams Sent, General James R. Chalmers' Command, February, 1862–April, 1865, Ch. II, Vols. 288–90

Letters, Telegrams, and Orders Received and Sent, General J. C. Breckinridge's Command, December, 1861–November, 1865, Ch. II, Vol. 311

Letters and Telegrams Sent, General P. G. T. Beauregard's Command, 1862–64, Ch. II, Vol. 35

Letter Book of General Gideon J. Pillow's Command, 1861–62, Ch. II, Vol. 18

Correspondence of the Western Department and the Army of the Mississippi, 1861–62, Ch. II, Vol. 271

Western Department, Letters Sent, 1861–62

Western Department, Telegrams Received, September to December, 1861

Western Department, Telegrams Received, January to May, 1862

Letters, Orders and Circulars Sent and Received, Medical Director's Office, Army of Tennessee, 1862–65, Ch. VI, 748

Letters Sent, Ordnance Officer, Army of Tennessee, June, 1862–February, 1864, Ch. IV, Vols. 141–43

Communications Received by Major General P. R. Cleburne's Division, Hardee's Corps, Army of Tennessee, 1862–64, Ch. II, Vol. 265

Orders, Army of Mississippi, Western Department No. 2, and Army of Tennessee, 1862–63, Ch. VIII, Vol. 342

Extracts of Special Orders Issued by Adjutant and Inspector General at Richmond, Virginia, and forwarded to General Polk's Command, 1862–63, Ch. II, Vol. 53½

Letters Sent, Department of East Tennessee, 1862, Ch. II, Vol. 237

Letters and Telegrams Sent and Received by Colonel T. W. Newman's (17th Tennessee and 23rd Battalion) Infantry, 1862–63, Letter Book, Ch. II, Vol. 238

Orders, 7th Tennessee Volunteers, 1861–62, Ch. VIII, Vol. 348

Letters Sent, Chief of Engineers, Western Department, 1861–62, Ch. III, Vol. 8

Letters and Telegrams Sent, Ordnance Offices, Nashville, Tennessee, and Atlanta, Georgia, December, 1861–April, 1862, Ch. IV, Vol. 8

Letters and Telegrams Sent and Circulars Issued, Central Division of Kentucky, September, 1861–February, 1862, Ch. III, Vol. 226

Militia Laws of Tennessee, Ch. VII, Vol. 278½

Register of Letters Received by General Polk's Corps, Army of Tennessee, 1861–62, Ch. II, Vol. 12

Index to Letters Sent by General Polk's Command, 1861–62, Ch. II, Vol. 13½

Index to Special Orders, Commands of Generals Leonidas Polk, D. H. Maury, S. D. Lee, and Richard Taylor 1862–64; Special Orders, same commands, 1862–64, Ch. II, Vol. 15

Special Orders, Letters Sent and Battle Reports, First Division, Western Department; and First Brigade, First Division of General William J. Hardee's Corps, Brigadier General Gideon J. Pillow Commanding, 1861–63, Ch. II, Vol. 18

Letters and Telegrams Sent, Department of East Tennessee, March–November, 1862, Ch. II, Vol. 51

Endorsements on Letters Received, Department of East Tennessee, 1862–63, Ch. II, Vol. 51½

Letters and Telegrams Sent, Department of East Tennessee, 1862, Ch. II, Vol. 52

Index to Endorsements, Major General Polk's Command, 1861–63; Endorsement Book, Major General Polk's Command, 1861–63, Ch. II, Vol. 52½

Letters and Telegrams Sent and Special Orders, Department of East Tennessee, 1862, Ch. II, Vol. 52½

Register of Letters Received, Western Department and Army and Department of Mississippi, 1861–63, Ch. II, Vol. 158½

Special Orders, Army of the Mississippi, Department No. 2 and Department and Army of Tennessee, 1862–64, Ch. II, Vol. 221

General and Special Orders, Central Division of Kentucky, 1861–62, Ch. II, Vol. 225

Letters and Telegrams Sent, Headquarters, Confederate Forces at Chattanooga and Department of Western Virginia, 1862–63, Ch. II, Vol. 233

Orders and Circulars, Army of Tennessee and Subordinate Commands, 1863–64, Ch. II, Vol. 53

Letters Sent, General Leonidas Polk's Command, 1862–64, Ch. II, Vol. 13

Miscellaneous Records, Army of Tennessee, 1863–65

Letters Sent, Department of the West, 1863, Ch. II, Vol. 18¼

Letters Sent and Endorsements on Letters Received, Army of Tennessee, 1863–64, Ch. II, Vol. 158¼

Century Collection, New York Public Library.
Thomas Jordan Letters
Joseph E. Johnston Letters

North Carolina Department of Archives and History, Raleigh.
Patton Anderson Papers

Southern Historical Collection, University of North Carolina, Chapel Hill.
James Lusk Alcorn Papers
E. P. Alexander Papers
J. F. H. Claiborne Papers
Alexander Donelson Coffee Papers
Jeremy F. Gilmer Papers
Daniel C. Govan Papers
James Iredell Hall Papers
G. A. Henry Papers
Daniel Harvey Hill Papers
J. A. Hinkle Papers
Edmund Kirby Smith Papers
Stephen Dill Lee Papers
H. C. Lockhart Papers
W. W. Mackall Papers
John Hunt Morgan Papers
Leonidas Polk Papers (microfilm of collection at University of the South, Sewanee, Tenn.)
Samuel H. Stout Papers
Marcus J. Wright Papers
Unknown Union Soldier's Diary, 1862

Historical Society of Pennsylvania, Philadelphia.
  Simon B. Buckner Letters
  John B. Floyd Letters
  William J. Hardee Letters
  Albert Sidney Johnston Letters
  Gideon J. Pillow Letters

Fondren Library, Rice University, Houston, Texas.
  Don Carlos Buell Papers

Rosenberg Library, Galveston, Texas.
  John A. Wharton Papers

South Caroliniana Library, University of South Carolina, Columbia.
  Williams–Chesnut–Manning Papers

Tennessee State Library and Archives, Nashville.
  Benjamin Franklin Cheatham Papers
  Sherrell Figuers Papers
  Isham G. Harris Papers
  Medical Board of Tennessee Papers
  Military and Financial Board of Tennessee Papers
  Field Notes of Francis Mohrhardt, U.S. Topographical Engineer, Moore
    Federal Collection
  Confederate Collection:
    George Thompson Blakemore Diary
    W. J. Brigham Letters
    Governor John C. Brown Autograph Album, Fort Warren
    David Clark Letters, 13th Tennessee Infantry
    W. E. Coleman Letters, 5th Kentucky Infantry
    Jefferson Davis Letters
    James Caswell Edenton Diary, 13th Tennessee Regiment
    George P. Faw Letters
    Captain Alfred Fielder Diary
    Thomas Julian Firth Letters, 4th Tennessee Infantry
    Enoch Hancock Letters
    Gustavus A. Henry Papers
    F. B. Kendrick Memoir
    James C. Malone Letters
    James M. Ollar Letters
    Gideon J. Pillow Letters
    Brigadier General James Rains Letters
    W. W. Searcy Letters
    S. R. Simpson Letters, 30th Tennessee Infantry
    S. R. Simpson Diary, February 6–November 29, 1862
    William E. Sloan Diary
    S. T. Williams Letters
    George Winchester Diary
    Papers of Corps of Artillery, State of Tennessee
    Miscellaneous File
    Fifth Tennessee Infantry Papers

Thirteenth Tennessee Infantry Papers
Fifteenth Tennessee Infantry Papers
Fifty-fifth Tennessee Infantry Papers
Fifth Tennessee Cavalry Papers
John Johnston Reminiscences

Howard–Tilton Memorial Library, Tulane University, New Orleans.
The Mrs. Mason Barret Collection of Albert Sidney and William Preston Johnston Papers
Jefferson Davis Papers, Louisiana Historical Association Collection
Correspondence between General A. S. Johnston and General P. G. T. Beauregard
Albert Sidney Johnston Papers, Louisiana Historical Association, Headquarters Book, 1861–62
Albert Sidney Johnston Papers, Louisiana Historical Association, Order Book, 1861–62
Samuel Rankin Latta Papers

Western Reserve Historical Society, Cleveland, Ohio.
William P. Palmer Collection of Braxton Bragg Papers
William P. Palmer Collection of Confederate Papers

United States Military Academy Library, West Point, N.Y.
Braxton Bragg Papers

MAPS

Alabama State Department of Archives, Montgomery.
Map collection of Major General Henry D. Clayton

Tennessee State Archives, Nashville.
Benjamin F. Cheatham Papers

Fondren Library, Rice University, Houston, Texas.
Asher and Company, The Historical War Map. Indianapolis, 1863.
Asher and Company, The Historical War Map. Indianapolis, 1864.
P. S. Duval and Son, Military Map of the United States Showing the Location of the Military Posts, Arsenals, Navy Yards and Ports of Entry. Philadelphia, 1861.
Hunt, John and R. H. Long. *Hunt's Gazetteer of Border and Southern States, and a Handbook and Reliable Guide for the Soldiers.* Pittsburgh, 1863.
Perrine's New Topographical War Map of the Southern States With a Chronology of the Great Rebellion. Boston, 1865.
Railroad Map of the Southern States, 1863.
United States Coast Survey, Map of Southern Mississippi and Alabama. Washington, 1863.
United States Coast Survey, Map of Southern Georgia and South Carolina. Washington, 1865.
United States Engineer Corps. Map of East Tennessee North of Loudon. Washington, 1864.
United States Engineer Corps. Map of West Tennessee. Washington, n.d.
United States Engineer Corps. Military Map of Kentucky and Tennessee, November 1863. Washington, 1863.

NEWSPAPERS

Chattanooga *Daily Rebel*
Cincinnati *Daily Enquirer*
Knoxville *Weekly Register*
Memphis *Daily Appeal*
Richmond *Examiner*

PRINTED PRIMARY SOURCES, PUBLIC DOCUMENTS, AND REMINISCENCES

Alderson, William T. (ed.). "Civil War Diary of Captain James Litton Cooper, September 30, 1861, to January, 1865," *Tennessee Historical Quarterly,* XV (June, 1956), 141–73.
————. "Civil War Reminiscences of John Johnston, 1861–1865," *Tennessee Historical Quarterly,* XIII (March, 1954), 65–82 (June, 1954), 156–78 (September, 1954), 244–76 (December, 1954), 329–54; XIV (March, 1955), 43–81 (June, 1955), 142–75.
Army Service Schools. *Donelson Campaign Sources.* Fort Leavenworth, Kan., 1912.
Boggs, William R. *Military Reminiscences of General Wm. R. Boggs, C.S.A.* Ed. William K. Boyd. Durham, 1913.
Buell, Don Carlos. *Statement of Major General Buell in Review of the Evidence before the Military Commission Appointed by the War Department.* n.p., n.d.
Carter W. C. *History of the First Regiment of Tennessee Cavalry in the Great War of the Rebellion.* Knoxville, 1902.
Davis, Jefferson. *Rise and Fall of the Confederate Government.* 2 vols. New York, 1881.
Duke, Basil. *A History of Morgan's Cavalry.* Ed. Cecil F. Holland. 3rd ed. Bloomington, 1960.
————. *Reminiscences of General Basil W. Duke, C.S.A.* Garden City, N.Y., 1911.
Field, Henry. *Blood is Thicker than Water: A Few Days Among Our Southern Brethren.* New York, 1886.
————. *Bright Skies and Dark Shadows.* New York, 1890.
Freeman, Douglas Southall (ed.). *Lee's Dispatches: Unpublished Letters of General Robert E. Lee, C.S.A. to Jefferson Davis and the War Department of the Confederate States of America, 1862–1865.* New York, 1915.
George, Henry. *History of the Third, Seventh, Eighth and Twelfth Kentucky, C.S.A.* Louisville, 1911.
Goodloe, Albert T. *Some Rebel Relics from the Seat of War.* Nashville, 1893.
Gorgas, Josiah. "Ordnance of the Confederacy. Notes of Brigadier General Josiah Gorgas, Chief of Ordnance, C.S.A.," *Army Ordnance,* XVI (January–February, March–April, 1936), 212–16, 283–88.
Grant, Ulysses Simpson. *Personal Memoirs of U. S. Grant.* 2 vols. New York, 1885.
Guild, G. B. *Brief Narrative of the Fourth Tennessee Cavalry Regiment, Wheeler's Corps, Army of Tennessee.* Nashville, 1913.
Hancock, R. R. *Hancock's Diary: Or, A History of the Second Tennessee Cavalry.* Nashville, 1887.

Head, Thomas A. *Campaigns and Battles of the Sixteenth Regiment, Tennessee Volunteers, in the War Between the States, with Incidental Sketches of the Part Performed by Other Tennessee Troops in the Same War, 1861–1865.* Ed. Stanley F. Horn. 2nd ed. McMinnville, Tenn., 1961.

Johnson, Robert U. and Clarence C. Buel (eds.). *Battles and Leaders of the Civil War.* 2nd ed., 4 vols. New York, 1956.

Johnston, Joseph E. *Narrative of Military Operations Directed During the Late War Between the States.* Ed. Frank E. Vandiver. 2nd ed. Bloomington, 1959.

Jones, John B. *A Rebel War Clerk's Diary at the Confederate States Capital.* Ed. Howard Swiggett. 2 vols. New York, 1935.

Jordan, Thomas P. and J. P. Pryor. *Campaigns of Lieut-Gen. N. B. Forrest, and of Forrest's Cavalry.* New Orleans, 1868.

Lindsley, John Berrien (ed.). *Military Annals of Tennessee, Confederate.* Nashville, 1886.

Lord, Walter (ed.). *Fremantle Diary, Being the Journal of Lieutenant Colonel James Arthur Lyon Fremantle, Coldstream Guards, on His Three Months in the Southern States.* Boston, 1954.

Lyon, Hylan B. "Memoirs of Hylan B. Lyon, Brigadier General, C.S.A." Ed. Edward M. Coffman. *Tennessee Historical Quarterly,* XVIII (March, 1959), 35–53.

McMurray, W. J. *History of the Twentieth Tennessee Regiment Volunteer Infantry, C.S.A.* Nashville, 1904.

Merrill, James W. (ed.). " 'Nothing to Eat But Raw Bacon': Letters From A War Correspondent, 1862," *Tennessee Historical Quarterly,* XVII (June, 1958), 141–55.

Mitchell, Enoch (ed.). "Letters of a Confederate Surgeon in the Army of Tennessee to His Wife," *Tennessee Historical Quarterly,* V (March, 1946), 60–81; (June, 1946), 142–81.

Moore, Frank (ed.). *Rebellion Record: A Diary of American Events with Documents, Narratives, Illustrative Incidents, Poetry, Etc.* 11 vols. and supplement. New York, 1861–68.

Mosgrove, George D. *Kentucky Cavaliers in Dixie: Reminiscences of a Confederate Cavalryman.* Ed. Bell Wiley. Jackson, Tenn., 1957.

Mott, Charles R. Jr. (ed.). "War Journal of a Confederate Officer," *Tennessee Historical Quarterly,* V (September, 1946), 234–48.

Noll, Arthur H. (ed.). *Doctor Quintard, Chaplain C.S.A. and Second Bishop of Tennessee; Being His Story of the War (1861–1865).* Sewanee, Tenn., 1905.

Partin, Robert. "A Confederate Sergeant's Report to His Wife During the Bombardment of Fort Pillow," *Tennessee Historical Quarterly,* XV (September, 1956), 243–52.

————. "The 'Momentous Events' of the Civil War as Reported by a Confederate Private-Sergeant," *Tennessee Historical Quarterly,* XVIII (March, 1959), 69–86.

Rennolds, Edwin. *A History of the Henry County Commands Which Served in the Confederate States Army.* Kennesaw, Ga., 1961.

Richardson, James D. *A Compilation of the Messages and Papers of the Confederacy, Including the Diplomatic Correspondence, 1861–1865.* 2 vols. Nashville, 1905.

Ridley, Bromfield (ed.) . *Battles and Sketches of the Army of Tennessee*. Mexico, Mo., 1906.

Rowland, Dunbar. *Jefferson Davis, Constitutionalist: His Letters, Papers and Speeches*. 10 vols. Jackson, Miss., 1923.

Russell, William H. *My Diary North and South*. Boston, 1863.

Scott, Samuel and Samuel Angel. *History of the Thirteenth Regiment, Tennessee Volunteer Cavalry, U.S.A*. Knoxville, 1903.

Sheridan, Philip H. *Personal Memoirs of P. H. Sheridan, General United States Army*. 2 vols. New York, 1888.

Sorrel, G. Moxley. *Recollections of a Confederate Staff Officer*. Ed. Bell I. Wiley. Jackson, Tenn., 1958.

Southern Historical Society Papers. 52 vols. Richmond, 1914–59.

Stevenson, William. *Thirteen Months in the Rebel Army*. New York, 1862.

Tarrant, Sergeant. *The Wild Riders of the First Kentucky Cavalry: A History of the Regiment in the Great War of the Rebellion 1861–1865*. Louisville, 1894.

Taylor, Richard. *Destruction and Reconstruction; Personal Experiences of the Late War*. New York, 1879.

Tennessee, State of. *House Journal 1861–1862 of the First Session of the Thirty-Fourth General Assembly of the State of Tennessee*. Nashville, 1957.

————. *Tennessee House and Senate Journals, 1861–1862*. Nashville, 1862.

————. *House Journal of the Extra Session of the Thirty-Third General Assembly of the State of Tennessee, Which Convened at Nashville, on the First Monday in January A.D., 1861*. Nashville, 1861.

————. *Senate Journal of the Extra Session of the Thirty-Third General Assembly of the State of Tennessee, Which Convened at Nashville, on the First Monday in January, A.D., 1861*. Nashville, 1861.

————. *House Journal of the Second Extra Session of the Thirty-Third General Assembly of the State of Tennessee, Which Convened at Nashville on Thursday, the 25th Day of April, A.D., 1861*. Nashville, 1861.

————. *Senate Journal of the Second Extra Session of the Thirty-Third General Assembly of the State of Tennessee, Which Convened at Nashville on Thursday, the 25th Day of April, A.D., 1861*. Nashville, 1861.

————. *Public Acts of the State of Tennessee Passed at the Thirty-Third General Assembly for the Year 1861*. Nashville, 1861.

Toney, Marcus B. *Privations of a Private*. Nashville, 1907.

United States Bureau of Census. *Agriculture of the United States in 1860; Compiled from the Original Returns of the Eighth Census*. Washington, 1864.

United States. 59th Cong., 1st Sess. *Senate Document Number Eighty-Three*. "Navigation of the Tennessee River." Washington, 1906.

————. 40th Cong., 2nd Sess. *House Executive Document Number 271*. William Gaw. "Report on the Examination and Survey of the Tennessee River." Washington, 1868.

————. 75th Cong., 1st Sess. *House Executive Document Number 254*. J. H. Alldredge *et. al. A History of Navigation on the Tennessee River System*. Washington, 1937.

————. 62nd Cong., 2nd Sess. *House Document Number 360*. William W. Harts. "Tennessee River: Tennessee, Alabama and Kentucky." Washington, 1912.

_____. 29th Cong., 1st Sess. *House Document Number 167*. S. H. Long. *Summary of the Tennessee River*. Washington, 1846.

United States Naval War Records Office. *Official Records of the Union and Confederate Navies in the War of the Rebellion*. 30 vols. Washington, 1894–1914.

Vandiver, Frank E. (ed.). *Civil War Diary of General Josiah Gorgas*. University, Ala., 1947.

Vaughan, Alfred J. *Personal Record of the Thirteenth Regiment, Tennessee Infantry, by Its Old Commander*. Memphis, 1897.

War of the Rebellion: A Compilation of the Official Records of the Union and Confederate Armies. 73 vols. Washington, D.C., 1880–1901.

Watkins, Sam R. *"Co. Aytch," Maury Grays, First Tennessee Regiment or A Side Show of the Big Show*. Ed. Bell I. Wiley. 2nd ed. Jackson, Tenn., 1952.

White, Robert. *Messages of the Governors of Tennessee*. 6 vols. Nashville, 1952–63.

Worsham, W. J. *Old Nineteenth Tennessee Regiment, C.S.A.: June, 1861–April, 1865*. Knoxville, 1902.

Wright, Marcus J. *Diary of Brigadier-General Marcus J. Wright, C.S.A. April 23, 1861–February 26, 1863*, n.p., n.d.

Young, J. P. *Seventh Tennessee Cavalry, A History*. Nashville, 1890.

Younger, Edward (ed.). *Inside the Confederate Government: The Diary of Robert Garlick Hill Kean, Head of the Bureau of War*. New York, 1957.

SECONDARY SOURCES

Adams, Ephraim Douglass. *Great Britain and the American Civil War*. 2 vols. London, 1925.

Allen, James Lane. *The Blue-Grass Region of Kentucky and Other Kentucky Articles*. New York, 1911.

Ambler, Charles Henry. *A History of Transportation in the Ohio Valley, with Special Reference to Its Waterways, Trade, and Commerce from the Earliest Period to the Present Time*. Glendale, Calif., 1932.

Ambrose, Stephen E. *Halleck: Lincoln's Chief of Staff*. Baton Rouge, 1962.

Amick, H. C. "The Great Valley of East Tennessee," *Economic Geography*, X (January, 1934), 35–40.

Anderson, Charles C. *Fighting by Southern Federals*. New York, 1912.

Armes, Ethel. *The Story of Coal and Iron in Alabama*. Birmingham, 1910.

Armstrong, Zella. *The History of Hamilton County and Chattanooga, Tennessee*. 2 vols. Chattanooga, 1931.

Arnow, Harriette Simpson. *Seedtime on the Cumberland*. New York, 1960.

Bayley, W. S. *Magnetic Iron Ores of East Tennessee and Western North Carolina*. Tennessee Department Geology, *Bulletin Number 18*. Nashville, 1923.

Bettersworth, John. *Confederate Mississippi: The People and Policies of a Cotton State in Wartime*. Baton Rouge, 1943.

Black, Robert C., III. "The Railroads of Georgia in the Confederate War Effort," *Journal of Southern History*, XIII (November, 1947), 511–34.

_____. *Railroads of the Confederacy*. Chapel Hill, 1952.

Brown, Dee Alexander. *The Bold Cavaliers: Morgan's 2nd Kentucky Cavalry Raiders*. Philadelphia, 1959.

Buck, Irving A. *Cleburne and His Command*. Ed. Thomas Robson Hay. 2nd ed. Jackson, Tenn., 1959.

Burchard, Ernest F. *Brown Iron Ores of the Western Highland Rim, Tennessee.* Tennessee Department Geology, *Bulletin Number 39.* Nashville, 1934.

Burt, Jesse C. *Nashville: Its Life and Times.* Nashville, 1959.

Butler, Mann. *A History of the Commonwealth of Kentucky.* Louisville, 1834.

Buttgenbach, Walter J., and John L. Holcombe. "Coast Defense in the Civil War; Fort Henry, Tennessee," *Journal of the United States Artillery,* XXXIX (January, 1913), 83–90.

Campbell, Mary. *Attitude of Tennesseans Toward the Union 1847–1861.* New York, 1961.

Campbell, T. J. *The Upper Tennessee.* Chattanooga, 1932.

Capers, Gerald. *Biography of a River Town; Memphis: Its Heroic Age.* Chapel Hill, 1939.

Case, E. C. *Valley of East Tennessee.* Tennessee Department Geology, *Bulletin No. 36.* Nashville, 1925.

Catton, Bruce. *Grant Moves South.* Boston, 1960.

Cist, Henry M. *The Army of the Cumberland.* Vol. VII of *The Campaigns of the Civil War.* New York, 1882.

Clark, Thomas D. *A History of Kentucky.* Lexington, 1950.

————. *The Kentucky.* New York, 1942.

Clarke, Blanche Henry. *Tennessee Yeoman, 1840–1860.* Nashville, 1942.

Clayton, W. W. *History of Davidson County Tennessee.* Philadelphia, 1880.

Cleaves, Freeman. *Rock of Chickamauga: The Life of General George H. Thomas.* Norman, Okla., 1948.

Conger, A. L. "Fort Donelson," *Military Historian and Economist,* I (January, 1916), 33–62.

Connelley, William E., and E. Merton Coulter. *History of Kentucky.* 5 vols. Chicago, 1922.

Connelly, Thomas Lawrence. "Gateway to Kentucky: The Wilderness Road, 1748–1792," *Register of the Kentucky Historical Society,* LIX (April, 1961), 109–32.

Cook, W. L. "Furnaces and Forges," *Tennessee Historical Magazine,* IX (October, 1925), 190–92.

Corlew, Robert. *A History of Dickson County.* Dickson, Tennessee, 1956.

————, Stanley Folmsbee and Enoch Mitchell. *History of Tennessee.* 4 vols. New York, 1960.

Cotterill, Robert S. "The Louisville and Nashville Railroad, 1861–1865," *American Historical Review,* XXIX (July, 1924), 700–15.

Coulter, E. Merton. *Civil War and Readjustment in Kentucky.* Chapel Hill, 1926.

————. "Commercial Intercourse with the Confederacy in the Mississippi Valley, 1861–1865," *Mississippi Valley Historical Review,* V (March, 1919), 377–95.

————. "Effects of Secession upon the Commerce of the Mississippi Valley," *Mississippi Valley Historical Review,* III (December, 1916), 273–300.

Crabb, Alfred Leland. "The Twilight of the Nashville Gods," *Tennessee Historical Quarterly,* XV (December, 1956), 291–305.

Creekmore, Betsey Beeler. *Knoxville.* Knoxville, 1958.

Crego, Arthur. "The Organization and Function of the Staff of the Confederate Army of Tennessee." M.A. Thesis, Louisiana State University, 1965.

Cunningham, H. H. *Doctors in Gray: The Confederate Medical Service.* Baton Rouge, 1958.

Davenport, F. Garvin. *Cultural Life in Nashville on the Eve of the Civil War.* Chapel Hill, 1941.

Davidson, Donald. *The Tennessee: The New River, Civil War to TVA.* New York, 1948.

Davis, Darrell H. *Geography of the Jackson Purchase.* Frankfort, 1923.

Dowdey, Clifford. *Experiment in Rebellion.* Garden City, N.Y., 1946.

Du Bose, John Witherspoon. *General Joseph Wheeler and the Army of Tennessee.* New York, 1912.

Duncan, Charles F. "Confederate Military Organization," *Military Engineer,* XXX (1938), 441–45.

Dyer, John P. *"Fightin' Joe" Wheeler.* Baton Rouge, 1941.

———. "Some Aspects of Cavalry Operations in the Army of Tennessee," *Journal of Southern History,* VIII (May, 1942), 210–25.

Eckenrode, Hamilton J. *Jefferson Davis, President of the South.* New York, 1930.

Evans, Clement (ed.). *Confederate Military History.* 12 vols. Atlanta, 1899.

Fertig, James Walter. *Secession and Reconstruction of Tennessee.* Chicago, 1898.

Fink, Paul. "The Bumpass Cove Mines and Embreeville," *East Tennessee Historical Society's Publications,* XVI (1944), 48–64.

Fish, Carl Russell. "The Decision of the Ohio Valley," *American Historical Association. Annual Report, 1910.* Washington, 1912, 155–64.

Fiske, John. *The Mississippi Valley in the Civil War.* Boston, 1900.

Fleming, Walter L. *Civil War and Reconstruction in Alabama.* New York, 1949.

Force, M. F. *From Fort Henry to Corinth.* Vol. II of *The Campaigns of the Civil War.* New York, 1881.

Frank, John G. "Adolphus Heiman: Architect and Soldier," *Tennessee Historical Quarterly,* V (March, 1946), 35–57.

Freeman, Douglas Southall. *Lee's Lieutenants, A Study in Command.* 3 vols. New York, 1942–44.

———. *R. E. Lee: A Biography.* 4 vols. New York, 1934–35.

Fuller, J. F. C. *The Conduct of War, 1789–1961; A Study of the Impact of the French, Industrial, and Russian Revolutions on War and Its Conduct.* New Brunswick, N.J., 1961.

Gibson, J. Sullivan. "The Land Economy of Warren County, Kentucky," *Economic Geography,* X (January, 1934), 74–98.

Goodspeed, Weston A., *et al.* (eds.). *History of Tennessee.* Nashville, 1883.

Govan, Gilbert E., and James W. Livingood. *A Different Valor: The Story of General Joseph E. Johnston, C.S.A.* New York, 1956.

———. *The Chattanooga Country, 1540–1951: From Tomahawks to TVA.* New York, 1952.

Guyot, Arnold. "On the Appalachian Mountain System," *American Journal of Science and Arts.* Second Series, XXXI (March, 1861), 157–87.

Hamer, Philip M. (ed.). *Tennessee: A History, 1673–1932.* 4 vols. New York, 1933.

Harmer, Marguerite B. "The Presidential Campaign of 1860 in Tennessee," *East Tennessee Historical Society's Publications,* III (1931), 3–22.

Hawkins, A. W. *Handbook of Tennessee.* Nashville, 1882.

Hay, Thomas Robson. "Braxton Bragg and the Southern Confederacy," *Georgia Historical Quarterly,* IX (December, 1925), 267–316.

———. *Hood's Tennessee Campaign.* New York, 1929.

_____. "The Campaign and Battle of Chickamauga," *Georgia Historical Quarterly,* VII (September, 1923), 213–50.

Henderson, G. F. R. *The Science of War: A Collection of Essays and Lectures, 1891–1903.* Ed. Neill Malcolm. London, 1906.

Hendrick, Burton J. *Statesmen of the Lost Cause: Jefferson Davis and His Cabinet.* Boston, 1939.

Henry, J. Milton. "The Revolution in Tennessee, February, 1861, to June, 1861," *Tennessee Historical Quarterly,* XVIII (June, 1959), 99–119.

Henry, Robert Selph. *"First with the Most" Forrest.* Indianapolis, 1944.

Hesseltine, William B. "The Underground Railroad from Confederate Prisons to East Tennessee," *East Tennessee Historical Society's Publications,* II (1930), 55–69.

Hittle, J. D. (ed.). *Jomini and His Summary of the Art of War.* Harrisburg, Pa., 1952.

Holland, Cecil Fletcher. *Morgan and His Raiders: Biography of the Confederate General.* New York, 1943.

Holland, James W. "The Building of the East Tennessee and Virginia Railroad," *East Tennessee Historical Society's Publications,* IV (1932), 83–101.

Horn, Stanley F. *Army of Tennessee.* 2nd ed., Norman Okla., 1955.

_____. "Nashville During the Civil War," *Tennessee Historical Quarterly,* IV (March, 1945), 3–22.

_____. *The Decisive Battle of Nashville.* Baton Rouge, 1956.

Hughes, Nathaniel Cheairs, Jr. *General William J. Hardee: Old Reliable.* Baton Rouge, 1965.

Humes, Thomas W. *The Loyal Mountaineers of East Tennessee.* Knoxville, 1888.

Jeffries, C. C. *Terry's Rangers.* New York, 1961.

Jillson, Willard Rouse. *The Topography of Kentucky.* Frankfort, 1927.

Johnson, Richard W. *Memoir of Maj.-Gen. George H. Thomas.* Philadelphia, 1881.

Johnston, William Preston. *The Life of Gen. Albert Sidney Johnston, Embracing His Services in the Armies of the United States, the Republic of Texas, and the Confederate States.* New York, 1879.

Jones, Archer. *Confederate Strategy from Shiloh to Vicksburg.* Baton Rouge, 1961.

_____. "Tennessee and Mississippi; Joe Johnston's Strategic Problem," *Tennessee Historical Quarterly,* XVIII (June, 1959), 134–47.

Kegley, Tracy M. "Bushrod Rust Johnson: Soldier and Teacher," *Tennessee Historical Quarterly,* VII (September, 1948), 249–58.

Killebrew, J. B. *Middle Tennessee As An Iron Centre.* Nashville, 1879.

_____. *Tennessee: Its Agricultural and Mineral Wealth.* Nashville, 1876.

_____, and J. M. Safford. *Introduction to the Resources of Tennessee.* Nashville, 1874.

Kincaid, Robert L. *The Wilderness Road.* 2nd ed. Harrogate, Tenn., 1955.

Lesley, J. P. *Iron Manufacturer's Guide to the Furnaces, Forges and Rolling Mills of the United States.* New York, 1859.

Liddell Hart, B. H. *Sherman: Soldier, Realist, American.* New York, 1958.

Lindsay, G. W. "The Memphis Branch of the Louisville and Nashville Railroad, (1850–1871)," *Railway and Locomotive Historical Society Bulletin,* LXXXI (October, 1950), 55–57.

Livingood, James. "Chattanooga: Rail Junction of the Old South," *Tennessee Historical Quarterly*, VI (September, 1947), 230–50.

McFarlan, Arthur. *Geology of Kentucky*. Lexington, 1943.

McKinney, Francis F. *Education in Violence: The Life of George H. Thomas and the History of the Army of the Cumberland*. Detroit, 1961.

McMurtry, R. Gerald. "Zollicoffer and the Battle of Mill Springs," *Filson Club History Quarterly*, XXIX (October, 1955), 303–19.

McRaven, Henry. *Nashville: Athens of the South*. Chapel Hill, 1949.

McWhiney, Grady. "Braxton Bragg and the Shiloh Campaign," *Tennessee Historical Quarterly*, XXI (March, 1962), 19–30.

————. "Controversy in Kentucky: Braxton Bragg's Campaign of 1862," *Civil War History*, VI (March, 1960), 5–42.

Martin, William. *Internal Improvements in Alabama*. Johns Hopkins University Studies in History and Political Science, XX, Fourth Series. Baltimore, 1902.

Maurice, Sir Frederick. *Statesmen and Soldiers of the Civil War: A Study in the Conduct of the War*. Boston, 1926.

Military Historical Society of Massachusetts. *Papers Read Before the Military Historical Society of Massachusetts*. 12 vols. Boston, 1881–1912.

Moore, Albert Burton. *Conscription and Conflict in the Confederacy*. New York, 1924.

Moore, John Trotwood, and Austin P. Foster. *Tennessee, The Volunteer State: 1769–1923*. 4 vols. Chicago, 1923.

Nevins, Allan. *The War for the Union: War Becomes Revolution 1862–1863*. Vol. VI of *Ordeal of the Union*. New York, 1960.

Nichols, James L. *Confederate Engineers*. Tuscaloosa, 1957.

————. "Confederate Map Supply," *Military Engineer*, XLVI (January–February, 1954), 28–32.

Noll, Arthur H. *General Kirby-Smith*. Sewanee, Tenn., 1907.

Odum, Howard W. *Southern Regions of the United States*. Chapel Hill, 1936.

Owsley, Frank Lawrence. *King Cotton Diplomacy: Foreign Relations of the Confederate States of America*. Chicago, 1931.

————. *State Rights in the Confederacy*. Chicago, 1925.

————, and Harriet C. Owsley. "The Economic Structure of Rural Tennessee, 1850–1860," *Journal of Southern History*, VIII (May, 1942), 161–82.

Parks, Edd Winfield. "Zollicoffer: Southern Whig," *Tennessee Historical Quarterly*, XI (December, 1952), 346–55.

Parks, Joseph Howard. *General Edmund Kirby Smith, C.S.A.* Baton Rouge, 1954.

————. *General Leonidas Polk, C.S.A., The Fighting Bishop*. Baton Rouge, 1962.

Patton, James Welch. *Unionism and Reconstruction in Tennessee, 1860–1869*. Chapel Hill, 1934.

Polk, William. *Leonidas Polk, Bishop and General*. 2 vols. New York, 1915.

Pollard, Edward. *Lee and His Lieutenants*. New York, 1867.

————. *The First Year of the War in America*. London, 1863.

Ramsdell, Charles. "The Confederate Government and the Railroads," *American Historical Review*, XXII (July, 1917), 794–810.

Reid, Whitelaw. *Ohio in the War: Her Statesmen, Generals and Soldiers*. 2 vols. Columbus, Ohio, 1893.

Robinson, William, Jr. "The Confederate Engineers," *Military Engineer*, XXII (July–November, 1930), 297–305.

Roland, Charles P. *Albert Sidney Johnston: Soldier of Three Republics*. Austin, 1964.

Roman, Alfred. *The Military Operations of General Beauregard in the War Between the States 1861 to 1865; Including a Brief Personal Sketch and a Narrative of His Services in the War with Mexico, 1846–8*. 2 vols. New York, 1883.

Ropes, John Codman. *The Army under Pope*. Vol. IV of *The Campaigns of the Civil War*. New York, 1881.

Rothrock, Mary U. (ed.). *The French Broad–Holston Country: A History of Knox County, Tennessee*. Knoxville, 1946.

Safford, James. *Geology of Tennessee*. Nashville, 1869.

Sauer, Carl Ortwin. *Geography of the Pennyroyal: A Study of the Influence of Geology and Physiography Upon the Industry, Commerce, and Life of the People*. Frankfort, 1927.

Seitz, Don. *Braxton Bragg, General of the Confederacy*. Columbia, S.C., 1924.

Shaler, Nathaniel S. *Kentucky: Pioneer Commonwealth*. Boston, 1885.

Sheppard, Eric William. *Bedford Forrest, The Confederacy's Greatest Cavalryman*. London, 1930.

Shortridge, Wilson P. "Kentucky Neutrality in 1861," *Mississippi Valley Historical Review*, IX (March, 1923), 282–301.

Smith, Edward Conrad. *The Borderland in the Civil War*. New York, 1927.

Speed, Thomas. *The Union Cause in Kentucky, 1860–1865*. New York, 1907.

_____, R. M. Kelley, and Alfred Pirtle. *The Union Regiments of Kentucky*. Louisville, 1897.

Steuart, Richard D. "Armories of the Confederacy," *Confederate Veteran*, XXXV (January, 1927), 9–10.

_____. "Confederate Swords," *Confederate Veteran*, XXXIV (January, 1926), 12–14.

_____. "How Johnny Got His Gun," *Confederate Veteran*, XXXII (May, 1924), 166–69.

_____. "The Long Arm of the Confederacy," *Confederate Veteran*, XXXV (July, 1927), 250–53.

Stickles, Arndt M. *Simon Bolivar Buckner, Borderland Knight*. Chapel Hill, 1940.

Strobridge, Thurman R. (ed.). "The Letters of D. C. Donnohue, Special Agent for the Procuring of Cotton Seed," *Tennessee Historical Quarterly*, XXI (December, 1962), 379–86.

Swanton, Eva. "Military Railroads During the Civil War," *Military Engineer*, XXII (January, 1930), 13–21.

Swiggett, Howard. *The Rebel Raider: A Life of John Hunt Morgan*. Garden City, N.Y., 1937.

Tapp, Hambleton. "The Battle of Perryville, 1862," *Filson Club History Quarterly*, IX (July, 1935), 158–81.

Tatum, Georgia Lee. *Disloyalty in the Confederacy*. Chapel Hill, 1934.

Temple, Oliver P. *East Tennessee and the Civil War*. Cincinnati, 1899.

Thomas, David Y. "Missouri in the Confederacy," *Missouri Historical Review*, XVIII (April, 1924), 382–91.

Thompson, Edwin Porter. *History of the First Kentucky Brigade*. Cincinnati, 1868.

Turner, George Edgar. *Victory Rode the Rails: The Strategic Plan of Railroads in the Civil War*. Indianapolis, 1953.

Vandiver, Frank E. "Jefferson Davis and Confederate Strategy," in *The American Tragedy: The Civil War in Retrospect*. Ed. Bernard Mayo. Hampden–Sydney, Va., 1959.

————. *Ploughshares Into Swords: Josiah Gorgas and Confederate Ordnance*. Austin, 1952.

————. *Rebel Brass, The Confederate Command System*. Baton Rouge, 1956.

Van Horne, Thomas V. *History of the Army of the Cumberland: Its Organization, Campaigns, and Battles*. 2 vols. Cincinnati, 1875.

————. *The Kentucky Mountains, Transportation and Commerce 1750–1911: A Study in the Economic History of a Coal Field*. Filson Club Publications No. 26. Louisville, 1911.

————. *The Life of Major-General George H. Thomas*. New York, 1882.

Verhoeff, Mary. *The Kentucky River Navigation*. Filson Club Publications No. 28. Louisville, 1917.

Walker, Peter Franklin. "Building a Tennessee Army: Autumn, 1861," *Tennessee Historical Quarterly*, XVI (June, 1957), 99–116.

————. "Holding the Tennessee Line: Winter 1861–1862," *Tennessee Historical Quarterly*, XVI (September, 1957), 228–49.

————. "Command Failure: The Fall of Forts Henry and Donelson," *Tennessee Historical Quarterly*, XVI (December, 1957), 335–60.

Weller, Jac. "Nathan Bedford Forrest: An Analysis of Untutored Military Genius." *Tennessee Historical Quarterly*, XVIII (September, 1959), 213–51.

Williams, Kenneth P. *Iuka to Vicksburg*, Vol. IV of *Lincoln Finds a General: A Military Study of the Civil War*. New York, 1956.

Williams, Samuel Cole. *General John T. Wilder, Commander of the Lightning Brigade*. Bloomington, 1936.

Williams, T. Harry. *P. G. T. Beauregard, Napoleon in Gray*. Baton Rouge, 1955.

Wood, W. Birbeck, and J. E. Edmonds. *A History of the Civil War in the United States, 1861–5*. London, 1905.

Wright, Marcus J. *Tennessee in the War, 1861–1865*. New York, 1908.

Wyeth, John Allen. *That Devil Forrest: Life of General Nathan Bedford Forrest*. 2nd ed. New York, 1959.

Young, Bennett H. *Confederate Wizards of the Saddle; Being Reminiscences and Observations of One Who Rode with Morgan*. Kennesaw, Ga., 1958.

————. "Zollicoffer's Oak," *Southern Historical Society Papers*, XXXI (1903), 165–72.

Index